North Carolina's Outer Banks and Crystal Coast

Bodie Island Lighthouse towers over Coquina Beach.

A COMPLETE GUIDE

FIRST EDITION

North Carolina's Outer Banks and Crystal Coast

Renee Wright

The Countryman Press
Woodstock, Vermont

To my Mom, Betty Lou, better known to her many "kids" across the country as RV Momma, who gave me the great gift of travel. Without her, this book could never have been written.

ISBN 978-1-58157-037-3

Cover photo © Laurence Parent Photography
Cover and interior photos by the author unless otherwise specified
Book design by Bodenweber Design
Composition by Chelsea Cloeter
Maps by Mapping Specialists, Ltd., Madison, WI, © The Countryman Press

Published by The Countryman Press, P.O. Box 748, Woodstock, Vermont 05091

Distributed by W. W. Norton & Company, Inc., 500 Fifth Avenue, New York, NY 10110

Manufactured in the United States of America

10 9 8 7 6 5 4 3 2 1

GREAT DESTINATIONS TRAVEL GUIDEBOOK SERIES

Recommended by *National Geographic Traveler* and *Travel + Leisure* magazines

[A] CRISP AND CRITICAL APPROACH, FOR TRAVELERS WHO WANT TO LIVE LIKE LOCALS.
—*USA Today*

Great Destinations™ guidebooks are known for their comprehensive, critical coverage of regions of extraordinary cultural interest and natural beauty. The authors in this series are professional travel writers who have lived for many years in the regions they describe. Each title in this series is continuously updated with each printing to ensure accurate and timely information. All the books contain more than one hundred photographs and maps.

Current titles available:

THE ADIRONDACK BOOK

ATLANTA

AUSTIN, SAN ANTONIO
 & THE TEXAS HILL COUNTRY

THE BERKSHIRE BOOK

BERMUDA

BIG SUR, MONTEREY BAY &
 GOLD COAST WINE COUNTRY

CAPE CANAVERAL, COCOA BEACH
 & FLORIDA'S SPACE COAST

THE CHARLESTON, SAVANNAH
 & COASTAL ISLANDS BOOK

THE CHESAPEAKE BAY BOOK

THE COAST OF MAINE BOOK

COLORADO'S CLASSIC MOUNTAIN TOWNS

COSTA RICA: GREAT DESTINATIONS
 CENTRAL AMERICA

THE FINGER LAKES BOOK

THE FOUR CORNERS REGION

GALVESTON, SOUTH PADRE ISLAND
 & THE TEXAS GULF COAST

THE HAMPTONS BOOK

HAWAII'S BIG ISLAND

HONOLULU & OAHU:
 GREAT DESTINATIONS HAWAII

THE JERSEY SHORE: ATLANTIC CITY TO CAPE MAY

KAUAI: GREAT DESTINATIONS HAWAII

LAKE TAHOE & RENO

LOS CABOS & BAJA CALIFORNIA SUR:
 GREAT DESTINATIONS MEXICO

MAUI: GREAT DESTINATIONS HAWAII

MICHIGAN'S UPPER PENINSULA

MONTREAL & QUEBEC CITY:
 GREAT DESTINATIONS CANADA

THE NANTUCKET BOOK

THE NAPA & SONOMA BOOK

NORTH CAROLINA'S OUTER BANKS
 & THE CRYSTAL COAST

PALM BEACH, FORT LAUDERDALE, MIAMI
 & THE FLORIDA KEYS

PALM SPRINGS & DESERT RESORTS

PHOENIX, SCOTTSDALE, SEDONA
 & CENTRAL ARIZONA

PLAYA DEL CARMEN, TULUM & THE RIVIERA MAYA:
 GREAT DESTINATIONS MEXICO

SALT LAKE CITY, PARK CITY, PROVO
 & UTAH'S HIGH COUNTRY RESORTS

SAN DIEGO & TIJUANA

SAN JUAN, VIEQUES & CULEBRA:
 GREAT DESTINATIONS PUERTO RICO

SAN MIGUEL DE ALLENDE & GUANAJUATO:
 GREAT DESTINATIONS MEXICO

THE SANTA FE & TAOS BOOK

THE SARASOTA, SANIBEL ISLAND & NAPLES BOOK

THE SEATTLE & VANCOUVER BOOK

THE SHENANDOAH VALLEY BOOK

TOURING EAST COAST WINE COUNTRY

WASHINGTON, D.C., AND NORTHERN VIRGINIA

YELLOWSTONE & GRAND TETON NATIONAL PARKS
 AND JACKSON HOLE

YOSEMITE & THE SOUTHERN SIERRA NEVADA

If you are traveling to, moving to, residing in, or just interested in any (or all!) of these enchanting regions, a Great Destinations guidebook is a superior companion. Honest and painstakingly critical, full of information only a local can provide, Great Destinations guidebooks give you all the practical knowledge you need to enjoy the best of each region. Why not own them all?

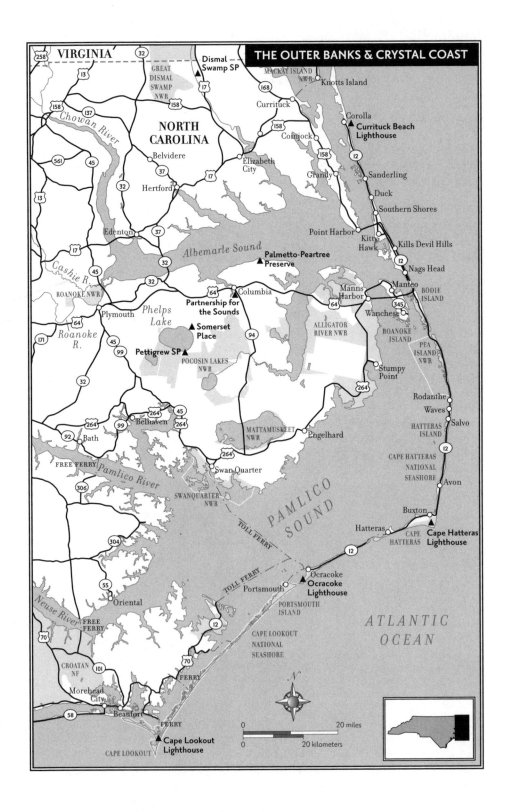

Contents

ACKNOWLEDGMENTS

A book such as this, bringing together so much information on so many different topics, required the help and insight of numerous people, both those who live on the Outer Banks and those who have visited and loved the place.

My thanks to all those who shared their favorite things about the Banks, including A. C. and Dot Hall at the Atlantis Lodge Inn; Linda Molloy and James Charlet at the Chicamacomico Historic Site; Carolyn Peifer, Bob White, and the staff at the Inn at Corolla Light; Sterling Webster, at the helm of the Hilton Garden Inn and Ramada Plaza; Tanya Young at Roanoke Island Festival Park; Miss Barbara Hird and lebame houston, of Elizabeth R & Company, for their outstanding Elizabethan scholarship and their continuing advocacy of the arts and history of the area; Ivy Hanes and Toby Gonzalez of Outer Banks Concierge; William "Billy" K. Brown, founder of the Oregon Inlet Fishing Center, and master storyteller and artist; Captain Aaron Kelly for the thrilling ride aboard the *Rock Solid*; Fran and Jerry Delu at the Ocean Club; Dave and Allison DuBuisson at the Pecan Tree Inn; Larry and Debby Jones at the Inlet Inn; Quinn Capps and Jackie Myers, head of Ocracoke Island Realty, for sharing their insights on Ocracoke; Jim and Bonnie Stewart of the Culpepper Inn, Russell Hadad and Jessica Faulkingham, all in Elizabeth City, truly the "Harbor of Hospitality"; Aaron Tuell at the Outer Banks Visitors Bureau; Ervin Angell at the Whalebone Information Center; and Carol Lohr and Elizabeth Barrow at the Carteret County Tourism Development Authority.

A special thanks to Joan and Wally Sprague at the Welcome Center on Roanoke Island for their kind help to a traveler in distress.

Thanks also to all those anonymous strangers who took the time to answer questions posed by a slightly crazy writer.

My friends and family have been especially supportive during my writing frenzy. To Kaylee and Paul, Holley and Tom, Irene, Jan, Linda, and especially my Mom, thanks for your understanding and encouragement.

A special thanks to Allan Maurer for his continuing support and fine writing advice.

Special thanks also to Caitlin Snead, my research assistant, who helped me look up addresses, kindly posed for pictures, and gave me her honest opinions and valuable time.

In addition, I'd like to thank Kim Grant, Jennifer Thompson, Kermit Hummel, Collette Leonard, and all the people at The Countryman Press who helped make this book a reality.

Introduction

Poised between sky and water, North Carolina's Outer Banks stand as a thin bulwark protecting the rest of the continent behind. A spearhead facing into the wind, a narrow wall marking the separation of land and sea, the Banks exist as they have for centuries, yet are never the same, season to season.

Hurricanes and storms created the Outer Banks, mounding up sand scraped from the ocean floor. But Mother Nature is never satisfied. The face of the Banks changes constantly as nature resculpts this work of art.

Behind the dunes, along the seashore shelters the rich brackish water of the Sounds, where North Carolina's great rivers mingle their fresh waters with the incoming tides. The Sounds—Pamlico, Roanoke, and Bogue—are home to a teaming richness of sea life, including many varieties of shellfish and some of the best sportfishing to be found on the globe.

In this land of sky, sand, and water, it takes a special kind of people to thrive. Despite the flood of visitors that now visit the Banks, the families who have lived here for generations remain, practicing their traditions, preserving their heritage. They welcome, as they always have, the castaways that wash up on their shores, fall in love with the place, and stay.

In this book, we introduce you to some of these people and help you seek out the authentic experiences the Outer Banks have to offer. Whether you're looking for a classic beach vacation, the thrill of extreme sports, immersion in a unique ecosystem, or a walk through history, the coast of North Carolina can be the destination of your dreams.

The Way This Book Works

Our guide covers an area stretching from the Virginia border south to the great Marine base of Camp Lejeune, outside Jacksonville, North Carolina. Between the two, you'll find as much water as land, and often a ferry offers a more direct route than a road.

We'll island hop from north to south, with a chapter for each of the main destinations on the North Carolina Banks. Scattered throughout, we'll take closer looks at some common denominators, such as Banker ponies, lighthouses, and lifesaving stations that stretch all along the coast. You'll also find a special section on the Inner Banks, perfect for daytrips and rich in history.

Special chapters on the history of the region, and the best ways to get there and get around, are at the beginning. Toward the end, you'll find lots of useful information, including a Calendar of Annual Events around the region.

Our special Wright Choices section suggests specific itineraries for different interests. And watch for our Wright Choice selections throughout the book, marked with a star ★.

All cities and towns mentioned in this guide are in North Carolina, unless otherwise noted.

Wherever possible, we've included a Web site address for more information. We've also included places you can get connected with free WiFi access.

We provide lots of specific information on hours and days of operation for most of the attractions on the Outer Banks, and the information was checked as close to publication as possible. However, the Banks change from month to month and season to season. Please use the phone numbers provided to check for current hours before you set out on a long trip to a particular place.

The Outer Banks no longer close down in the winter, as was once the norm. Seasonal closures now are quite random. Most everyone takes a month or two off during the winter; they just don't take the *same* month off. Even locals sometimes find themselves sitting in front of a favorite restaurant looking at a CLOSED sign. Telephone first to avoid disappointment.

A Note on Prices

While summer rates on accommodations still are the highest of the year, various special events or holiday weeks can bump up prices when you might not expect it. Most places go full tilt from Memorial Day to Labor Day, but we'll steer you to places where you won't notice the crowds.

While the Outer Banks traditionally offered mostly weekly rentals, this is changing. Increasingly, options include long weekend specials on cottages as well as hotels, motels, and bed-and-breakfast inns renting rooms by the night.

The listings of both accommodations and restaurants include a wide selection of price points. Rather than give specifics, we use a code based on a range of prices. This range is based on nightly room rates for hotels and per unit for cottages or other rental units. For meals, the range represents entrée prices, tax and tip not included. Most restaurants on the Outer Banks will add a gratuity to bills for large groups.

Price Codes

Code	Lodging	Dining
Inexpensive	up to $80	under $10
Moderate	$80 to $150	$10 to $20
Expensive	$150 to $200	$20 to $25
Very Expensive	$200 and up	$25 and up

Credit card abbreviations used in this book are:

AE—American Express
CB—Carte Blanche
D—Discover Card
DC—Diners Club
J—JCB International Credit Card
MC—Master Card
V—Visa

The forces of wind and water continue to build and destroy dunes along the coast.

1

The History of North Carolina's Banks

A Story of Wild Waters and Independent Souls

The Outer Banks, an isolated string of islands thrust into the Atlantic Ocean, stretch for about 175 miles from the Virginia border to Beaufort Inlet. These fragile bits of land are made entirely of shifting sand, exposed to extremes of wind and water.

To keep a foothold on this uncertain terrain takes a special breed of people. And though they've seen their homesteads washed over with sand, water, and most recently by developers, the Bankers remain—independent, full of stories, and just a bit salty.

The Barrier Islands: A Fragile Ribbon Made of Sand

The island chain now called the Outer Banks juts into the ocean like the bow of a great ship. Here the two great currents of the western Atlantic—the warm, cobalt-blue waters of the Gulf Stream flowing north, and the cold, murky green Labrador Current traveling south— meet and mingle.

It is not a peaceful encounter. The maelstrom where the currents meet extends some 8 miles off the tip of Cape Hatteras. The dreaded Diamond Shoals are a place of fog, shifting sand bars, and sudden surf that have led many ships to their ruin and caused the area to be called "the Graveyard of the Atlantic."

The banks are in constant motion, changed by every storm. Made almost entirely of sand, the land here is forever rolling westward, driven by waves, wind, and rising sea level.

During storms, waves wash across the barrier islands carrying sand from the ocean beach into the sound waters, moving the islands a little westward, and creating new salt marsh. It is a process called "overwash" and is now considered a necessary part of the health of the island ecology. It is also the reason most cottages stand on tall legs above the sand.

This process has been going on for thousands of years and repeats as sea levels rise and fall. Other bands of barrier islands in the past have formed and moved west until they collided with the mainland. Roanoke Island, now situated between the outer islands and the mainland, is one example.

Viewed from above, the temporary nature of the Outer Banks is revealed. The pounding ocean surf is just yards away from the quiet sound waters at some points. Often these are sites where old inlets have closed—or where new ones are in the process of opening.

Other evidence of the moving islands can be found in the ocean surf. In some places, the remnant stumps of forests long drowned emerge from the surf to slash the tires of unwary motorists. One large area of these "wash woods" can be found on the beach just north of the final beach ramp in Corolla.

Blackened oyster shells and chunks of brownish peat sometimes found on beaches provide further clues. These developed in the brackish waters of the sound, then were slowly buried as the island moved west, only to be uncovered by the ocean surf.

THE WINDSWEPT DUNES

Although it is the ocean that provides the material, it is the wind gives shape to the great dunes of sand that are the most notable feature of the Outer Banks. Jockey's Ridge, at nearly 100 feet, is the largest dune on the East Coast and the most southern in a line of dunes that once stretched north over the Virginia border.

Like all dunes, Jockey's Ridge began life with a wind shadow—a tree usually, or even a building—that blocked the wind. Sand behind the obstruction does not blow away, and a dune begins to form. The prevailing winds of the area come from opposite directions. From March through August, roughly, the winds come from the southwest, off the mainland. The rest of the year, September to February, the winds whistle in off the open ocean, across the cold Atlantic. These opposite winds are ideal for the formation of dunes.

The winter winds are stronger, causing the dunes to move slowly to the southwest, usually just inches a year. Jockey's Ridge has slowly swallowed a hamburger stand and a miniature golf course since it became a state park in 1975. You can see the final turrets of a castle on the mini-golf course poking above the sand just across the street from Kitty Hawk Kites.

Jockey's Ridge State Park presents good exhibits on the processes that form the dunes, as well as a spectacular view from the top of the ridge. Dunes also shelter the land at their base from the salt spray, and rich pockets of maritime forest develop in their lee. The nature trails at Jockey's Ridge lead through pockets of forest called "blowouts," where fox, deer, and rabbits make their homes.

North of Jockey's Ridge, **Nags Head Woods** is a mature maritime forest full of pines, bayberry, wax myrtle, cedar, and live oaks. On its north side stands Run Hill, the next in the line of dunes; it can be accessed from West Airfield Road off US 158.

From the top of Run Hill, you can see the sand slowly swallowing the forest on the soundside of the dune, while to the north the next dune in line can be seen. This is **Kill Devil Hill**, the dune used by the Wright Brothers for their experiments in flight. No longer technically a dune, since it has been planted entirely with grass to stabilize it for the monument on top, in the Wright Brothers' day it was as nude as Jockey's Ridge.

The line of dunes continues on toward Virginia, looming to the west as you drive along NC 12 through Duck and beyond. Past the end of the road in Corolla stands the second largest of the untamed dunes, variously called Penny's or Lewark's Hill. The old settlement of Seagull, long buried, is slowly emerging from beneath the ever-traveling sand.

Another undisturbed dune system can be found on Bear Island, part of **Hammocks Beach State Park** near Swansboro.

On Hatteras Island, **Buxton Woods** is the remnant of the great forest of cedar and live oaks laced with grape vines that once covered this island. The trees were timbered off for use in shipbuilding by the mid-1800s, and grazing livestock kept vegetation from regrowing.

Huge dunes, called "whaleheads" by locals, developed on Hatteras during this time and swept across the island. Today they are gone, dissipated into the sound, leaving a relatively flat landscape behind. The low dunes along the oceanfront today are the work of a Civilian Conservation Corps project, which constructed sand fences and planted sea grass to rebuild the dune line in the 1930s.

INLETS AND SOUNDS

While the great dunes are the most obvious work of wind and water, inlets that break up the island chain are the most troubling. A single storm can change the face of the Outer Banks, destroying roads and stranding residents.

In fact, Ocracoke Inlet and Beaufort Inlet are the only breaks in the barrier island chain that remain the same from the time the earliest explorers drew maps of the region in the 1500s. A great hurricane in September of 1846 opened the Hatteras and Oregon Inlets we know today.

The process that gives birth to new inlets originates not from the action of the ocean but from the combination of wind and the fresh water flowing into the sounds from the rivers of the region. Pamlico Sound, the largest lagoon-style body of water on the East Coast, receives vast amounts of water from the Roanoke/Chowan river systems, via Albemarle Sound in the north, as well as the Tar/Pamlico and Neuse rivers farther south. All of this water reaches the ocean through the inlets that pierce the barrier islands.

Hand-carved decoys once were essential to the retail wildfowl trade.

The Wash Woods on the beach at Carova are remnants of ancient forests.

During a hurricane, the water in Pamlico Sound is often driven far northwest during the early hours of the storm, then returns with devastating force as the winds shift to the southeast during the later stages of the hurricane. It is this huge storm surge coming from the landside that opens new inlets in the Outer Banks.

Inlets may close naturally or they may get some help. In September 2003, with the Centennial of Flight celebration fast approaching, Hurricane Isabel opened a new inlet just east of Hatteras Village, isolating the community and its ferry dock. The United States Army Corps of Engineers moved swiftly to pump sand into the breach, closing it within a month, and rebuilding NC 12. By contrast, inlets are generally allowed to open and close as nature dictates on uninhabited Core Banks, within the Cape Lookout National Seashore.

Because of the prevailing winds, inlets tend to migrate southwest, along with the rest of the barrier island chain. This process can be seen at work at Oregon Inlet. Since the 2.5-mile long Herbert C. Bonner Bridge opened over Oregon Inlet in 1965, Bodie Island on the north side of the bridge has extended nearly a mile south while, on the opposite shore,

Pea Island retreated until the southern end of the bridge was threatened and the Army Corps of Engineers was forced to build a rock seawall to protect the underpinnings of the bridge. This is seen as a temporary measure however, and plans for a new bridge are in the works. Meanwhile, dredging continues year round to keep Oregon Inlet open for the sport and commercial fishing fleets that depend on this route to reach the open ocean.

THE INNER BANKS

The sounds to the west of the Outer Banks vary in width from just a few hundred yards to more than 50 miles. Beyond lie the shores, if you can call them that, of the Inner Banks. Here brackish and fresh waters mix together in broad tidal estuaries, marshes, and wetlands, creating one of the richest breeding grounds for sea life on the planet.

These swamps provide some of the last refuges for endangered species, such as the red wolf and red-cockaded woodpecker, and are at the northern limit of the American alligator. Black bear, deer, raccoon, turkey, squirrel, rabbits, quail, mink, and otter make this their home, as do a large variety of poisonous snakes and biting insects. Winter is considered the best time to visit. That's when the region's most beautiful visitors arrive for their winter vacations. Some 100,000 tundra swans—plus many more geese, ducks, coots, and other migrating waterfowl—make the lakes of this region their cold-weather home.

The Carolina bays are unusual features found within this wilderness. These round or oval depressions have been variously attributed to giant prehistoric beavers, an ancient asteroid shower, or—most likely—a remnant of falling sea level at the height of the last Ice Age. Found scattered all along the southern Atlantic seaboard, these bays, also called *pocosins*, are most numerous in eastern North Carolina, where thousands have been identified. Rimmed with sand, pocosins often contain acidic lakes surrounded by thick layers of peat. Bay trees, vines, and briars survive best in this nutrient poor soil, and cypress trees grow along the water's edge.

Some pocosin plants have developed unusual behaviors to supplement their diets. This ecosystem is the evolutionary cradle of carnivorous plants, including the Venus fly-trap and the less well-known pitcher plant and sundew. In fact, the Croatan National Forest is home to the nation's largest collection of carnivorous plants.

"A LAND OF PLENTIE"

Raleigh's explorers brought back stories of great abundance to entice settlers to make the voyage into the unknown. They described a land "so full of grapes as the very beating and surge of the Sea overflowed them." These grapes were the native scuppernongs, of which the 400-year-old Mother Vine on Roanoke Island is the oldest surviving example. Scientists speculate that the native tribes in the area began the cultivation of grapes, even before the arrival of the English settlers.

The Banks, then and now, are home to white-tailed deer and the occasional black bear that makes the swim from the mainland. Today's bears have been known to make use of the causeways to reach the Banks.

The ecosystem found along these shores is unique. Buxton Woods, at the base of Cape Hatteras Lighthouse, supports a population of rare plants and the greatest diversity of mammals of any barrier island along the East Coast. The forests, marshes, and freshwater ponds of the Banks also play host to a vast variety of birds, from migrating songbirds to waterfowl, and are the year-round home of ospreys and other raptors, as well as many wading birds. Rare pelagic species are found off-shore on the Gulf Stream. Some 400 species have been spotted in this region, making it one of the prime birding destinations along the East Coast. Several beach areas provide important nesting grounds for the endangered piping plover.

Endangered sea turtles also come to the Banks to nest from May to August. Loggerhead and Green are the species most commonly found, with Kemp's Ridley, Hawksbill, and Leatherback turtles making occasional appearances. The Network for Endangered Sea Turtles (252-441-8622;

The Scotch Bonnet, state shell of North Carolina and a rare find

www.nestonline.org) maintains a 24-hour hotline for turtle sightings.

Beachcombers will find plenty to spark their interest on these shores. Although the heavy surf pounds many shells to fragments, a stroll along the beach, especially in early spring at low tide, may yield a trove of shells, including quahog clams, scallops, pen shells, olives, moon snails, Atlantic giant cockles, and Scotch bonnets, the state shell of North Carolina. Shelling is generally best at the ends of the islands, along the inlet shores.

An excellent collection of shells is on permanent display at the **North Carolina Maritime Museum** in Beaufort. On the North Banks, the **Hampton Inn and Suites Corolla** displays a fine private collection in its lobby.

NATIVE TRIBES

By the time the English first arrived off the Outer Banks, the area had been occupied for thousands of years by tribes of Native Americans. The coast of North Carolina had villages belonging to all three major linguistic groups then inhabiting eastern North America.

The most numerous were the Algonquian-speaking tribes occupying the northern Banks and the shores of Albemarle Sound. Although often warring among themselves, the Roanoke, Croatan, and the tribes of the Chowan river valley spoke languages related to those of the tribes of Virginia and the Chesapeake Bay.

To the west, the Tuscarora tribes spoke an Iroquoian language, indicating their origin in the eastern Great Lakes region.

The southern Banks and the area around today's New Bern were home to tribes speaking Siouan dialects. The Woccon occupying Ocracoke, and the Coree who lived in Carteret County and gave their name to the Core Banks, belonged to this group.

Early maps created by English explorers show dozens of native villages occupying the Banks and the shores of adjacent sounds and rivers. Population at the time of first contact is estimated to have been in the neighborhood of 10,000 souls.

The coastal regions occupied by the native tribes offered a rich selection of foods. In addition to deer, waterfowl, and much other game, the Indians depended on the ample fish and shellfish, including crabs, oysters, clams, scallops, and mussels, found in the waters of the sounds.

Great piles of shells mark the location of many Indian villages on the Banks. Today these can be found in Wanchese; on Colington Island adjacent to Kill Devil Hills; at Indian Town near Buxton; and at Shell Point on Harkers Island. Many of the tribes apparently occupied their coastal encampments for just part of the year, retiring to mainland villages to grow crops of various tubers and root vegetables, as well as corn, squash, pumpkins, gourds, beans, and sunflowers. They also gathered wild walnuts, hickory nuts, and chinquapins, wild grains, and fruits.

Early explorers reported that the local tribes drank wine made from local grapes, as well as a tea made from the leaves of the yaupon tree, still found abundantly in the maritime forests. Tobacco was grown as a sacred herb.

Much of our knowledge of how the Indians lived comes from drawings made by John White in 1585. The Indian Village recreated at **Roanoke Island Festival Park** is based on White's research.

Roanoke Island was a center of Native American activity in precolonial times. Its name indicates it was a manufacturing center for making the shell money used by the native tribes in trade. *Roanoke* was a type of wampum that consisted of round disks of shell cut from whelk and clamshells. White was the most common color, but black or purple beads were worth more. The name seems to come from the Algonquian word that means to rub, smooth, or polish—a reference to how the beads were made.

The Croatan Indians had their main village, called Croatoan, on what is now the island of Hatteras, near the village of Buxton. Recently, archeologists conducted excavations, discovering many pottery shards and a few English artifacts amid enormous numbers of discarded oyster shells. Like most tribes, the Croatans also held land on the mainland more suitable for agriculture. Growing crops on the Banks themselves was difficult because of the high salt content of the soil. Hatteras is derived from an Algonquian word, *hatorask,* which has been translated as "place where nothing will grow."

Hatteras-style clam chowder, a unique dish found on the Outer Banks

European diseases decimated the tribes, a process completed by the Tuscarora War. This uprising began in 1711 as the tribes protested the taking of their lands, as well as the capture and enslavement of their people. Most tribes in the area joined the rebellion, in a last ditch effort to expel the English and preserve their traditional ways of life. The natives were utterly defeated in 1715, and the survivors enslaved or driven inland.

Most of the Tuscarora migrated north to join with their cousins in the Iroquois Confederacy. The surviving Coree settled near Lake Mattamuskeet, while many of the Croatan people disappeared into the deep swamps surrounding

Wild Horses: Free Spirits of the Banks

Manes flying in the wind, hooves leaving their imprint in sand, the herds of wild horses that make their home among the dunes are some of the most popular—and most endangered—tourist attractions of the Outer Banks. Once the herds roamed at will from Virginia to Shackleford Banks. Today they are confined to narrow stretches of land and a few islands, their numbers controlled by park rangers often more concerned with the survival of native grasses than that of the horses, which they consider "exotic species."

These attitudes are at odds with the beliefs and wishes of most of the local inhabitants. Early settlers reported that the horses were there before them, and the old families of the Banks tell tales of taming the local horses. They pulled pony carts and plows, helped the surfmen of the Life-Saving Service rescue shipwrecked sailors, and raced around Jockey's Ridge.

On Ocracoke, locals held a pony penning on July 4th every year, rounding up the native ponies and selecting some to be sold off-island, thus stabilizing the size of the herd. The island's Boy Scout Troop, established in 1956, was the first mounted troop in the country. Each boy caught, tamed, and trained his own horse.

When most of Ocracoke, including the area where the herds roamed free, became part of the Cape Hatteras National Seashore, the park rangers wanted to remove all the ponies to prevent overgrazing and to protect the ponies themselves from the traffic on NC 12. Local Ocracokers organized a protest and managed to keep some of the ponies on the island. About 25-30 ponies remain on Ocracoke, now confined to a 180-acre "pony pen."

Wild or feral horses are still found at several other locations on North Carolina's Banks. About 90 individuals live north of Corolla in the off-road area next to the Virginia state line. Once free-roaming, the Corolla herd is now confined to about 12,000 acres north of a fence and cattle guard near the end of NC 12. The horses were moved behind the fence after collisions with auto-mobiles led to numerous fatalities. In one accident alone, six horses were killed. The Corolla Wild Horse Fund (www.corollawildhorses.com) operates an educational museum and store to support the herd.

Further south, the horses of Shackleford Banks (www.shacklefordhorses.org) live much as their ancestors did, running free on a barrier island with no road or other traffic to threaten them. Nearby, an unrelated herd of feral horses, descended from a herd released here by a local farmer in the 1940s, occupies Carrot Island.

The origin of the Banker ponies and horses has been much debated, but scientific evidence is mounting to support the theory that they are descended from Spanish horses brought to these shores in great numbers by early explorers, as well as from ships wrecked along the coast. Horses are great swimmers and, according to records, were often driven overboard to lighten a ship stuck on a sandbar.

The Corolla, Ocracoke, and Shackleford horses all exhibit typical Spanish traits, including five rather than six lumbar vertebrae. In addition, a unique and rare blood variant found only in horses of Spanish descent is carried by the Shackleford herd. DNA tests are ongoing, but the Horse of the Americas organization recently officially recognized the Corolla and Shackleford herds as Heritage Herds of Colonial Spanish Horses. On a less positive note, the American Livestock Breed Conservancy in 2008 moved both herds from the threatened to the critical category, on the verge of extinction.

Alligator River. Other Croatans migrated to the shores of the Lumbee River close to the South Carolina border and joined with the remnants of other tribes to become the forefathers of today's Lumbee Indians.

Early Explorers and First Contact

Spanish explorers visited coastal Carolina as early as 1520, and in 1524, Giovanni da Verrazano, a Florentine captain sailing under the French flag in search of the Northwest Passage, landed on the Bogue Banks in Pine Knoll Shores, and again near today's Kitty Hawk. He was the first to comment on the vast quantities of grapes growing along the shore, but he mistook Pamlico Sound for the Pacific Ocean.

In 1584, Sir Walter Raleigh received a patent from his queen "for the discovering and planting of new lands not possessed by any Christian Prince nor inhabited by Christian People . . . to continue for the space of 6 yeeres and no more." Raleigh sent a reconnaissance voyage out that very summer. Captains Amadas and Barlowe brought back two young Indians, a Croatan named Manteo and a Roanoke brave named Wanchese, and gave such a glowing report about the new land that Queen Elizabeth allowed Raleigh to name his colony Virginia, in her honor.

Subsequent voyages in 1585 and 1586 didn't go as smoothly. Sir Richard Grenville

No one knows the origin of the wild ponies that live on the Outer Banks.

Raleigh's Lost Colony: Theories and Clues to Its Fate

Despite the 400 years since the colonists of the short-lived "Citie of Ralegh" disappeared, the mystery continues to attract public interest as well as scientific research and speculation.

Certainly the colonists died, but when and by what means remain matters of debate. Perhaps they perished through starvation, disease, or massacre, at the hands of either the Spanish or the native tribes. Perhaps some trusted to the sea, and tried to sail home on their small pinnace. Perhaps some joined the Croatan tribe, the friendliest of the natives, thanks to the continuing good will of Manteo. Most likely several of these theories are correct and their fates took them down different roads.

In the 1930s, a series of stones emerged that seemed to be engraved with messages from Eleanor Dare to her father John White, as she moved southwest with Indian friends. They passed several scientific tests in the beginning, but today are generally considered bogus.

In 1701, the Indians then inhabiting Hatteras Island told naturalist John Lawson that they were descended from English ancestors, and Lawson noted that many of the group had light hair and grey eyes.

The Jamestown colonists made several efforts to find traces of the Roanoke Island group less than 30 years after their disappearance. They discovered nothing conclusive, but an abundance of rumors about men who dressed in European clothes and lived in two-story houses or who could "talk in a book." One chief claimed to have sent several youths and a "younge maide" to beat copper at his mine up the Roanoke River, but they were never found. Powhatan, the father of Pocahontas, when consulted on the missing colonists' fate, claimed they had been massacred after taking refuge with a Chesapeake tribe.

The political situation back in England gives perspective to these findings. It was to the benefit of the newcomers and their sponsor King James I if the colonists could be proved to have perished. A surviving colony would further Sir Walter Raleigh's continued claim to Virginia.

Certainly, John White, who had perhaps the most reason to seek his daughter and granddaughter, initially felt minimal concern for their fate. The carved letters he found at the abandoned stockade indicated clearly to him that the colonists had taken refuge with the friendly Croatan tribe, and were not in immediate danger, since he found no carved cross—the agreed upon sign of distress.

Research into the fate of the colony picked up speed around the 400th anniversary of its

grounded his ship in Ocracoke Inlet, the sailors spread smallpox through the native villages, and the men left on Roanoke Island were soon in conflict with the local tribe.

In 1587, John White, an artist who had accompanied one of the earlier voyages, arrived with a party of colonists at Roanoke Island. Among the colonists were the first English women to cross the ocean, including White's pregnant daughter Eleanor. Abandoned on Roanoke Island by the captain of their transport vessel, White's group soon found themselves reliant on the good will of Manteo and his mother, head of the Croatan people. Using the superiority of British arms, White drove off the local Roanoke tribe and installed Manteo as Duke of much of the Albemarle Peninsula, including the Alligator River region.

After the birth and christening of his granddaughter, Virginia Dare, White was persuaded to return to London for additional supplies, but was unable to return to "Virginia" until 1590, because of the attack of the Spanish Armada on England. When he finally set foot once again on Roanoke Island, he found only the letters CRO and CROTOAN carved in the logs of the colonists' palisade. A hurricane drove his ship back across the Atlantic before he could visit Manteo's people.

Despite extensive investigations, nothing certain was ever heard of the 117 colonists and the enduring mystery of the Lost Colony was born.

disappearance. In the early 1990s, an archeological dig at the Fort Raleigh site found a metallurgical workshop used by the 1585 expedition, but no trace of the living area of the colonists. Researchers speculate that the site may have washed away and is now underwater.

In 1998, excavations conducted on Hatteras Island at the site of large Indian village, believed to be the Croatan capital, turned up an English signet ring with ties to the English colonists.

Two separate research organizations continue to investigate the mystery. The **First Colony Foundation** (www.firstcolonyfoundation.org), a group of historians, archeologists, and concerned citizens, are concentrating their efforts on finding the area occupied by the 1587 colonists at the north end of Roanoke Island. They have conducted underwater surveys in the nearby sound, as well as archeological digs within the National Historic Park.

The Lost Colony Center for Science and Research (www.lost-colony.com), a group of interested amateur scientists and historians, is looking farther afield for evidence of the Lost Colony. Using satellite technology, remote sensing, oral histories, and primary sources, they are exploring the fate of the lost colonists on several fronts. Currently they are conducting DNA studies in America and Britain, attempting to find mitochondrial and Y-chromosome matches among several populations.

One of the Center's most intriguing theories is based on John White's statement that the colonists planned to move 50 miles into the mainland after his departure. Using old maps and other records, Philip McMullan speculates that the colonists relocated to a Croatan village about 50 miles away on the Alligator River, where abundant stands of sassafras trees were located.

Sassafras was the main cash crop of the early years of American colonization, before tobacco came to the fore. The roots of the sassafras were at the time believed to cure syphilis, a newly introduced disease then running rampant through Europe.

While Raleigh's early voyages are well-known, few are aware of the later voyages he sponsored to bring home cargos of sassafras. In 1602, sassafras was selling for up to 2,000 British pounds per ton, and the profits from one voyage in that year permitted Raleigh to fit out two more ships in 1603. The location where Raleigh's captains found these cargos, ready for shipment, was a closely guarded secret, and may well have been the Alligator River region.

LORDS PROPRIETORS AND THE IRON MEN OF ALBEMARLE

By the 1650s, planters from Jamestown began to move down the Chowan River and into the Albemarle area, spreading gradually south. In 1662 Charles II granted the lands south of Virginia to eight of his cronies, called the Lords Proprietors, who named the region Carolina in his honor.

Over the next several decades, the new owners of Carolina took measures to tighten their control over the Albemarle colonists, decreasing the power of elected officials. A series of clashes between the Proprietory and anti-Proprietory parties culminated in Culpeper's Rebellion in 1677, the first uprising against British tyranny in the colonies. The planters that inhabited the banks of Albemarle Sound earned the name of "Iron Men," thanks to their stiff determination on self-rule.

About 1696, settlers moved to the region of Bath on Pamlico Sound and, in 1706, the village became the first incorporated town in North Carolina.

In 1710, Baron Christoph von Graffenried led a group of Swiss and German Protestants to Carolina where they founded the town of New Bern. In doing so, they displaced an important American Indian town and precipitated the Tuscarora War, which killed hundreds of white settlers in the following years.

Beaufort, named for Henry Somerset, Duke of Beaufort, one of the Lords Proprietors, was established in 1713 next to the deep-water inlet then called Topsail, making it the third oldest town in the colony.

Most of the action in the Carolinas during the War for American Independence took place further south and west, however North Carolinians across the state formed Committees of Safety to prepare for the coming war and protests by the "Sons of Liberty" began as early as 1765. In 1774, the ladies of Edenton organized a boycott of English tea in support of American Independence. Their Edenton Tea Party is one of the earliest political actions on record organized by women.

Josiah Martin, the royal governor, was forced to flee his palace in New Bern in 1776 after the North Carolina militia defeated Tory forces at Moore's Creek Bridge near Wilmington. This battle, which took place on February 27, 1776, was the first decisive patriot victory of the war and ended British control of North Carolina.

THE CIVIL WAR ON THE BANKS

The Confederates built numerous fortifications along the Banks in the early days of the Civil War. Gun batteries were built on Huggin's Island (now part of Hammocks Beach State Park), on Beacon Island in Ocracoke Inlet, at the southern end of Hatteras Island, and on Roanoke Island. In April 1861, the Confederates occupied Fort Macon, built in 1826 to defend the port of Beaufort.

Union General Ben Butler attacked the forts on Hatteras Island at the end of August 1861, the first amphibious attack of the war. Confederate troops based on Roanoke Island attempted to retake Hatteras in September. The armies chased each other up and down the island for several days, causing the locals to dub the battle the "Chicamacomico Races."

Union forces took Roanoke Island on February 7, 1862, and that spring New Bern and Fort Macon fell. The Confederate "mosquito fleet" was defeated off Elizabeth City, and Plymouth and other towns in North Carolina's northeast soon were under Union control. The Confederates managed to defend the Dismal Swamp Canal and the Wilmington & Weldon Railroad, keeping the supply lines to Richmond open. The port of Wilmington, defended by Fort Fisher at the mouth of the Cape Fear River, remained open until the final months of the war.

During the war, the Confederates built many ironclads in the rivers of North Carolina and sent them downstream to do battle with Union gunboats. In April of 1864, the Confederates successfully recaptured the port of Plymouth with the support of the ironclad *CSS Albemarle*. This was the last major Confederate victory of the Civil War.

Civil War Trail markers dot the eastern North Carolina landscape. You can find a list of sites at www.civilwartraveler.com. A working replica of the *CSS Albemarle* still patrols the river at Plymouth.

During the war, Roanoke Island hosted a unique social experiment, the **Freedmen's Colony** (www.roanokefreedmenscolony.com). Many slaves from nearby regions escaped and made their way behind Union lines. Declared "contraband" by the U.S. military, these men, women, and children settled in a New England–style village, which included a sawmill, church, and schools. By war's end, the population reached an estimated 3,500. The village was dismantled after the war, but many inhabitants of Roanoke Island today trace their family history back to the Freedmen's Colony.

Blackbeard and the Age of Pirates

Although the name of Blackbeard looms large in North Carolina history, his actual career of piracy was relatively short. Like many eventual pirates, Edward Teach, a.k.a. Blackbeard, originally served aboard a privateer with letters of marque from Queen Anne of Britain. These permitted him to capture French and Spanish ships during the War of Spanish Succession, called Queen Anne's War in North America.

After the war ended in 1714, many of the privateers continued to attack foreign ships, only their actions were now considered piracy. In 1717, the royal government offered a one-time pardon to English privateers turned pirates, and most of the active pirates accepted.

Teach, which may or may not have been Blackbeard's true name, first rose to prominence as the magistrate of the short-lived Pirate's Republic on the island of Nassau. In 1717, he and his associate Captain Benjamin Hornigold captured the French slave ship *Le Concorde*. Teach equipped the ship with 20 guns and made it his flagship, renaming it the *Queen Anne's Revenge* (*QAR*). In May 1718, he committed his most daring feat—a blockade of Charleston harbor. Blackbeard's demand was unusual: he would release his hostages and leave the harbor in return for a box of medicine.

Pirates provide some of the region's most colorful history.

Shortly after Charleston met his demands, Blackbeard sailed his fleet of four vessels north, loaded with treasure taken from Spanish ships of the line. The *QAR* ran aground in Beaufort Inlet. Historians speculate that Teach purposely beached the vessel to rid himself of most of his crew. Certainly the flagship could never navigate the shallow inshore waters of the Outer Banks. Divers found what is believed to be the wreck of the *QAR* in 1996 in waters off Fort Macon.

The Meka II, based in Beaufort, is an authentic reproduction of a pirate ship, captained by Horatio Sinbad.

Teach off-loaded most of his treasure onto the *Adventure*, a smaller vessel, left the majority of the crew on a convenient sandbar, and sailed up Pamlico Sound to Bath, where he accepted the royal pardon from Governor Charles Eden and reportedly married a local girl. The area was a familiar one for Teach. Legend says he had houses in both Beaufort and Bath at various times.

His domestic bliss was short-lived however, and by the fall of 1718 he was once again under sail. By November, reports located him at Ocracoke Inlet, roasting pigs, drinking meal wine, the local liquor, and partying with other pirates. Here Lt. Robert Maynard, of the Royal Navy, caught up with Blackbeard, and in a pitched battle at a spot called Teach's Hole, cut off the pirate's head, ending the career—but not the fame—of North Carolina's most notorious pirate.

GREAT STORMS, LOST SHIPS, AND HEROIC RESCUES

No one knows how many ships have been lost off the North Carolina Banks. Estimates range from the hundreds to many thousands. All agree, however, that this shore richly deserves its reputation as "Graveyard of the Atlantic." Bodie (pronounced "body") Island seems to have been named for the many shipwreck victims washing up on its shores. From the famous ironclad, *USS Monitor,* lost off Cape Hatteras in 1862, to the latest fishing trawler that fails to return to port, the ocean continues to exact its toll.

Storms are the greatest danger, and hurricanes arriving from the tropics June through November cause widespread devastation. But residents of the Banks fear the northeasters that blow in just as much. Storms, such as the Ash Wednesday storm of 1962, the Halloween storm of 1991, and the Thanksgiving storm of 2006, live on in local lore.

As early as 1792, the United States Congress authorized the building of lighthouses along this coast to aide navigation. Wooden light towers were constructed at Bald Head Island on the Cape Fear River in 1795, and on Shell Castle Island in Ocracoke Inlet in 1798. The first Cape Hatteras Lighthouse was completed in 1803, and a light tower began operation at Cape Lookout three years later.

The lighthouses were upgraded over the years, but ships continued to run ashore, with crew and passengers perishing just yards from safety. The local fishermen and farmers along the Banks frequently came to the aide of shipwreck victims. Many of them were descendants of mariners who survived earlier wrecks and stayed to make a life on this harsh shore.

In 1874 the U.S. Life-Saving Service (www.lifesaving service.org), a division of the U.S. Department of the Treasury, established seven stations along the Outer Banks. One of the earliest was the **Chicamacomico Station** (www .chicamacomico.net) in Rodanthe, where the original buildings have been beautifully restored. Several other early stations survive, although not in their original forms. The Kitty Hawk station today houses the Black Pelican Restaurant; the Caffey's Inlet station serves as the Boathouse Restaurant at the Sanderling Resort; and the Kill Devil Hills station was moved to Corolla to become a real estate office. The Little Kinnakeet station near Avon is being restored by the National Park Service.

Most of the surfmen manning these stations were locals, seeking to supplement their incomes and carrying on a tra-

Lifesaving stations once lined the coast, giving aide to sailors in distress.

Bodie Island Light

Currituck Beach Light

Cape Hatteras Light

Ocracoke Light

Cape Lookout Light

dition of service to those in peril at sea. A series of devastating wrecks during 1877 and 1878 caused Congress to authorize an additional 11 stations along the North Carolina coast. Lifesaving stations were eventually located about 4 miles apart along the entire Outer Banks.

The surfmen patrolled every mile of beach on foot or horseback 24 hours a day. When a ship in distress was sighted, they launched lifeboats through the surf or used a small cannon to send a line from the beach to the wreck, allowing them to bring survivors to safety using the breeches buoy apparatus or a metal life car.

Many of the Life-Saving Service's most daring rescues took place on the Outer Banks. Some of the most notable include the rescue of the crew of the schooner *E. S. Newman* in 1896 by the men of the Pea Island Life-Saving Station, the only station staffed by African Americans, and the rescue by the Chicamacomico station of the crew of the British tanker *Mirlo*, after it was torpedoed by a German U-boat in 1918. In 1899, Rasmus Midgett of the Gull Shoal Station single-handedly rescued the 10-man crew of the barkentine *Priscilla*.

The men of the Life-Saving Service had a motto: "You have to go out, but nothing says you have to come back." This same brave spirit and commitment continue today in the U.S. Coast Guard, a service established in 1915 by the merger of the Life-Saving Service and the Revenue Cutter Service. One of the Coast Guard's largest bases is located at Elizabeth City.

TAKING TO THE AIR

The first years of the 20th century were important ones on the Outer Banks. The work of the Wright Brothers that led to the first airplane flight at Kill Devil Hills in 1903 is well-known. However, not far away, inventor Reginald Fessenden was developing another important invention—the wireless telegraph, which led directly to radio and today's wireless technology. Working for the U.S. Weather Bureau, Fessenden successfully sent a message from Hatteras Island to Weirs Point on Roanoke Island on April 26, 1902, a demonstration witnessed by several Navy officers. The development of wireless technology proved a great advance in weather forecasting and an important new aide to keep ships safe at sea.

Wilbur and Orville Wright began coming to Kitty Hawk in 1900 to conduct glider experiments. They returned to test improved gliders the next two years, and in the fall of 1903 arrived with a powered flyer equipped with a wooden propeller and an aluminum engine created in their bicycle shop. On December 17, they successfully left the ground, and the Age of Flight began.

The Wright Brothers returned to their campsite on Kill Devil Hill in 1908, to test a new airplane with improved controls and two upright seats. Mechanic Charlie Furnas flew as the first air passenger on May 14, the beginning of air travel.

THE GERMAN U-BOAT INVASION

During World War II, a major battle raged off the Outer Banks, still largely unknown to the American people. From the time of Pearl Harbor and the American declaration of war, dozens of German U-boats were active along the Atlantic Coast. Some came so close they reported seeing the lights from U.S. cities.

Afraid of causing panic, the U.S. government did not call for a blackout until August 1942. Sinking tankers and cargo boats along the coast was so easy that German commanders referred to it as "the great American turkey shoot." The U-boats sank nearly 400 Allied ships off the North Carolina coast during this period, with over 5,000 lives lost. The seas off Diamond Shoals earned yet another ominous name: Torpedo Junction.

Sharks now haunt the wrecks of German U-boats in the Graveyard of the Atlantic.

Winged Horses of the Outer Banks

During the Centennial of Flight in 2003, 99 life-sized fiberglass winged horses and foals, decorated by local artists, lined the streets of the Outer Banks. The sponsor of the project, the Outer Banks Press, selected the horses to represent both the iconic herds of wild mustangs that still roam the Banks and the development of flight. The resulting works of art, each unique, were tremendously popular with residents and visitors alike. Seventy of the winged horses, some a bit battered by wind and rain, can still be seen at locations around the region, from Corolla to Ocracoke. A full listing of the current locations of the Winged Horses can be found on the Outer Banks Press Web site, www.outerbankspress.com.

The war in the shipping lanes was no secret to the residents of the Outer Banks, who witnessed great explosions and fires off the coast and found the bodies of burned and drowned seamen washed up on their beaches. The people of Ocracoke buried several British sailors when a submarine sank the *HMS Bedfordshire*. The British Cemetery there is the only official bit of British soil in the United States, outside of the embassy in Washington, DC.

By mid-1942, the U.S. military began to counterattack against the German subs. Air submarine patrols took off from the Manteo airport and naval stations were established on Ocracoke and at Morehead City. The top-secret **Loop Control Station** on Ocracoke intercepted transmissions from the German U-boats that helped locate them.

The U.S. Coast Guard and U.S. Navy finally got the better of the German fleet. Four U-boats are known to rest on the ocean bottom off the Banks, and are now favorite destinations for divers.

TOURISM—PAST, PRESENT, FUTURE

The first seasonal visitors to the Outer Banks arrived in the early 1800s as planters in the Albemarle region looked for a healthier place for their families to spend the summer. Francis Nixon, a Perquimans County planter, is the first on record. He brought his family to the Banks village at the base of Jockey's Ridge in 1830 to escape an outbreak of malaria. Soon after, Nixon bought 200 acres stretching across the Banks from the sound to the ocean, and Nags Head, the first resort destination on the Outer Banks was born.

In 1838, the 200-room Nags Head Hotel, located on the shore of the sound, opened. Visitors arriving at its dock could look forward to a season of balls and formal dinners, as well as bowling, card games, and ocean bathing. A boardwalk connected the hotel with the ocean, and local Bankers made good incomes transporting visitors to the shore in their pony carts. Today that hotel lies buried beneath the dunes of Jockey's Ridge, which slowly swallowed the property in the 1870s. By then, the vacation village had shifted its focus to the ocean beach.

Around 1855, Elizabeth City physician Dr. W. G. Pool bought 50 acres of oceanfront property from the Midgetts, who were then, as they are now, a prominent Banker family. Pool paid a reported $30 and sold lots to his neighbors in Elizabeth City for $1 each. By 1885 there were 13 cottages lining the shore, the first of the "Unpainted Aristocracy" of Nags Head. Several of these historic cottages still survive, although most have been moved back from the ocean several times, as storms washed away the sand in front of them.

In the years following the Civil War, Northern businessmen discovered the superb waterfowl hunting available in the region. Much of the land around the sounds was bought by hunt clubs, where sportsmen were accommodated in varying degrees of luxury during their annual winter visits.

The 1920s brought a new group of tourists to the Outer Banks as the first waves of motorists arrived in their Model Ts, crossing the sounds on ferries or taking an adventurous route along the tide line. The year of 1928 saw two causeways built to make access to the Banks easier. In Morehead City, a toll bridge linked the end of the rail line to an ocean bathing pavilion on Bogue Banks, in today's Atlantic Beach. And in the same year, the Washington Baum Bridge linked Roanoke Island with Nags Head.

Now a water sports capital, the Outer Banks attracts windsurfers from around the world.

The Baum project was a true leap of faith. At the time, the only way to reach Roanoke Island was by a lengthy journey on a rough road through Alligator Swamp and then by ferry from the mainland. On the Nags Head end, the bridge ended in sandy ruts leading north and south; no roads had yet been paved on the Banks. However, Baum, then chairman of the Dare County Board of Commissioners, was a big believer in the philosophy "if you build it, they will come."

National attention was focused on the Outer Banks in 1928. It was the 25th anniversary of the Wright Brothers' first flight and the National Aeronautic Association commemorated the event by placing a 10-ton boulder at the point of takeoff. The next year, work began on the 60-foot tall Wright Memorial pylon, which was dedicated in 1932, the beginning of the **Wright Memorial National Historic Site.**

W. O. Saunders, founder and editor of the Elizabeth City *Independent* newspaper, was another of the area's notable boosters. He advocated the development of the Wright Memorial, and helped organize the group of Elizabeth City businessmen who built the Wright Memorial Bridge from the Currituck mainland to Kitty Hawk. The 3-mile bridge was completed in 1930, and in 1931, the state paved the Beach Road, now NC 12, between the Nags Head and Kitty Hawk bridges.

Dubbed the **Virginia Dare Trail**, the new road made it possible for motorists to drive on pavement from the mainland all the way to the gates of the "Citie of Ralegh" on Roanoke Island. This re-creation of Raleigh's colony, originally built by local history buffs, became part of the National Park system in 1941.

The Lost Colony outdoor drama, another Saunders idea, was first performed in 1937. Franklin D. Roosevelt attended a performance and the drama, originally intended to be a one-season affair to celebrate the 250th anniversary of Virginia Dare's birth, continues to be produced today, more than 70 years later.

In 1933, Saunders and one of his columnists, Frank Stick, began promoting another project in the *Independent*, this one for a coastal park that would restore and protect the rapidly eroding beaches of the Outer Banks. The idea caught on and funds for the restoration of the dunes along the bald beaches were allocated at the federal level.

The Civil Works Administration and its successor, the Civilian Conservation Corps, began work constructing sand fences and planting sea grasses to rebuild the dunes in late 1933. The project was a success, and by 1940 a barrier dune as much as 25 feet high ran from the Virginia state line all the way to Hatteras Inlet, and along about half of the Ocracoke Island beachfront. It proved impossible to build dunes as far as Cape Lookout because the Core Banks were still being used as pasturage for free-roaming horses and cattle.

Meanwhile, the Cape Hatteras Seashore Commission sought donations of land for the proposed seashore park. In 1935, the owners of a hunt club on Hatteras donated 999 acres surrounding the Cape Hatteras Lighthouse to the project. Other donations followed, until the beginning of World War II put seashore protection on hold.

The post-war years brought a boom in tourism and a rise in property values that almost put an end to the project, but in 1952 an anonymous donation for the purchase of park lands made the **Cape Hatteras National Seashore** a reality nearly 20 years after it was first approved by the U.S. Congress.

The Cape Lookout National Seashore followed in 1966. Together, these national parks preserve a unique and ever-changing ecosystem that continues to attract visitors from around the world.

A North Carolina state ferry

2

Transportation

A Maritime Tradition

Once, not so long ago, a trip to the Outer Banks required a voyage by water. The first inhabitants arrived in dugout canoes made from cypress logs. The area was a popular stop for the Native American tribes of the East Coast who lived well on the plentiful shellfish and numerous waterfowl. Later, English settlers arrived in ships much like the *Elizabeth II,* docked today on Manteo's waterfront.

The colonial settlers eventually found the Native American canoe a more practical boat than the English-style vessel. The North Carolina sounds required a boat that could navigate shallow waters, so the colonists fitted out a cypress dugout with two masts and sails, inventing the periauger.

With time, the periauger evolved into other shallow-draft vessels suitable for the unique conditions and lifestyles of the Banks. The shad boat and the sharpie are two of the best known, and have influenced the Carolina Custom fishing boats still built on Harkers Island and in Wanchese, where strong boatbuilding traditions continue today.

The **North Carolina Maritime Museums** in Beaufort and Manteo have recreated the wooden boats of old. You can see modern examples at their docks, and perhaps go for a sail. The region's boats are on display at Beaufort's annual Wooden Boat Festival, Day at the Docks in Hatteras Village, and other regional celebrations.

As tourism got underway in the years before the Civil War, packet boats brought families from inland ports to spend a week or a season on the Banks. On the islands themselves, horse carts were the preferred method of transportation.

The invention of the automobile caused a great change on the Outer Banks, as elsewhere. Ferries, at first just adapted fishing boats, replaced the packet boats. Motorists swarmed to the Banks, despite the very real danger of getting stuck in the sand.

Eventually many of the ferries gave way to long causeways that crossed the shallow sounds. The sandy tracks behind the dunes were paved and became state roads.

TRAVELING BY LAND

Most of the more than 7 million visitors who come to North Carolina's Outer Banks each year arrive by private automobile. Some drive from home; others fly into Norfolk, Newport News, Raleigh/Durham, Wilmington, or some other airport, and hire a rental car.

An automobile is almost required for a vacation on the Outer Banks, except for the most

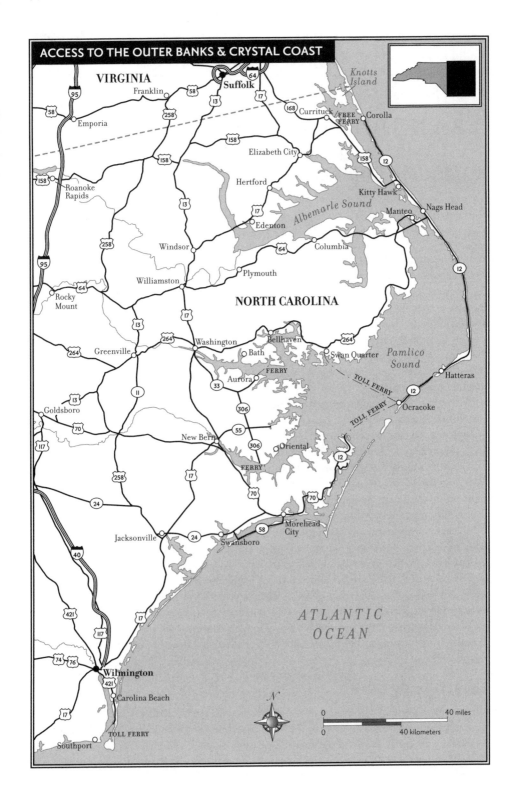

ACCESS TO THE OUTER BANKS & CRYSTAL COAST

intrepid biker or confirmed homebody. The Banks are narrow but deceptively long, and there is no public transportation at this time, although bus service is being discussed in Dare and Carteret Counties.

The exceptions to the vehicle-required rule are the historic towns of Beaufort, Manteo, Ocracoke, and Hatteras Village, all ideal for a weekend—or longer—getaway. Once you reach these destinations, you can easily walk or bike to plenty of attractions and restaurants, or catch a boat taxi. All have inns located in the historic district. Not by coincidence, these are also the popular ports in the area, with power yachts and sailboats tied up at downtown docks and marinas.

Major Routes to the Banks

The scarcity of causeways and bridges limit automobile access to the Banks to just a few routes. Despite their popularity, the Banks are a bit off the beaten track, far from the major interstates, so allow extra time to reach them, especially if you have an appointment to make. You can download current maps of North Carolina from the state Department of Transportation Web site, www.ncdot.org; or you can order a free state transportation map to be sent by mail, either from the Web site or by calling 877-DOT-4YOU or 800-VISIT NC.

From the North

There are two main routes from Virginia and points north, and one delightful "back way."

Approaching from the Norfolk airport or I-64E, the fastest route to the Outer Banks is VA/NC 168, a toll road. It joins US 158 in Barco, North Carolina, running down to the Wright Memorial Bridge and Kitty Hawk. This route is about 90 miles from airport to bridge, but may be slow in summer, especially on weekends when people are coming in for their weekly rentals. A new causeway across Currituck Sound in the Jarvisburg/Grandy vicinity, intended to cut down on the congestion, begins construction in 2010.

A second route from Virginia follows US 17, which has four lanes from the North Carolina border running parallel with the historic Dismal Swamp Canal. At Elizabeth City, a charming harbor town, you pick up US 158 out to Barco and beyond.

To sneak into the region via the scenic "back way," take VA/NC 618 from Virginia Beach through the **Mackay Island National Wildlife Refuge** and Knott's Island, noted for its vineyards, then cross via a free ferry to join NC 168. Call ahead to make sure the ferry is running (252-232-2683), as low water sometimes keeps it at the dock.

From the East

To reach Roanoke Island and the Central Banks from the east, you have your choice of two major roads, US 64 and US 264, both of them now four-lane, limited-access highways for most of the distance. The roads start out together from Raleigh, then separate to sweep along either shore of the great Albemarle Peninsula, joining again in Manns Harbor, on the mainland opposite Roanoke Island.

US 64 is the most direct and fastest route, being four-lane as far as Columbia. The trip from Raleigh to Roanoke Island takes about four hours via this route, with a rest stop in Columbia, or about three hours from I-95.

US 264 is currently four-lane as far as Washington. Beyond, it makes its winding way past Lake Mattamuskeet and tiny fishing villages on the peninsula's southern and eastern shores. You can turn off US 264 at Swan Quarter to catch a toll ferry to Ocracoke.

Two bridges link Roanoke Island with the mainland, the newer and longer Virginia Dare

Mileage to the Outer Banks from United States and Canadian Cities

Atlanta, GA . . . . 607 mi.	Nashville, TN . . . . . . 732 mi.	Rocky Mount, NC . . 154 mi.
Charleston, SC . . . . 450 mi.	Norfolk, VA . . . . 90 mi.	Toronto, Ontario . . . 827 mi.
Charlotte, NC . . . . . 359 mi.	New York City, NY . . 500 mi.	Washington, DC . . . 270 mi.
Montreal, Quebec . . 780 mi.	Raleigh, NC . . . . 192 mi.	

Memorial (US 64/264) and the older William B. Umstead (US 64 Business). These routes join just outside Manteo and run over the Washington Baum Causeway to Nags Head, meeting NC 12 and US 158 at Whalebone Junction.

US 70E, a good four-lane, is the most direct route from Raleigh to the Crystal Coast, crossing both I-40 and I-95 along the way. Drive time to Beaufort is about three hours.

From the South

US 17 runs from Wilmington north to the Virginia border, passing through many old Inner Banks towns. To reach the Crystal Coast, turn east on NC 24 in Jacksonville.

NAVIGATING ON THE BANKS

Once you are in the region, navigation is relatively easy. All the major roads run parallel with the ocean.

Navigating along the roads closest to the ocean is made easier by a series of mile markers found along US 158, NC 12, and NC 58. Addresses are often given just by milepost (MP) or mile marker (MM) number, especially along US 158 and NC 12. These generally increase from north to south, except in Currituck County, where the MP numbers on NC 12 running up the North Banks get higher as you approach Corolla and the end of the road.

Car Rentals

Most rental cars are available at airports. Check the Web sites listed below to find rental companies serving your arrival point.

Rental Cars at Airports

Alamo 800-462-5266; www.alamo.com
Avis 800-331-1212; www.avis.com
Budget 800-527-0700; www.budget.com
Dollar 800-800-3665; www.dollar.com
Enterprise 800-261-7331; www.enterprise.com
Hertz 800-654-3131; www.hertz.com
National 800-227-7368; www.nationalcar.com
Thrifty 918-669-2168, 800-847-4389; www.thrifty.com

Rental Cars on the North and Central Banks

ABCO Auto Rental 252-473-4508; 1088 US 64, Manteo
B&R Rent-a-Car 252-473-2141, 888-869-4983; www.rdsawyer.com; R D Sawyer Motor
   Co., 404 US 64S, Manteo

Beach Jeeps of Corolla 252-453-6141; www.beachjeepsofcorolla.com; 1210 Ocean Trail, Corolla Light Town Center, Corolla

Beach Ride 4x4 Rentals 252-916-0133; www.ocracoke4x4rentals.com; 1070 Irvin Garrish Hwy., Ocracoke

Cape Point Exxon 252-995-5695; 47153 NC 12, Buxton

Corolla Jeep Rentals & Tours 252-453-6899; www.outerbanksjeeprentals.com; 1070 Ocean Trail, Corolla

Enterprise Rent-A-Car 252-480-1838; www.enterprise.com; 1818 N. Croatan Hwy., Kill Devil Hills

Island Cruisers 252-987-2097; www.hatterasjack.com; 23902 NC 12, Rodanthe

Midgette Auto 252-491-8500, 800-685-9938; www.midgetteauto.com; 9022 Caratoke Hwy., Harbinger

Outer Banks Chrysler-Dodge-Jeep 252-441-1146; 3000 N. Croatan Hwy., Kill Devil Hills

Victory Chevrolet-Buick-Pontiac 252-261-5900; www.victorychevroletbuickpontiac.com; 6166 N. Croatan Hwy., Kitty Hawk

Rental Cars on the South Banks

Avis 252-247-5577; www.avis.com; Morehead City

Enterprise 252-240-0218; www.enterprise.com; Morehead City

Morehead City Ford 252-247-2132; www.moreheadcityford.com; 5557 US 70W, Morehead City

Stars Auto Rentals 252-728-2323; 150 Airport Rd., Beaufort

Taxi and Limousine Services

NORTH AND CENTRAL BANKS

Bayside Cab 252-480-1300; Kill Devil Hills

Beach Cab 252-441-2500, 800-441-2503; Kill Devil Hills

Coastal Cab Company 252-449-8787; www.coastalcab.com; Kill Devil Hills

The Herbert C. Bonner Bridge connects Hatteras Island with the rest of the world.

The Beach Road in Kitty Hawk

The Connection 252-441-5488, 252-449-2777; www.calltheconnection.com; Kill Devil Hills

Island Hopper Shuttle 252-995-6771; Buxton

Island Limousine 252-441-5466, 800-828-5466; www.islandlimo.com; Kill Devil Hills

Karat Limo Service 252-473-9827; www.karatlimo.com; Manteo

Luxury Limousine 252-202-8436; www.luxurylimousineobx.com

Manteo Cab Company 252-473-6500; Manteo

Outer Banks Limousine & Taxi 252-256-1343, 252-256-3696; www.outerbankslimousine .com; Nags Head

SOUTH BANKS

A-1 Yellow Cab 252-240-2700, 252-504-3680; Atlantic Beach

Atlantic Beach Taxi 252-240-3555; Atlantic Beach

Carteret Cab 252-247-4600; Morehead City

Crystal Coast Classic Cadillac Limousine Service 910-381-0656, 877-VIP-ROLL; www.4c limo.com; Jacksonville

Crystal Coast Yellow Cab Co. 252-728-3483, 252-728-5365, Beaufort; 252-726-3125, Morehead City

Diamond Limousine Service 252-240-1680, 800-840-4070;
www.adiamondlimousine.com; Morehead City
Presidential Limousine Service 252-726-8109; Morehead City

Getting There By Bus

Greyhound (214-849-8100, 800-231-2222; www.greyhound.com) offers scheduled bus
service along US 17. Jacksonville (910-346-9832), New Bern, Washington (252-946-
3021), and Elizabeth City (252-335-5183) are the closest terminals to the Outer Banks
and Crystal Coast. No tickets are sold at the New Bern station, but you can order tickets
by mail through the main Greyhound contact numbers.

Getting There By Train

Amtrak (800-872-7245; www.amtrak.com) offers daily rail service from Boston, New York,
and Washington, DC, to Newport News, Virginia, with bus connections to Norfolk and
Virginia Beach. *The Palmetto, Silver Meteor,* and *Silver Star* trains offer service from New
York City, Washington, DC, Charleston, South Carolina, and Florida, with stops in Richmond, Virginia, where you can connect with the train to Newport News. The *Carolinian*
running daily between New York City and Charlotte, North Carolina, also stops at Richmond, Virginia, as well as Rocky Mount, North Carolina.

Driving Tour Itineraries

Several special interest tours will guide you through the Outer Banks, the South Banks, and beyond.
Select the itinerary that best suits your interests.

Charles Kuralt Trail www.northeast-nc.com/kuralt. Signboards identify II national wildlife refuges
and a national fish hatchery in eastern North Carolina and along the Virginia border.

Historic Albemarle Tour www.historicalbemarletour.org. Founded in 1975, this rambling journey
follows brown signs to over 25 sites, most of historical significance, along with natural history and
eco-tourism highlights. The entire guide can be printed from the Web site for easy reference.

HomeGrownHandMade Art Roads & Farm Trails www.homegrownhandmade.com. This Web site
guides you to treasures scattered along the state's back roads, with listings of art studios, pick-
your-own farms and farmers markets, hiking trails, and unique events. Trails that feature the Outer
Banks and its immediate region include "High Tide on the Sound Side," "Coastal Treasure
Chest," "Front Porch to Back Forty," and "Rock Stew Ramble."

North Carolina Birding Trail www.ncbirdingtrail.org. Detailed maps identify dozens of top birding
spots in the region.

North Carolina Civil War Trails www.civilwartraveler.com. Markers tell of little known battles
fought on Roanoke, Ocracoke, and Hatteras islands.

North Carolina Scenic Byways www.ncdot.org. The **Outer Banks Scenic Byway** runs III miles
from Whalebone Junction in Nags Head to Beaufort. Other routes cross Roanoke Island, circle
the Albemarle Peninsula, and loop through many towns on the Inner Banks. Maps and descrip-
tions of the various routes can be downloaded from the North Carolina Department of Transportation Web site.

You can also view sample tour itineraries on the Outer Banks and elsewhere in Northeast North
Carolina at www.visitncne.com.

Touring

By Bicycle

Eastern North Carolina is one of the most popular bicycling destinations in the country. In addition to many local bike paths, the area is included in several longer North Carolina Department of Transportation bike trails that lead across the state. **Bike Route 2, Mountains to Sea,** leads from the Great Smoky Mountains to Manteo. **Bike Route 7** runs from Wilson to Cedar Island and the Ocracoke Ferry.

The **Wright Brothers Bike Route** runs the length of the Outer Banks, 45 miles from Corolla to Hatteras Village, then over the ferry to Ocracoke. Most of the distance requires on-road riding.

A popular 100-mile round-trip can be made by traveling from Manteo, down Hatteras Island, over the ferry to Ocracoke, then the ferry to Swan Quarter, connecting with US 264, and returning to Manteo. It can be done in one day if you start early in the morning.

You can order free maps of statewide and regional bicycling routes from the North Carolina Department of Transportation Web site: www.ncdot.org.

By Car, Bus, or Minivan

Hatteras Tours 252-475-4477; www.hatterastours.com. Native historian Danny Couch conducts tours of Hatteras Island and other destinations.

Our Tour Guide www.ourtourguide.net. A series of self-guided audio tours of the Outer Banks are available on CD or audiotape. You can order from the Web site or buy the tours at local outlets.

Sandy Beach Tours 252-441-9800; www.sandybeachtours.com; Kill Devil Hills. Groups can tour the sights in a 12-, 15-, or 35-passenger coach. This company also provides shuttle service to Norfolk International Airport and transportation for weddings and other parties.

By Foot

Part of the 900-mile **North Carolina Mountains-to-Sea Hiking Trail** (www.ncmst.org) traverses the length of the Crystal Coast and Outer Banks, crossing the Croatan National Forest via the Neusiok Trail in Carteret County, then leaping to Ocracoke and Hatteras islands on the state ferries, before ending at Jockey's Ridge State Park in Nags Head. The sections of trail on Ocracoke, Hatteras, and Bodie islands run along the beach. Camping is available at established campgrounds within the Cape Hatteras National Seashore.

TRAVELING BY WATER

Although most of North Carolina's outer islands are now linked by bridge and causeway to the mainland, quite a few still require a journey by boat.

The state of North Carolina maintains a fleet of ferries that runs year round on routes throughout the eastern part of the state. These link Ocracoke Island with Hatteras Island to the north, Cedar Island to the south, and Swan Quarter on the Hyde County mainland to the west. They also cross rivers and sounds, linking the sometimes isolated communities of the Inner Banks, in addition to creating interesting options for visitors.

To reach other islands, including the Core Banks, Cape Lookout, the Shackleford Banks, and Bear Island, you have to take a smaller craft, one of the swarm of private ferries that crisscross the sounds of North Carolina. Look for listings within our destination chapters.

North Carolina Ferry System

Captain Toby Tillett began the state's ferry system in the 1920s, taking residents and visitors across Oregon Inlet. The state bought his business in 1950, adding it to the ferry across Croatan Sound linking Manns Harbor and Roanoke Island, which it bought from T. A. Baum in 1947. Both of the old ferry routes are served by bridges now, but the North Carolina Department of Transportation's Ferry Division continues to operate ferries on seven other routes. Over one million vehicles and 2.5 million passengers use the state ferries each year.

Only one of the state ferries operates outside of the Outer Banks/Crystal Coast region—the ferry from Fort Fisher to Southport across the Cape Fear River in the far south of the state.

Any size vehicle can be accommodated on the ferries and pedestrians and bikers are welcome. Pets must be on a leash or remain in the vehicle. The ferries have restrooms, but no food service beyond vending machines, so a box lunch is recommended for the longer voyages.

The state ferries run on regular schedules all year and in most weather, although they may be canceled because of high seas or strong winds. Call the terminal in advance to check on current conditions.

State Ferry Routes

Call 800-BY FERRY or visit www.ncferry.org for current schedules and routes. No reservations are taken for free ferries.

Bayview—Aurora Crosses the Pamlico River near Bath. Crossing time: 30 minutes. Fare: Free.
Cherry Branch—Minnesott Beach Crosses the Neuse River below New Bern. Crossing time: 20 minutes. Fare: Free.

The North Carolina state ferry system runs every day all year.

Any size vehicle can be accommodated on the state ferries.

Currituck—Knotts Island Crosses Currituck Sound. Crossing time: 45 minutes. Fare: Free.
Hatteras—Ocracoke Crossing time: 40 minutes. Fare: Free.
Ocracoke—Cedar Island Crossing time: 2.25 hours. Fare: $15 for vehicles less than 20 feet;
    $1 for pedestrians; $3 for bicycle and rider; $10 for motorcycles; price increases with
    length of vehicle. Reservations recommended, especially during the summer season.
Ocracoke—Swan Quarter Crossing time: 2.5 hours. Fare: Same as Cedar Island Ferry.
    Reservations recommended.

State Ferry Terminals

Aurora/Bayview 252-964-4521
Cedar Island Reservations and information: 252-225-3551, 800-856-0343
Cherry Branch/Minnesott 252-447-1055, 800-339-9156
Currituck/Knotts Island 252-232-2683
Hatteras 252-986-2353, 800-368-8949
Ocracoke Reservations and information: 252-928-3841, 800-345-1665
Swan Quarter Reservations and information: 252-926-1111, 800-773-1094

The Atlantic Intracoastal Waterway

Although most visitors arrive by car, an increasing number of travelers tour North Carolina's shores by boat. A steady stream of power yachts and sailing vessels makes its way up
the Atlantic Intracoastal Waterway (ICW), the great, 3,000-mile-long water highway that
stretches from Boston, Massachusetts, to Key West, Florida. The ICW has one of its longest
stretches in North Carolina, making its way down black-water rivers and salt estuaries. The

towns of Elizabeth City, Belhaven, Oriental, and Beaufort are major stops for mariners passing through, as well as for in-state boaters. An alternate route runs down the backside of the Banks. Visit the Web site of the Atlantic Intracoastal Waterway Association (www.atl intracoastal.org) for information and updates.

Many marinas lie along the ICW. We include listings in each section of facilities that welcome transient boaters. You can request a free copy of the official *North Carolina Coastal Boating Guide* by calling 877-368-4968, or by visiting www.ncwaterways.com.

North Carolina Paddle Trails

The coastal region of North Carolina offers a wealth of paddling opportunities for canoes and kayaks. You can browse hundreds of trails on the North Carolina Paddle Trails Association Web site (www.ncpaddletrails.info).

The **North Carolina Coastal Plain Paddle Trails** range from easy paddles on Lake Mattamuskeet, to challenging trips across the open waters of the sounds. You can download maps at www.ncsu.edu/paddletrails, or order a copy by calling 919-778-9499, or by contacting the North Carolina Division of Parks and Recreation (345-B Park Entrance Rd., Seven Springs, NC 28578).

One of the state's longest paddle trails, the 128-mile **Roanoke River Trail,** is also one of the best developed. It begins near Roanoke Rapids and follows the river to its mouth in Albemarle Sound, near Plymouth. Along the way, it passes through the **Roanoke River National Wildlife Refuge,** home of black bear, river otters, bobcats, and bald eagles. Camping platforms and boat ramps have been built the length of the river by the Roanoke River Partners. You can find more information, including links to outfitters offering rentals and guided tours, at: www.roanokeriverpartners.org.

BY AIR

Although no scheduled commercial flights touch down at the small airports that dot the Outer Banks, the heritage of flight is strong here. Kill Devil Hill, where the Wright Memorial now stands, is a place of pilgrimage for many pilots. They come to fly over the memorial, and to land and take off at the **First Flight Airport** next to the national monument, flying in the contrail of the Wright Brothers themselves.

Pilots can request free copies of the current North Carolina Aeronautical Chart or North Carolina Airport Guide from the North Carolina Department of Transportation's Aviation Division Web site (www.ncdot.org), or by calling 919-840-0112.

Commercial Airports

Albert J. Ellis Airport (OAJ) 910-324-1100; www.co.onslow.nc.us/airport; Richlands. This airport operated by Onslow County is served by US Airways Express and Delta Connection, with daily non-stops to Charlotte and Atlanta. About 60 miles from Beaufort.

Craven Regional Airport (EWN) 252-638-8591; www.newbernairport.com; New Bern. Served by Delta Connection and US Airways Express with daily non-stop flights to Atlanta, Charlotte, and Philadelphia. About 45 miles from Beaufort.

Newport News/Williamsburg International Airport (PHF) 757-877-0221; www.fly newportnews.com; Newport News, Virginia. Served by AirTran, Delta, and US Airways. Driving distance is about 90 miles from Kitty Hawk.

The Dismal Swamp Canal

One of the most scenic sections of the Intracoastal Waterway, and certainly the most historic, is the Dismal Swamp Canal. Begun in 1793 by a group of investors that included George Washington, the canal connects Albemarle Sound with Chesapeake Bay. Along the way it traverses a great cypress swamp that stretches across the Virginia–North Carolina border. US 17 parallels the canal for much of its length.

The Great Dismal Swamp served as an escape route and refuge for enslaved individuals during the years before the Civil War and today is recognized as part of the National Underground Railway Network to Freedom. The canal's strategic position caused Union forces to try to destroy the locks during the Civil War. The Battle of South Mills was fought nearby.

In 2008, 14,000 acres within North Carolina became the **Dismal Swamp State Park.** The visitor center, a few miles south of the state border along US 17, gives visitors access to 16 miles of hiking and mountain-bike trails.

The canal is also popular for kayaking and canoeing. At the annual Paddle for the Border held in early May, hundreds of craft make the run from South Mills, North Carolina, to Chesapeake, Virginia. For more information, contact the Dismal Swamp Welcome Center (252-771-8333, 877-771-8333; www.dismalswamp.com)

Norfolk International Airport (ORF) 757-857-3351; www.norfolkairport.com; Norfolk, Virginia. The closest major airport to the Outer Banks, about two hours from Kitty Hawk. Carriers include American, Continental, Delta, Independence Air, Southwest, and US Airways. Car rental companies serving this airport have over 3,000 vehicles available.

Raleigh-Durham International Airport (RDU) 919-840-2123; www.rdu.com; Morrisville. Airlines serving RDU include Air Canada, AirTran, American, Continental, Delta, ExpressJet, JetBlue, Midwest, Southwest, United, and US Airways. Direct flights are available from London and Canada. Driving distance to Nags Head is about 200 miles.

Wilmington International Airport (ILF) 910-341-4125; www.flyilm.com; Wilmington. Carriers include Allegiant Air, Delta, and US Airways with non-stops available to New York (LGA), Atlanta (ATL), Charlotte (CLT), Cincinnati (CVG), Orlando Sanford (SFB), and Philadelphia (PHL). About 85 miles from Beaufort.

General Aviation Airports

Billy Mitchell Airfield (HSE/HNC) 252-995-3646; www.nps.gov/caha; Frisco. Unattended airfield has 3,000 feet of runway. No facilities. Air tours available.

Currituck Regional Airport (ONX) 252-453-8032, 252-453-2876; www.co.currituck.nc.us, Maple. Public-use general aviation facility located off US 158 has a 5,500-foot concrete runway. Facilities include an Automated Weather Observing System, self-service fuel, free overnight tie-downs, and new terminal. Hang gliding available.

Dare County Regional Airport (MQI) 252-475-5570; www.fly2mqi.com; Manteo. General aviation airport offers car rentals, air tours, an aviation museum, 24-hour fuel service, two lighted runways of 3,300 and 4,300 feet, and amenities for visiting pilots.

Elizabeth City–Pasquotank Regional Airport (ECG) 252-335-5634; www.ecgairport.com; Elizabeth City. Full service facility shares its 7,200-foot runway with the U.S. Coast Guard. Rental cars, 24-hour fuel service, pilot's lounge and flight planning room, courtesy car, and tie-downs available.

First Flight Airport (FFA) 252-441-7430, 252-473-2111; www.nps.gov/wrbr; Kill Devil Hills. Unattended airfield next to the Wright Brothers Memorial. Unlighted 3,000-foot runway. Amenities include a weather and flight planning pilot's facility and free 24-hour tie-downs.

Michael J. Smith Field Airport (MRH) 252-728-1928; www.beaufortairport.com; Beaufort. Car rentals, fuel, and tie-downs available, as well as air tours and aircraft rentals.

Ocracoke Island Airport (W95) 919-571-4904, 252-473-2111; Ocracoke. This 3,000-foot asphalt strip is unattended and unlighted. Tie-downs available.

Charter Air Services

Barrier Island Aviation 252-473-4247; www.fly2mqi.com; Dare County Airport, Manteo. Air tours and charters available.

FlightGest 252-453-3656, 919-840-4443; www.flightgest.com; Corolla. Offering charter service from Norfolk to Pine Island's private airfield near the Sanderling, and other destinations; formerly Sea Air.

Linear Air 781.860.9696, 877.254.6327; www.linearair.com. Catch flights from Manassas, Virginia (suburban Washington, DC), to Manteo and other Outer Banks locations.

Outer Banks Airways 252-441-8687; www.flyobx.com; Dare County Airport, Manteo. Air tours, flight camp, and charters available.

Pelican Airways 252-928-1661, 888-7PELICAN; Ocracoke Island Airport.

Segrave Aviation 252-728-2323; www.beaufortairport.com; Beaufort. Offering air tours, charters, training, and aircraft rentals.

The Dismal Swamp Canal is part of the Intracoastal Waterway.

IBX: North Carolina's Inner Banks

Once you've made your journey down the Outer Banks, jumping by bridge and ferry from Nags Head to Hatteras to Ocracoke to the Crystal Coast, loop back via an inland route, traveling US 17, once the major route down the East Coast in pre-interstate days. In North Carolina, it passes through many of the early ports, located on the great rivers and sounds of the Inner Banks, North Carolina's secret shore. Here history blends seamlessly with eco-tourism, offering paddling trails, historic and walk-able downtowns, public docks, and interesting inns.

We present these towns south to north along US 17, starting from Jacksonville, just a few miles inland from Swansboro, and ending at Elizabeth City, close to the Virginia border. Most of US 17 is now four-lanes, and limited access highways, such as US 264 and US 64, provide quick "escape routes" out to I-95, if time runs short. Where destinations are located off US 17, we give brief directions.

Although the list is arranged south to north, the itinerary could as easily be followed north to south, starting in Virginia. Numerous shorter routes, or day trips from the Outer Banks, can be devised with the help of a map.

Jacksonville (US 17; www.onslowcountytourism.com, www.jacksonvilleonline.org) The support community for the Marine Corps Base Camp Lejeune and Marine Air Station New River, Jacksonville is home to the moving **Beirut Memorial** (www.beirut-memorial.org), and the oldest USO in the nation still in operation.

New Bern (US 17 & US 70; www.visitnewbern.com) The second oldest town in North Carolina and the home of royal governor William Tryon, this historic town has several house museums in addition to the reconstructed 1770 governor's palace surrounded by gorgeous gardens. Walking and trolley tours visit colonial and Civil War sites, the soda fountain where Pepsi-Cola was invented, and the numerous bear mascots that dot the town.

Oriental (NC 55 east of New Bern; www.visitoriental.com) The Sailing Capital of North Carolina, located on the tip of the Pamlico Peninsula, hosts regattas nearly every weekend. Popular with visiting yachters, this dog-friendly town sits in the heart of over 300 miles of marked paddling trails.

Aurora (NC 33 east of Washington; www.co.beaufort.nc.us, www.aurorafossilmuseum.com) The **Aurora Fossil Museum** exhibits huge shark skeletons and other ancient relics found in the nearby phosphate mines. **Bennett Vineyards** makes muscadine wines using colonial techniques. From here, catch a free ferry north to Bath, or south to Havelock and the Crystal Coast.

Washington (US 17 & US 264; www.originalwashington.com) Located in Washington's historic downtown, the **North Carolina Estuarium** explains the unique ecology of the estuary system and offers free boat tours on the Pamlico-Tar River. Nearby, the **Beaufort County Arts Council** displays local artwork in the former Atlantic Coastline Train Depot.

Bath (US 264 & NC 92 east of Washington; www.nchistoricsites.org/bath) North Carolina's oldest town incorporated in 1705, and was home, briefly, to both Blackbeard and the Royal Governor. The **Bath Historic Site** preserves several buildings dating from the 18th century. Just west of town, you can swim or hike at **Goose Creek State Park**.

Belhaven (US 264 east of Bath; www.belhavennc.us) A popular stop on the ICW, Belhaven is a picture-perfect harbor town with commercial and sport fishing fleets. The **Belhaven Memorial Museum**, on the second floor of city hall, contains a unique collection of oddities. Plan a stop at the 1899 **River Forest Manor,** today a world famous restaurant, hotel, and marina.

Engelhard (US 264 east of Belhaven; www.hydecounty.org) The unique eight-sided **Octagon House** offers information on Hyde County attractions. Just west of Engelhard, historic **Mattamuskeet**

Lodge presides over one of the country's largest gatherings of swans and other waterfowl every winter.

Williamston (US 17 & US 64; www.visitmartincounty.com) The Martin County seat, located on the Roanoke River, is a nexus of hiking and paddling trails. Nearby attractions range from the Old-West town of **Deadwood** to the **East Carolina Speedway.** A self-guided walking tour begins at the 1831 **Asa Biggs House,** now a visitor's center. Along the way, enjoy a heritage meal at the **Cypress Grill** or the **Sunny Side Oyster Bar**.

Plymouth (US 64 east of Williamston; www.visitplymouthnc.com) The **Port O' Plymouth Museum** follows the history of the area from the Native Americans to the Civil War. There's a working 63-foot replica of a Confederate ironclad tied to the dock outside, and in season it cruises the river, firing its guns. Stroll down Water Street to discover the **Roanoke River Lighthouse and Maritime Center** and the **Rail Switch Nature Trail,** plus unique eateries and shops.

Columbia (US 64 east of Plymouth; www.visittyrrellcounty.com) The **Tyrrell County Visitor Center** provides a welcome stop at the foot of the bridge on US 64, offering restrooms and travel information. Next door is the **Walter B. Jones Center for the Sounds,** with exhibits on red wolves and other native species, as well as the **Scuppernong River Interpretive Boardwalk** along the waterfront. A few blocks away on Main Street, the **Pocosin Arts & Crafts gallery** and the **Columbia Theater Cultural Resources Center,** located in a renovated movie palace, provide insight into life along the Scuppernong.

Windsor (US 17 & US 13; www.co.bertie.nc.us) The **Roanoke/Cashie River Center** interprets both the ecology and history of these river bottomlands, with special emphasis on the native wild turkey. The adjacent **Cashie Wetlands Walk** leads through a cypress swamp. **Hope Plantation,** just west of town, recreates 19th century Bertie County life.

Edenton (US 17, www.visitedenton.com) Often called "the prettiest town in the South," Edenton overlooks an idyllic harbor off Albemarle Sound. The site of the 1774 Edenton Tea Party, one of the earliest political actions organized by women, the colonial town preserves a collection of bed-and-breakfast inns, historic sites, and house museums, including the distinctive **Cupola House.** Guided walking and trolley tours begin at the State Historic Site.

Hertford (US 17, www.visitperquimans.com) Another of North Carolina's lovely harbor towns, Hertford is home to the 1730 **Newbold-White House,** the oldest dwelling in the state open to the public, and a replica periauger, a form of boat used by early colonists. A stroll of the historic downtown takes you past antique stores, Queen Anne mansions, and a unique S-shaped swing bridge—the only one of its type remaining in the United States—that inspired the classic song "Carolina Moon."

Elizabeth City (US 17 & US 158; www.discoverec.org) Known as the "Harbor of Hospitality," Elizabeth City is a favorite stop for boaters traveling the ICW and a popular weekend getaway for visitors from Virginia. The quiet streets of the town, perfect for a walking tour, are lined with historic houses and inns, revitalized shops, even a restored movie palace. On the waterfront, exhibits at the free **Museum of the Albemarle,** one of the state museums of history, explore 10,000 years of ecology and culture in the region. Elizabeth City is also the home of one of the country's largest U.S. Coast Guard bases, and TCOM, a company that builds lighter-than-air craft, otherwise known as blimps. Tours of both are available on a limited basis.

These Web sites provide more information on the attractions and events of the Inner Banks: www.partnershipforthesounds.org, www.visitncne.com, www.historicalbemarletour.org, www.homegrownhandmade.com, www.ibxarts.com.

Wild horses roam free in Carova.

3

THE NORTH BEACHES:
Southern Shores to Carova

Where the Road Ends

The North Beaches of the Outer Banks are not islands, but they have been. The original northern boundary of North Carolina was set at Currituck Inlet back in 1663. When the inlet closed in 1828, the island became a peninsula, connected with the Virginia mainland.

In the mid-1900s, many of the inhabitants of the North Beaches commuted up the beach to jobs in Virginia. But in 1974, a fence at the border blocked the route. On the Virginia side lie False Cape State Park and the Back Bay National Wildlife Refuge, neither of which allow any vehicular access. The fence was built to protect this pristine area. The border fence has become a tourist attraction in its own right for visitors on the North Carolina side.

Numerous proposals were made over the years to build a paved road connecting the Virginia and North Carolina coastlines. But these all came to nothing, and NC 12 today ends at a beach access ramp about 12 miles south of the Virginia line.

The human history of the North Beaches is largely the story of this road. NC 12, today called Ocean Boulevard in Southern Shores, Duck Road in Duck, and Ocean Trail in Corolla, was originally just a sandy track behind the dunes. Most locals drove on the beach. But when the Wright Memorial Bridge joined the mainland with the Banks in 1930, attention inevitably turned to the stretch of Banks to the north, more than 30 miles of dunes and marshes dotted here and there with fishing villages and lifesaving stations. As NC 12 was paved farther north over the following four decades, tourism moved with it up the Banks.

SOUTHERN SHORES

In 1947, naturalist Frank Stick established the Kitty Hawk Land Company and began the first planned community on the Outer Banks, Southern Shores. Interested buyers were advised to cross the Wright Memorial Bridge and turn left at the ocean, directions that still hold true today. This left turn onto NC 12 leads through the heart of the original development, today an incorporated town in Dare County.

The 4-square-mile community stretches from the oceanfront to the sound. Many of the largest homes are built along the sound side, and many year-round residents live here. Most vacation rentals are located closer to the ocean, along NC 12. Scattered between the newer cottages are some survivors of the original homes built by Stick and his son David, who took over the company in 1955. Designed to withstand the local weather, these are

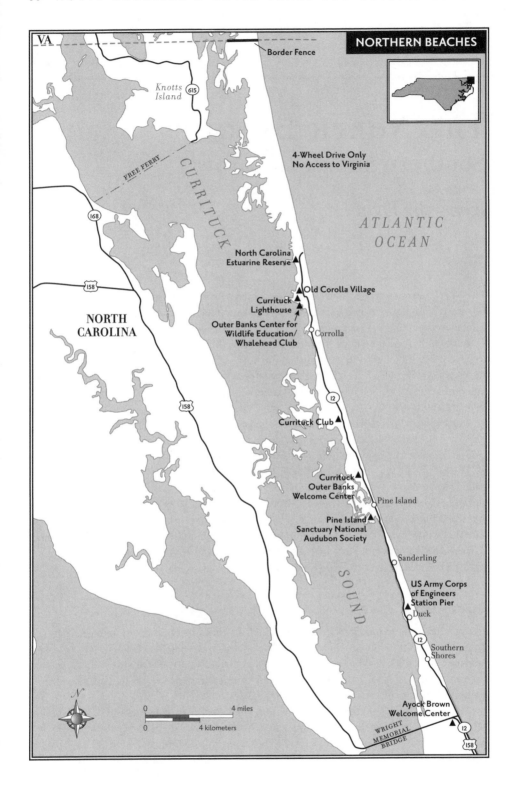

generally flat-topped houses built of concrete made with local sand. Inside, they are paneled in native juniper (white cedar).

David Stick took a great interest in Southern Shores, laying out many of the roads himself to take full advantage of the contour of the land. Today, the community is known for its natural beauty, with roads winding between tall pines, dogwoods, and live oaks draped with Spanish moss. Beautiful lagoons and canals intertwine along the sound.

The local civic association owns and maintains the town's beach accesses and other community resources. No one can park a car inside the town limits except residents, property holders, and those renting cottages here, keeping the beaches free of crowds.

While Southern Shores is a planned community, most of it is not gated. A system of bike trails, both paved and unpaved, runs throughout Southern Shores, connecting on the north with the Duck Path and US 158 to the south. These provide the best way to explore this unique beach community.

Duck

Today a scenic destination noted for exceptional shopping and gourmet dining, this small fishing village first appears on maps dating to the 1790s. The local folks, who traveled mostly by boat, developed the first crab-shedding business in the area, founding the commercial soft-shell crab industry. In the 1940s local residents and crabs alike were subjected to the sound of bombing practice on military land just north of the village.

The bombing range is long gone. Its sole remnant is an impressive pier built by the U.S. Army Corps of Engineers, now used to conduct scientific studies of waves and currents. The village burgeoned in the 1950s when the main road, now NC 12, was paved, linking it with Southern Shores and the beaches farther south.

Duck is Dare County's newest town, having incorporated in 2001. The new Town Waterfront Park lies along NC 12 on the sound side of the village. Public parking is available here, as well as at the numerous shopping villages that stretch along the road all the way through town.

Most of the town's many rental condominiums and houses are tucked out of sight amid the maritime forest that makes Duck such a shady, pleasant place in the summer. The town has no public beach access but is still extremely popular as a destination for day trips. This stretch of coast is renowned for its sunsets, and many establishments look west over Currituck Sound.

Sanderling

Just north of Duck is one of the narrowest parts of the Banks, once the site of Caffey's Inlet. Today the **Sanderling Resort** occupies this prime property. The old Life-Saving Station has been restored as a restaurant.

Although officially part of Duck, Sanderling is often thought of as a separate community. The hotel's builder, Earl Slick, was the first to push the paved road north of Duck, and he put a gate across the road, protecting the exclusive neighborhoods he developed beyond it. The gate remained from 1975 until 1984, when the road became part of NC 12 and the state bulldozed the barrier.

COROLLA

North of Sanderling lies the Outer Banks portion of Currituck County, where waterfowl hunt clubs once held huge tracts of land. With the coming of the paved road, many of these properties were developed into exclusive communities of vacation homes.

NC 12 soon reached Corolla, pronounced "cuh-RAH-la" by locals. Originally it was a small fishing village and home of the **Currituck Beach Lighthouse,** built in 1875. Located on the sound side of NC 12, **Currituck Heritage Park** includes the Lighthouse, the **Whalehead Club,** and the **Outer Banks Center for Wildlife Education**, all surrounding a boating lagoon and picnic area. On the north side of the lighthouse, the old village of Corolla houses a shopping district of charming shops with an off-the-beaten-track appeal. **The Wild Horse Museum** occupies the renovated schoolhouse.

CAROVA

A mile past the lighthouse, NC 12 comes to its end at a beach access ramp. Beyond a fence and livestock grate lie 12 miles of unpaved North Carolina, variously called the outback, the off-road area, and, most commonly, Carova, thanks to its position between the two states.

The land is a patchwork of public and private wildlife refuges, traveling sand dunes, and communities where owners and renters travel by four-wheel drive along sandy tracks or on the beach. Wild ponies and 12-bedroom vacation cottages exist here side-by-side, along with a sprinkling of beachcomber shacks and year-round homes.

Several villages were located here in the past, among them Seagull, just now emerging from beneath Penny's Hill, the second largest untamed sand dune along the Banks after Jockey's Ridge. Today the communities along this coast are Swan and North Swan, close to the ramp, and Carova, near the fence on the Virginia border.

Wild horses co-exist with development in Carova.

Once all roads on the Outer Banks were sandy lanes like this one in Carova.

Commercial businesses are not allowed in this area. All groceries and other supplies must be brought in by four-wheel-drive vehicle from Corolla.

Bridge to the Future

As the summer population in Corolla multiplied, so did the traffic trying to reach the area up narrow, two-lane NC 12. Calls came to expand the road to four lanes, a move much opposed in Duck, where it would mean the sacrifice of a considerable portion of the trees that line the road through town.

An alternative solution to the problem was found: a new bridge and causeway across Currituck Sound. Stretching from US 158 to NC 12 at Pine Island north of Sanderling, it will join mainland Currituck County with its beachfront area, diminish drive-through traffic farther south, and cut the drive time to Corolla. The bridge, scheduled to begin construction in 2010 with completion by 2014, will probably charge a toll.

Lodging

The Northern Beaches have just a handful of hotels and inns available to overnight travelers. Most accommodations are single-family homes, plus some condominiums, represented by a number of different real estate companies.

Corolla has some of the most luxurious and high-priced homes on the Banks. During the last decades, the entire Atlantic side of NC 12 became lined with tall beach houses, many with private pools, hot tubs, and elevators, well suited to large family get-togethers.

Southern Shores also has mostly rental houses, while Duck offers a mix of single-family homes, condominiums, and time-shares.

The Charles Kuralt Trail

Television journalist Charles Kuralt's love of America, and especially his native state of North Carolina, is well documented in his books *Charles Kuralt's America* and *North Carolina Is My Home*. One of the memorials to him that he might have liked best is the Charles Kuralt Trail, linking 11 national wildlife refuges and a national fish hatchery. Located on barrier islands, blackwater swamps, and inland waterways in eastern North Carolina and along the Virginia border, these refuges provide homes for a host of species, many endangered by habitat loss. Each also offers special opportunities for nature lovers to enjoy the splendor and solitude that left Kuralt, in his own words, "a dazzled Odysseus, dizzy with the wonders of the world."

The following stops along the trail are located in and near the Outer Banks:

Mackay Island, the birthplace of Ducks Unlimited, once a famous hunt club, now a National Wildlife Refuge (NWR).

The Great Dismal Swamp NWR parallels US 17 as it crosses the Virginia border. A canal begun by George Washington is still open to watercraft.

Currituck NWR, with tracts north of Corolla and on Knotts Island.

Back Bay NWR, at the northern end of Currituck Sound in Virginia.

Alligator River NWR, home to black bear and red wolves.

Mattamuskeet, Pocosin Lakes, and Swan Quarter NWRs, winter home of some 100,000 swans, snow geese, and ducks.

Pea Island NWR, located along NC 12 on Hatteras Island, home of nesting sea turtles and numerous birds.

Cedar Island NWR, a maritime forest on the south side of the state ferry from Ocracoke.

For more information on the Charles Kuralt Trail, look for red-roofed signboards at each location detailing hiking and paddling routes, boardwalks, observation towers, and scenic drives. Or contact the Coastal Wildlife Refuge Society, 252-473-1131, www.northeast-nc.com. An audio tour of the refuges, narrated by Kuralt's brother, Wallace, is available and highly recommended.

Rate Categories

Inexpensive	up to $80
Moderate	$80 to $150
Expensive	$150 to $200
Very Expensive	$200 and up

These rates are per room, based on double occupancy. They do not include room taxes or any special service fees that may apply. In Dare County, taxes add an additional 11.75 percent, and in Currituck County, 13 percent.

The range of prices is due to seasonal fluctuation. Rates during the busy summer season and holiday weekends are often double or more the winter off-season rates. Prices peak on Memorial Day, Fourth of July, and Labor Day weekends.

Properties listed are open year round and are air-conditioned, unless otherwise noted.

Credit Cards

AE—American Express
CB—Carte Blanche
D—Discover Card
DC—Diners Club
E—Enroute
J—JCB International Credit Card
MC—Master Card
V—Visa

Resorts and Inns

COROLLA
HAMPTON INN AND SUITES OUTER BANKS COROLLA
252-453-6565
www.hamptoninn-outerbanks.com
333 Audubon Dr., NC 12, Pine Island 27927
Price: Moderate to Expensive
Credit Cards: AE, CB, D, DC, E, J, MC, V
Internet Access: Free high speed

Located north of the Sanderling, this low-rise hotel sits just behind the dune line, halfway between Corolla and Duck. The spacious 123 guest rooms and studio suites all have balconies or patios, microwaves, refrigerators, cable TV, and coffeemakers, and most have a sleeper sofa. Complimentary breakfast is served daily in the lobby, where you can browse an extensive seashell

A bed-and-breakfast in Duck

collection. An indoor pool and hot tub are open all year, while outdoors a pool, kids' pool, and one of the few lazy rivers on the Banks are open seasonally. The hotel has its own game room, coin laundry, and fitness center, and guests also have access to the facilities at the Pine Island Racquet and Fitness Club.

★ THE INN AT COROLLA LIGHT
252-453-3340, 800-215-0772
www.corolla-inn.com
1066 Ocean Trail, NC 12, Corolla 27927
Price: Inexpensive to Very Expensive
Credit Cards: D, MC, V
Internet Access: Free WiFi

The farthest north of all Outer Banks hotels, this inn sits within the expansive Corolla Light community and shares its extensive amenities, including oceanfront and soundfront activity centers, and an inside sports center with pool, hot tub, and racquetball and tennis courts. The inn itself is charming, with friendly staff and a complimentary continental breakfast buffet served daily in the sunny dining room. Each of the 43 rooms and suites is unique, many with views of Currituck Sound, all with pillowtop beds, refrigerator, TV, and coffeemaker. All guests can enjoy the intimate hot tub and pool with views of the sound, or watch spectacular sunsets from the inn's gazebo, which sits at the end of a 400-foot pier. In the summer, kayaks, personal watercraft, sailboats, and other craft are available for rent. Bicycles are free for guests. Pet-friendly and special-needs rooms are available. Bob's Off-Road Wild Horse Adventure Tours begin at the inn.

DUCK
★ THE DUCK INN, A BED AND BREAKFAST
252-261-2300
www.theduckinnbnb.com
1158 Duck Rd., NC 12, Duck 27949
Price: Moderate to Very Expensive

Credit Cards: AE, D, MC, V
Internet Access: Free WiFi

A comfortable house with a great location in the heart of Duck village rents three rooms, one handicapped accessible with its own entrance. All have private baths, cable TV, and DVD players. The breakfast here is special, with hot items such as omelets, quiches, pancakes, or French toast accompanied by bacon, ham, or sausage, joining the usual cold cereals and pastries. The inn is decorated cleverly throughout. Expect to find rubber duckies in your bath. Views of the sunset are spectacular from the inn's decks and dock. Guests can borrow the inn's bikes and kayaks to explore by land or sea.

★ THE SANDERLING RESORT & SPA

252-261-4111, 800-701-4111
www.thesanderling.com
1461 Duck Rd., NC 12, Duck 27949
Price: Moderate to Very Expensive
Credit Cards: AE, D, DC, MC, V
Internet Access: Free WiFi

The Sanderling serves up luxurious resort amenities with laid-back Outer Banks style 5 miles north of Duck village. Two-story, cedar-shingled buildings keep a low profile on this stretch of land between sound and sea. The public rooms of the inn are virtual galleries of art featuring birds and wildfowl. The property recently enjoyed a $4 million refit that equipped guest rooms with king-sized beds, 32-inch TVs, wireless Internet, and walk-in showers. Many rooms have private porches where guests can enjoy water views. The 88 guestrooms and suites, plus a conference center, the Lifesaving Station Restaurant, and several Jacuzzis, are located along the oceanfront, where a big deck and boardwalk provide access to the beach. Across the road, a full-service spa, indoor pool, and the elegant Left Bank restaurant overlook the sound. Guests also have access to the championship golf course at the Currituck Club and the indoor courts at the Pine Island Racquet Club. The eco-center conducts guided kayak trips and bird-watching hikes in the adjacent Audubon Nature Preserve. The resort also rents five oceanfront villas and the rustic Pine Island Hunt Club Cottages and Clubhouse. A suite atop the Conference Center with balconies that face both the sunrise and sunset is a favorite with honeymooners.

Beach Cottage and Condo Rentals

Real estate companies offer a wide variety of different properties for weekly rental. Shorter stays are sometimes available, especially off-season. Cottages generally have from two to eight bedrooms; some have as many as 18, making them suitable for large family reunions. Most real estate companies rent only to families.

Hot tubs and wireless Internet are standard amenities; some houses have their own private swimming pools. Depending on the location, your cottage rental may include access to community pools, tennis courts, fitness centers, and golf courses. As an extra incentive, some companies offer an amenities package that includes free rounds of golf, beach umbrellas, and complimentary tickets to activities.

With so many properties now available for rental in this area, many management companies are increasing their efforts to make renting from them hassle free. Linens and towels are now included with many rentals, formerly a separate charge, and some companies even make up the beds for you in advance. Companies are also dropping some of the many fees that traditionally have been added on, so that the price you see in brochures or online is actually what you pay, without the hundreds of extra dollars in administrative fees, damage waivers, and fees to use a credit card.

Increasingly, you can browse available properties online and make your reservations there as well.

Atlantic Realty 252-261-8340; www.atlanticrealty-nc.com; 1180 Duck Rd., NC 12, Duck 27949. Over 200 properties from Corolla to South Nags Head, including some pet-friendly. All renters enjoy the company's Family Fun amenities package.

Carolina Designs Realty 252-261-3934, 800-368-3825; www.carolinadesigns.com; 1197 Duck Rd., NC 12, Duck 27949. Specializing in some of the finest houses in the area. Free weekly homebuyer seminars are offered for those thinking of buying a vacation home.

Corolla Classic Vacations 252-453-9660, 866-453-9660; www.corollaclassicvacations.com; 1196 Ocean Trail, NC 12, Corolla 27927. This property management company represents more than 200 properties in the Corolla area, many equipped with elevators, private pools, and hot tubs. Holiday rentals and partial week rentals available.

Corolla Light Resort 252-453-2455; www.corollalightresort.com; 1197B Franklyn St., Corolla 27927. The largest and most amenity-laden community on the North Beaches, this resort includes 400 homes on 250 acres that stretch from the ocean to the sound. Renters enjoy, among other amenities, an oceanfront recreation center with two pools; a sound-side swimming pool, pier, and gazebo; kayak rentals; mini-golf; an ecology trail; fishing pond; an indoor sports center; a free summer trolley service; and weekly planned activities during the summer season.

Elan Vacations 252-491-8787, 866-760-3526; www.elanvacations.com; 8624 Caratoke Highway, US 158, Powells Point 27966. Early arrival policy lets you pick up your keys at the check-in office on the mainland. Three-day off-season getaways can be booked in advance.

Karichele Realty 252-453-2377, 800-453-2377; www.karichele.com; 705 Sunset Blvd., TimBuck II Shopping Village, Corolla 27927. Lists many properties, some pet-friendly, in Swan Beach and Carova, where you may see wild ponies in your yard.

Outer Banks Blue Realty 252-255-1220, 888-623-2583; www.outerbanksblue.com; 1245 Duck Rd., Duck 27949. Unique "check in by mail" program eliminates that time-consuming visit to the real estate office to pick up keys.

Resort Realty 252-453-8700, 800-458-3830; www.resortrealty.com; 791A Sunset Blvd., TimBuck II, Corolla 27927. Resort Club properties offer check-in as early as noon, and personal caretakers at your rental on check-in day. Event packages available.

ResortQuest Outer Banks Vacation Rentals 252-453-3033; www.resortquest.com; 1023 Ocean Trail, Corolla 27927. Large national company lists hundreds of rental properties from condos to 12-bedroom estates all along the Outer Banks.

Seaside Vacations 252-261-5500, 888-884-0267; www.outerbanksvacations.com; 1070D Ocean Trail, Corolla 27927. This full-service management company handles rentals at over 300 properties from the off-road area in Carova to Nags Head. Last-minute specials available.

Southern Shores Realty 252-261-2000, 800-334-1000; www.southernshores.com; 5 Ocean Blvd., Southern Shores 27949. This real estate company handles 400 rentals in Southern Shores. Long-term rentals available.

Sun Realty 252-453-8822, 800-334-4745; www.sunrealtync.com; 1135 Ocean Trail, Corolla 27927. One of the largest rental companies on the Outer Banks.

Twiddy & Company Realtors 252-457-1100, 866-457-1190; www.twiddy.com; 1127A

Schoolhouse Ln., Corolla 27927; 1181 Duck Rd., Duck 27949. Twiddy specializes in the North Beaches and lists over 700 properties, including more than 100 beyond the end of the road, some truly immense, with 16 to 18 bedrooms sleeping up to three dozen people.

Village Realty 252-453-9650, 877-546-5362; www.villagerealtyobx.com; 501 Hunt Club Dr., Ocean Club Centre, Corolla 27927. Represents properties at Corolla Light and the exclusive Currituck Club. Last-minute specials available.

DINING

Duck has a national reputation for fine dining, thanks to restaurants such the Left Bank, Elizabeth's, and the Blue Point. Many restaurants here are oriented toward adults, and several don't welcome children. Most are open year round, although they may cut back hours in the winter.

Dining in Corolla, on the other hand, is far more casual and aimed at large family groups. The emphasis here is on beach food and take-out. Most restaurants in the area can accommodate large groups with advance reservations. Many establishments close during the off-season or limit their hours.

Corolla is also more of a party town than either Duck or Southern Shores, with several bars and nightspots offering entertainment and late-night hours.

Rate Categories

Inexpensive	under $10
Moderate	$10 to $20
Expensive	$20 to $25
Very Expensive	$25 and up

These ratings represent the average cost of an entrée, not including higher-priced specials, that super-size steak or rack of lamb. They also do not include appetizers, desserts, beverages, taxes, or gratuities. When a range of ratings is offered, it usually indicates the difference in price between lunch and dinner entrées.

Credit Cards

AE—American Express
D—Discover
DC—Diners Club
MC—Master Card
V—Visa

Meal Abbreviations

B—Breakfast
L—Lunch
D—Dinner
SB—Sunday brunch

Restaurants

COROLLA
GROUPERS GRILLE & WINE BAR

252-453-4077
www.grouperswinebar.com
7901 Sunset Blvd., TimBuck II, Corolla 27927
Price: Expensive
Children's Menu: Yes
Cuisine: Seafood
Liquor: Full
Serving: D
Credit Cards: MC, V
Handicapped Access: Yes
Special Features: Wine bar; no smoking

Award-winning chef and owner Matthew Fretwell prepares creative, elegant entrées using fresh seafood. Specialties include Hawaiian sunfish, stuffed catfish crusted with pecans, and grilled romaine salad topped with feta. Angus steaks and an awesome 12-ounce pork chop fill out the menu. The wine list has received many awards, including seven straight years of *Wine Spectator*'s Award of Excellence. Many interesting wines are served by the glass.

MIKE DIANNA'S GRILL ROOM

252-453-4336

www.grillroomobx.com
796A Sunset Blvd., TimBuck II, Corolla
27927
Price: Expensive
Children's Menu: Yes
Cuisine: Steaks, chops, and seafood
Liquor: Full
Serving: D
Credit Cards: AE, D, MC, V
Handicapped Access: Yes
Special Features: Live music; outdoor bar;
open seasonally

Mesquite-grilled meats and seafood, plus
some pasta entrées, are the specialties at
this popular spot in TimBuck II that can
accommodate large groups. USDA Prime
beef, chicken, lamb, pork, and veal seared
on the grill come with your choice of homemade sauces. A big wine list recognized by
Wine Spectator complements the menu with
vintages in every price range, including
many bottles under $40. Try the mesquite-
grilled banana split for dessert. You can eat
inside in the white-tablecloth dining room,
or outside on the casual deck. Live music on
the deck in season. Reservations recommended, especially for large groups.

NORTH BANKS
RESTAURANT & RAW BAR

252-453-3344
100G Sunset Blvd., TimBuck II, Corolla
27927
Price: Inexpensive to Very Expensive
Children's Menu: Yes
Cuisine: Steaks and seafood
Liquor: Full
Serving: L, D
Credit Cards: MC, V
Handicapped Access: Yes
Special Features: Bar; drink specials; take-
out available

This popular spot on the upper deck of Tim-
Buck II's west building offers drink specials
and a wide variety of steamed seafood.
Lunch features casual sandwiches and

salads. At dinner the specialties are lobster
and filet mignon. The small dining room
does not accept reservations, so you may
have to wait.

PINE ISLAND DINER

252-453-4828
www.thesanderling.com
345 Audubon Dr., NC 12, Corolla 27927
Price: Inexpensive to Moderate
Children's Menu: Yes
Cuisine: All-American
Liquor: Beer, wine
Serving: L, D
Credit Cards: AE, D, DC, MC, V
Handicapped Access: Yes

This classic 1950s diner located next to the
Hampton Inn in Pine Island features a family-friendly menu, with pizzas, burgers,
fries, and grilled sandwiches, at family-
friendly prices. Come for a meal, or sit at
the counter and enjoy a milkshake, banana
split, or old-fashioned malt. Beer and wine
are available for Mom and Dad, plus roasted
chicken and a cold salad plate.

ROUTE 12 STEAK & SEAFOOD CO.

252-453-4644
www.rt12restaurant.com
786C Ocean Trail, TimBuck II, Corolla
27927
Price: Moderate to Expensive
Children's Menu: Yes
Cuisine: All-American and seafood
Liquor: Full
Serving: L, D
Credit Cards: MC, V
Handicapped Access: Yes
Special Features: Take-out menu; martini
menu; raw bar

Chef Ron Davidson prepares a wide variety
of popular dishes, from steak or tuna au
poivre to pastas, duck, and shrimp, at this
casual spot next to the BrewThru. Try the
crab bisque or the Big Kahuna combo:
clams, oysters, shrimp, and crab legs from

the steamer. The pork ribs are locally famous. Reservations recommended.

THE BLUE POINT BAR & GRILL

252-261-8090
www.goodfoodgoodwine.com
1240 Duck Rd., Waterfront Shops, Duck 27949
Price: Moderate to Very Expensive
Children's Menu: Yes
Cuisine: Southern coastal
Liquor: Full
Serving: L, D
Credit Cards: MC, V
Handicapped Access: Yes
Special Features: Reservations accepted a month in advance and online

Nationally recognized for its innovative cuisine, the Blue Point recently expanded to accommodate more of its avid fans but retains its diner charm, complete with checkerboard floors, red leather stools and booths, and the atmospheric screen porch overlooking Currituck Sound. An extensive wine list complements the menu designed by Chef Sam McGann and his team. While there are seasonal changes in the lineup, you'll want to try the much-praised Carolina She-Crab Soup laced with sherry. The crowds—and prices—max out at dinner, but you can eat lunch here for a much more moderate check. Locals are crazy about the meat loaf. Reservations are accepted only for dinner and are very much recommended.

ELIZABETH'S CAFÉ & WINERY

252-261-6145
www.elizabethscafe.com
1117 Duck Rd., Scarborough Faire, Duck 27949
Price: Very Expensive
Children's Menu: No
Cuisine: Country French
Liquor: Wine
Serving: D
Credit Cards: MC, V
Handicapped Access: Yes
Special Features: Wine bar; prix fixe wine menus; wine gallery next door; no smoking or cell phones

Named "Best Fine Dining Wine Restaurant in the United States" by *Santé* magazine in 2003, Elizabeth's is top of the line when it comes to wining and dining on the Banks. Owner Leonard Logan, an accepted expert in the world of wine, is on hand most evenings. Pairing wine with food is his area of expertise, and the nightly six-course prix fixe wine dinners are educational as well as delicious. An à la carte menu is also served. Menus change nightly; however, flame-seared barbecue shrimp served with mango chutney—a dish Logan developed himself—and a lobster, scallop, and brie bisque are house specialties. Although definitely in the splurge category, Elizabeth's strives for a casual beach feel. Two seatings are offered for the prix fixe dinners each night, and reservations are recommended.

FISHBONES RAW BAR & RESTAURANT

252-261-6991
www.fishbonessunsetgrille.com
1171 Duck Rd., Scarborough Lane Shoppes, Duck 27949
Price: Inexpensive to Expensive
Children's Menu: Yes
Cuisine: Creative Caribbean
Liquor: Full
Serving: L, D
Credit Cards: MC, V
Handicapped Access: Yes
Special Features: Tiki bar; specialty cocktail menu; raw bar

A fun Tiki bar with a thatched roof serves specialty cocktails in collectible glasses, as well as all the standard libations. The big menu of appetizers with Caribbean flair, such as Oysters St. Thomas topped with a lobster mushroom sauce, conch fritters, and coconut shrimp, is served all day and night. Seafood dominates the menu, but you'll find burgers, pastas, jerk pork and chicken, and a brie-stuffed filet mignon as well. The chowders here are award-winning.

RED SKY CAFÉ

252-261-8646
www.redskycafe.com
1197 Duck Rd., Duck Landing, Duck 27949
Price: Inexpensive to Expensive
Children's Menu: Yes
Cuisine: Southern coastal
Liquor: Full
Serving: L, D, SB
Credit Cards: MC, V
Handicapped Access: Yes
Special Features: Outdoor seating; early dinner specials; specialty cocktail menu; Chefs-on-Call service

Chef Wes Stepp puts his wood-burning oven to good use, roasting everything from Vidalia onions and tomatoes to crab cakes and pizza. Burgers, quesadillas, and pressed sandwiches are lunch fare. Dinner leans to seafood and steaks. The Unlucky Duck, served with redneck risotto, is one popular favorite. Breads and desserts are baked in house. The Chefs-on-Call service will bring your selected meal to you; no waiting for a table. Reservations available.

SUNSET GRILLE & RAW BAR

252-261-3901
www.fishbonessunsetgrille.com
1270 Duck Rd., Duck 27949
Price: Moderate to Very Expensive
Children's Menu: Yes
Cuisine: Creative Caribbean
Liquor: Full
Serving: B, L, D
Credit Cards: MC, V
Handicapped Access: Yes
Special Features: Tropical drink menu; outside seating; sushi bar; live entertainment in season; watersports rentals

If you like Fishbones in Duck Village, you're going to love its big sister. It's hard to miss this edifice along the sound side of NC 12 north of Duck, and usually one look at the Tiki bars and long dock stretching out to a gazebo is enough to make travelers hit the brakes. If you like a partying good time and spectacular sunsets, you'll come away singing this spot's praises. White tablecloth dining it's not, but take a seat at one of the outdoor Tiki bars, order up a martini in a neon glass, hum along to a Jimmy Buffet tune, and you'll soon catch the Key West vibe. The menu has a lot of fun appetizers like blackened tuna bites and grilled shrimp skewers. Lunch features burgers, sandwiches, and fried seafood baskets. For dinner, treat yourself to a whole stuffed Caribbean lobster, prime rib, or steak. Raw and steamed seafood is available all day, and sushi is served nightly on the upper level. The restaurant also offers an interesting and very reasonably priced breakfast menu.

SANDERLING

★ THE LEFT BANK

252-261-8419
www.thesanderling.com
1461 Duck Rd., Sanderling Resort, Duck 27949
Price: Very Expensive
Children's Menu: No
Cuisine: Contemporary American
Liquor: Full
Serving: D
Closed: Sunday, Monday
Credit Cards: AE, D, DC, MC, V
Handicapped Access: Yes
Special Features: Bar; specialty drink menu; Doughty "Birds of North America" Royal Worchester collection; no children under 13

Cleanly elegant decor highlighted by a bank of windows overlooking Currituck Sound sets off the seven- and three-course tasting menus created by the talented culinary team in the Left Bank's exhibition kitchen. Seasonal ingredients combine with foie gras, lamb, truffles, seafood, or quail, with spectacular results. Each course can be paired with a suitable wine by the sommelier, or you can order from the bar. *Santé* magazine named this the "Culinary Hospitality Restaurant of the Year," and the wine list won approval from *Wine Spectator.* The most magical time here occurs at sunset when the blond onyx bar reflects the sun's glow. Muddle the mint in your mojito and enjoy. The dress code is "beachy casual": Men are asked to wear shirts with collars and "dress shorts" or slacks. Reservations are requested.

THE LIFESAVING STATION

252-449-6654
www.thesanderling.com

1471 Duck Rd., Sanderling Resort, Duck 27949
Price: Inexpensive to Expensive
Children's Menu: Yes
Cuisine: Contemporary American
Liquor: Full
Serving: B, L, D
Credit Cards: AE, D, DC, MC, V
Handicapped Access: Yes
Special Features: Private wine room; Swan Bar upstairs

The Sanderling's casual restaurant, the Lifesaving Station, occupies the renovated 1899 Caffey's Inlet boathouse. The paneled interior, beautifully restored, is studded with maritime memorabilia, historical

The Lifesaving Station Restaurant at the Sanderling Resort

objects, bird decoys, and culinary awards. Menus vary with the season but always feature local fish and shellfish. At breakfast, the Eggs Sanderling and the Sweet Potato and Country Ham Hash topped with poached eggs are both standouts. The lunch menu of sandwiches, salads, and wraps includes several vegetarian options. Upstairs you'll find the Swan Bar, a great place for a quiet drink and a bowl of the Sanderling's signature chowder, a creamy blend of shrimp, crab, and corn.

SOUTHERN SHORES

MERIDIAN 42

252-261-0420

www.meridian42.com

1 Ocean Blvd., Southern Shores Crossing, Southern Shores 27949

Price: Expensive

Children's Menu: No

Cuisine: Coastal Mediterranean

Liquor: Full

Serving: D

Credit Cards: AE, D, MC, V

Handicapped Access: Yes

Special Features: Bar; martini menu; drink specials

Wines by the glass at reasonable prices, a big menu of tapas, plus a friendly bar, healthy Mediterranean-inspired cuisine, and ocean views from the upstairs balcony, make this place a hit with locals and visitors. Tapas range from a plate of olives to handmade ravioli. Dinner entrées might range from a pot-au-feu of beef, duck, and foie gras, to a Piquillo pepper stuffed with Gruyere cheese bread pudding. Desserts, including ice cream and sorbet, are made in house. Reservations are recommended. If you want to make them more than two weeks in advance, you can do so on the Internet.

Food Purveyors

Bakeries and Coffee Shops

Cravings Coffee Shoppe 252-261-0655; 1211 Duck Rd., Duck Common, Duck 27949. Coffee shop serving pastries, coffee, and espresso drinks, is also a WiFi hot spot.

★ **Duck's Cottage Coffee and Books** 252-261-5510; www.duckscottage.com; 1240 Duck Rd., Waterfront Shops, Duck 27949. Run by java junkies, the historic, cedar-shingled cottage that once housed the Powder Ridge Gun Club now provides an early morning stop for residents and visitors who come to browse the book selection, enjoy an espresso or herbal tea, or hang out on the porch with a Mucky Duck specialty drink.

Maui Wowi Hawaiian Coffees and Smoothies 252-457-0222; www.mauiwowi.com; 603 Currituck Clubhouse Dr., Shoppes at Currituck Club, Corolla 27927. Kona espresso and kiwi fruit smoothies put the "aloha" in this Hawaiian-themed café.

Northern Light Pastries and Coffee 252-453-0201; www.obxcoffee.com; 109A Austin St., Corolla Light Town Center, Corolla 27927. Chef Zack Grumet's European-style croissants, plus doughnuts, and other pastries baked fresh daily, are available both here and at sister stores **Outer Banks Coffee** and **Corolla Bagels** 252-453-8877; Corolla Light Town Center. Free WiFi access.

Outer Banks Coffee Company 252-453-0200; www.obxcoffee.com; 807L Ocean Trail, Monteray Plaza, Corolla 27927. Beans are fresh roasted on-site, adding to the wake-up aroma as you walk through the door. Free WiFi access.

Tullio's Pastry Shop www.tulliospastry.com; two Duck locations: 252-261-7111, Scarborough Faire; 252-261-7112, Loblolly Pines Shopping Plaza. Award-winning cakes, pies, and other baked goods featured at some of the area's top restaurants are available at these retail outlets.

Breakfast

Big Mama's Breakfast, Seafood, Ice Cream & Yogurt 252-453-4960; 1152 Ocean Trail, NC 12, Corolla 27927. Big Mama's breakfast biscuits and sausage gravy keep the locals coming back.

First Light Breakfast & Burger 252-453-4664; 793C Sunset Blvd., TimBuck II, Corolla 27927. Serves a full breakfast menu until 2 PM in season.

Lighthouse Bagels & Smoothies 252-453-9998; www.lighthousebagels.com; 807 Ocean Trail, Monteray Plaza, Corolla 27927. New Jersey natives bring authentic bagels to the beach.

Candy and Ice Cream

★ **Big Bucks Homemade Ice Cream & Coffee Bar** 252-453-3188; 794F Sunset Blvd., TimBuck II, Corolla 27927. More than 50 flavors of homemade ice cream, sherbets, fat free frozen yogurt, fruit smoothies, milk shakes, and espresso drinks, plus ice cream cakes to die for.

The Fudgery www.fudgeryfudge.com; Corolla locations: 252-453-8882, Shoppes at Currituck Club; 252-261-8882, TimBuck II; Duck location: 252-261-8283, Scarborough Faire. This national chain born on the Outer Banks originated "fudge theater." On hot days, order the chiller fudge, with your choice of fudge blended into ice cream.

Paradise Sweets 252-453-3500; 793D Sunset Blvd., TimBuck II, Corolla 27927. Coffee, Hawaiian shave ice, ice cream, and a wall of candy are available in this old-fashioned sweet shop.

Delis and Specialty Foods

Bagels to Beef Café by Tommy's Market 252-255-2888; www.bagelstobeef.com; The Marketplace, Southern Shores. Second location of Tommy's expands the takeout menu with subs, paninis, and burgers.

Coastal Provisions 252-480.0023; www.coastalprovisionsmarket.com; 1 Ocean Blvd., Southern Shores 27949. Gourmet groceries or dishes prepared by talented chefs, to-go or delivered.

Duck Deli To Go 252-261-7032; www.duckdelitogo.com; The Marketplace, Southern Shores 27949. Duck Deli's popular menu of smoked barbecue pork, chicken, and ribs available for takeout.

Tommy's Gourmet Market and Wine Emporium 252-261-8990; www.tommysmarket.com; 1242 Duck Rd., Duck 27949. Personal service and convenience are the hallmarks of this longtime Duck store that lets you order your groceries, or entire prepared meals, online or by phone.

Try My Nuts Nut Company www.trymynuts.com; three locations: 252-453-4955, TimBuck II, Corolla; 252-261-0900, Scarborough Lane Shoppes, Duck; 252-995-7000, Hatteras Island Plaza, Avon. Local company, home of "the world's hottest nuts," hovers on the edge of fame for its Dirty White Trash snack mix.

Wee Winks Market 252-261-2937; 1213 Duck Rd., Duck 27949. The first store ever in Duck, and still much beloved for its convenience and wide variety of necessities.

Winks of Corolla 252-453-8166; 1152 Ocean Trail, Corolla 27927. Once the only spot in Corolla to get groceries, beer, wine, gas, and just about everything else, Winks anchors the shops in the Austin building, all local favorites.

Farmers Markets and Vegetable Stands

Green Acre Market 252-261-8687; 1216 Duck Rd., Wee Winks Square, Duck 27949. Produce stand sells sweet corn, vine-ripened tomatoes, watermelons, hot peppers, berries, and more, direct from farms in Currituck County. Open daily from Memorial Day to Labor Day.

Seaside Farm Market 252-453-8285; home.earthlink.net/~seasidemarkt; 787 Sunset Blvd., TimBuck II, Corolla 27927. Family-run open-air market at the entrance to Tim-Buck II offers locally grown produce, baked pies and breads, local seafood, and beer and wine.

Pizza

Corolla Pizza and Deli 252-453-8592; 1152 Ocean Trail, Austin Complex, Corolla 27927. Serving hand-tossed stone-oven pizza, plus a variety of hot and cold subs, this is a favorite with locals. Free delivery in season.

Cosmo's Pizzeria 252-453-4666; www.cosmospizzeria.com; 110C Corolla Light Town Center, Corolla 27927. This popular spot with a great location offers fresh-made New York-style pizzas, salads, and subs. Cold beer on tap.

The Pizza Guy 252-453-9976; 501 Old Stoney Rd., Pine Island 27927. Located near the Pine Island water tower, the Pizza Guy offers free delivery in both Duck and Corolla.

Pizzazz Pizza Company www.pizzazzpizza.net; three locations: 252-453-8858, 603E Currituck Clubhouse Dr., Shoppes at Currituck Club, Corolla 27927; 252-261-8822, Loblolly Pines, Duck 27949; 252-255-0050, 4146 N. Croatan Highway, Bypass, MP 3.5, Kitty Hawk 27949. Locally owned and operated pizzerias offer buffets with salad bar, online ordering and a wide delivery area.

Tomato Patch Pizzeria 252-453-4500; www.obxpizza.com; 802 Albacore St., Monteray Plaza, Corolla 27927. The menu goes way beyond your typical pizza place, offering crab dip, Italian classics, seafood baskets, hot subs, gyros, po' boys, and vegetarian specials.

Sandwiches

Bad Bean Taqueria 252-453-4380; www.badbeanobx.com; 785A Sunset Blvd., TimBuck II, Corolla 27927. The flavors of Baja California inspire the menu at this casual spot with a big-screen TV and a large selection of Mexican beers and margaritas.

Guava Jelly's 252-453-6777; 887 Albacore St., TimBuck II, Corolla 27927. This cool spot grooves to a reggae beat. Enjoy a healthy sandwich or wrap inside or out on the deck.

Zero's Subs 252-453-0060; www.zerossubs.com; 603B Currituck Club Dr., Shoppes at Currituck Club, Corolla 27927. Popular with surfers since its founding back in 1967, Zero's receives many "Best of the Beach" awards from loyal customers.

Takeout

Corolla Village Barbecue 252-457-0076; 1129 Corolla Village Rd., Corolla 27927. Serving Carolina pork barbecue, ribs, BBQ chicken, soft serve ice cream, and homemade sides in the heart of Old Corolla Village, this local favorite offers takeout only, but you can eat at the picnic tables out front.

Fat Crabs Rib Company 252-453-9931; 1159A Austin St., Corolla Light Town Center, Corolla 27927. A large selection of steamed seafood, including stone and Dungeness crab and lobster, is available à la carte or in steamer pot combos for takeout only. St. Louis–style ribs and North Carolina pork barbecue make up the flip side of the menu.

Smokey's Restaurant 252-453-4050; www.smokeysrestaurant.com; 811 Ocean Trail, Monteray Plaza, Corolla 27927. Fried chicken, North Carolina–style pork barbecue, and ribs available in large combos for pickup.

Sooey's BBQ and Rib Shack www.sooeysbbq.com; two locations: 252-453-4423, 807B Ocean Trail, Corolla 27927; 252-449-2271, Scarborough Faire, Duck 27949. Eat in or take out.

Steamers Shellfish To Go 252-453-3305; www.steamersshellfishtogo.com; 798B Sunset Blvd., TimBuck II, Corolla 27927. Steamer pots of seasoned seafood, red bliss potatoes, corn on the cob, and onions, are this spot's specialty. There's also a long list of gourmet dishes and a low-priced lunch menu served before 4 PM.

Seafood Markets

Bluewater Seafood Market 252-453-9921; 508 Hunt Club Dr., Ocean Club Centre, Corolla 27927. Fresh fish and shellfish, including lobster and crabs, plus everything else you need for an eat-in evening.

Dockside N Duck Seafood Market 252-261-8687; 1216 Duck Rd., Wee Winks Square, Duck 27949. Down East clambakes to steam on your stovetop, raw and steamed seafood, crab cakes, live Maine lobsters, and blue crabs, along with prime cuts of beef, breads, and desserts.

Dockside North Seafood Market 252-453-8112; www.docksidenorth.com; 819C Ocean Trail, Monteray Plaza, Corolla 27927. Full service market will steam lobster, shrimp, king and snow crab to order, or you can get a Down East clambake, ready to go.

Wine, Beer, and Spirits

ABC Store 252-453-9628; www.ncabc.com; Ocean Club Centre, Corolla; 252-261-6981, Wee Winks Square, Duck. These state-run stores are the only places where you can buy a bottle of the hard stuff.

Bacchus Wine & Cheese 252-453-4333; www.bacchuswineandcheese.com; 891 Albacore St., Monteray Plaza, Corolla 27927. This entertaining place stocks over 750 vintages from around the world, and all the extras to go with them, from imported cheeses, to steaks, lobster tails, pasta, and desserts, plus after-dinner cigars. Weekly wine tastings in season.

Brew Thru Beverage Store 252-453-2878; www.brewthru.com; NC 12, TimBuck II, Corolla 27927. The ultimate in convenience: You don't even have to get out of your car to score a six-pack.

Elizabeth's Wine Gallery 252-261-6145; www.elizabethscafe.com; 1117 Duck Rd., Scarborough Faire, Duck 27949. Elizabeth's extensive wine selection is displayed in a unique, temperature and humidity controlled, walk-in wine cellar.

North Banks Wine Shop 252-453-6019; www.nbxwine.com; 794 I Sunset Blvd., TimBuck II, Corolla 27927. Shop with a view stocks wines from around the world, as well as local vintages, wine-related gifts, and many hard-to-find beers. Frequent wine tastings.

TOURING

Tourism to the North Beaches boomed in the first years of the 21st century, with many outfitters entering the market to provide vacation activities for the huge increase in visitors. **The Currituck Outer Banks Visitor's Center** (252-453-9612, 877-287-7488; www.visit currituck.com; 500 Hunt Club Rd., Ocean Club Centre, Corolla 27927) provides a wealth of information on the area. Information on Southern Shores and Duck can be found at the Dare County welcome centers. The closest is the **Aycock Brown Welcome Center** (877-629-4386; www.outerbanks.org), located at MP 1 in Kitty Hawk on US 158.

By Four-Wheel-Drive

The area past the end of the road in Corolla offers more than a dozen miles of off-road adventure. The wild ponies that make this their home are an added bonus to a fascinating and unforgettable experience. The best way to explore this area is with one of the local outfitters who know how to get around, where to find the ponies, and how to avoid getting stuck in the sand.

Back Country Outfitters and Guides 252-453-0877; www.outerbankstours.com; Corolla Light Town Center, NC 12, Corolla 27927. Led by experienced guides, **Wild Horse Safaris** explore the sandy roads of Carova in family-size, air-conditioned four-wheel-drive SUVs. The half-day **4WD & Kayak Expedition** adds a guided paddle through canals in the Horse Sanctuary.

Barrier Island Eco-Tours 252-457-0224, 252-256-8371; www.barrierislandecotours.com; 795 Sunset Blvd., TimBuck II, Corolla 27927. The **Monster Bus Beach Tour** takes you up the beach to Carova aboard a big-tire, four-wheel-drive bus that seats up to 34 passengers. From there, you can take an airboat or WaveRunner tour across Back Bay to the Virginia Beach community of Sandbridge or enjoy an eco-tour of the marsh.

Beach Jeeps of Corolla 252-453-6141; www.beachjeepsofcorolla.com; Corolla Light Town Center. Drive your family on a GPS-guided tour of the 12,000 acres "north of the fence." Vehicles with automatic transmission available.

★ **Bob's Corolla Wild Horse Adventure Tours** 252-453-8602; www.wildhorsetour.com; Inn at Corolla Light, NC 12, Corolla. Family-friendly two-hour tour aboard comfortable, air-conditioned four-wheel-drive SUVs guarantees you will see ponies, or your money will be refunded.

Corolla Jeep Rentals and Tours 252-453-6899; www.outerbanksjeeprentals.com; 1070 Ocean Trail, Corolla 27927. Do-it-yourself tours in a four-wheel-drive Jeep of the off-road area. GPS coordinates lead you to horse hot spots as well as Penny's Hill and the Wash Woods Coast Guard Station. Escorted, sunset, and group tours also available.

Corolla Outback Adventures 252-453-4484; www.corollaoutback.com; 1150 Ocean Trail, Corolla 27927. Drive a vintage Land Cruiser into the outback as part of a convoy of retro vehicles that visits several exclusive areas of the Wild Horse Reserve before heading back down the beach for some serious beachcombing. Tour guide Jay Bender's family has been leading off-road adventures since 1962, when the road ended south of Duck.

By Boat, Kayak, or Jet Ski

Barrier Island Eco-Tours 252-457-0224, 252-256-8371; www.barrierislandecotours.com; 795 Sunset Blvd., TimBuck II, Corolla 27927. Take an airboat or personal watercraft tour of the marsh, or cross to Knotts Island to tour the vineyards. Two- and three-passenger WaveRunners available.

Coastal Kayak 252-261-6262, 800-701-4111; www.outerbankskayaktours.com. Guided paddle trips explore the intricate marsh maze of the Pine Island Audubon Sanctuary.

Corolla Water Sports 252-453-6900; www.corollawatersports.com. Departing from the Kitty Hawk Water Sports dock behind TimBuck II, kayak eco-tours paddle north to the Whalehead Club or south through the protected marsh waterway owned by the Currituck Hunt Club, one of the best paddling routes on the Banks.

Kitty Hawk Kites 877-FLY-THIS; www.kittyhawk.com. Popular tours are a sunset paddle around the lagoon at Historic Corolla, and a family-friendly paddle along the Duck waterfront.

Nor'Banks Sailing Center 252-261-2900; norbanks.com; 1314 Duck Rd., Duck 27949. Guided tours of Currituck Sound via personal watercraft.

Outer Banks Charter Fishing Adventures/Corolla Bait and Tackle 252-453-9500; www.corollabaitandtackle.com. Relaxing tours aboard the pontoon boat *Currituck Queen* include a two-hour sunset cruise and a trip around Monkey Island, once a famous hunt club. A wine tasting cruise takes you across Currituck Sound to a visit a winery on Knotts Island.

By Segway

★ **Back Country Outfitters and Guides** 252-453-0877; www.outerbankstours.com; Corolla Light Town Center, NC 12, Corolla 27927. Segways are the newest way to explore Historic Corolla Village. This guided tour includes instruction in operating your two-wheeled vehicle before a gliding trip past the village's historic buildings. Tours of the company's private Spanish Mustang Preserve are offered aboard fat-wheeled off-road Segways.

CULTURE

Formerly an area of small fishing villages and a scattered population, the North Beaches have had little time to develop cultural amenities such as theater companies and symphonies. However, the rich history of the area has inspired preservationists to restore and protect several historic structures, from hunt clubs to lifesaving stations.

Architecture

The Outer Banks Conservationists (www.currituckbeachlight.com) led the drive to preserve the area's history. Starting in the late 1970s, the group raised more than $1.5 million in private dollars to restore the **Currituck Beach Lighthouse** and its keepers' quarters. The buildings had been standing open to the elements for over 40 years and several had been hauled away by local residents, a time honored Outer Banks tradition.

The restoration of these buildings dating to the late 1800s gives the area a unique group of what is today called "stick style" Queen Anne. Architectural features are notable in the keeper's house, now used as a museum store, and a storage building topped with sharp finials, now used for offices, as well as the 1878 Life Saving Station on NC 12, today the office of Twiddy Realty. The design elements found in these buildings have provided inspiration for more recent architects and can be seen reflected in many new buildings in the area.

Historic Lighthouses of North Carolina

Beginning in Corolla and stretching nearly to the South Carolina border, the North Carolina coast has seven historic lighthouses. Built between 1818 and 1958, the lighthouses each sported a distinctive color pattern to help ships distinguish between them during the day; at night each flashed an individual light signature. Most of the North Carolina beacons are still in operation. This list travels north to south.

Farthest north, the **Currituck Beach Light** (www.currituckbeachlight.com), a 162-foot redbrick tower completed in 1875, operates under the stewardship of the Outer Banks Preservationists. Climbing is permitted seasonally.

Bodie Island Light (www.nps.gov/caha), 156 feet tall, is painted in horizontal black and white stripes. Completed in 1872, it is still in operation under the care of the National Park Service (NPS) and retains its first-order Fresnel lens. The base of the lighthouse reopened for tours in 2007, and the NPS plans to eventually reopen the tower for climbing.

Cape Hatteras Light (www.nps.gov/caha), at 198 feet, is the tallest and most famous lighthouse in America. Painted in a black and white spiral pattern, it was moved to a new location in 1999 and continues to flash its signal out to sea. The National Park Service opens the lighthouse to climbers during the summer season.

Ocracoke Light (www.nps.gov/caha), a 65-foot white tower built in 1823, is the oldest continuously operating lighthouse in North Carolina, and the second-oldest in the United States. Still owned by the U.S. Coast Guard, the lighthouse is maintained by the National Park Service. Climbing is not permitted; however, the base is open for limited hours during the summer months.

Cape Lookout Light (www.nps.gov/calo), completed in 1859, is painted in a pattern of black and white diamonds. At 163 feet, it was the first tall lighthouse to be built and served as a model for later construction. The lighthouse can be reached by boat from Harkers Island, where the Cape Lookout National Seashore headquarters are located. The lighthouse is still operational, and climbing has been permitted during quarterly open houses, if you are lucky enough to get a reservation, although closures for repairs are frequent. The NPS plans to open it for climbing on a regular schedule in the future.

The remaining two lighthouses marked the treacherous entrance to the Cape Fear River in southern North Carolina: **Bald Head Island Light** (www.oldbaldy.org), no longer in service, was built in 1818, making it the oldest lighthouse still standing in the state. The 109-foot octagonal structure is built of brick covered with concrete. Open for climbing during the summer months, Old Baldy, as it's called by its fans, can be reached by ferry from Southport, North Carolina.

Oak Island Light (www.oakislandlighthouse.org), a poured concrete 158-foot structure striped gray, white, and black, was built in 1958 to replace several earlier beacons and was one of the last manually operated lighthouses in the world. Tours of the first and second levels are conducted by the Friends of Oak Island Lighthouse.

Several other aids to navigation were used in North Carolina waters. Lightships, the most famous of which was anchored off Cape Hatteras on the Diamond Shoals until torpedoed by German submarines, helped mark extremely shallow waters. In the sounds, screw-pile lighthouses helped guide ships. Replicas of the screw-pile cottage-style lights can be found in Manteo on Roanoke Island and in Plymouth on Albemarle Sound.

For more information, visit the Web site of the Outer Banks Lighthouse Society (www.outerbanks lighthousesociety.org).

Another building of interest is the Whalehead Club, which houses exceptional examples of Art Nouveau decorative details.

Art Galleries and Exhibits

Dolphin Watch Gallery 252-453-2592; www.dolphinwatchgallery.com; 793 Sunset Dr., TimBuck II, Corolla 27927. Features a wide variety of arts and fine crafts, including gallery owner Mary Kaye Umberger's original works depicting wild horses and local landmarks.

Eclectic Treasures 252-453-0008; www.eclecticgallery.net; 794K Sunset Blvd., Corolla 27927. Unique selection of fine art and crafts runs the gamut from blessing bowls to martini glasses. Standouts are watercolors by former lighthouse keeper Lloyd Childers.

Greenleaf Gallery 252-261-2009; www.outer-banks.com/greenleaf; 1169 Duck Rd., Duck 27949. Large gallery on the south side of Duck showcases paintings, ceramics, jewelry, woodcraft, and art glass primarily created by North Carolina and Virginia artists. Monthly openings in season.

Ocean Treasures 252-453-2383; www.oceantreasures.net; 785 Sunset Blvd., TimBuck II, Corolla 27927. A 6-foot bronze dolphin welcomes you to the only gallery on the Banks representing Wyland, painter of whales, and Thomas Kinkade, Painter of Light. Both are represented by new releases and some sold-out items, as well as licensed gifts and collectibles.

The Sanderling Resort 252-261-4111, 800-701-4111; www.thesanderling.com; 1461 Duck Rd., NC 12, Duck 27949. The public rooms of this landmark resort display an outstanding collection of wildfowl art, including porcelain birds by Gunter Granget, the Boehm Studio, and Dorothy Doughty's "Birds of North America" Royal Worchester collection, as well as many impressive wood and metal bird sculptures by South Carolina artist Grainger McKoy. The main inn lobbies display 18 original Audubon prints in addition to a complete baby elephant folio.

Spry Creek Dry Goods 252-453-0199; www.sprycreek.com; 1122 Corolla Village Rd., Historic Corolla Village. From the outside the unpresuming building may look like the auto repair shop it once was, but inside Corolla native Karen Whitfield has gathered a colorful collection of local art and jewelry, combining it with handmade crafts from around the world. Look for the exclusive line of toiletries made locally just for this shop.

Tarheel Trading Company 252-441-6235; www.tarheeltrading.com; two locations: TimBuck II, Corolla; Scarborough Lane Shoppes, Duck. Handcrafted jewelry, gifts, and decorative art from over 300 American artists, including many from North Carolina. The store in Corolla is more contemporary, while the Duck location tends toward the traditional.

★ **Whalehead Club Museum Shop** 252-453-9040; Currituck Heritage Park, Corolla 27927. Unique jewelry, ornaments, birdhouses, and other art objects created from the house's original copper shingles join a nice collection of books, posters, and other gifts. Proceeds benefit historic preservation.

The Wooden Feather 252-261-2808; www.woodenfeather.com; 1171 Duck Rd., Scarborough Lane Shoppes, Duck 27949. Decoys hand carved by local artists and wildlife art in wood and metal, plus artistic birdhouses, starfish, and sea urchins crowd this interesting gallery in Duck Village.

Historic Gardens, Homes, and Sites

Corolla Surfing Museum 252-453-9283; www.corollasurfshop.com; TimBuck II and Monteray Plaza, Corolla. Classic surfboards, including a 1930s hollow-wood board and many experimental designs from the 1960s, are on display in the stores at Monteray Plaza and TimBuck II (the shop next to the go-cart track, not the "surf lifestyles" shop in the west building).

★ **Currituck Beach Lighthouse and Keepers' Houses** 252-453-4939, 252-453-8152; www.currituckbeachlight.com; 1101 Corolla Village Rd., Corolla 27927. The Outer Banks Conservationists have done a magnificent job restoring the lighthouse itself and the surrounding buildings. The 162-foot lighthouse was the last one built along this coast, illuminating the final "dark spot" starting in 1875. You can climb the 214 steps to the top to enjoy an unsurpassed view of the Corolla area from Easter to Thanksgiving weekend (closed Thanksgiving Day) for a fee of $6 a person. Children under eight years old climb for free. The original keeper's cottage is now a museum gift shop. The buildings are arranged around a shady green lawn that is a magnet for artists and photographers.

Currituck Heritage Park 252-453-9040; NC 12, MP 11, Corolla. The 39-acre park is a small fraction of the original grounds of the Whalehead Club, but it seems pretty spacious amid today's development. Launch at the free boat ramp to access the sound. Or just admire the sunset from the arching bridge and gazebo. Many special events, from concerts and wine tastings to Halloween hayrides, are held here annually. Plenty of free parking.

Historic Corolla Village 252-453-9612. Old Corolla, once a fishing village that was the largest town between the Virginia border and Kitty Hawk, has been renovated into a district of charming shops. Highlights include the **1900 Corolla School House** (1126 Schoolhouse Rd.), the **1930 Parker House** (252-453-0171; 1129 Corolla Village Rd.), the **1895 Lewark-Gray House** (252-453-4388; 1130 Corolla Village Rd.), the **Corolla Post Office** in the Austin Building on NC 12, and the **1885 Corolla Chapel** (252-453-4224; 1136 Corolla Village Rd.). Most now house shops and offices, but services are still conducted in the chapel. Refreshments are available at Village Bar-B-Que.

Historic Corolla Village Garden 252-452-0171; www.lighthouse-garden.com; 1129 Corolla Village Rd., Corolla 27927. Behind the Lighthouse Garden shop, you'll find this delightful retreat with many native and heirloom species. Visitors are welcome.

U.S. Life Saving Station / Twiddy & Company Realtors 252-457-1100, 866-457-1190;

The historic schoolhouse in Corolla Village, now a museum and headquarters of the Wild Horse Fund

www.twiddy.com; NC 12, Corolla. Pick up information on Corolla's historic district and view memorabilia at this real estate office, housed in the 1878 Kill Devil Hills station that preservationist Doug Twiddy moved to Corolla and restored.

Wash Woods Coast Guard Station 252-457-1100, 866-457-1190; www.twiddy.com; North Swan Beach. This landmark in the off-road area served as a lifesaving and Coast Guard Station from 1878 and was restored by Twiddy & Company. Close by, the stumps of ancient trees poke out of the beach, giving the area the name of Wash Woods.

★ **The Whalehead Club** 252-453-9040, www.whaleheadclub.org, 1100 Club Rd., Corolla 27927. With copper roof shingles, cork floors, Tiffany light fixtures, duck-head door-knobs, and many art nouveau details, the Whalehead Club stands as a monument to a former age. This imposing 21,000-square-foot edifice began life in 1922 as the winter cottage of northern industrialist Edward Knight and his bride, then became the most elegant hunt club on the southeast coast. After decades of other uses, ranging from a boys' school to a rocket-testing facility, the sumptuous structure has been restored to pristine condition. A variety of tours are offered daily, including a self-guided audio tour. Ghost tours and children's treasure hunts require reservations. Tours range from $7 to $15.

Nightlife and Entertainment

During the summer season, many local restaurants add music to their menus. In Corolla, bands play regularly at Mike Dianna's Grill Room, Guava Jelly's, Dr. Unk's, and Sundogs Sports Bar. In Duck, the Sunset Grill has live music daily during high season and, true to its name, celebrates the sunset Key West–style every evening. A free summer music series takes place at the Duck Town Park. Concerts are held in the early evening several times each week. Seating is not provided; bring a chair or blanket. For a schedule, visit www.townof duck.com or call the town's event hotline: 252-255-1286.

Currituck Heritage Park 252-453-9040; www.whaleheadclub.org; Corolla. The Whale-head Club sponsors a free Summer Concert Series on the Lawn Thursday evenings in July and August, and Wine Festivals with live music on Wednesday afternoons.

Dr. Unk's Bar 252-457-0053; www.obxpizza.com; Monteray Plaza, Corolla. Bar attached to the Tomato Patch Pizzeria serves up a late-night menu and a full selection of cocktails, plus frequent live music by regional and local bands, June to September.

Roadside Raw Bar & Grill 252-261-5729; 1923 Duck Rd., Duck 27949. Charming cottage serves fresh seafood, great chowder, and live jazz on its deck.

Sundogs Sports Bar and Grill 252-453-4263; www.myspace.com/sundogger; Monteray Plaza, Corolla. Full service bar, with a bar food menu, pool table, and late night hours, is a favorite spot to watch sports on the big screen. Bands play several nights a week during the summer season.

RECREATION

With extensive marshes on Currituck Sound and unspoiled beaches on the Atlantic, plus the off-road playground beyond the end of the road, the North Beaches have some of the best recreational opportunities on the Banks.

Note that no ATVs are allowed in the off-road area, and drivers are requested to stay on the established sand roads through the communities. No access is available to the Virginia

The Whalehead Club, once the most elegant hunt club on the Banks, now restored to its Art Deco splendor

side of the state line through the locked gates.

You must keep 50 feet away from any wild ponies you come upon. Do not feed them any kind of food, even hay or apples. Ponies have died in recent years from well-meaning visitors feeding them food that their digestive systems are not adapted to handle.

Beaches

The beaches at the northern end of the Banks are wide, inviting, clean, and generally not crowded. An excursion onto the beach north of Corolla at the end of NC 12 is a fascinating journey, best taken with a local who knows how to navigate the maze of largely unmarked sand tracks. If you venture in with your own four-wheel drive vehicle, stick to the beach and you can't get lost. There are no public facilities in the off-road area, and commercial development is forbidden. You can buy T-shirts, and perhaps get directions, at the fire station.

Here are some hints for driving on the beach that may keep you from getting stuck. Lower the pressure in your tires to 20 psi. Be sure you know the weather forecast and the tide tables. High surf can cut you off. Avoid getting too close to the water. If your tires do begin to spin, back up in your tracks for several car lengths, then move forward slowly. You may need to let out more air. Locals usually take along a shovel, wooden planks, and a tow-rope. Don't forget the suntan lotion, hat, cell phone, and extra water.

If you do get stuck, don't call 911. This is not considered an emergency. Instead, use your cell phone to call the local tow service (**A-1 Towing and Recovery**, 252-452-4002).

When you come off the beach, re-up your tires with air, and your cooler with beverages, at Winks.

Beach Access

Most beach access points from Southern Shores to Corolla are in private communities and can be used only by people renting or owning there. The beaches themselves are public, and it's possible to bike or walk from Kitty Hawk to Corolla along the water's edge, a distance of more than 20 miles, if you have the stamina.

You can drive, walk, or bike onto the beach from Corolla's North Beach Access ramp where NC 12 ends, 24 hours a day, 365 days a year, and drive north on the beach all the way to the Virginia line. Beware of the many stumps that protrude from the sand, the remnants of an ancient forest, as well as other hazards. You cannot drive south from the North Beach Access May through September.

Elsewhere in Corolla, you can access the beach via East Corolla Village Road, a sand road across NC 12 from the Lighthouse, also called the Lighthouse Ramp Road.

The Currituck County Southern Beach Access at 471 Ocean Trail (NC 12) has bathrooms, showers, and parking. There is a lengthy walk to the ocean.

Parking lots are available in Corolla near public beach walkways about a block from the ocean on Whalehead Drive at Sailfish, Bonito, Perch, Barracuda, and Shad Streets. The ban on parking on the shoulders of streets is vigorously enforced.

At Pine Island there is a public bathhouse operated by Currituck County located just off NC 12.

Bonfires, glass, personal watercraft, camping, and ATVs are all prohibited on Currituck County beaches. Pets must be on a leash.

No driving is permitted on the beaches of Duck and Southern Shores, and neither town provides any public ocean beach accesses.

Beach Buggy and Four-Wheel-Drive Rentals

Beach Jeeps of Corolla 252-453-6141; www.beachjeepsofcorolla.com; Corolla Light Town Center, Corolla. Vehicles with automatic or standard transmissions are available, as are GPS self-guided tours.

Corolla Jeep Rentals and Tours 252-453-6899; www.outerbanksjeeprentals.com; 1070 Ocean Trail, Corolla 27927. Daily and weekly four-wheel-drive Jeep and Chevy Suburban rentals can include a surfboard or kayak strapped on top.

Bicycling

Best Bike Routes

The North Beaches are great for biking, with dedicated multi-use paths stretching along NC 12 from Corolla all the way to the junction with US 158. Bike paths wind through historic Corolla Village and Currituck Heritage Park, then paved paths parallel both sides of NC 12 as it heads south, reverting occasionally to a wide shoulder. A paved path runs along the road from the Dare County line through Duck and Southern Shores to the US 158 intersection, then turns west along 158 to Kitty Hawk Elementary School. From there you can cross 158 to the Woods Road Multi-Purpose Path through Kitty Hawk Woods. Other paved and unpaved paths lace the neighborhoods in Southern Shores, Duck, Sanderling, and Corolla.

Bike Rental Shops

These companies will deliver a wide-tired beach cruiser to your door. Tricycles, child seats, and tag-a-longs are also available from most outfitters. Some also offer bikes with gears.

The Sunset Grill north of Duck celebrates Key West–style every evening.

Duck Village Outfitters 252-261-7222; www.duckvillageoutfitters.net; 1207 Duck Rd., Duck 27949.

Just for the Beach Rentals 877-FOR-JFTB; www.justforthebeach.com; 501 Hunt Club Dr., Currituck Club, Corolla 27927.

Ocean Atlantic Rentals www.oceanatlanticrentals.com; two North Beaches locations: 252-453-2440, Corolla Light Town Center, Corolla; 252-261-4346, 1194 Duck Rd., Duck 27949.

Boats and Boating

Boat and Personal Watercraft Rentals

Corolla Kayak Company 252-453-0077; www.outerbanksjeeprentals.com; 1070 Ocean Trail, Corolla 27927. Take a guided or self-guided paddling tour of the Whalehead Club area, or hop the "mothership" shuttle for an easy paddle with the wind at your back.

Corolla Water Sports 252-453-6900; www.corollawatersports.com; Kitty Hawk Water Sports, TimBuck II, Corolla. You can rent a kayak here to explore the nearby shore, or have a kayak delivered. WaveRunner rentals are available at the dock behind TimBuckII.

Duck Village Outfitters 252-261-7222; www.duckvillageoutfitters.net; 1207 Duck Rd., Duck 27949. Single or double, surf or touring kayaks and canoes, delivered free. Rentals by the day or week.

Grog's Watersports 252-261-6866; www.grogswatersports.com; 1264 Duck Rd., at Sunset Grille. In addition to the standard sit-on-top kayaks, Grog's rents the Hobie Mirage that

you can pedal as well as paddle. Two- and four-stroke Yamaha personal watercraft and
pontoon boats for rent

Just for the Beach Rentals 877-FOR-JFTB; www.justforthebeach.com; 501 Hunt Club Dr.,
Currituck Club, Corolla 27927. Single, double, and triple kayaks by the day or week. Free
delivery.

Nor'Banks Sailing Center 252-261-2900; www.norbanks.com; 1314 Duck Rd., Duck
27949. In addition to surf and touring kayaks, Nor'Banks rents Stealth Angler kayaks
fully equipped for fishing. Quiet and fast four-stroke WaveRunners are available for
rent, as well as motor boats and sailboats.

North Duck Water Sports 252-261-4200; www.corollawatersports.com; 1446 Duck Rd.,
NC 12, 2.5 miles north of Duck. Kayaks and personal watercraft for rent.

Ocean Atlantic Rentals www.oceanatlanticrentals.com; two locations: 252-453-2440,
Corolla Light Town Center, Corolla; 252-261-4346, 1194 Duck Rd., Duck 27949. Large
selection of different surf and ocean kayak models. Free delivery.

Soundside Water Sports 252-261-0855; 1566 Duck Rd., NC 12, across from the Sanderling. Kayak and personal watercraft rentals available.

Public Boat Ramps

The North Beaches suffer from a lack of public boat ramps, and Currituck Sound is shallow
and weedy, so flat-bottom boats or very shallow draft vessels work best here. A free boat
ramp is located at Currituck Heritage Park next to the Whalehead Club. You can also launch
a canoe or kayak into the sound at the Duck Town Waterfront Park.

Sailboat Charters

Grog's Watersports 252-261-6866; www.grogswatersports.com; 1264 Duck Rd., Duck
27949. Hobie catamarans for rent by the hour at Sunset Grille.

Nor'Banks Sailing Center 252-261-2900; www.norbanks.com; Duck Rd., Duck 27949.
This full-service sailing center offers rentals and instruction. Kids' sailing camp and a
weekly racing series are open to visitors.

Family Fun

Biking, beachcombing, flying kites, and building sand castles are some of the most popular
family activities on the North Beaches. Try crabbing or fishing at Currituck Heritage Park,
or paint a horse at the **Corolla Wild Horse Museum** (252-453-8002).

The **Outer Banks Center for Wildlife Education** (252-453-0221; www.ncwildlife.org;
Currituck Heritage Park, Corolla) offers free classes geared for children as young as three
throughout the year. Registration is required.

The free **SEAL for Kids Program** (safety education and aquatic safety), offered by Corolla
Ocean Rescue, teaches kids ages 7–14 about ocean safety, first aid, and physical fitness.
Parent/guardian seminars are offered at the same time. Call 252-453-3242 for reservations.

Corolla has two mini-golf options: the **Grass Course at Corolla Light Resort** (252-453-
4198) and the **Golf Links** (252-453-6900; www.corollawatersports.com) behind TimBuck II.

Turtles and waterfowl are abundant at the paddleboat pond at **Kitty Hawk Water Sports**
(252-453-6900; www.corollawatersports.com) behind TimBuck II, next door to the
Corolla Raceway (252-453-9100) go-kart track, bumper boats, and video arcade. **Kitty
Hawk Kites** (252-453-8845, 877-FLY-THIS; www.kittyhawk.com), also at TimBuck II,
offers free kite-flying lessons.

Island Revolution Skate Park (252-453-9484; www.islandrevolution.com), at Corolla Light Town Center, challenges boarders with dual bowls, grind pipes, and jumps. Rental boards and safety equipment are available.

Public playgrounds in Corolla are located at **TimBuck II Shopping Center** and **Corolla Light Town Center**. The **Duck Town Waterfront Park** also has a public playground.

In Southern Shores, a playground, basketball court, and soccer field can be found at **Sea Oats Park**. The **Soundside Wading Beach** has a playground and picnic area. The water here is shallow and suitable for young children. Both facilities are under the management of the Southern Shores Civic Association.

Carolina Outdoors in Corolla's Monteray Plaza (252-453-3685; www.kittyhawk.com) has a 26-foot climbing wall in the courtyard.

RC Theaters Corolla Movies 4 (252-453-2999; Monteray Plaza, Corolla) presents four first-run movies every week and adds extra shows on rainy days.

In Duck, the town's two bookstores sponsor **Children's Story Time** geared to ages three to seven on the Town Green (252-255-1286; www.townofduck.com) during the summer.

In Corolla Light Town Center, **Beach Bag Book & Music** (252-453-2900; www.visit finnegan.blogspot.com) schedules low-fee summer activities, such as Hogwarts Activity Hours and jewelry making.

Fishing

Most of Currituck Sound is too shallow for oceangoing charter boats. However, fishing in the sound with light tackle is very good. This was once the sea bass capital of the world. On the beaches, surf fishing reigns.

Fishing Charters and Outfitters

Corolla Bait and Tackle 252-453-9500; www.corollabaitandtackle.com; two locations: Corolla Light Town Center and Shoppes at Currituck Club. This full-service store can set you up for offshore, inshore, backcountry, wreck fishing, or big game safari fishing. They also offer surf fishing classes, rod and reel and crab pot rentals, plus a huge selection of tackle and bait. Drop by either store for free local fishing advice. Introductory crabbing and fishing trips aboard their pontoon boat are family favorites.

Sharky's Bait, Tackle and Charters 252-255-2248; www.sharkyscharters.com; 1245 Duck Rd., Barrier Island Station, Duck 27949. Stocks bait, tackle, and fishing supplies, and arranges charter-fishing trips. Rod and reel rentals, surf fishing clinics, and fishing licenses also available.

TW's Bait & Tackle and Fish Emporium 252-453-3339; www.twstackle.com; 815B Ocean Trail, Monteray Plaza, Corolla 27927. Top of the line fishing equipment for sale or rent, plus plenty of free fishing advice.

Fishing Piers

No public ocean piers are available along the north coast, but you can fish or crab in the sound from the pier and gazebo at Currituck Heritage Park.

Golf

The Currituck Club 252-453-9400, 888-453-9400; www.thecurrituckgolfclub.com; 620 Currituck Club Dr., Corolla 27927. Set amid dunes and marsh, this award-winning Rees Jones course is a links-style par 72, considered one of the top golf experiences in the state. Jones's design makes superb use of the land, formerly part of the legendary Currituck Hunt Club, yielding awesome views of the ocean, sound, and nearby lighthouse. **Bunkers Grill and Bar** serves lunch and after-golf libations. Call well in advance for tee times.

Duck Woods Country Club 252-261-2609; www.duckwoodscc.com; 50 South Dogwood Trail, Southern Shores 27949. Semiprivate course designed by Ellis Maples accepts public play on a limited basis. The course's traditional layout is sheltered by trees along the fairways, making this a good choice for windy days.

Hunting

The 35-mile-long Currituck Sound is shallow and grassy, ideal habitat for the migrating ducks, geese, and swans that visit in great numbers every winter. Currituck County makes a limited number of blinds available to hunters with waterfowl hunting permits from the state. Contact the **Currituck County Game Commission** (252-429-3472; www.currituck gamecommission.org) and the **N.C. Wildlife Resources Commission** (888-248-6834; www.ncwildlife.org) to start the process.

You can also arrange a hunt with a local guide service. One of the best known in the region is **Stuart's Hunting Lodge** (252-232-2309), run by Watson Stuart, world swan-calling champion.

Nature Preserves and Eco-attractions

CAMA Sound Boardwalk, Currituck Heritage Park, Corolla. Short boardwalk just west of the lighthouse leads through an abundance of native plants to a great view over the marsh.

Currituck Banks National Estuarine Preserve 252-261-8891; www.ncnerr.org; NC 12, Corolla. Just before the end of the road, a boardwalk and hiking trail lead from a parking lot through several barrier island habitats. Interpretive signs explain the ecology of the area.

Duck Town Waterfront Park A boardwalk and trail lead through coastal willow swamp and maritime forest in downtown Duck. Free launch ramp for kayaks and canoes.

Duck Research Pier/Field Research Facility 252-261-3511; frf.usace.army.mil; 1261 Duck Rd., Duck 27949. The equipment on this pier does important research into waves, currents, and other processes that create the Outer Banks. You can visit the facility on weekday mornings during the summer. Free tours begin promptly at 10 AM.

★ **Outer Banks Center for Wildlife Education** 252-453-0221; www.ncwildlife.org; 1160 Village Ln., Currituck Heritage Park, Corolla 27927. Spacious center explores the region's rich heritage of waterfowl hunting and fishing. Exhibits include a life-size duck blind in a salt marsh, an 8,000-gallon aquarium stocked with native fish, and the 250-piece Neal Conoley collection of antique decoys, one of the finest in the country. The center provides a year-round schedule of classes suitable for ages three through adult, including decoy carving, crabbing, kayaking, and nature photography. The classes are mostly free, but registration in advance is highly recommended. The center is open daily all year, including many holidays. Admission is free.

Pine Island Audubon Sanctuary 910-686-7527; www.ncaudubon.org. Occupying one of the last undeveloped parcels of land between Kitty Hawk and Corolla, this 6,000-acre sanctuary stretches from the ocean dunes to the marshes of the sound. A 2.5-mile, self-guided nature trail runs along the sound side of the sanctuary, beginning at the north end of the Sanderling Resort.

Seahawk Overlook Sound Viewing Area West Seahawk Dr., Duck. Short hiking trail on the south side of Duck Village leads to an outstanding sound view.

★ **Wild Horse Museum** 252-453-8002; www.corollawildhorses.com; 1126 Old School-house Ln., Corolla 27927. The restored Corolla Village Schoolhouse now serves as the headquarters and information center for the **Corolla Wild Horse Fund**, dedicated to preserving and protecting the wild herd of some 100 horses that makes its home north of the protective sound-to-sea fences just beyond Corolla Village. In the schoolhouse, exhibits tell the history of the wild herd. Children's activities are offered in summer for a small fee. Admission to the museum is free. The Wild Horse Fund also operates a **Wild Horse Museum Store** selling horse-themed gift items and offering information on the horses in the Corolla Light Town Center.

Racquet Sports and Tennis

Just for the Beach Rentals 877-FOR-JFTB; www.justforthebeach.com; 501 Hunt Club Dr., Currituck Club, Corolla 27927. Some of the private communities along NC 12 have ter-rific tennis facilities. Rent racquets from this outfit if you forgot your own.

Pine Island Racquet and Fitness Center 252-453-8525; www.thesanderling.com; NC 12, Pine Island. This full-service fitness and racquet sport center is open to the public, offering day and weekly memberships. Tennis facilities include two outdoor clay courts and three indoor cushioned courts.

Currituck Heritage Park provides the perfect setting for crabbing, picnics, and sunset views.

Spas and Fitness

Diva's Day Spa and Salon 252-255-1772; www.divasdayspa.com; 1 Ocean Blvd., Southern
Shores Crossing, Southern Shores 27949. Massages, facials and peels, waxing, plus full
services for hair, feet, and nails, are offered at this award-winning spa. Couple massages
available.

Eden Day Spa and Salon www.edendayspasalon.com; two locations: 252-255-0711, 1225
Duck Rd., Duck 27949; 252-453-0712, 817 Ocean Trail, Monteray Plaza, Corolla 27927.
Each of the Edens is a little different—the Corolla location has a Far Eastern slant while
the Duck Eden takes you on a trip south of the border—but both are dedicated to
refreshing and rejuvenating their clients.

★ **The Sanderling Spa** 252-261-4111, 800-701-4111; www.thesanderling.com; Sanderling
Resort. This elegant spa overlooking the tranquil waters of Currituck Sound is the perfect setting for the signature Serenity Ritual, in which two therapists work in tandem
giving clients a hydro massage, facial, scalp treatment, sea salt glow, and sea mud wrap,
then finish up with a Swedish hose massage and Vichy rain shower. The spa features
products made from the native Russian olive tree and offers yoga and Pilates classes.
Couple's suite available.

Tai Chi 252-255-1286; www.townofduck.com. Free drop-in tai chi classes are offered at
Duck's waterfront park during good weather.

Water Sports

Most water-sport emporiums on the North Beaches offer a wide variety of water-based fun.
Surfing and kayaking are huge here, and parasailing is literally taking off. Kayaks and personal watercraft, such as Jet Skis and WaveRunners, are widely available. On the other
hand, the area is just beginning to explore the sports of windsurfing and kiteboarding.
Here are a few of the best places to play. Most are open seasonally, May to October, or as
weather permits.

Corolla Water Sports 252-453-6900; www.corollawatersports.com; Kitty Hawk Water
Sports, TimBuck II, Corolla 27927. Truly a one-stop shop for fun, this complex behind
TimBuck II rents WaveRunners, kayaks, paddleboats, and a flat-bottom party boat, will
take you parasailing, even turn you on to miniature golf. The shopping plaza is right next
door, and there's plenty of shady seating if you just want to watch.

Duck Village Outfitters 252-261-7222; www.duckvillageoutfitters.net; 1207 Duck Rd.,
Duck 27949. Rent surfboards, skateboards, kayaks, or bikes here or sign up for a surf
lesson or kayak eco-tour.

Grog's Watersports 252-261-6866; www.grogswatersports.com; 1264 Duck Rd., Duck
27949. Lots of fun at a great location behind the Sunset Grille, party place of the North
Banks. Rent a WaveRunner, catamaran, kayak, or pontoon boat, or go parasailing.

Nor'Banks Sailing Center 252-261-2900; www.norbanks.com; 1314 Duck Rd., Duck
27949. Sailing rules at Nor'Banks, but you can also go parasailing, or rent kayaks and
WaveRunners. Grassy lawn, with picnic tables, umbrellas, and restrooms, and a 200-
foot pier, make this a great place to spend the day.

North Duck Water Sports 252-261-4200; www.corollawatersports.com; NC 12, 2.5 miles
north of Duck, near the Sanderling Resort. Island beach with plenty of seating and shade
is a fun spot to spend time on a summer day. You can parasail, or rent kayaks, WaveRunners, sailboats, or pontoon boats. Windsurfing rentals and instruction are also available.

Surfing

The beach at Corolla forms many long, flat sandbars close to shore, making it an easy and safe place to enter the water with your board. *Outside* magazine rated Corolla one of the six best places in the United States to learn how to surf.

The off-road beaches north of town are favorites with the surf crowd. Another popular break is found at the end of the Lighthouse Ramp Road, across NC 12 from the lighthouse.

★ **Corolla Surf Shop** 252-453-9283; www.corollasurfshop.com; TimBuck II, Monteray Plaza, and Currituck Shops, Corolla 27927. With four locations in Corolla and over a dozen years of experience, this outfit is the most knowledgeable on local surf conditions. Its team of professional surfers offers classes for all ability levels. If you are coming during the busy summer season, make your reservations online, as classes fill up fast. You can also reserve rental equipment online. New and used boards are for sale, including the shop's private-label boards made by top shapers.

Duck Village Outfitters 252-261-7222; www.duckvillage outfitters.net; 1207 Duck Rd., Duck 27949. Rents surfboards, body boards, skim boards, fins, and wet suits, and will deliver for free to your rental property. Two-hour surf lessons include board rental.

The Island Revolution Surf Company and Skatepark 252-453-9484; www.islandrevolution.com. Cool shop in Corolla Light Town Center schedules surfing lessons and rents surfboards and wet suits.

Just for the Beach Rentals 877-FOR-JFTB; www.justfor thebeach.com; 501 Hunt Club Dr., Currituck Club, Corolla 27927. Reasonable rates for surfboard rentals by the day or week. Delivery available.

Kitty Hawk Surfin' Sports 252-261-8770; www.kitty hawksports.com; 1213 Duck Rd., Wee Winks Square, Duck 27949. Rent surfboards, body boards, and kayaks from this location in the heart of Duck. Surfing lessons and three-day surf camps are available.

A historic board on display at one of the Corolla Surf Shops

Ocean Atlantic Rentals www.oceanatlanticrentals.com; two locations: 252-453-2440, Corolla Light Town Center, Corolla; 252-261-4346, 1194 Duck Rd., Duck 27949. Soft top surfboards as well as the more standard epoxy models are available. Free delivery.

SHOPPING

Each of the towns on the North Beaches offers different kinds of shopping, but in general if you enjoy browsing and walking from store to store, you'll enjoy shopping here. If you prefer national chains with big parking lots, you'll probably want to shop on the Bypass in Kitty Hawk.

Duck's main claim to fame has always been its collections of unique and eclectic shops, making it one of the prime shopping destinations on the Outer Banks. The stores here are linked by paved walkways and boardwalks, many of them shaded by old live oaks, making for excellent daylong browsing. Most of the boutiques, shops, and galleries are locally owned and operated, with a smattering of regional chains and high-end nationals.

Scarborough Faire Shopping Center (www.scarboroughfaireducknc.com) was one of the first shopping destinations in Duck and set the standard. Next door is **Scarborough Lane Shoppes**, with ample parking beneath the building, and even more eclectic shops.

Within a half-mile or so along either side of NC 12 (called Duck Road on this stretch), you'll find Duck Common, Duck Landing, Loblolly Pines, and Wee Winks Square. **Duck Soundside Shops** and **Osprey Landing** both have pleasant decks and great views of the sound.

The Waterfront Shops, located on the sound at the north end of the village, occupy atmospheric buildings, some of them rescued from old hunt clubs, all joined by an expansive deck. This is a great place for lunch, and an even better one at sunset when nature puts on a show. A boardwalk connects the shops with Duck Waterfront Park.

All of the retail in Southern Shores is concentrated along its southern edge. No freestanding retail exists in this community once you start up NC 12. **Southern Shores Crossing**, where NC 12 splits with US 158, is the town's premiere shopping destination, with high-end restaurants, shops, and services.

In Corolla, retail is concentrated into shopping centers that sit along NC 12, often at the entrance of gated communities. The first, and still the most extensive, shopping destination here is **TimBuck II Shopping Village** (www.timbuckii.com), a complex including over 60 shops and restaurants spread through several buildings, with ample parking. The complex backs up to the sound with a water-sports complex, go-kart track, paddleboat pond, and miniature golf course along the waterfront.

The Ocean Club Centre and the **Shoppes at Currituck Club** lie at the entrance to the exclusive Currituck Club community, location of one of the state's top golf courses. The main shopping attraction is the **Harris Teeter Grocery Store**, noted for its deli and wine selection.

A short distance farther north, **Monteray Plaza** is anchored by a **Food Lion** grocery. Here you'll also find the North Beaches' only cinema and a climbing wall.

Situated directly across the street from Currituck Heritage Park, the **Corolla Light Town Center** (www.corollacompanies.com) has a skate park hidden in its center amid pizza shops, bakeries, and ice cream parlors.

For a very special shopping experience, walk along the sandy streets of **Old Corolla Village**, poking your head into the various shops. Most of them are run by locals, born and bred, and they all have stories to tell.

Books and Music

Beach Bag Book & Music 252-453-2900; www.visitfinnegan.blogspot.com; 1109 Ocean Trail, Corolla Light Town Center, Corolla 27927. Huge selection of books and used CDs. Check out summer activities for kids, and other events, on the blog "written" by the store's resident black Lab.

Duck's Cottage Coffee and Books 252-261-5510; www.duckscottage.com; 1240 Duck Rd., Waterfront Shops, Duck 27949. Handpicked selection of fiction and nonfiction fills this historic, cedar-shingled cottage. Summer signing series and monthly reading group, plus newspapers from up and down the East Coast and great coffee, make this a special spot.

★ **The Island Bookstore** www.islandbooksobx.com; three locations: 252-453-2292, 1130 Corolla Village Rd., Historic Corolla; 252-261-8981, 1177 Duck Rd., Scarborough Faire

Shops, Duck; also in Kitty Hawk, MP 4.5, US 158, Bypass. This independent bookstore with three locations features carefully selected books for every interest. Over 5,000 *New York Times* bestsellers, local and regional books, audio books, and children's titles are kept in stock. The location in Duck was the original. The Corolla store occupies a reproduction of the village's original general store. Signings and readings are frequent in season.

Clothing

Ally & Maddy www.allyandmaddy.com; two locations: 252-453-6322, TimBuck II, Corolla; 252-261-4005, 1187 Duck Rd., Loblolly Pines, Duck 27949. Voted "Best of the Outer Banks" by its many fans, this boutique carries bright, whimsical women's clothing, at reasonable prices.

Birthday Suits www.birthday-suits.com; four locations: 252-453-4862, Monteray Plaza, Corolla; 252-261-7297, Scarborough Lane Shoppes, Duck; 252-986-2282, Hatteras Landing; 252-441-5338, Beach Barn Shops, MP 10, Bypass, Kill Devil Hills. Another "Best of the Beach" winner, this store with several locations has been selling swimwear for over half a century.

Gray's Department Store www.grays-sportswear.com; several locations: 252-453-4994, 252-457-1058, TimBuck II, Corolla; 252-453-0852, Monteray Plaza, Corolla; 252-261-1740, Scarborough Faire, Duck; 252-255-5768, Waterfront Shops, Duck; 252-261-1776, MP 4, Bypass, Kitty Hawk. The Outer Banks's homegrown department store chain carries the largest selection of Tommy Bahama and Fresh Produce on the Banks, and stocks a huge Vera Bradley collection, said to be the largest in the mid-Atlantic region.

Plum Crazy 252-261-1125; www.ruplumcrazy.com; two locations: NC 12, Soundside Shops, Duck; 252-255-2799, Ocean Plaza, MP 4.5, Bypass, Kitty Hawk. Step through the looking glass at this local favorite stocking one-of-a-kind jewelry, accessories, and functional art furniture, much of it by local artists, plus the hippest national brands.

Soundfeet Shoes www.soundfeet.com; three locations: 252-453-9787, TimBuck II, Corolla; 252-261-0490, 1194 Duck Rd., Duck 27949; 252-441-8954, Croatan Centre, MP 14, Bypass, Nags Head. The only full-service shoe stores on the Banks, Soundfeet carries all the top brands and styles, from sheepskin boots to sandals.

Crafts

Funtastic Fabrics 252-261-7393; www.funtasticfabrics.com; 1 Ocean Blvd., Suite 107, Southern Shores Crossing. With over 5,000 bolts of cloth, this is the largest quilting supply shop on the Banks.

Knitting Addiction 252-255-5648; www.knittingaddiction.com; 1 Ocean Blvd., Suite 111, Southern Shores Crossing. A huge selection of yarns, including many organics, and every sort of supply for knitting and crocheting. Classes available.

Stained Glass and Mosaic 252-261-5010; www.stainedglassvisions.com; 1187 Duck Rd., Loblolly Pines, Duck 27949. Designs on display include glass lighthouses and ship models. Stained-glass kits and free lessons available.

Gifts

Christmas Mouse 252-261-5404; www.christmasmouse.com; Scarborough Lane Shoppes, Duck. Specializes in nautical and beach-themed ornaments.

Corolla Candles 252-457-0233, www.corollacandles.com; TimBuck II, Corolla. Owners are

Carova residents who handcraft candles adorned with local shells.

Currituck Beach Lighthouse Museum Shop 252-453-6778; www.currituckbeachlight
.com; Little Lightkeeper's House, Currituck Beach Lighthouse, Corolla. Sales of lighthouse and wild horse souvenirs benefit their respective charitable foundations. Look
beyond the gifts to see the amazing architecture of this beautifully restored building.

Dog Nutz 252-453-9955, 866-364-6887; www.dognutz.com; Timbuck II, Corolla. Make
your dog the best-dressed barker on the beach in OBK9 gear.

Outer Barks 252-261-6279, 888-870-6279; www.outerbarks.com; 1171 Duck Rd., Scarborough Lane Shoppes, Duck 27949. Huge selection of gifts for dogs and dog-lovers. Bring
your pampered pooch to the Outer Barks Yappy Hour.

Rub-A-Dub Duck Bath & Body 252-261-0833; www.culinaryduck.com; Scarborough
Faire, Duck. No vacation in Duck is complete without a rubber ducky to take home.

Jewelry

Cara Magnus Celtic 252-261-8110; www.caramagnus.com; Scarborough Faire, Duck. Step
through the door and into Dublin. Brother and sister team Michael and Joan Young
import fine Celtic jewelry and gifts to create this unique environment.

The Mystic Jewel www.themysticjewel.com; two locations: 252-453-3797, TimBuck II,
Corolla; 252-255-5515, Scarborough Lane Shoppes, Duck. Handcrafted sterling silver
jewelry set with semiprecious stones comes with information on the mystical powers of
the gems.

Yesterday's Jewels 252-261-4869; www.yesterdaysjewels.com; Loblolly Pines, Duck. Specializing in antique and estate jewelry, as well as gold and silver charms.

Kitchenware and Home Decor

Diane's Lavish Linens 252-255-0555; www.dianeslavishlinens.com; Scarborough Lane
Shoppes, Duck. Bed, bath, and table linens, window treatments, and more.

The Glass Shop 252-453-3999; www.theglassshopobx.com; TimBuck II, Corolla. Hand-
painted glassware by designer Renee Hilimire.

Lighthouse Garden 252-453-0171; www.lighthouse-garden.com; 1129 Corolla Village Rd.,
Corolla 27927. Country pine antiques, silk flower arrangements, Italian ceramics, and
hand-thrown Guy Wolff garden pottery displayed in a historic cottage.

Nags Head Hammocks 800-344-6433; www.nagsheadhammocks.com; 252-261-1062,
1212 Duck Rd., Duck 27949; 252-453-4611, TimBuck II, Corolla; also in Avon (252-995-
3744) and Kill Devil Hills (252-441-6115). Selling relaxation since 1974, the nation's
largest retailer of hammocks still produces its products on the Outer Banks. At the Duck
location, you can see the company's full line on display and watch hammocks being
made.

Old Corolla Trading Co. & Outer Banks Style 252-453-9942, 252-453-4388; www.outer
banksstyle.com; 1129 & 1134 Old Corolla Village Rd., Corolla 27927. Two shops in Historic Corolla Village join forces to decorate your home. The Trading Company specializes in nautically themed accents and antiques, while Outer Banks Style focuses on
artisan-made furniture, local art, and wines.

Sporting Goods and Clothing

Ocean Threads 252-453-8967; www.ocean-threads.com; 102 Corolla Light Town Center, Corolla 27927. Fashion forward surf and skate apparel plus an expanded selection of swimwear for every age and body type.

Outer Banks Running Company 252-255-5444; www.outerbanksrunningcompany.com; 1187 Duck Rd., Loblolly Pines, Duck 27949. Top brand running shoes and apparel, as well as information on upcoming running events and suggestions on where to stretch your legs.

KITTY HAWK OCEAN RESCUE

GUARD *Molly & Brad*
HIGH TIDE 4PM
LOW TIDE 9AM
H2O TEMP 73°
SURF 2-4ft
ADVISORIES
STRONG lateral current! u will drift
to the South, Possible RIP CURRENTS
can pull u out! Shorebreak can still
beat u up....
WWW.KITTYHAWKFD.COM

KHOR CALL 911
OVERCAST BUT
STILL USE SUN
BLOCK

Numerous lifeguards make the Central Beaches the most family-friendly on the Outer Banks.

4

THE CENTRAL BEACHES:
Kitty Hawk to Oregon Inlet

Taking Wing

One hundred years ago, tall sand dunes, migrating with the wind, dominated the landscape. Today, this is the most accessible—and the most visited—region of North Carolina's
Outer Banks. On this part of the coast, you will find the greatest variety of accommodations,
the most restaurants, and the most active nightlife.

These beaches have an intimate connection with the history of flight. Orville and Wilbur
Wright first took to the air from a tall dune in Kill Devil Hills, a flight that changed the
world.

The persistent breezes that helped lift the Wright brothers into the air today make this
one of the premiere destinations for air sports on the East Coast. In the 1940s, aeronautical
engineer Francis Rogallo invented the flexible wing, a design that led to high performance
kites, hang gliders, and powered light aircraft. Rogallo, a resident of Southern Shores,
makes frequent appearances at local events.

John Harris, an early proponent of the sport of hang gliding, established Kitty Hawk
Kites in 1974. Today he heads the largest hang gliding school in the world and, with 11 locations, is one of the guiding forces on the Outer Banks. Over the years, Harris has branched
out into many other sports that combine the area's unique blend of wind and water, helping
to popularize surf kayaking, parasailing, and the latest extreme sport, kiteboarding.

Kitty Hawk Kites sponsors numerous festivals, competitions, and workshops throughout the year. Its 35 instructors introduce 10,000 visitors annually to the thrills of hang gliding. Instruction takes place at Jockey's Ridge State Park atop the highest dune on the East
Coast. After a lesson, you can spread your nylon wings to the breeze and, like Wilbur and
Orville and a million birds before you, take to the sky.

NORTH OF THE BRIDGE

On the northern side of the Wright Memorial Bridge, the mainland of Currituck County is
the gateway to the Central Beaches. Here US 158 and NC 168 run along Currituck Sound,
providing the most direct route to the Banks from Norfolk and points north. Locals consider this area "north of the bridge" an extension of the Outer Banks, and as property values
on the Banks themselves have soared some businesses have relocated there. It's a region of

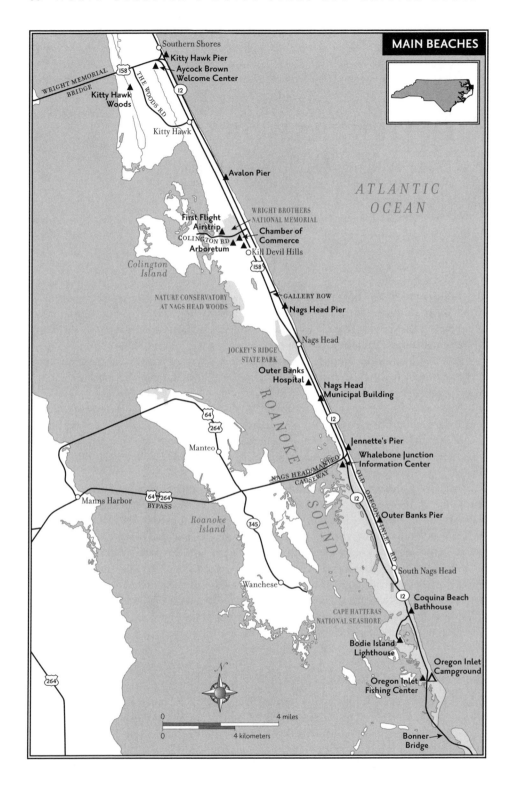

MAIN BEACHES

ATLANTIC OCEAN

Southern Shores
Kitty Hawk Pier
Aycock Brown
Welcome Center
WRIGHT MEMORIAL BRIDGE
Kitty Hawk Woods
THE WOODS RD.
Kitty Hawk
Avalon Pier
WRIGHT BROTHERS NATIONAL MEMORIAL
First Flight Airstrip
COLINGTON RD.
Chamber of Commerce
Arboretum
Kill Devil Hills
Colington Island
NATURE CONSERVATORY AT NAGS HEAD WOODS
GALLERY ROW
Nags Head Pier
Nags Head
JOCKEY'S RIDGE STATE PARK
Outer Banks Hospital
Nags Head Municipal Building
Manteo
Jennette's Pier
Whalebone Junction Information Center
NAGS HEAD/MANTEO CAUSEWAY
ROANOKE SOUND
OLD OREGON INLET RD.
Manns Harbor
BYPASS
Roanoke Island
Outer Banks Pier
Wanchese
South Nags Head
Coquina Beach Bathhouse
CAPE HATTERAS NATIONAL SEASHORE
Bodie Island Lighthouse
Oregon Inlet Campground
Oregon Inlet Fishing Center
Bonner Bridge

0   4 miles
0   4 kilometers

many farms, as well as shopping opportunities, often with prices less than you'll find on the beaches. Many of the area's golf courses are located here as well.

A ferry connects Currituck with Knotts Island, one of the most isolated parts of the Outer Banks, today a hot spot for wineries.

Getting Around

Two causeways, the only mainland access to the Outer Banks, join the Central Beaches with the rest of the world. In the north, the Wright Memorial Bridge leaps Albemarle Sound, connecting Kitty Hawk and Southern Shores with mainland Currituck County. About 20 miles south, the Nags Head–Manteo Causeway leads to Roanoke Island and the Albemarle Peninsula beyond.

Between the two causeways, two highways run north and south, NC 12 and US 158, otherwise known as the Beach Road and the Bypass.

The Beach Road, now NC 12 and the Virginia Dare Trail, is the older and narrower of the two, also the most scenic. Sand frequently blows in little drifts across the two lanes, there are few traffic lights, and bicycles are as popular as cars for getting around. Take your time as you drive, and you'll spot raw bars and taverns lining the west side of the road, and beach cottages about to wash into the sea on the east. While large hotels and condominiums have made inroads along the beachfront, the coast here is far from being lined with high-rises. Dare County imposes a 35-foot maximum height on most new development. Numerous public beach accesses make it easy to find a quiet piece of beach, and small family-run cottage courts preserve the beach vacation of an earlier day.

The Bypass, just a block or two west, is quite the opposite: a large, fast-moving highway with two lanes in each direction. Although not many hotels are located here, the majority of the newer retail stores and restaurants line both sides, in a sometimes bewildering procession of shopping centers and strip malls. The Bypass is officially US 158 and also the Croatan Highway.

To add to the confusion, street numbers get higher on both highways as you go north and south, starting from the Ocean Bay Boulevard/Colington Road intersection, just south of the Wright Brothers Memorial in Kill Devil Hills.

Fortunately for visitors, the milepost system is well established along both these roads, and looking for the "MP" signs will speed locating your destination. MP 0 is at the foot of the Wright Memorial Bridge. The milepost distances are not quite the same on the Beach Road and Bypass, but are helpful anyway. Street addresses can also help with locations. Even-numbered establishments are on the west side of the highways; odd numbers are on the east or ocean side.

Traveling south, you pass through three separate incorporated towns, all part of Dare County, plus a national park, before reaching Oregon Inlet and the Bonner Bridge to lonely Hatteras Island. The towns may appear alike, but each has its individual personality, history, laws, and attractions. All three, Kitty Hawk, Kill Devil Hills, and Nags Head, stretch across the Banks from the ocean beaches to the waters of the sound.

Kitty Hawk

Originally a quiet fishing village and port for arriving visitors, among them the Wright brothers, Kitty Hawk became the gateway to the Outer Banks with the completion of the

Wright Memorial Bridge. The old village lies west of the Bypass, hidden in a deep maritime forest and marsh, with many year-round residences set back in the trees. The Beach Road lies very close to the ocean here, and many seaside cottages have been lost to the sea.

The area appears on the earliest maps as "Chickahauk," a native Indian name meaning "goose hunting grounds," which may have evolved into both Kitty Hawk and Currituck, the county across the bridge on the mainland. Certainly, the Native Americans considered the area essential to their welfare and once complained to the colonial government when incoming settlers kept them from hunting there. Other historians speculate that the name Kitty Hawk came from the skeeter hawk, a local name for the dragonflies that gathered to feast on the mosquitoes so plentiful in earlier days. The name Kitty Hawk was well established by the 1790s.

At the base of the Wright Memorial Bridge, MP 0, Kitty Hawk is on the south side of the highway and Southern Shores is on the north for about 2 miles to the junction with NC 12. One of the oldest developed parts of the coast lies around Winks Store at MP 2 on the Beach Road.

Kill Devil Hills

Referred to by locals as KDH, Kill Devil Hills occupies the middle portion of the Central Beaches, and was the first town in Dare County to incorporate, taking that step in 1953. The Wright Brothers Memorial was the area's first non-beach attraction, and many hotels located close to it. More chain hotels and condominiums are found in this part of the beach than any other.

The Wrights took flight from a dune called Kill Devil Hill by locals, some say because it was used as a hiding place for scavenged rum that would "kill the devil."

Avalon, centered on the Avalon fishing pier in KDH, was one of the first beachfront neighborhoods on the coast. Today, KDH is Dare County's largest municipality, with over 7,000 year-round residents and a distinctly family focus.

KDH runs roughly from MP 5 to MP 10. The town offices, as well as the Outer Banks Chamber of Commerce, a library, recreation facilities, and an arboretum are located at Ocean Bay Boulevard/Colington Road, the first street south of the Wright Brothers Memorial.

Colington Island

Located west of the Wright Memorial, this island—about 2 miles long by 2 miles wide—is connected by bridges and a single road to Kill Devil Hills and is a part of that township. Named for Sir John Colleton, one of Carolina's Lords Proprietors, Colington was the location of one of the earliest plantations on the Banks and eventually became the home of a thriving fishing village where crab-shedding was a major industry.

Development was slow to come to the island, but recently many upscale subdivisions have appeared among the more modest homes of families who have lived here for generations. The few restaurants and inns set among the old live oaks are worth seeking out for an Outer Banks experience different from both the beach and the Bypass.

NAGS HEAD

The unusual name of this area of the Outer
Banks appears on maps as early as 1738.
Some say it was named for the wild horses
that roamed the area, others that it reminded
an early settler of a place on the coast of England that bears the same name. The most colorful tale attributes the name to the practice
of placing a lantern around a horse's head and
leading it along the shore to lure ships to
their destruction. In those early days, much
of the wood for building homes, as well as
other supplies, came ashore from shipwrecks. The practice of luring ships, called
"wrecking," has not actually been documented along this coast.

The region became the earliest summer
resort on the Outer Banks in the 1830s, when
a planter from nearby Perquimans County
brought his family to Nags Head to avoid the
fevers and insects of the interior. The area
along the sound soon housed hotels and cottages with docks extending far out to accommodate the steamers that put in with
vacationing families. By the 1860s, families
began to build cottages along the oceanfront,
some of which still survive in the historic
Nags Head Beach Cottage Row, otherwise
known as the Unpainted Aristocracy.

The largest surviving dune along the
Banks is located in Nags Head. Named

*The Wright Brothers Memorial provides a focal
point for the Central Beaches, and a starting
point for their modern history.*

Jockey's Ridge, possibly for the horse races once held there, the dune is moving slowly
southwest with the prevailing wind. The sand has buried many things over the years,
including a church and a hotel. Along the Bypass opposite Jockey's Crossing, the top turrets
of a castle, all that remains of a mini-golf course, can be seen peeking above the sands.

WHALEBONE JUNCTION

No one knows where the name for this area came from, but the area where the Beach Road
joins the Bypass, as well as the causeway coming from Manteo, does provide the backbone
and nerve center of the area. Whalebone Junction is the oldest developed part of Nags Head,
where you'll find long-lived establishments such as Sam and Omie's and Owens' Restaurant.

From the causeway, NC 12 continues south through the National Park lands along an
inland route, while the Beach Road, now named Old Oregon Inlet Road, continues south
along the coast for a few miles before rejoining NC 12. This area, almost completely composed of residential and rental properties, is called South Nags Head.

BODIE ISLAND

Pronounced "body" island by natives, and named supposedly for the many bodies that washed up here during the worst years of the Graveyard of the Atlantic, this end of the peninsula forms the northernmost segment of Cape Hatteras National Seashore. The Bodie Island Lighthouse, Coquina Beach, and a campground are maintained by the park rangers.

Bodie Island comes to an end at Oregon Inlet and the Bonner Bridge, stretching to Pea Island, Hatteras Island, and beyond. The Bonner is scheduled to be rebuilt and perhaps replaced with a bridge taking a different route across the inlet, a matter of great debate among local residents and national wildlife advocates.

Just before the Bonner Bridge, Oregon Inlet Fishing Center is home to one of the world's most storied fishing fleets. Crowds gather here in the afternoons to see what the boats bring in.

LODGING

Not so long ago, vacations to the Outer Banks took a predictable course. Small cottages arranged in "courts" or units connected into "motor courts," the forerunners of motels, were the only accommodations available in 1950s and 1960s. Families rented a cottage or unit with kitchen facilities, then packed the car with bed linens and towels and headed out for a week of sun, sand castles, surf fishing, and Mom's cooking.

Today, you can still find those cottages and motor courts scattered among the many hotels, motels, condominiums, and larger rental houses that have since filled the coast from the Wright Memorial Bridge all the way to South Nags Head, some 20 miles south.

This region of the Outer Banks offers more variety of accommodations, as well as greater numbers, than any other. Bed-and-breakfasts are a growing trend in the area, both along the Beach Road and along Roanoke Sound. While weekly cottage and house rentals are still the norm during the summer season, overnight and weekend accommodations are now available year-round, although two- and three-night minimums are still the rule on holiday weekends at all but the most expensive hotels. During the off-season, many shorter rentals are available, and most prices drop dramatically.

Nearly every rental unit and hotel room on the Central Beaches has a refrigerator, and many include a microwave. Some accommodations are now pet-friendly, often with an additional pet fee required.

While the majority of lodgings on the beach in Kitty Hawk and Nags Head are privately owned, the bigger chain hotels are present as well, mostly along the oceanfront in Kill Devil Hills. You can find accommodations that are part of the Quality Inn, Budget Inn, Comfort Inn, Clarion, Travelodge, Best Western, Days Inn, and Ramada Inn families. The new Hilton Garden Inn pioneered high-rise accommodation in Kitty Hawk.

Pay close attention to cancellation policies wherever you rent, including hotels. Many require early notice of cancellations to refund deposits. Trip insurance may be a good idea, especially if you are making a considerable outlay in advance.

Another thing to take note of is the hurricane or storm policy followed by your accommodation. These vary widely, but very few offer refunds, even for mandatory evacuations. You may receive a rain check or other compensation, or nothing at all. If you cancel before you arrive, or leave because of the forecast before an evacuation is announced, you will generally not be compensated. Locals know that storms predicted often don't actually arrive, and will expect you to pay for your reservation.

Rate Categories

Inexpensive	up to $80
Moderate	$80 to $150
Expensive	$150 to $200
Very Expensive	$200 and up

These rates are per room, based on double occupancy. They do not include room taxes, currently about 11.75 percent in Dare County, or any special service fees that may apply. The range is usually due to seasonal changes. Rates during the busy summer season and holiday weekends are often double or more the winter off-season rates. Prices peak on Memorial Day, Fourth of July, and Labor Day weekends.

What you see out of your window may affect the price of your room. Ocean view and oceanfront rooms will cost more than pool view or so-called "dune view" rooms that may look out on the parking lot. Prices are also often higher on the upper floors of hotels for rooms with ocean views, even though you may have to walk up several flights of stairs to get there. If stairs are a problem, it's a good idea to ask specifically whether a property has an elevator.

For last-minute vacations, you can check current vacancies at the official **Outer Banks Visitor Center** site, www.outerbanks .org. The information is updated weekly from Memorial Day to Labor Day and during holiday periods.

Properties listed are open year round and are air-conditioned, unless otherwise noted.

Credit Cards

AE—American Express
CB—Carte Blanche
D—Discover Card
DC—Diners Club
J—JCB International Credit Card
MC—Master Card
V—Visa

Resorts and Hotels

COLINGTON ISLAND
COLINGTON CREEK INN
252-449-4124
www.colingtoncreekinn.com

Bodie Island Lighthouse, one of three lighthouses located in the Cape Hatteras National Seashore

1293 Colington Rd., Kill Devil Hills 27948
Price: Moderate to Very Expensive
Credit Cards: MC, V
Internet Access: Free WiFi

Enjoy waterfront views from the two-story screened porch at this cedar-shingled bed-and-breakfast on Colington Island, or take a dip in the private pool. The inn's four bedrooms all have private baths, spacious beds, and excellent water views. Boat dockage is available along Colington Creek if you arrive by water. A continental breakfast is served during the week, with a full breakfast on weekends. Every evening, innkeepers Bob and Mae Lunden serve hors d'oeuvres on the porch after taking guests on an evening cruise aboard their private boat to enjoy the sunset. The inn has an elevator for handicapped access; children and pets cannot be accommodated. Although the inn enjoys a secluded location off the main highway, public beach access is an easy drive away, without getting into traffic. Rates here remain the same all year.

KILL DEVIL HILLS

ATLANTIC STREET INN

252-441-2965, 252-305-0246
www.atlanticstreetinn.com
205 E. Atlantic St., MP 9.5, Kill Devil Hills 27948
Price: Inexpensive to Moderate
Credit Cards: MC, V
Internet Access: Free WiFi

Six comfortable suites, all with refrigerator, microwave, cable TV, phone, coffeemaker, and a personally controlled heating and air-conditioning unit, are available in this recently renovated beach house. Located close to all the action in KDH, the inn is also just down the street from the Atlantic Street Beach Access. Bright colors and local art decorate the suites, which are available by the day or week. Backyard grill, full kitchen, and enclosed outdoor showers are available for guest use. Two-night minimum stay required.

BEST WESTERN OCEAN REEF SUITES

252-441-1611, 800-WESTERN
www.bestwestern.com
107 Virginia Dare Trail, MP 8.5, Beach Rd., Kill Devil Hills 27948
Price: Inexpensive to Very Expensive
Credit Cards: AE, CB, D, DC, J, MC, V
Internet Access: Free high-speed

The only all-suite hotel directly on the beach in the Outer Banks, this five-story Best Western received a three-diamond rating from AAA. Each suite accommodates up to six people, and has a completely equipped kitchen. To get above it all, book the hotel's penthouse suite, where the rooftop deck with Jacuzzi offers an unimpeded view. Room rates include a full continental breakfast daily, free local calls, cable TV, and access to the hotel's hot tub, sauna, steam room, fitness center, and outdoor heated pool (open seasonally). The hotel also has a guest laundry room open 24 hours. Most rooms in the hotel are non-smoking, and several are equipped for handicapped access. Children under 13 stay free with paying adult. Pets are not allowed.

COLONY IV BY THE SEA

252-441-5581, 800-848-3728
www.motelbythesea.com
405 S. Virginia Dare Trail, MP 8.5, Beach Rd., Kill Devil Hills 27948
Price: Inexpensive to Very Expensive
Credit Cards: MC, V
Internet Access: Free high-speed

Freshly refurbished with new bedding, furniture, and carpet, the Colony IV offers four floors of rooms with two double beds and efficiencies with full kitchens on the oceanfront. All accommodations have microwaves, refrigerators, free local calls, radios, hair dryers, and cable TV with HBO. Amenities include a new indoor heated pool, whirlpool, and exercise room, in addition to an outdoor pool, gazebo, and walkway to the beach. Rooms on the second

through fourth floors have private balconies. Rates include a deluxe continental
breakfast.

CYPRESS HOUSE INN
252-441-6127, 800-554-2764
www.cypresshouseinn.com
500 N. Virginia Dare Trail, MP 8, Beach Rd.,
Kill Devil Hills 27948
Price: Moderate to Expensive
Credit Cards: AE, D, MC, V
Internet Access: Free WiFi

The six guest rooms in this 1940s hunting
lodge feature cypress tongue-and-groove
paneled ceilings and walls, as well as more
modern amenities, including private baths,
small refrigerators, ceiling fans, air-conditioning, and cable TV. Bicycles, beach
chairs, and towels are complimentary. A
public beach access is located directly
across the street. Innkeepers Bill and Veda
Peters place coffee, tea, and fresh-baked
muffins outside each door in the morning
for guests to enjoy on the inn's wraparound porch or in front of the fireplace in
nippy weather. Room rates include a full
breakfast served in the dining room and
afternoon tea and cookies.

DAYS INN OCEANFRONT—
WILBUR AND ORVILLE WRIGHT
252-441-7211, 800-329-7466
www.obxlodging.com
101 N. Virginia Dare Trail, MP 8.5, Beach
Rd., Kill Devil Hills 27948
Price: Inexpensive to Expensive
Credit Cards: AE, D, DC, J, MC, V
Internet Access: Free WiFi

The longest continuously operating hotel on
the beach, this 52-room property opened in
1948 and has a nostalgic "Old Nags Head"
appeal. Built in the style of a mountain
lodge, the inviting lobby features a big fireplace where guests gather for hot cider and
popcorn in the cooler months. In summer,
lemonade and cookies are the afternoon
refreshments.

A full continental breakfast with waffles
is included in the room rate. Double,
queen, and king rooms, plus efficiencies
each with a full kitchen, microwave, refrigerator, cable TV, coffeemaker, and hair
dryer, as well as nonsmoking and handicapped-accessible rooms, are available.
Children under 13 stay free. No pets are
allowed.

The property has a large outdoor pool,
open seasonally, and a boardwalk to the
beach. Guests also can take advantage of
free passes to the local YMCA. Oregon Inlet
Fishing Center parties qualify for special
discounted rates.

The same company operates a number of
other properties nearby, including the **Days
Inn Mariner,** located on the oceanfront at
MP 7, and the budget conscious **Driftin'
Sands** motor court, across the street from
the ocean at MP 6.5.

RAMADA PLAZA
RESORT AND CONFERENCE CENTER
252-441-2151, 800-635-1824
www.ramadaplazanagshead.com
1701 S. Virginia Dare Trail, MP 9.5, Beach
Rd., Kill Devil Hills 27948
Price: Moderate to Very Expensive
Credit Cards: AE, D, DC, J, MC, V
Internet Access: Free WiFi

This five-story hotel offers a host of amenities in a convenient, oceanfront location.
Rooms have a king or two queen beds, private balconies, wireless Internet access,
microwaves, refrigerators, coffeemakers,
hair dryers, and irons. Cable TV is connected to the LodgeNet system with current
movie releases. Free guest laundry, fitness
center, and business center are located off
the spacious lobby, where complimentary
morning coffee and newspapers are available. Large indoor pool and Jacuzzi are open
all year. Outdoors, guests enjoy lots of deck
space, a seasonal gazebo bar, and a boardwalk to the beach. Free passes to the nearby
YMCA by request. Most rooms are non-

Yellowfin tuna at Oregon Inlet Fishing Center

smoking; special-needs rooms and pet-friendly rooms are available.

The on-site restaurant and bar, **Peppercorns**, offers nightly specials, frequent entertainment, and full cocktail service with an ocean view. The breakfast served here, both buffet and à la carte, is a real bargain.

KITTY HAWK
CYPRESS MOON BED AND BREAKFAST
252-261-5060, 877-905-5060
www.cypressmooninn.com.
1206 Harbor Court, MP 2, Kitty Hawk 27949
Price: Moderate to Expensive
Credit Cards: AE, D, MC, V
Internet Access: Free WiFi in common areas

Innkeepers Greg and Linda Hamby rent three guest rooms that open directly onto the sound. The elegantly appointed inn, furnished with antiques and Greg's professional photography, sits tucked into the maritime forest in Kitty Hawk Village. Rooms each have private bath, private dining area, and semi-private porch looking out on the water, as well as satellite TV, stereo, and refrigerator. Hot breakfast is served daily, and vegetarian requests can be accommodated. Take one of the inn's complimentary kayaks for a tour of the shoreline or relax in the comfortable hammock chairs on the porch. The inn is nonsmoking and does not accept guests under 18. You must climb stairs to reach the rooms. The Hamby's also rent two fully equipped cottages nearby at the same nightly rate.

★ HILTON GARDEN INN
252-261-1290, 877-629-4586
www.hiltongardeninn.com
5353 N. Virginia Dare Trail, MP 1, Beach Rd., Kitty Hawk 27949
Price: Moderate to Very Expensive
Credit Cards: AE, CB, D, DC, J, MC, V
Internet Access: Free WiFi

Conveniently located at the northern end of Kitty Hawk where the Beach Road and the Bypass meet, this Hilton has an added amenity unique on this stretch of beach—its own private fishing pier. You can fish 24 hours a day on the former Kitty Hawk Pier as a hotel guest. This new hotel, which opened in 2006, offers every amenity with the Hilton emphasis on quality, including an indoor pool and whirlpool, fitness center, outdoor seasonal pool, 24-hour convenience shop, and a lobby restaurant serving breakfast, lunch, and dinner. Room service is available in the evenings. The 180 rooms and suites all have private balconies with views of the ocean, and the beach is right out the back door. Standard equipment in each room includes a hospitality center with refrigerator, microwave, and coffeemaker, large-screen cable TV, telephones with voice mail, a large desk with ergonomic chair, and both wired and wireless Internet access. A free Business Center, open around the clock with remote printing and complimentary fax, make this a good place to stay when traveling on business. Guest laundry is available. Children under 18 stay free with parents. Open all year.

NAGS HEAD
COLONIAL INN MOTEL

252-441-7308
www.colonialinnmotel.com
3329 S. Virginia Dare Trail, MP 11.5, Beach
Rd., Nags Head 27959
Price: Inexpensive to Moderate
Credit Cards: MC, V
Internet Access: Free WiFi in office

This low-rise classic enjoys an excellent
location directly on the ocean and next door
to the Nags Head Fishing Pier and Restaurant. The motel is now open all year, and
serves a continental breakfast included in
the room rate. Thirty-one rooms and efficiencies, plus 12 one- and two-bedroom
apartments, many paneled in knotty pine,
are all first or second floor, with parking in
front. Hanging baskets and window boxes
full of blooming flowers lend a colorful note
to the traditional brick buildings. Each
room has a refrigerator and a TV. The outdoor pool is open seasonally. Free YMCA
passes are available to guests. Fall and winter specials provide real bargains.

FIRST COLONY INN

252-441-2343, 800-368-9390
www.firstcolonyinn.com
6720 S. Virginia Dare Trail, MP 16, Beach
Rd., Nags Head 27959
Price: Inexpensive to Very Expensive
Credit Cards: MC, V

A Grand Old Lady of the Outer Banks, this
inn first welcomed guests in 1932, and is
the sole survivor of the era of shingle-style
beach hotels. In 1988, the revered inn was
rescued from the ocean by moving it to the
other side of the Beach Road, and an extensive renovation began. Placed on the
National Register of Historic Places, the inn
received an award from the Historic Preservation Society of North Carolina. Charm-
ingly decorated throughout, the inn is a
great favorite for wedding parties and other
romantic occasions.

Today the two stories of rocking chair-
lined verandas that circle the building once
again look out on sunrise and sunset. Each
of the 27 rooms is decorated with antiques
and wicker, and bears the name of one of
the original colonists in the Lost Colony. All
rooms are equipped with remote-con-
trolled heat and A/C, TVs, microwaves,
refrigerators, phones, and coffeemakers,
and some have wet bars and Jacuzzi tubs, as
well. Outside, a large swimming pool and
hot tub sit amid award-winning landscaping next to a croquet court. Beach chairs
and towels are provided. The inn has its
own gazebo on the oceanfront and a boardwalk leading to it.

A hot breakfast buffet and afternoon tea
are both included in the daily rate. The
property is nonsmoking and kid friendly.
Babysitting service and cribs are available.
AAA, AARP, and military discounts offered.
Open all year.

NAGS HEAD BEACH INN
BED AND BREAKFAST

252-441-8466, 800-421-8466
www.nagsheadbeachinn.com
303 E. Admiral St., off the Beach Rd., MP
10.5, Nags Head 27959
Price: Inexpensive to Expensive
Credit Cards: MC, V
Internet Access: Free WiFi

Eight guest rooms are available in this historic cottage, once used as a dance pavilion.
Rooms have wooden floors and knotty-pine
paneling, pillow-top mattresses, TVs, private baths, and individual heat and air controls. Larger rooms have Jacuzzi tubs.
Continental breakfast is served daily in the
lobby, which is decorated with pictures of
the building during its days as a dance hall.
The Admiral Street beach access is a short
walk away, and beach chairs, body boards,
and bikes are available. Innkeepers Ken and
Lisa are a fount of knowledge about the
many nearby restaurants and shops. Closed
in winter.

SEA FOAM MOTEL

252-441-7320
www.seafoam.com
7111 S. Virginia Dare Trail, MP 16.5, Beach
Rd., Nags Head 27959
Price: Inexpensive to Moderate
Credit Cards: AE, MC, V

Now on the National Register of Historic
Places, this 1948 landmark is hard to miss—
it's painted the color of its name. Noted by
the register as "one of the last and best preserved" motor courts of the post–World War
II era, it's better noted by guests for its
well-kept, clean rooms, friendly service,
and oceanfront location. On the first floor,
you can walk from your car, in the front
door, out the back door, and onto the beach.
On the floor above, you can leave the door
open to your private balcony to catch the
ocean breezes. Poolside rooms are available
at slightly lower rates. All rooms have
refrigerators, microwaves, cable TV, and
phones. Cottages, one- and two-bedroom
apartments, and efficiencies are available
with fully equipped kitchens. During the
summer season, these are only rented by
the week and have a loyal repeat clientele.
The motel wraps around a heated swimming
pool, shuffleboard court, and children's
playground. No pets are allowed. Children
under 12 stay free.

WHALEBONE JUNCTION AND THE CAUSEWAY

FIN 'N FEATHER WATERSIDE INN

252-441-5353, 888-441-5353
www.finnfeather.com
7740 S. Virginia Dare Trail, Nags
Head–Manteo Causeway, Nags Head 27959
Price: Inexpensive to Moderate
Credit Cards: MC, V

Located on the Causeway, this straightfor-
ward two-story inn is a hit with anglers,
who can launch their boats at the ramp
here, then tie up at the 160-foot dock for
the rest of their stay. Standard rooms have
double beds, phones, and cable TV; efficiencies with kitchens are also available.
Most rooms have windows looking out on
the sound. Rooms are nonsmoking and dog
friendly. Rental kayaks and fishing charters
available.

OASIS SUITES

252-441-5211
www.oasissuites.com
7721 S. Virginia Dare Trail, Nags
Head–Manteo Causeway, Nags Head 27959
Price: Expensive to Very Expensive
Credit Cards: MC, V
Internet Access: Free WiFi

This new boutique hotel offers luxurious
suites on the north side of the Causeway.
Leather furniture and oriental rugs, beds
topped with poofs, flat-screen plasma TVs,
full kitchens with stainless steel appliances,
and Jacuzzi tubs are standard in the family
and executive suites, most of which sleep
six. The honeymoon suite features a heart-
shaped Jacuzzi for two. All suites have private balconies with great views. Pool and
outdoor hot tub are fenced for privacy.
Guests can dock their boats behind the
hotel, or fish from the dock. A fishing table
is available for cleaning your catch.

Cottage and Motor Courts

To experience an "old Nags Head" vacation, make reservations for a week at one of the cottage courts that date from the 1950s to 1970s. A few still survive along the Beach Road
where you can enjoy the simple life filled with traditional beach activities. Cottages typically have kitchen facilities, private baths, and porches. Amenities usually begin and end
with air-conditioning and a TV hooked to cable. Linens are usually provided; phones and

pools are generally not. Fish-cleaning stations and grills are available for cooking up the daily catch. Some so-called cottages may actually be attached units. Cottage and motor courts usually close during the off-season.

Cahoon's Cottages 252-441-5358; www.cahoonscottages.com; 7213 S. Virginia Dare Trail, MP 16.5, Beach Rd., Nags Head 27959. Oceanfront cottages located next to Cahoon's Variety Store, a longtime landmark on the beach, have between two and four bedrooms. No pets.

Manor Motel & Cottages 252-441-5464; www.manormotelnc.com; 6321 S. Virginia Dare Trail, MP 15.5, Beach Rd., Nags Head 27959. Oceanfront. Telephones provided. Pet-friendly.

Ocean Side Court 252-441-6167; www.oceansidecourt.com; 6401 S. Virginia Dare Trail, MP 15.5, Beach Rd., Nags Head 27959. No pets. Oceanfront.

Pelican Cottages 252-441-2489; www.pelicancottages.com; 3513 S. Virginia Dare Trail, MP 12, Beach Rd., Nags Head 27959. Two- and three-bedroom cottages on oceanfront. Outdoor hot showers. Complimentary bikes. Free YMCA passes. Pet-friendly. Linens are not furnished.

Saltaire Cottage Court 252-261-3286; www.saltairecottages.com; 4618 N. Virginia Dare Trail, MP 2.5, Beach Rd., Kitty Hawk 27949. Recently renovated two-bedroom apartments and three-bedroom cottages available year round are across the street from the beach. All have screened porches. Nightly rentals available off-season. Linens not included with weekly rentals. Pool, beach access, deck, BBQ pit, coin laundry. No smoking or pets in units.

The Sandspur Motel & Cottage Court 252-441-6993, 800-522-8486; www.sandspur.net; 6607 S. Virginia Dare Trail, MP 15.5, Beach Rd., Nags Head 27959. Two-night cottage rentals available off-season. Linens and towels are not provided. Outdoor pool, hot tub, playground, pay phone, coin laundry. Efficiencies and motel rooms also available. No pets.

Sea Kove Motel 252-261-4722; 4600 Lindburgh Ave., MP 3, Kitty Hawk 27949. Efficiencies and cottages across the street from the ocean. Outdoor pool and playground. Handicapped-accessible units. No pets.

Beach House and Condo Rentals

Many of the real estate companies listed for the North Beaches also have houses available in this area. Check there for additional options.

Beach Realty and Construction/Kitty Hawk Rentals 252-441-7166, 800-635-1559; www.beachrealtync.com; 2901 N. Croatan Hwy., MP 6, Bypass, Kill Devil Hills 27948. Amenity package with some rentals. Partial weeks and long-term rentals available.

Bodie Island Realty 252-441-9443, 800-862-1785; www.bodieislandrealty.com; MP 11, Bypass, Nags Head 27959. Weekly and year-round rentals.

Cola Vaughan Realty 252-449-2652, 877-247-2652; www.obxcola.com; 324 W. Soundside, Nags Head 27959. Pet-friendly cottages from Southern Shores to South Nags Head.

Cove Realty 252-441-6391, 800-635-7007; www.coverealty.com; 105 E. Dunn St., MP 13.5, Nags Head 27959. Weekly, yearly, and winter rentals, with many located in Nags Head, including Old Nags Head Cove. Some cottages have negotiable rates.

Joe Lamb Jr. & Associates 252-261-4444, 800-552-6257; www.joelambjr.com;

5101 N. Croatan Hwy., MP 2, Bypass, Kitty Hawk 27949. Over 500 properties available, most in the Central Beaches.

Nags Head Realty 252-441-4315, 800-222-1531; www.nagsheadrealty.com; 2405 S. Croatan Hwy., MP 10.5, Bypass, Nags Head 27959. Over 200 rentals; some three-day packages.

Outer Banks Beach Club 252-441-6321; www.spmresorts.com; 1110 S. Virginia Dare Trail, Beach Rd., MP 9, Kill Devil Hills 27948. One of the largest condominium groups directly on the ocean rents completely equipped one-, two-, and three-bedroom units by the week year round. Amenities include indoor and outdoor pools and hot tubs, tennis and shuffleboard, barbecue grills, and a large clubhouse with planned activities all year.

Outer Banks Resort Rentals 252-441-2134; www.outerbanksresorts.com; Croatan Center, MP 13.5, Bypass, Nags Head 27959. Specializes in rentals and re-sales at over a dozen time-share properties on the Banks. Weekly rental units are completely equipped, with pools and other amenities.

Rentals on the Ocean 252-441-5005; www.rentalsontheocean.com; 7128 S. Virginia Dare Trail, MP 16.5, Beach Rd., Nags Head 27959. Group of pet-friendly cottages in South Nags Head are available all year.

Seaside Vacations 252-261-5500, 800-395-2525; www.outerbanksvacations.com; two locations: 3852 N. Croatan Hwy., MP 2, Bypass, Kitty Hawk 27949; 4727 S. Croatan Hwy., Nags Head 27959. Handles rentals at over 300 properties from condominiums to large oceanfront houses. Last-minute specials and dedicated-event properties available.

Sun Realty www.sunrealtync.com; Kitty Hawk office: 252-261-3892, 800-404-3892, 6385 N. Croatan Hwy.; Kill Devil Hills office: 252-441-8011, 800-801-7861, 1500 S. Croatan Hwy.. One of the largest rental companies on the Outer Banks. Rate includes all fees except taxes.

Wright Property Management 252-261-2186, 800-276-7478; www.wpmobx.com; 3719 N. Croatan Hwy., MP 4.5, Bypass, Kitty Hawk 27949. Over 100 properties, most in Kitty Hawk and South Nags Head. Three- and four-night rentals available off-season.

Camping and RV Resorts

Adventure Bound Campground 252-255-1130, 877-453-2545; 1004 W. Kitty Hawk Rd., MP 4.5, Kitty Hawk 28949. Tent-only campground has 20 sites, hot water showers, laundry, large lawn for games, campfire area. No pets.

Joe & Kay's Campground 252-441-5468; 1193 Colington Rd., west of the Bypass at MP 8.5, Kill Devil Hills 27948. Dump station, restrooms with hot water, boat ramp. One mile from the Wright Memorial. Most of the full-hookup sites are rented by the year. Several tent sites available during summer.

Kitty Hawk RV Park 252-261-2636; Beach Rd., MP 4, Kitty Hawk 27949. The last survivor of the oceanside campgrounds rents just eight RV sites with full hookups, including cable. No tents or pop-ups. Open all year; longer leases available.

Oregon Inlet Campground 252-473-2111; www.nps.gov/caha; NC 12, Nags Head 27959. The 120 sites at the NPS campground opposite the Oregon Inlet Marina have no utility hookups but are located on level ground. Campground amenities include modern restrooms, potable water, unheated showers, grills, and tables. The ocean is just across the dune line. Open from April to October; 14-day maximum. Reservations not accepted.

DINING

Once visitors to the Outer Banks had just a handful of restaurants to choose from, and most of those closed after Labor Day. Today, literally hundreds of eateries line both the Bypass and the Beach Road. New restaurants open every year, and the chains have arrived in force. Visitors won't have trouble finding something to eat on the Central Beaches, although lines can be long during the summer months if you don't have reservations.

Despite increasing development during the last decade or so, there are still many eating establishments located along the Beach Road, mostly across the street from the water. These provide convenient neighborhood hangouts that visitors can enjoy within an easy walk of their hotel or cottage. Nearly all are child friendly and have kids' menus.

Our listing includes spots that have consistently pleased both visitors and local residents and that offer a special dining experience.

Rate Categories

Inexpensive	under $10
Moderate	$10 to $20
Expensive	$20 to $25
Very Expensive	$25 and up

These ratings represent the average cost of an entrée, not including higher-priced specials, that supersize steak or the rack of lamb. They also do not include appetizers, desserts, beverages, taxes, or gratuities. When a range of ratings is offered, it usually indicates the difference in price between lunch and dinner entrées.

Smoking policies differ with each establishment, but in most Outer Banks restaurants, smoking is not allowed in the dining room of restaurants, but probably is at the bar or in the lounge. Our listings note when there is any change from this policy.

Credit Cards

AE—American Express
D—Discover
DC—Diners Club
MC—Master Card
V—Visa

Meal abbreviations

B—Breakfast
L—Lunch
D—Dinner
SB—Sunday brunch

Restaurants

COLINGTON ISLAND
COLINGTON CAFÉ
252-480-1123
www.colingtoncafe.com
1049 Colington Rd., Kill Devil Hills 27948
Price: Moderate to Expensive
Children's Menu: Yes
Cuisine: Continental
Liquor: Full
Serving: D
Credit Cards: MC, V
Handicapped Access: Yes
Special Features: Nightly specials; no smoking

Located in a lovely Victorian house well away from the crowds on the Bypass, this local favorite is not such a secret since *Southern Living* named it the "Best Restaurant for the Best Price" on the Outer Banks. Inspired by owner Carlen Pearl's French background, the cuisine here features the freshest seafood and other local ingredients in classic preparations. Many wonderful shrimp, chicken, and pork dishes are joined by a selection of dishes built around filet mignon grilled over an open flame. The she-crab bisque is legendary, and the homemade desserts, especially the white chocolate crème brûlée, leave guests raving. The atmosphere is romantic, with several small rooms downstairs. However, larger family groups can be accommodated in the upstairs room. Reservations are highly recommended, especially during the busy summer season. The Colington is open mid-March through Thanksgiving weekend and usually reopens for the week between Christmas and New Year's and for Valentine's Day.

★ HIDDEN CREEK GRILL

252-480-3298
1469 Colington Rd., Kill Devil Hills 27948
Price: Inexpensive to Moderate
Children's Menu: Yes
Cuisine: Seafood
Liquor: Beer, wine
Serving: L, D
Credit Cards: D, MC, V
Handicapped Access: Yes
Special Features: Daily specials; heated screened porch; boat dock; takeout available

Inexpensive menu, fresh seafood, and swift service make this a real find several miles out winding Colington Road, or arrive by boat at the dock off Colington Creek. Eat inside at tables or at the counter in the air-conditioned dining room, or take a table on the screened porch, where you can listen to the cicadas sing. A big fan keeps the porch cool in summer, and in winter it's heated. The porch is rimmed with strands of tiny white lights, casting an atmospheric glow. More lights lead from the boat dock up the garden path. Steamed spiced shrimp, oyster po' boys, and specialty salads are some of the most popular menu items. At dinner, rib eye and prime rib join a menu of fresh seafood, available fried or broiled. The broiled crab cakes, made with no filler, are worth the drive by themselves. Desserts here are homemade and excellent. Try the Snowball, a memorable concoction of coffee ice cream, Heath-crunch candy, whipped cream, and chocolate syrup, if it's on offer. Open all year.

KILL DEVIL HILLS
AWFUL ARTHUR'S OYSTER BAR

252-441-5955
www.awfularthursobx.com
2106 S. Virginia Dare Trail, MP 6, Beach Rd., Kill Devil Hills 27948
Price: Inexpensive to Moderate
Children's Menu: Yes
Cuisine: Seafood

The remains of a mini-golf course peek through the sands of the largest dune on the Banks.

Liquor: Full
Serving: L, D
Credit Cards: AE, D, DC, MC, V
Handicapped Access: Yes
Special Features: Gift shop; upstairs lounge; copper oyster bar; outside takeout window

Serving steamed oysters the authentic North Carolina way for two decades, Arthur's has a casual, kicked-back atmosphere much beloved by locals and the regulars who return here each year. Between peeling the famous spiced shrimp (*Esquire* named them one of "67 Things Worth a Detour" in the United States) and cracking crab legs, things may get a little messy. During summer, the crowds and the smoke can get thick as the sun heads west. At this point, adopt the local strategy: Head upstairs to the lounge, order some steamed shrimp and a cold beverage, and enjoy the view of the ocean. If you want to sit at a table, you may have a long wait. Locals usually opt for a stool at the copper-topped bar. Besides the many selections available from the raw bar, Arthur's serves fried seafood, soft-shell crabs, burgers, BBQ, steaks, and pasta. Open every day of the year (another reason the locals love it) for lunch and dinner.

KILL DEVIL GRILL

252-449-8181
www.thecoastalexplorer.com/killdevilgrill
2008 S. Virginia Dare Trail, MP 9.5, Beach Rd., Kill Devil Hills 27948
Price: Inexpensive to Moderate
Children's Menu: Yes
Cuisine: American
Liquor: Full
Serving: L, D, SB
Closed: Seasonally
Credit Cards: MC, V
Handicapped Access: Yes
Special Features: Jukebox; bar with TV; takeout available

Located in an authentic railroad dining car listed on the National Registry for Historic Places, this Beach Road family favorite offers meals that far surpass typical diner fare. Talented chefs create daily seafood and blue-plate specials, white pizza topped with goat cheese and fresh basil, wood-roasted chicken, steaks and chops, all with nice culinary touches. Popular dishes include the chicken wings, cheese steak eggrolls, and the Kahuna burger. Sunday brunch features several unusual dishes, including the Cajun Bubble & Squeek (spicy fried chicken topped with poached eggs and sausage gravy) and Devil's Got a Brand New Mess. Desserts are real treats, from an authentic key lime pie with Nilla wafer crust to a root beer float.

MAKO MIKE'S

252-480-1919
www.makomikesobx.com
1630 N. Croatan Hwy., MP 7, Bypass, Kill Devil Hills 27948
Price: Moderate
Children's Menu: Yes
Cuisine: American, seafood
Liquor: Full
Serving: D
Credit Cards: AE, D, MC, V
Handicapped Access: Yes
Special Features: Gift shop; bar with TVs; early bird specials; catering; private dining room

Promising "killer food" at reasonable prices, Mako Mike's serves all the family favorites, from pizza cooked in a wood oven and a variety of pasta dishes to standard beef, chicken, and pork entrées. Prime rib is a specialty. The long list of seafood runs from blackened Mako shark to lobster thermidor. No surprises in the preparations here, which are geared to family taste buds, but the decor makes up for any plainness in the menu. Wildly painted furniture, walls, and ceilings create an underwater atmosphere popular with children. The restaurant occupies three levels and can accommodate large groups. This is the sister restaurant of **Kelly's** farther down the Bypass. Mike Kelly owns both. Reservations available. Open all year.

OUTER BANKS BREWING STATION

252-449-2739
www.obbrewing.com
600 S. Croatan Hwy., MP 8.5, Bypass, Kill Devil Hills 27948
Price: Inexpensive to Moderate
Children's Menu: Yes
Cuisine: American fusion
Liquor: Full
Serving: L (summer only), D
Credit Cards: AE, MC, V
Handicapped Access: Yes
Special Features: Angry Hour; on-site brewery; food and drink specials; bar with TV; late-night menu; live entertainment; free WiFi

Fresh award-winning beer, frequent specials and live entertainment, plus the daily "Angry Hour" of low-priced appetizers, keep the crowds coming to one of the Outer Banks's most popular establishments. Grilled or beer-battered seafood, rotisserie chicken, and grilled chops and steaks fill out the dinner menu. Steamed seafood is available all day, as well as an above-average "pub grub" menu featuring gumbo, beer-steamed brats, and soft-shell crabs. Vegetarian entrées are nicely thought out. The kids' menu is special too, featuring a filet mignon and home-brewed root beer. An in-house pastry chef creates the desserts. Stop by for a beer sampler and check out the week's entertainment lineup. This is a hot spot for live regional and national bands. The building itself is inspired by one of the old life-saving stations that once dotted the Banks.

KITTY HAWK

★ BAREFOOT BERNIE'S TROPICAL GRILL & BAR

252-261-1008
www.barefootbernies.com
3730 N. Croatan Hwy., MP 4.5, Bypass, Kitty Hawk 27949
Price: Inexpensive to Moderate
Children's Menu: Yes
Cuisine: American
Liquor: Full
Serving: L, D
Credit Cards: D, MC, V
Handicapped Access: Yes
Special Features: Bar with TVs, satellite sports; surf videos; deck; live entertainment; gift shop; happy hour; late-night menu; WiFi access

The menu at Bernie's features all the popular favorites presented with interesting tropical flavors drawn from Caribbean, Cajun, and Thai cuisines, with a bit of Greek thrown in. Fish tacos, gyros, hot subs, pizzas and pastas, Thai lettuce wraps, steamed seafood, and Cuban-style steak are on the menu all day. At night these are joined by well-prepared entrées such as pecan-crusted flounder, Tequila lime chicken, and Grouper in a Bag. In addition to satisfying meals, this casual spot books live entertainment and is a gathering place for sports fans. Bernie's subscribes to NFL's Season Pass and has a dozen or so TVs so you can watch your favorite game. Tabletop Sound Dog wireless receivers let you tune in to the audio, too.

BLACK PELICAN OCEANFRONT CAFÉ

252-261-3171
www.blackpelicancatering.com
3848 N. Virginia Dare Trail, MP 4, Beach Rd., Kitty Hawk 27949
Price: Inexpensive to Moderate
Children's Menu: Yes
Cuisine: American
Liquor: Full
Serving: L, D
Credit Cards: MC, V
Handicapped Access: Yes
Special Features: Outdoor deck and bar with TVs; late-night menu; live entertainment

Located in an 1876 lifesaving station, the Black Pelican makes a great destination before, during, or after a day at the beach. A beach access is just across the street, and you can even shower off at the adjacent bathhouse. The restaurant has three levels and a lofty deck with a view of the ocean. Wood-oven pizzas, fresh seafood, steamed, grilled and blackened, and pasta dishes are among the most popular menu items. Open all year.

★ OCEAN BOULEVARD BISTRO & MARTINI BAR

252-261-2546
www.ocean-boulevard.com
4700 N. Virginia Dare Trail, MP 2, Beach Rd., Kitty Hawk 27949
Price: Inexpensive to Very Expensive
Children's Menu: Yes
Cuisine: Eclectic
Liquor: Full
Serving: D
Credit Cards: AE, D, MC, V
Handicapped Access: Yes
Special Features: Bar; martini menu; tapas and sushi specials; live jazz; catering; private dining room; deck

A casual spot just steps from the beach, this bistro serves artfully designed dishes that appeal to the upscale palate. *Southern Living* described it as "beachy and swanky all at once." The menu is divided into "Big Plates," which are serious entrées of lamb, fresh fish, duck, or beef, sold at equally serious prices, and "Small Plates," a nicely varied tapas menu that may range from gourmet macaroni and cheese to an antipasto plate with goat cheese, olives, and cured duck. Menus change with the season. Martinis are a specialty, and the wine list received the *Wine Spectator* Award of Excellence. This is the sister restaurant of **1587** at Manteo's Tranquil House Inn and enjoys the same fresh, local ingredients and emphasis on quality. Open all year for dinner; seasonal hours. Reservations recommended.

RUNDOWN CAFÉ & TSUNAMI SURF BAR

252-255-0026
www.thecoastalexplorer.com/RundownCafe
5218 N. Virginia Dare Trail, MP 1, Beach Rd., Kitty Hawk 27949
Price: Inexpensive to Moderate
Children's Menu: Yes
Cuisine: Caribbean fusion
Liquor: Full
Serving: L, D
Closed: Winter season
Credit Cards: AE, D, MC, V
Handicapped Access: Yes
Special Features: Raw and steamer bar; surf videos; live entertainment; takeout available

Named for the traditional Jamaican fish-and-coconut soup that tops the menu, this cool spot right at the head of the Beach Road provides a gathering spot for locals and a favorite dinner stop for everyone who discovers its laid-back charm and eclectic menu. Known for its huge dinner salads and Oriental sesame noodle bowls, both available with a wide variety of toppings, the Rundown successfully combines the flavors of the Caribbean with Asian influences. Vegetarians will be pleased with the numerous offerings designed for them, and special dietary requests can be accommodated. The dining room downstairs is smoke free. Upstairs a bar offers ocean views, cold brews, and a surfer vibe.

NAGS HEAD
OWENS' RESTAURANT

252-441-7309
www.owensrestaurant.com
7114 S. Virginia Dare Trail, MP 16.5, Beach Rd., Nags Head 27959
Price: Very Expensive
Children's Menu: Yes
Cuisine: Southern coastal
Liquor: Full
Serving: D
Credit Cards: MC, V

Handicapped Access: Yes
Special Features: Gift shop; AAA three-diamond rating

Bob and Clara Owens opened a 24-seat café on the beach back in 1946, among the first to gamble on the oceanfront property opened up by the causeways. Today, Owens' is one of the most storied restaurants on the coast, highly praised for its cuisine, fresh seafood, attentive service, and elegant decor. The entrées here are classic preparations of soft-shell crab, shrimp, crabmeat, lobster, and beef, served with salad and seasonal vegetables, as well as a crock of cheese and crackers as a before-meal treat, an old southern tradition. Ordering fried seafood here is a waste; there are so many delicious and original dishes to choose from. Built to resemble a lifesaving station, Owens' exhibits a collection of logbooks, photographs, and historic memorabilia. The elegant upstairs lounge is a great place for a before-dinner drink. Sometimes a piano player will entertain while you wait.

PENGUIN ISLE SOUNDSIDE BAR & GRILLE

252-441-2637
www.penguinisle.com
6708 S. Croatan Hwy., MP 16, Bypass, Nags Head 27959
Price: Moderate to Very Expensive
Children's Menu: Yes
Cuisine: Steaks and seafood
Liquor: Full
Serving: D
Closed: Winter months
Credit Cards: AE, D, MC, V
Handicapped Access: Yes
Special Features: Outdoor deck; live entertainment; early dining specials

Enjoy a fabulous sunset view from the dining room, huge lounge, or outdoor deck at this sound-side landmark. Certified Angus beef served in a variety of preparations, and fresh fish and seafood occupy the high end of the menu, but there's also a big selection of "lighter fare," from burgers and wraps to salads and some interesting appetizers. The signature fresh basil jalapeño bean-cake sautéed with snails in brandy will give you something to talk about all winter. The restaurant's wine cellar has over 400 wines from around the world and has received the *Wine Spectator* Award of Excellence many times.

PIER HOUSE RESTAURANT

252-441-4200
www.nagsheadpier.com/food.htm
3335 S. Virginia Dare Trail, MP 11.5, Beach Rd., Nags Head 27959
Price: Inexpensive to Moderate
Children's Menu: Yes
Cuisine: Seafood
Liquor: Full
Serving: B, L, D
Closed: Winter
Credit Cards: MC, V
Handicapped Access: Yes
Special Features: Screened dining room; daily lunch specials

The last of its kind along this stretch of coast, this restaurant sits above the surf on the Nags Head fishing pier. The view can't be beat, even on a stormy day. This is a popular breakfast spot, where you'll find some unusual local dishes on the menu, such as salt herring. Lunch specials are homemade. Local seafood is the specialty here. You can bring your own catch if you like, and the kitchen will prepare if for you. Dinner includes a free pass to the pier for an after-dinner stroll.

WINDMILL POINT RESTAURANT

252-441-1535
www.windmillpointrestaurant.com
6800 S. Croatan Hwy., MP 16.5, Bypass, Nags Head 27959
Price: Expensive
Children's Menu: Yes

Cuisine: Steaks and seafood

Liquor: Full

Serving: D, weekend brunch

Credit Cards: AE, D, MC, V

Handicapped Access: Yes

Special Features: Piano bar; specialty drink menu; catering available

The distinctive windmill, the last survivor of an energy source once common in the area, helps you find this unusual and lovely restaurant. Much of the interior decor was salvaged from the *SS United States*, one of the largest and fastest ocean liners ever built. Dinner is served nightly, featuring land-and-sea combinations that pair fresh seafood with steak, prime rib, or veal. Daily chef's specials include an ever-changing Fish Trio, three fillets of the freshest fish in the kitchen, topped with unique sauces. The sunset views here are superb, especially from the upstairs lounge. A combined breakfast and lunch menu is served all day on Saturday and Sunday. Open all year.

WHALEBONE JUNCTION AND THE CAUSEWAY

★ **BASNIGHT'S LONE CEDAR CAFÉ**

252-441-5405

www.lonecedarcafe.com

7623 S. Virginia Dare Trail, Nags Head–Manteo Causeway, Nags Head 27959

Price: Moderate to Expensive

Children's Menu: Yes

Cuisine: Seafood and steaks

Liquor: Full

Serving: L, D

Closed: Seasonally

Credit Cards: D, MC, V

Handicapped Access: Yes

Special Features: Bar; outdoor seating; gift shop; live entertainment

President pro tem of the North Carolina Senate Marc Basnight and his family operate this longtime local favorite located on the causeway. Basnight is a native of Manteo and a strong supporter of the local fishing and farming industries. This is one place where you can be sure the fish is fresh and from local waters, the vegetables are locally grown, and both the pork and chicken come from local farms. When the restaurant burned to the ground in May 2007, contractors worked around the clock to replace this essential spot on the local dining scene, getting it reopened before Labor Day. Fortunately, none of the restaurant's famous recipes were lost, and the she-crab soup and many other favorites are as good and as generously portioned as ever. Fresh grilled seafood comes sizzling to the table on metal plates. All steaks are certified U.S. Prime. Every table has a water view over the sound, where birds are frequently spotted feeding in the marsh. Senator Basnight himself can often be spotted in the restaurant, greeting guests and helping clear tables.

SUGAR CREEK SOUNDFRONT SEAFOOD RESTAURANT

252-441-4963

Nags Head–Manteo Causeway, MP 16.5, Nags Head 27959

Price: Moderate

Children's Menu: Yes

Cuisine: Seafood

Liquor: Full

Serving: L, D

Closed: Winter

Credit Cards: MC, V

Handicapped Access: Yes

Special Features: Early bird specials; gazebo bar; indoor lounge with TV; seafood market

Located on the north side of the causeway, the former RV's has been expanded to offer more great views and extra seating for groups. A favorite with families, thanks to all the wildlife visible from the dock and outdoor walkways, Sugar Creek also offers great sunset views. The menu includes a variety of steaks, ribs, pasta, salads, sandwiches, and soups, as well as fresh seafood.

Food Purveyors

Bakeries and Coffee Shops

★ **The Beach Bread Company** 252-261-7711; www.beachbread.com; 3712 N. Croatan Hwy., MP 4.5, Bypass, Kitty Hawk 27949. Serving organic fair-trade coffee and delectable breakfast Danish and croissants, plus a full selection of desserts and breads, this place is a retail store and self-serve deli during the day and in the evening, a martini bar, bistro, and live entertainment venue. Smoke-free and open all year.

Front Porch Café www.frontporchcafeonline.com; two locations: 252-449-6616, 2200 N. Croatan Hwy., Milepost 6 Plaza, MP 6, Bypass, Kill Devil Hills 27948; 252-480-6616, 2707 S. Croatan Hwy., MP 10.5, Bypass, Nags Head 27959. Home of the Kill Devil Coffee Roasters. Fresh-roasted beans have been voted best on the beach.

The Good Life Gourmet 252-480-2855; www.goodlifegourmet.com; 1712 N. Croatan Hwy., Dare Center, MP 7.5, Bypass, Kill Devil Hills 27948. A real find in a little strip mall, this place is a bakery and coffee shop in the morning, a deli at lunchtime, and a bistro with occasional live music at night. A wine shop is on premises, and the whole place is a free WiFi hot spot.

La Isla Bakery & Latin Market 252-441-7710; 3723 N. Croatan Hwy., Ocean Plaza, MP 4.5, Bypass, Kitty Hawk 27949. Pastries filled with tropical mango and pineapple flavors, Tres Leche, Latin coffee drinks, and groceries.

Majik Beanz 252-255-2700; 4107 S. Virginia Dare Trail, Surfside Plaza, MP 13, Beach Rd., Nags Head 27959. Full espresso bar plus ice cream, fruit smoothies, and wireless Internet, right across from the beach.

N.Y. Bagels two locations: 252-480-0106, Outer Banks Mall, MP 14, Bypass, Nags Head 27959; 252-480-0990, 1708 Croatan Hwy., the Dare Center, MP 7.5, Bypass, Kill Devil Hills 27948. Twelve flavors of bagels are made daily at two locations. Breakfast and lunch sandwiches are available on bagels or bread, plus a variety of spreads and salads.

Southern Bean 252-261-JAVA; Dunes Shops, MP 4.5, Bypass, Kitty Hawk 27949. Locally owned coffee shop serves fresh-brewed coffee, along with vegetarian and seafood sandwiches and salads, pastries, fresh-squeezed fruit juices, and ice cream. Open all year.

★ **The Village News** 252-441-7748; www.village-news.com. A bag of coffee to brew up will be delivered right to your door along with your daily paper. Daily, weekly, and summer rates are available for papers from up and down the East Coast. Delivery available from Carova to South Nags Head.

Barbecue

In North Carolina, barbecue is a noun, and no vacation would be complete without a big order of takeout from one of the local joints. Be sure to order plenty, since ribs and chopped pork are favorite leftovers for many families.

High Cotton Barbeque 252-255-2275; www.highcottonbbq.com; 5230 N. Virginia Dare Trail, MP 1, Beach Rd., Kitty Hawk 27949. Authentic North Carolina–style pulled pork flavored with vinegar and hot pepper shares the menu with Texas beef brisket, St. Louis–style ribs, and chicken, smoked or fried. The big family packages are a real bargain. Dine in or take out.

Jockey's Ribs 252-441-1141; 3948 S. Virginia Dare Trail, MP 13, Beach Rd., Nags Head 27959. One of the two barbecue joints that flank Kitty Hawk Kites across from Jockey's

Jockey's Ridge, a favorite launch point for hang gliders

Ridge State Park, this place is known for its ribs but serves a full menu and full bar as well. Dine in or take out.

Pigman's Bar-B-Que and Ye Olde Ham Shoppe 252-441-6803; www.pigman.com; 1606 S. Croatan Hwy., MP 9.5, Bypass, Kill Devil Hills 27948. Besides the usual pork and beef barbecue, this place offers heart-healthy 'cue made from tuna, catfish, and turkey, plus smoked chicken and ribs, homestyle sides, and sweet potato fries. Eat in or take out. Second carry-out location at Wee Winks Square in Duck, 252-261-2660.

Sooey's BBQ and Rib Shack 252-449-6465; www.sooeysbbq.com; MP 12.5, Jockey's Ridge Crossing, Nags Head. Dine in or take out.

Breakfast and More

Locals also like to eat breakfast at the Pier House Restaurant on Nags Head Pier. The Beach Bread Company serves a popular Sunday brunch.

Art's Place 252-261-3233; 4624 N. Virginia Dare Trail, MP 2.5, Beach Rd., Kitty Hawk 27949. Tiny spot on the Beach Road serves great breakfast and lunch all year to a loyal clientele. Upper deck with ocean view. Full bar.

Bob's Grill 252-441-0707; 1219 S. Croatan Hwy., MP 9, Bypass, Kill Devil Hills 27948. Breakfast is served all day at this restaurant, where the motto is "Eat and Get the Hell Out!" Big servings arrive fast, but the line can be long midmorning. Full lunch and dinner menu, plus full bar. Smoke-free.

The Dunes Restaurant 252-441-1600; www.thedunesrestaurant.com; 7013 S. Croatan Hwy., MP 16.5, Bypass, Nags Head 27959. Big all-you-can-eat breakfast buffet with lots of fresh fruit is served every morning in summer, weekends in spring and fall. The breakfast menu also offers many special platters noted for their huge portions and reasonable prices. Smoke-free.

★ **Grits Grill** 252-449-2888; 5000 S. Croatan Hwy., Outer Banks Mall; MP 14, Bypass, Nags Head 27959. Retro diner serves breakfast and lunch from 6 AM to 3 PM. Huge biscuits, fresh Krispy Kreme doughnuts, and reasonable prices on everything from corned-beef hash to shrimp and grits. Open all year.

Henry's Beef & Seafood Restaurant 252-261-2025; 3396 N. Croatan Hwy., MP 5, Bypass, Kitty Hawk 27949. A local favorite for breakfast, served until 1 PM. Open all year.

Jolly Roger Restaurant 252-441-6530; www.jollyrogerobx.com; 1836 N. Virginia Dare Trail, MP 6.5, Beach Rd., Kill Devil Hills 27948. While most visitors come to the Jolly Roger for huge servings of pasta, karaoke, and pirate ambience, locals know this is a great spot for breakfast, served from 6 AM to 2 PM. Pier-style eggs and Belgian waffles topped with ice cream are specialties, and for the true pirate, homemade bread pudding with a hearty bourbon sauce.

Sam & Omie's 252-441-7366; www.samandomies.net; 7228 S. Virginia Dare Trail, MP 16.5, Beach Rd., Nags Head 27959. Opened in 1937 by a couple of fishermen as a place to eat breakfast before the Oregon Inlet charter fleet set out for the day, Sam & Omie's is still serving breakfast more than 70 years later. Breakfast features "Omie"-lettes and Bloody Marys. Later in the day attention shifts to steamed seafood and cold ones.

The Ships Wheel Restaurant 252-441-2906; 2028 S. Virginia Dare Trail, MP 9.5, Beach Rd., Kill Devil Hills 27948. Breakfast-only spot, located in front of the Ebb Tide Family Motel, wins rave reviews from regulars and locals for huge portions at reasonable prices served from 6 AM to noon. Home of the world's, or at least the beach's, largest pancakes.

Stack 'Em High www.stackemhigh.com; two locations: 252-441-7064, 1225 S. Croatan Hwy., MP 9, Bypass, Kill Devil Hills 27948; 252-261-8221, 3801 N. Croatan Hwy., MP 4.5, Bypass, Kitty Hawk 27949. Family-owned and -operated cafeteria-style breakfast restaurants offer made-to-order French toast, pancakes, omelets, and eggs, plus unusual items such as clam hash from 7 AM to 1 PM daily.

Candy and Ice Cream

Fat Boyz Ice Cream & Grill 252-441-6514; 7208 S. Virginia Dare Trail, MP 16.5, Beach Rd., Nags Head 27959. Full line of ice cream delights, plus hand-patted burgers, veggie burgers, great onion rings, and other takeout favorites are served at this pink landmark on the Beach Road. Shady side deck has tables where you can eat.

Forbes Candy & Gift Shop two locations: 252-441-2122; 1700 S. Croatan Hwy., MP 9.5, Bypass, Kill Devil Hills 27948; 252-441-7293, 321 S. Croatan Hwy., MP 15.5, Bypass, Nags Head 27959. Fifteen flavors of Outer Banks saltwater taffy, plus fudge, peanut brittle, and penny candy.

How Sweet It Is 252-441-4485, 3941 S. Croatan Hwy., Jockey's Ridge Crossing, MP 12.5, Bypass, Nags Head 27959. Ice cream shop conveniently located across from the often burning sands of Jockey's Ridge.

Kill Devil's Frozen Custard & Beach Fries 252-441-5900; 1002 S. Croatan Hwy., MP 8.5, Bypass, Kill Devil Hills 27948. Real frozen custard, made fresh hourly, and so much better than ordinary soft-serve ice cream, served along with never-frozen, hand-cut fries, Coney Island hot dogs, BBQ, and burgers, both meat and veggie. Open seasonally.

Outer Banks Fudge Company 252-449-8484; www.fudgeman.com; 2236 S. Croatan Hwy., Plaza Del Sol, MP 10.5, Bypass, Nags Head 27959. Handcrafted fudge, cooked in copper kettles the old-fashioned way, plus Dolly's Beach Glass candy and unique saltwater fudge.

★ **The Snowbird** 252-441-0000; 3522 S Virginia Dare Trail, MP 12, Beach Rd., Nags Head 27959. Try your choice of 24 different flavors of soft-serve ice cream at this sweet little takeout spot on the Beach Road. Cool penguin T-shirts. Stays open very late in summer.

Delis and Specialty Foods

Butcher Block Fine Meats & Delicatessen 252-441-8787; www.obxbutcherblock.com; 3022 S. Croatan Hwy., Pirate's Quay Shopping Center, MP 11.5, Bypass, Nags Head 27959. Top-quality beef, pork, racks of ribs, and chicken cut to order by an experienced butcher. Also homemade sausage and hoop cheese, plus hot and cold sandwiches and salads.

Cahoon's Variety and Gourmet 252-441-5358; www.cahoonsvariety.com; 7213 S. Virginia Dare Trail, MP 16.5, Beach Rd., Nags Head 27959. Cahoon's, for four decades a one-stop shopping destination along the Beach Road, goes gourmet, adding cheese, pâté, and locally grown vegetables to its offerings of wine, beer, meats cut in-house, and other groceries, plus beach, fishing, and camping supplies.

Charlene's 252-441-1188; 1484 Colington Rd., Kill Devil Hills 27948. Combination grocery and grill stocks Boars Head deli items, a big selection of wine and beer, and lots of prepared foods, including breakfast specials, desserts, and the best Philly cheesesteaks on the Banks.

Country Deli 252-441-5684; 4107 S. Virginia Dare Trail, Surfside Plaza, MP 13, Beach Rd., Nags Head 27959. Overstuffed subs, deli meats, cheeses, and salads, plus a selection of beverages available to take out or delivered free along the Central Beaches.

Health-A-Rama Nutrition Center 252-261-9919; 3712 N. Croatan Hwy., MP 4.5, Bypass, Kitty Hawk 27949. This health food grocery stocks gluten-free products, organic produce, vitamins, and herbs.

★ **The Weeping Radish Farm Brewery & Eco Farm** 252-491-5205; www.weepingradish .com; 6810 Caratoke Hwy., Grandy 27939. The Farmer to Fork Natural Foods Market at the Weeping Radish's new Jarvisburg location just north of the Wright Memorial Bridge offers organic vegetables, as well as hormone-free beef, pork, and chicken from local farms, smoked local fish, homemade sausages, and fresh beer brewed in accordance with the strict Bavarian purity laws. Meals are served at the barn café, and brewery tours are available.

Winks Grocery 252-261-2555; 4626 N. Virginia Dare Trail, MP 2, Beach Rd., Kitty Hawk 27949. This family-run grocery has stood the test of time by providing what beachgoers need for more than 50 years. Deli sandwiches and specials at lunch.

Farms, Farmers Markets, and Vegetable Stands

A couple of produce stands are located on the Main Beaches, but most of the farming action is just over the Wright Memorial Bridge in Currituck County. There you'll find farm stands selling sweet white corn, vine-ripened tomatoes, strawberries, blueberries, blackberries, melons, tree-ripened peaches and other fruits, plus some more exotic items such as lavender and honey. All are open seasonally, so it's a good idea to call ahead for hours and availability.

Country Boys Farm Market on the corner of the Bypass and Woods Rd., Kitty Hawk; on the Outer Banks side of the Wright Memorial Bridge.

Grandy Farm Market 252-453-2658, 800-942-2658; 6264 Caratoke Hwy., Grandy 27939.

Harbinger Lavender Farm 252-491-2225; www.harbingerlavender.com; 187 Church Rd., Harbinger 27941. Family farm offers lavender products from wands to jellies, or you can pick your own.

Point Harbor Pick Your Own Strawberries 252-491-8266; 135 James Griggs Rd., Point Harbor 27964.

Roberts Ridge Farm Market 252-336-4793; 489 N. Indiantown Rd., Shawboro 27973. Farmers market and cornfield maze.

Rose Produce & Seafood 252-453-2911; 6378 Caratoke Hwy., Grandy 27939.

Tarheel Produce 252-491-8600; US 168, Powells Point and **Tarheel Too** at Seagate North Shopping Center, MP 5.5, Bypass, Kill Devil Hills.

Watkins Apiary 252-429-3134; 121 Wade Cove Ln., Knotts Island 27950. Honey fresh from the hive available in summer. Tours available.

Pizza

American Pie 252-441-3332; 1600 S. Virginia Dare Trail, MP 9.5, Beach Rd., Kill Devil Hills 27948. Homemade ice cream and hand-tossed New York–style pizza converge at this spot just across Beach Road from the Ramada.

Dare Devil's Authentic Pizzeria 252-441-6330, 252-441-2353; 1112 S. Virginia Dare Trail, MP 9, Beach Rd., Kill Devil Hills 27948. A landmark along the Beach Road since 1987, this cool spot shows surf videos while you wait for your pizza or stromboli. Full bar.

Maxximmuss Pizza 252-441-2377; 5205 S. Croatan Hwy., MP 14.5, Bypass, Nags Head 27959. Authentic Southern Italian pizza and calzones, plus paninis, hoagies, salads, and Middle Eastern specialties such as gyros and hummus, available to eat in or take out. Beer available. Delivery as far as Manteo and MP 8.

Stone Oven Pizza 252-441-7775; 7100 S. Croatan Hwy., Tanger Outlet Center, MP 16.5, Bypass, Nags Head 27959. Tasty pies baked in a stone oven, cold brews, and a sunset view make this a favorite with locals. Try the white pizza with garlic and pepper sauce topped with spinach and mozzarella. Free delivery to Nags Head and Pirate's Cove.

Seafood Markets

Austin Fish Company 252-441-7412; www.austinfishcompany.com; 3711 S. Croatan Hwy., MP 12.5, Bypass, Nags Head 27959. Family-owned and operated, Austin's has been selling fresh fish and seafood from the same location next to Jockey's Ridge for over 40 years. Freshness is guaranteed, and they will pack and ship your catch home for you. Seafood dinners to go also available.

Carawan Seafood 252-261-2120; 5424 N. Croatan Hwy., MP 1, Bypass, Kitty Hawk 27949.

Family-owned operation specializes in local seafood, steamed crabs and shrimp, plus beer, wine, and groceries.

Daniels Big Eye Seafood 252-441-5755; www.bigeyeseafood.com; 3213 N. Croatan Hwy., Bypass, MP 5, Kill Devil Hills 27948. Offerings here depend upon what's biting. Lots of game fish for sale, including the illustrious striped bass.

The Sugar Shack 252-441-3888; 7340 S. Virginia Dare Trail, Nags Head Causeway, Nags Head 27959. Get a bucket of seafood to "go-go" from the shack located at the edge of the sound next to sister restaurant **Sugar Creek**. Delivery of raw or steamed seafood available.

Takeout and Beach Fast Food

Capt'n Frank's 252-261-9923; 3800 N. Croatan Hwy., MP 4.5, Bypass, Kitty Hawk 27949. Don't let the boat out front fool you. Hot dogs, topped with everything imaginable, are the main event here, plus North Carolina barbecue, chicken and steak sandwiches, cheese fries, and steamed shrimp in season. Open all year.

Dune Burger 252-441-2441; 7304 S. Virginia Dare Trail, MP 16.5, Beach Rd., Nags Head 27959. Get your burgers, hot dogs, fries, and other fast-food favorites from the window at this throwback to another age, strategically placed in Whalebone Junction. Open seasonally.

Five Guys Burgers & Fries 252-255-0006; www.fiveguys.com; 1203 S. Croatan Hwy., MP 9, Bypass, Kill Devil Hills 27948. This chain has taken the burger market by storm, thanks to never-frozen beef and hand-cut fries.

John's Drive-In 252-261-6227; 3716 N. Virginia Dare Trail, MP 4.5, Beach Rd., Kitty Hawk 27949. A longtime favorite on the Beach Road, John's keeps busy all summer, making its signature milkshakes with added fruit, burgers, and fried fish sandwiches. Takeout only.

Seaside Gourmet To Go 252-255-5330; www.seasidegourmet.com; 3701 Croatan Hwy., Dunes Shops, MP 4.5, Bypass, Kitty Hawk 27949. Formerly the Seaside Vegetarian, this takeout-only spot has expanded its offerings to include seafood but retains a dedication to local and organic products.

Wine Stores, Vineyards, Brew Tours, and Spirits

Microbrew enthusiasts can find fresh brews and brewery tours at the **Outer Banks Brewing Company** in Kill Devil Hills, and at the **Weeping Radish Brewery** in Jarvisburg on the north side of the Wright Memorial Bridge. Several wineries are located in this area as well.

ABC Liquor Stores www.ncabc.com; two locations: 252-261-2477, MP 1, Bypass, Kitty Hawk; 252-441-5121, MP 10, Bypass, Nags Head 27959. All liquor by the bottle is sold at these state-run stores, which are closed on Sunday. Beer and wine, however, are available at a wide variety of outlets, after 12 noon on Sunday and until 2 AM every evening.

BrewThru www.brewthru.com; Kill Devil Hills location: 252-441-9190, 3101 N. Croatan Hwy., MP 5.5; Kitty Hawk location: 252-261-3948, 4728 N. Croatan Hwy., MP 2; two Nags Head locations: 252-441-5108, 2203 S. Croatan Hwy., MP 10; 252-480-2739, 3700 S. Virginia Dare Trail, MP 13. Wide selections of beer and wine, and "world famous" T-shirts, plus the convenience of drive-through service.

Chip's Wine and Beer Market 252-449-8229; www.chipswinemarket.com; 2200 N. Croatan Hwy., Milepost 6 Plaza, MP 6, Bypass, Kill Devil Hills 27948. With 2,000 different wines and the Great Wall of Beer offering 400 brews, Chip's may well have the largest selection of wine and beer on the Outer Banks.

Knotts Island: Between Two States

One of the most isolated communities on the East Coast lies on an island caught between North Carolina and Virginia. Connected by causeway to Virginia, Knotts Island is actually a part of North Carolina's Currituck County, although the only connection is by boat. A free state-run ferry takes 45 minutes to reach this island surrounded by marsh in Currituck Sound. From the ferry dock, NC 615 travels a dozen miles north to the Virginia border and then on to Pungo, Virginia. Several boat tours also visit the island from the Corolla area of the Outer Banks, just a few miles across the sound.

Once known as the home of duck-hunting preserves, Knotts Island today is a quiet, friendly community. In recent years several wineries have taken root in its sandy soil, and bed-and-breakfast inns now offer accommodations on the island. Peaches are the biggest crop here, and the community hosts an annual peach festival in July. The actual name of the town on Knotts Island is Fruitville.

The ducks and snow geese still come by the thousands, finding a winter home in Mackay Island National Wildlife Refuge along the Virginia border. The land was once the estate of publishing magnate and philanthropist Joseph P. Knapp, founder of Ducks Unlimited, the organization that has done more than any other to preserve the great migrating flocks for future generations. Throughout the refuge, hiking trails and observation decks invite visitors to see the rich wildlife that made this part of the world famous.

You can find out more about this unique community at its Web site, www.knottsislandonline.com. Here are some places to explore on the island:

Bay Breeze Lodge Bed and Breakfast 252-429-3234; www.baybreezelodge.com; Duck Lane, Knotts Island 27950.

Bay-Villa Marina and Restaurant 252-429-3559; 112 Bay-Villa Lane, Knotts Island 27950. Full-service restaurant and lounge, locally called Pearl's, on the shores of Knotts Island Bay.

Knotts Island Market 252-429-3305; 395 Knotts Island Rd., Knotts Island 27950. Established in 1937, this store carries a little bit of everything and is the only gas station on the island. Deli serves quick meals all day.

Mackay Island National Wildlife Refuge 252-429-3100; www.fws.gov/mackayisland; Marsh Causeway, NC 615, Knotts Island. Biking, hiking, paddling, fishing, crabbing, and bird-watching opportunities. Stop on the Charles Kuralt Trail.

Martin Vineyards 252-429-3542, 252-429-3564; www.martinvineyards.com; 213 Martin Farm Lane, Knotts Island 27950. Tastings available of dry reds and whites, plus fruit wines. Pick your own apples, peaches, scuppernong grapes, and pumpkins in season.

Moonrise Bay Vineyard 252-429-WINE, 866-888-WINE; www.moonrisebaywine.com; 134 Moonrise Bay Vineyard Rd., Knotts Island 27950. Dry reds and whites, as well as fruit wines made of berries and cherries. Tasting and tours available.

The Peach Basket 252-429-3317; 208 South End Rd., Knotts Island 27950. Peaches, plums, nectarines, pears, and apples, along with jams, jellies, peach pies and cobblers are available in season.

Sandy Point Resort Campground 252-429-3094; 176 Sandy Point Dr., Knotts Island 27950. Full RV hookups, rental cabins and campers available. Boat ramp, fishing supplies.

Stillwater Touring Company 252-429-2089; 101 Shepherds Way, Knotts Island 27950. Kayak instruction, rentals, and tours.

Moonrise Bay Vineyard, Knotts Island

★ **Native Vine I** 252-491-5311; www.nativevine.com; 9138 Caratoke Hwy., Point Harbor 27964 and **Native Vine II** 252-480-9991; www.nativevine.com; 3933 S. Croatan Hwy., Jockey's Ridge Crossing, MP 12.5, Bypass, Nags Head 27959. Featuring wine, beer, and gourmet food from around the world, Native Vine's two locations offer daily tastings of North Carolina wines and a huge selection of microbrews.

Outer Banks Wine University 252-449-8229; www.outerbankswineuniversity.com; 2200 N. Croatan Hwy., Milepost 6 Plaza, MP 6, Bypass, Kill Devil Hills 27948. Fun and informative wine classes conducted by a pro.

Sanctuary Vineyards 252-491-2387; www.sanctuaryvineyards.com; 6957 Caratoke Hwy., Jarvisburg 27947. Vineyards planted with Sangiovese, Norton, and French hybrids produces signature blends. Tasting room located in the Cotton Gin.

TOURING

The best place to begin any tour of the Outer Banks is one of the region's welcome centers. **Aycock Brown Welcome Center** (877-629-4386; www.outerbanks.org), located at MP 1 in Kitty Hawk, provides information for vacationers arriving on the Outer Banks via the Wright Memorial Bridge. The center offers an accommodations reservation service, restrooms, public phones, and a picnic area. The Outer Banks welcome centers close only two days a year, on Thanksgiving and Christmas.

Adjacent to the Aycock Brown Welcome Center, the **Monument to a Century of Flight** commemorates the accomplishments that led from Kitty Hawk to outer space. Stainless steel pylons and black granite panels chronicle the 100 most significant events of the first 100 years of flight. Admission to the monument is free.

At the entrance to the Cape Hatteras National Seashore on NC 12, the **Whalebone Welcome Center** dispenses friendly advice on activities in the National Park and on the route south.

During the busy summer months, many activities fill up early. It's a good idea to make reservations well in advance if your time is limited. Calling on a local concierge service, such as the **Outer Banks Concierge** (252-261-5817; www.outerbanksconcierge.com) can smooth the process of planning your vacation by arranging fishing charters and other activities, even stocking your rental's refrigerator with food before your arrival.

CULTURE

As one of the East Coast's earliest summer getaways, the Outer Banks helped define the beach vacation. The traditions of the Central Beaches are ones of laid-back summers spent in hammocks on the cottage porch, beachcombing, and dancing in the sand on warm summer nights. With the burgeoning of the tourism industry, steps have been taken to preserve reminders of these early days on the Banks.

A nightlife scene is growing here as well, with the action continuing well into the night at clubs and bars, a nice addition to the traditional all-night action on the fishing piers.

Architecture

Immortalized as the "Unpainted Aristocracy" in books such as Anne Siddons's best-selling *Outer Banks*, the historic beach cottages of Nags Head are monuments to survival in the face of generations of storms. Some of the older cottages, which date to the 1850s, have been moved westward numerous times as the ocean has taken the land out from under them.

About 40 structures along a 1.5-mile stretch of the Beach Road make up the **Nags Head Beach Cottage Row Historic District**. Many of them are listed on the National Register of Historic Places. Nine cottages built before 1885 survive today. Most of the others date from 1900 to 1940.

The cottages share design elements that have come to define the Nags Head style: unpainted cedar-shake siding, wide hip-roofed porches with built-in benches, and propped shutters on windows.

Cottage Row runs between MP 12 and MP 13.5, from the C. H. White Cottage at 3905 S. Virginia Dare Trail on the north end to the Outlaw Cottage at 4327 S. Virginia Dare Trail and Dove Avenue in the south. Besides the private cottages, historic buildings include **St. Andrew's By-the-Sea Episcopal Church** (1915), the **First Colony Inn** (1932), and **Mattie Midgette's Store** (1914), now a museum. The oldest surviving cottage is the 1859 Spider Villa at 4049 Virginia Dare Trail.

A paved multi-use path runs along the Beach Road past the historic cottages. To see the cottages from the beach side is more difficult, as there are no public beach accesses in the historic district. The closest are at Conch Street (3600 block, Beach Rd.) at the north end, and Small Street (4500 block, Beach Rd.) at the southern end.

This first cottage community was built close to the eastern flank of the Jockey's Ridge dune, and a fine overall view of the historic district can be gained from the observation tower at **Jockey's Crossing Shopping Center**, built on the site of the old dance pavilion.

In recent years, the Town of Nags Head has encouraged the use of local design elements, including cedar-shake siding, wraparound porches, wooden shutters, gable and hip roofs, cupolas, and lifesaving station watchtowers. These can now be seen in numerous new commercial and residential units along the Banks.

Art Museums and Galleries

A group of galleries can be found on **Gallery Row**, located around MP 10 between the Beach Road and the Bypass in Nags Head. This area, encompassing both Gallery Row Road and Driftwood Road, was set aside by the town especially to encourage local arts and crafts. Most artists here live on the property.

Ann's Beach Crafts 252-441-7459; 206 E. Driftwood St., Gallery Row, MP 10, Nags Head 27959. Consignment shop displays crafts hand-made by local residents, at very reasonable prices.

The Bird Store 252-480-2951; www.thebirdstore.biz; 807 S. Croatan Hwy., MP 8.5, Bypass, Kill Devil Hills 27948. Antique decoys and fishing and hunting equipment on display, plus new carvings, paintings, and prints of wildfowl and other wildlife by local and regional artists.

First Flight Shrine 252-441-7430; www.firstflight.org/shrine.cfm; US 158, MP 8, Bypass, Kill Devil Hills. Over 50 portraits of outstanding figures in the history of aviation hang in the Wright Brothers National Memorial Visitor Center. Reading their biographies is an education in itself.

★ **Glenn Eure's Ghost Fleet Gallery** 252-441-6584; 210 E. Driftwood St., Gallery Row, MP 10, Nags Head 27959. Unique gallery displays the sculptural watercolors and oils, woodcuts, and etchings of the talented Eure, a fixture for over 30 years on the local art scene.

Annual shows include the Frank Stick Memorial Art Show in February and the Icarus International show in December.

Jewelry by Gail 252-441-5387; www.jewelrybygail.com; 207 E. Driftwood St., Gallery Row, MP 10, Nags Head 27959. Award-winning jeweler Gail Kowalski creates original designs using diamonds, colored pearls, amethysts, and corals. The shop features a magnificent amethyst chandelier.

★ **KDH Cooperative Gallery & Studios** 252-441-9888; www.kdhcooperative.com; 502 S. Croatan Hwy., MP 8.5, Bypass, Kill Devil Hills 27948. Artist-operated gallery exhibits the works of over two dozen local artists. Frequent classes and openings are offered year round.

Lighthouse Gallery and Gifts 252-441-4232; www.seabeacons.com; 301 E. Driftwood St., Gallery Row, MP 10, Nags Head 27959. This replica lighthouse, a landmark on Gallery Row, houses a huge selection of lighthouse and nautical art, including the Harbour Lights and Lefton Lighthouse collections, and lace curtains with nautical themes.

Nags Head Town Hall 252-441-5508; www .townofnagshead.net; 5401 S. Croatan Hwy., MP 15, Bypass, Nags Head 27959. The town's ever-growing collection of local art in all media is on display free Mon.–Fri. 8:30 AM– 5 PM.

The Quacker Connection 252-441-2811; www.quackerconnection.com; 1720 Bay Dr., Seagate North Shopping Center, MP 5.5, Bypass, Kill Devil Hills 29748. Decoys, both new and antique, are for sale here, including many made by resident carver Doug Hevener.

Seaside Art Gallery 252-441-5418, 800-828-2444; www.seasideart.com; 2716 S. Virginia Dare Trail, MP 10, Beach Rd., Nags Head 27959. Established in 1961, this gallery carries over 2,000 originals by local and contemporary artists, as well as works by Picasso, Chagall, Whistler, and Renoir. Special collection of original animation art from

The Lighthouse Gallery, a landmark on Nags Head's Gallery Row

Disney, Hanna-Barbera, and others. Annual miniature art show in May.

SeaTree Gallery 252-441-6786; www.seatreegallery.com; 7332 S. Virginia Dare Trail, Whalebone Junction, Nags Head 27959. Operated by the current generation of an old Nags Head family, this gallery exhibits works by numerous local and regional artists, including lots of garden art, and sponsors frequent juried shows, monthly art openings, and classes.

Yellowhouse Galleries 252-441-6928; www.yellowhousegallery.com; 2902 S. Virginia Dare Trail, MP 11, Nags Head 27959. Housed in an authentic 1935 beach cottage along the Beach Road, this gallery invites you to browse through its huge collection of antique maps, charts, and prints, most over 100 years old, as well as many modern reproductions.

Museums and Historic Sites

Bodie Island Lighthouse and Keepers Quarters 252-473-2111; www.nps.gov/caha; NC 12, South Nags Head 27959. The 156-foot, black-and-white-striped tower, built in 1972, is not currently open for climbing. The Double Keepers Quarters building contains exhibits, a National Park Service visitor's center, and a bookstore. Follow the path behind the quarters to a boardwalk to spot wading birds and waterfowl.

Grave Digger Dungeon 252-453-4121; www.gravedigger.com; 5650 Caratoke Hwy., US 158, Grandy 27939. Fans visiting the home of the legendary monster truck can have their pictures taken sitting in the Grave Digger and pick up logo merchandise.

Nellie Myrtle Pridgen Beachcomber Museum in Mattie Midgette's Store 252-441-6259; www.osob.net, www.oldnagshead.org; 4008 S. Virginia Dare Trail, MP 13, Beach Rd., Nag's Head 27959. Housed in a 1914 grocery store listed on the National Register of Historic Places, this museum exhibits treasures gathered during a lifetime of beachcombing, including rare shells, sea glass, whalebone, messages in bottles, driftwood, and all sorts of curious artifacts. Call for hours.

USS Huron **Historic Shipwreck Preserve** 910-458-9042; www.arch.dcr.state.nc.us. North Carolina's first shipwreck preserve is the site of the wreck of the *Huron* just north of Nags Head Pier, about 250 yards off the beach. In summer, buoys mark the stern and bow of the wreck, now home to a great variety of sea life. Collecting artifacts from the wreck is prohibited.

Windmill Point 252-441-1535; www.windmillpointrestaurant.com; 6800 S. Croatan Hwy., MP 16.5, Bypass, Nags Head 27959. The last survivor of some 50 windmills that once ground grain along the Outer Banks stands on the sound side behind a restaurant. The original millstones lie close by. Wind power is returning to the Banks today. The National Park Service has a 70-foot-tall windmill supplying power at Coquina Beach, and the Outer Banks Brewing Station generates electricity with its new wind turbine.

★ **Wright Brothers National Memorial** 252-473-2111; www.nps.gov/wrbr; US 158, MP 7.5, Bypass, Kill Devil Hills 27948. Many improvements to the exhibits at this national shrine were made during the 2003 Centennial of Flight. The Centennial Pavilion houses exhibits on the history of aviation and an interactive area showing what the Outer Banks were like when Wilbur and Orville arrived. Close by, the park service has reconstructed the Wrights' living quarters and hangar. The 60-foot granite pylon, the memorial's most noticeable feature, stands atop Kill Devil Hill. On the far side, a life-size group of bronze statues, accurate down to the barefoot photographer snapping the most famous picture in history, captures the moment of the First Flight. During the summer months, park rangers give tours and talks throughout the park.

Music, Theater, and Dance

The Casino Remembered, a retrospective of the music played at Nags Head's famous dance pavilion, brings big-band jazz to the Outer Banks. Check local listings.

Center Front Theater Troupe 258-441-1181; 300 Mustian St., Kill Devil Hills 27948. Senior thespians at the Thomas A. Baum Center mount occasional, critically praised theatrical productions. *Wanchese, the Musical*, is one to watch for.

Outer Banks Music Showcase 252-261-7505; www.outerbanksmusicshowcase.com; 3848 N. Croatan Hwy., MP 4.5, Bypass, Kitty Hawk 27949. High-energy shows of country-western tunes and popular favorites are presented several night a week most of the year. Special shows include an annual Christmas show, Elvis tribute nights, and guest bands.

Outer Banks Shag Club 252-491-2645; www.obxshagclub.com; P.O. Box 1126, Kitty Hawk 27949. Dance with the locals to beach music every Monday night at Peppercorns in the Ramada Plaza Resort. Lessons available.

Nightlife and Entertainment

If late-night action is an important part of your vacation plans, then the Central Beaches are the right destination. During the summer season you'll find live music somewhere most nights of the week, as well as places to dance and romance. Things slow down on the entertainment scene during the off-season, but more and more places, especially the sports bars, now stay open all year. Many also have late-night menus and sushi or tapas nights. Call ahead for current entertainment schedules. Because of North Carolina's liquor laws, all bars also sell food.

Live music at sunset can be found at **Basnight's Lone Cedar Café** (252-441-5405; www.lonecedarcafe.com; 7623 S. Virginia Dare Trail, Nags Head–Manteo Causeway, Nags Head 27959), **Penguin Isle Soundside Bar & Grille** (252-441-2637; www.penguinisle.com; 6708 S. Croatan Hwy., MP 16, Bypass, Nags Head 27959), and **Tale of the Whale** (252-441-7332; www.taleofthewhalenagshead.com; 7575 S. Virginia Dare Trail, Nags Head–Manteo Causeway, Nags Head 27959). All have great water views on the sound.

Owens' Restaurant (252-441-7309; www.owensrestaurant.com; 7114 S. Virginia Dare Trail, MP 16.5, Beach Rd., Nags Head 27959), **Windmill Point** (252-441-1535; www.windmillpointrestaurant.com; 6800 S. Croatan Hwy., MP 16.5, Bypass, Nags Head 27959), and the **Clarion Oceanfront** (252-441-6333, 800-843-1249; www.outerbanksclarion.com; 1601 S. Virginia Dare Trail, MP 9.5, Beach Rd., Kill Devil Hills 27948) have elegant piano bars with occasional music.

For live jazz, check the schedules at **Ocean Boulevard Bistro & Martini Bar** (252-261-2546; www.ocean-boulevard.com; 4700 N. Virginia Dare Trail, MP 2, Beach Rd., Kitty Hawk 27949) and the **Beach Bread Company Bistro** (252-261-8692; www.beachbread.com; 3712 N. Croatan Hwy., MP 4.5, Bypass, Kitty Hawk 27949).

Other popular nightspots include:

Argyles Restaurant & Piano Bar 252-261-7325; www.argylesrestaurant.com; 4716 N. Croatan Hwy., MP 2.5, Bypass, Kitty Hawk 27949. Sophisticated tunes from the baby grand perfectly complement the cuisine and atmosphere at this longtime beach favorite.

Barefoot Bernie's Tropical Grill & Bar 252-261-1008; www.barefootbernies.com; 3730 N. Croatan Hwy., MP 4.5, Bypass, Kitty Hawk 27949. Bar with good food, live entertainment, TVs tuned to sports, late-night action.

Beach Road Grill 252-480-2228, 2519 S. Virginia Dare Trail, MP 10.5, Beach Rd., Nags Head 27959. Fun bar atmosphere, burgers, and steamed seafood at this place that backs up to the beach and frequently hosts live local acoustic acts.

Black Pelican Oceanfront Café 252-261-3171; www.blackpelicancatering.com; 3848 N. Virginia Dare Trail, MP 4, Beach Rd., Kitty Hawk 27949. While you're here, lift a glass to Wilbur and Orville. The Wright brothers came to this building, then a lifesaving station and telegraph office, to send word of their first successful flight out to the world. Frequent live entertainment in season.

Chilli Peppers 252-441-8081; www.chilli-peppers.com; 3001 N. Croatan Hwy., MP 5.5, Bypass, Kill Devil Hills 27948. Live entertainment some nights, along with a late-night menu featuring sushi and vegetarian options, steamer bar, and tapas nights, plus some of the spiciest food on the beach.

The Comedy Club 252-441-2151; www.comedyclubobx.com; Ramada Plaza Hotel, 1701 S. Virginia Dare Trail, MP 9.5, Beach Rd., Kill Devil Hills 27948. Touring comedians keep the laughs coming.

Goombay's Grille and Raw Bar 252-441-6001; www.goombays.com; 1608 N. Virginia Dare Trail, MP 7, Beach Rd., Kill Devil Hills 27948. Cool vibes, good food, big beer selection, and live music some nights. Jazz during Sunday brunch.

Hurricane Mo's Beachside Bar and Grill 252-255-0215; 120 E. Kitty Hawk Rd., MP 4, Beach Rd., Kitty Hawk 27949. Fun tropical bar just steps from the beach with nightly happy hours.

Jolly Roger Restaurant 252-441-6530; www.jollyrogerobx.com; 1836 N. Virginia Dare Trail, MP 6.5, Beach Rd., Kill Devil Hills 27948. Late-night bar hosts NTN Interactive Trivia and nightly shows by the Alan Ross Karaoke Roadshow.

Kelly's Outer Banks Restaurant & Tavern 252-441-4116; www.kellysrestaurant.com; 2316 S. Croatan Hwy., MP 10.5, Bypass, Nags Head 27959. Popular restaurant also has a spacious nightclub and the largest dance floor on the beach. Drink specials, NTN Trivia, and late-night menu, plus frequent live entertainment, everything from national touring bands to female impersonators.

Lucky 12 Tavern 252-255-LUCK; www.lucky12tavern.com; 3308 S. Virginia Dare Trail, MP 12, Beach Rd., Nags Head 27959. A neighborhood favorite for its reasonably priced food, TVs tuned to sports, pool table, laid-back attitude, and pizza served until 2 AM.

Mama Kwan's Tiki Bar & Grill 252-441-7889; www.mamakwans.com; 1701 S. Croatan Hwy., MP 9.5, Bypass, Kill Devil Hills 27948. A favorite hangout for the late-night crowd, Kwan's serves tasty food, tropical drinks, and occasional live entertainment with a laid-back vibe.

Outer Banks Brewing Station 252-449-2739; www.obbrewing.com; 600 S. Croatan Hwy., MP 8.5, Bypass, Kill Devil Hills 27948. Busy schedule of bands, DJs, open mikes, and special events keeps the good times rolling most nights.

Peppercorns 252-441-2151, 800-635-1824; www.ramadaplazanagshead.com; Ramada Plaza Resort, 1701 S. Virginia Dare Trail, MP 9.5, Beach Rd., Kill Devil Hills 27948. Oceanfront club hosts live bands, DJs, and the Comedy Club. Shag dance on Monday nights.

★ **The Pit Surf Shop, Bar & Boardriders' Grill** 252-480-3128; www.pitsurf.com; 1209 S. Croatan Hwy., MP 9, Bypass, Kill Devil Hills 27948. A hangout for surfers day and night, the Pit frequently hosts live bands. Food is served all day and includes a big vegetarian menu. Alcohol-free teen dance nights are held several times a week during the summer.

Port O' Call Restaurant & Gaslight Saloon 252-441-7484; www.outerbanksportocall.com; 504 S. Virginia Dare Trail, MP 8.5, Beach Rd., Kill Devil Hills 27948. Romantic atmosphere with frequent live music, dance floor, two levels of bar seating.

Prime Only Martini Bar 252-480-0047; www.primeonly.com; 2706 S. Croatan Hwy., MP 11, Bypass, Nags Head 27959. One of the Banks's best steakhouses has a popular martini and wine bar with live entertainment.

Red Drum Grille and Taphouse 252-480-1095; 2412 S. Virginia Dare Trail, MP 10.5, Beach Rd., Nags Head 27959. Over a dozen beers on tap, foosball, and pool, plus live entertainment and a late-night menu.

Rundown Café & Tsunami Surf Bar 252-255-0026; www.thecoastalexplorer.com/rundown cafe; 5218 N. Virginia Dare Trail, MP 1, Beach Rd., Kitty Hawk 27949. Laid-back music in the lounge.

Shuck U—Old School Raw Bar and Grill 252-449-6969; MP 9, Beach Rd., Kill Devil Hills 27948. A hang out for students of seafood, with live entertainment and pinball.

Slammin' Sammy's Offshore Grille and Stillery 252-449-2255; www.slamminsammys.com; 2407 S. Croatan Hwy., MP 10.5, Bypass, Nags Head 27959. More than 40 TVs make this a favorite stop for sports fans. Nonsmoking section available. Open all year.

Sunburn Sports Bar & Grill 252-261-7833; www.myspace.com/sunburns45; 3833 N. Croatan Hwy., MP 4, Bypass, Kitty Hawk 27949. Casual bar with food, live entertainment, pool tables, and plenty of TVs tuned to sports. Hosts Texas hold 'em poker and pool tournaments.

Tortuga's Lie Shellfish Bar and Grille 252-441-RAWW; www.tortugaslie.com; 3014 N. Virginia Dare Trail, MP 11, Beach Rd., Nags Head 27959. Beachside spot features great seafood, beach volleyball, and cool vibes year round.

RECREATION

The Central Beaches present two faces to the world. The most public face is the well-known beachfront, mile after mile of some of the finest sand and waves in the world. Here you'll find surfers, boogie boarders, sandcastle artists, beachcombers, and surf anglers having the time of their lives.

The other, more hidden face of the Central Beaches overlooks Roanoke Sound. The marshes are full of wildlife, attracting both hunters and bird watchers. The shallow water is perfect for Jet Skis and kayaks, while the steady winds make this an ideal location to learn to windsurf or kiteboard.

In between these two coasts, the Central Beaches hold a wealth of both history and natural wonders. The great dunes that brought the Wright brothers to this neighborhood now lift hang gliders on their own first flights. The deep maritime forests give nature lovers and bird watchers many pleasant options.

Beaches

Dozens of public access points line NC 12 (the Beach Road) and Old Oregon Inlet Road along the Central Beaches. Regional beach accesses have bathhouses with restrooms where you can shower and change.

Bathhouses in Kitty Hawk are located at Byrd Street and just south of Kitty Hawk Road. In Kill Devil Hills, you'll find a bathhouse at Ocean Bay Boulevard. In Nags Head, bathhouses are located at Bonnet Street, Hargrove Street, and Epstein Street. Most bathhouse locations have lifeguards during the summer months. Several other beach accesses in each town have open-air showers.

Handicapped access is available at many of the beach accesses. Beach wheelchairs are available from the Kitty Hawk Fire Department (252-261-2666; www.kittyhawkfd.com), the Kill Devil Hills Fire Department (252-480-4060), the Nags Head Fire Department (252-441-5909), Jockey's Ridge State Park (252-441-7132), and the Bodie Island Lighthouse Visitor Center (252-441-5711). These are also the places to apply for a fire permit.

Lifeguards are on duty at many beach access points along this stretch of coast from Memorial Day to Labor Day. Hours vary depending on the town. Roving beach patrols also are on duty.

Contact the Outer Banks Visitor Center (252-473-2138, 877-629-4386; www.outerbanks .org) for the latest information on lifeguards, handicapped access, and beach facilities.

The Cape Hatteras National Seashore maintains a large beach facility at Coquina Beach opposite the Bodie Island Lighthouse. Amenities include changing rooms, showers, walkway to the beach, large paved parking lot, handicapped access, and a lifeguard (in season). The remains of the *Laura A. Barnes*, which wrecked in 1921, are sometimes visible.

Sound Access

Kill Devil Hills has several places where the public can gain access to the sound. All are located along Bay Drive. The N.C. Wildlife Access, at Dock Street and Bay Drive, with boat-launching area, picnic tables, and free parking, is a popular spot to jump in the water.

In Kitty Hawk, Orville Beach can be found at the end of Moore Shore Road. This was the location of the historic village of Kitty Hawk when the Wright brothers arrived. The town of Kitty Hawk also has a handicapped-accessible public sound access at Windgrass Circle.

In Nags Head, Jockey's Ridge Sound Access, located at the end of Soundside Road, which runs along the state park's southern boundary, is a popular place for families to swim. The Nags Head Causeway Estuarine Access, on the south side of the Nags Head–Manteo Causeway near its east end, has a public dock, fishing gazebo, and kayak launch. Bring the chicken necks and string, because the crabbing is great here. Another sound access at MP 16 is a favorite with windsurfers and kiteboarders.

Beach Buggy and Four-Wheel-Drive Rentals

Outer Banks Chrysler Dodge Jeep 252-441-1146, 800-441-0352; www.outerbanksjeep .com; 3000 N. Croatan Hwy., MP 5.5, Bypass, Kill Devil Hills 27948.

Beach Equipment Rentals

You can rent just about anything from the companies that serve the area, and most deliver and pick up for free, with a minimum order. Linens and towels, beach chairs and umbrellas, baby equipment, bikes, kayaks, boogie boards, and surf boards are standard items, but you can also rent sports equipment, metal detectors, binoculars, basketballs, volleyball and horseshoe sets, beach wheelchairs, coolers, charcoal grills, and roll-away beds.

Lifesaver Rent-Alls 252-441-6048, 800-635-2764; 1006 S. Virginia Dare Trail, MP 9, Beach Rd., Kill Devil Hills 27948.

Moneysworth Beach Home Equipment Rentals 252-261-6999, 800-833-5233; www.mworth.com; 947 W. Kitty Hawk Rd., Kitty Hawk 27949.

Ocean Atlantic Rentals 252-441-7823; www.oceanatlanticrentals.com; MP 10, Beach Rd., Nags Head 27959. Surfboards are a specialty; lessons available.

Bicycling

Biking is great on the Central Beaches, and many families rent bikes to get around. Most of the shoulders along the Beach Road (NC 12) have been widened to make biking safer, but be sure to stay in single file, and avoid riding through deep sand that may have blown over the pavement. The Bypass (US 158) is not recommended for biking, as the traffic is often very heavy and moving fast. Use great caution when crossing the Bypass, even where crosswalks and crossing lights are available. State law requires that all bike riders under 16, including passengers, wear helmets on public roads or paths.

Best Bike Routes

The best bike route of all is along the beach, where you can travel for miles without encountering any motorized traffic during the summer months. However, each of the towns along the Central Beaches has excellent bike paths.

In Kitty Hawk, the **Pruitt Multi-Use Trail,** a separate paved path, runs along Woods Road through the maritime forest. It connects at its northern end with the Southern Shores bike path and at its southern end with a bikeway along the wide, paved shoulders of Kitty Hawk Road. A right on Moore Shore Road leads through the historic village of Kitty Hawk, where the Wright brothers first stayed when they came to the Banks. A monument marks the spot of their boarding house. Moore Shore Road leads down to the **Wright Brothers Multi-Use Path**, which follows a historic roadbed along the sound. This bikeway, a paved road not accessible to motorized traffic, leads to Bay Drive in Kill Devil Hills with a beautiful ride along the sound for several miles.

Another route through Kitty Hawk is along a multi-use path running beside Twiford and Kitty Hawk roads to Kitty Hawk Landing. Lindbergh Avenue, between the highways in north Kitty Hawk, is also a popular biking route.

Kill Devil Hills' main bike path runs along Colington Road on the south side of the Wright Brothers Memorial, from the Bypass out to First Street, Canal Road, and Bay Drive. These connect to paths through the **Centennial Park and Recreation Center.** Another path runs along Veteran's Drive.

Many bikers want to ride along the Beach Road, and the towns and state are working to make this safer. In Nags Head, a bike path extends along Old Oregon Inlet Road to Whalebone Junction, where it connects with a multi-use path running parallel to the Beach Road north to MP 11.5. There it joins a widened shoulder on the Beach Road through Kill Devil Hills. Shoulders are narrower in Kitty Hawk and often covered with sand, especially for northbound traffic.

For off-road biking, several miles of dirt roads are available through **Nags Head Woods;** however, bikes are not allowed on the preserve's trails.

Maps of bike routes and paths are available from the **Outer Banks Welcome Centers** in Kitty Hawk and on Roanoke Island. Contact the **Wheels of Dare Bicycle Club** (252-261-3068; 6072 Currituck Rd., Kitty Hawk 27949) or one of the local bike shops for advice and more information.

Bike Rental Shops

Most companies will deliver weekly rentals right to your cottage. Every size and style of bicycle is available, as well as child seats, various tag-a-longs, and tricycles for children and adults.

The Bike Barn 252-441-3786; 1312 Wrightsville Blvd., MP 9.5, Bypass, Kill Devil Hills 27948. Professional service on rentals, repairs, and sales.

Kill Devil Hills Cycle & Skate 252-480-3399; 203 S. Virginia Dare Trail, Beach Rd., MP 8.5, Kill Devil Hills 27948. Rentals, sales, and repairs. BMX, scooters, hybrids, and tandems also available.

Kitty Hawk Cycle Company 252-261-2060; www.kittyhawkcyclecompany.com; 203 E. Eckner St., MP 2.5, Beach Rd., Kitty Hawk 27949. Repairs, rentals, and sales of beach cruisers, road and mountain bikes. Group rides for road bikers offered most days.

Kayaks are the best way to explore the marsh on the soundside of the Banks.

Lifesaver Rent-Alls 252-441-6048, 800-635-2764; 1006 S. Virginia Dare Trail, MP 9, Beach Rd., Kill Devil Hills 27948.

Moneysworth Beach Home Equipment Rentals 252-261-6999, 800-833-5233; www.mworth.com; 947 W. Kitty Hawk Rd., Kitty Hawk 27949.

Ocean Atlantic Rentals 252-441-7823; www.oceanatlanticrentals.com; MP 10, Beach Rd., Nags Head 27959.

Boats and Boating

Kayaking

The Central Beaches offer some great spots to paddle. The marshes that stretch between Nags Head and Roanoke Island, both north and south of the Causeway, although very shallow, are full of waterfowl and wading birds. Kitty Hawk Bay and the canals and streams that surround Colington Island provide peaceful places to paddle. See our Public Boat Ramps listings for suggestions of places to put your craft in the water.

A canal, really a finger of Ginquite Bay, which runs into Kitty Hawk Woods close to the Wright Memorial Bridge, is one of the best paddles on the Banks. Narrow and lined by tall trees on either side, it is protected from the often strong winds that sweep the Banks, besides being a haven for wading birds, turtles, and other wildlife. A covered bridge is one of the trip's highlights. This trip is highly recommended and perfect for children and novice paddlers.

Kayak Rentals and Tours

Bodie Island Adventures 252-441-8875, 252-441-6822; www.waterworks.ws; 7649 S. Virginia Dare Trail, Nags Head–Manteo Causeway, Nags Head 27959. Single and double kayaks and canoes are available by the hour. Surf kayaks rent by the day. Eco-tours available.

Carolina Outdoors / Kitty Hawk Kites 877-FLY THIS; www.kittyhawk.com. Paddles around Kitty Hawk Bay, through the maritime forest of Kitty Hawk Woods, and along the sound side of Bodie Island, plus sunset and bioluminescence paddles, are among the tours offered. Rentals and sales of new and used kayaks.

Coastal Kayak 252-261-6262, 800-701-4111; www.outerbankskayaktours.com. Guided paddle trips follow several routes through the Kitty Hawk Maritime Forest and the adjacent marsh.

★ **Kitty Hawk Kayaks Paddling Center** 252-261-0145, 866-702-5061; www.khkss.com; 6150 N. Croatan Hwy., MP 1, Bypass, Kitty Hawk 27949. With a launch directly into the canal through Kitty Hawk Woods, this is a great place to rent or join a guided paddle. Exclusive tours exploring the Nags Head Woods Ecological Preserve, with proceeds benefiting the Nature Conservancy, and overnight kayak trips to platforms around Albemarle Sound, including some key birding areas, are also available.

Kitty Hawk Watersports 252-441-2756; www.kittyhawksports.com; 6920 S. Croatan Hwy., MP 16, Bypass, Nags Head 27959. Surf, ocean, and touring kayaks for rent or sale, as well as specialized fishing kayaks and new paddle boards.

The Promenade Watersports 252-261-4400; www.promenadewatersports.com; 105 Promenade Ln., MP 0, Bypass, Kitty Hawk 27949. Rentals launch from the Promenade's 600-foot dock just south of the Wright Memorial Bridge.

Personal Watercraft Rentals and Tours

Bodie Island Adventures / Waterworks Sports Center 252-441-8875, 252-441-6822; www.waterworks.ws; 7649 S. Virginia Dare Trail, Nags Head–Manteo Causeway, Nags Head 27959. WaveRunners rented by the hour and half-hour.

Carolina Outdoors / Kitty Hawk Kites 877-FLY THIS; www.kittyhawk.com. Jet Skis available for half-hour or hour rental at the Windmill Point and Whalebone locations. Jet Ski tours from Whalebone available to view Bodie Island Lighthouse or the Lost Colony on Roanoke Island.

Kitty Hawk Watersports 252-441-2756; www.kittyhawkwatersports.com; 6920 S. Croatan Hwy., MP 16, Bypass, Nags Head 27959. Rentals of Yamaha WaveRunners that seat three and will go up to 60 mph include instruction and patrol boat. Guided tours also available.

The Promenade Watersports 252-261-4400; www.promenadewatersports.com; 105 Promenade Ln., MP 0, Bypass, Kitty Hawk 27949. Jet Skis for rent near the Wright Memorial Bridge.

Powerboat Rentals

Fishing Unlimited 252-441-5028; www.fishingunlimited.net; 7665 S. Virginia Dare Trail, Nags Head–Manteo Causeway, Nags Head 27959. Rent an outboard skiff or pontoon boat for fishing, crabbing, or sightseeing on Roanoke Sound by the full or half-day.

The Promenade Watersports 252-261-4400; www.promenadewatersports.com; 105 Promenade Ln., MP 0, Bypass, Kitty Hawk 27949. Pontoon and fishing boats available for rent.

Public Boat Ramps

A Dare County public boat ramp is located at the end of Bob Perry Road in Kitty Hawk, where parking is available for about 30 vehicles. The 200-foot canal leading to the sound is approximately 5 feet deep.

The North Carolina Wildlife Boat Ramp and Access is located at Dock Street off Bay Drive in Kill Devil Hills, where there are docks, a breakwater, and 12 paved parking spaces.

The National Park Service operates a free boat ramp at Oregon Inlet behind the fishing center. About 75 vehicles and trailers can park here.

Kayaks can launch at the Nags Head Causeway Estuarine Access on the south side of the Causeway near its east end, where you'll also find a public dock and fishing gazebo.

Another good place to put your kayak in is behind Jockey's Ridge State Park at the Soundside Access area, found by following the road that runs along the southern boundary of the park to its end. This is also a popular swimming beach for families.

On Colington Island, put in at the foot of the second bridge, where you'll find a parking area.

Sandy Run Park, located on Woods Road in Nags Head, has a canoe and kayak launch that puts you in the heart of the maritime forest, as well as a short wetlands boardwalk.

Sailboat Charters

Kitty Hawk Watersports 252-441-2756; www.kittyhawkwatersports.com; 6920 S. Croatan Hwy., MP 16, Bypass, Nags Head 27959. Sailboat rentals and instruction on the sound using Hobie catamarans. This is the Outer Banks dealer for the Hobie Mirage Adventure Island, a combined kayak, pedal boat, and trimaran.

The Promenade Watersports 252-261-4400; www.promenadewatersports.com; 105 Promenade Ln., MP 0, Bypass, Kitty Hawk 27949. Catamarans and trimarans for up to 10 passengers for rent.

Family Fun

Dare County Youth Center 252-475-5850; www.dareyouthcenter.org; 602 Mustian St., Kill Devil Hills 27948. Two full-court gyms for open play of basketball or volleyball, TV room, foosball, Ping-Pong, pool table, and computer room. Visitors can use the facilities for a small daily or weekly fee.

Kitty Hawk Kites 252-441-4124, 877-FLY THIS; www.kittyhawk.com; 3933 S. Croatan Hwy., Jockey's Ridge Crossing, MP 13, Bypass, Nags Head 27959. Indoor 22-foot rock-climbing wall, lessons in kite flying, and kite-making workshops.

Kitty Hawk Watersports 252-441-2756; www.kittyhawkwatersports.com; 6920 S. Croatan Hwy., MP 16, Bypass, Nags Head 27959. Bumper boats, a 26-foot-tall climbing wall, plus WaveRunner rentals, parasailing, windsurfing, and more at this soundside mecca. This stretch of the Bypass around MP16 has a wealth of entertainment options, including several go-kart tracks and mini golf courses.

Nags Head Bowling & Billiards 252-441-7077; www.nagsheadbowling.com; 201 W. Satter-field Landing Rd., MP 10.5, Bypass, Nags Head 27959. Billiards and arcade games, as well as full-service bowling, snack bar with wine and beer, and bumper bowling for kids make this a fun rainy-day destination. Neon bowling, rock-and-bowl nights, and other special events.

Oregon Inlet Fishing Center & Marina 252-441-6301; 800-272-5199; www.oregon-inlet .com; 98 NC 12, Nags Head 27959. Head down to the south end of Bodie Island in the late afternoon when the charter boats come in to see the different fish that have been caught and watch the crews weigh the really big ones. The store here can provide an impromptu picnic.

Outer Banks Family YMCA Water Park 252-449-8897; www.ymcashr.org; 3000 S. Croatan Hwy., MP 11, Bypass, Nags Head 27959. Water park with two pools and a waterslide is open during the summer.

Play N Trade Video Games & DVDs 252-261-3838; www.playntrade.com; 3809 N. Croatan Hwy., MP 4, Bypass, Kitty Hawk 27949. Hard-core gamers will like this full-service store offering play-before-you-buy and trade-in options. Free advice and retro games for parental units.

The Weeping Radish Eco Farm 252-491-5205; www.weepingradish.com; 6810 Caratoke Hwy., Grandy 27939. During the Christmas holiday season, an indoor rink offers ice skating with all the traditional trimmings.

Go-karts

Colington Speedway 252-480-9144; 1064 Colington Rd., Kill Devil Hills 27948. Off the beaten track on Colington Island.

Dowdy's Go-Karts 252-441-5122; MP 11, Beach Rd., Nags Head 27959.

Nags Head Raceway 252-480-4639; 7000 S. Croatan Hwy., MP 16, Bypass, Nags Head 27959.

Speed-n-Spray Action Park 252-480-2877; MP 15.5, 6408 S. Croatan Hwy., Bypass, Nags Head 27959.

Mini Golf

Blackbeard's Golf and Arcade 252-441-4541; 6714 S. Croatan Hwy., MP 16, Bypass, Nags Head 27959.

Galaxy Golf 252-441-5875; 2914 S. Virginia Dare Trail, MP 11, Beach Rd., Nags Head 27959.

Jurassic Park 252-441-6841; 6926 S. Croatan Hwy., MP 16, Bypass, Nags Head 27959.

Lost Treasure Golf 252-480-0142; www.losttreasuregolf.com; 1600 N. Croatan Hwy., MP 7, Bypass, MP 7, Kill Devil Hills 27948. Wild West mining theme features a free train ride to the first hole.

Mutiny Bay Adventure Golf 252-480-6606; 6606 S. Croatan Hwy., MP 16, Bypass, Nags Head 27959. This 18-hole course next to Penguin Isle has an arcade and snack bar, plus a store with pirate souvenirs.

Paradise Golf & Arcade 252-441-7626; 3300 N. Croatan Hwy., MP 5.5, Bypass, Kill Devil Hills 27948. Play all day for one price at two 18-hole, natural grass courses that appeal to both kids and adults.

The Promenade 252-261-4900; www.promenadewatersports.com; MP 0, Bypass, Kitty Hawk. Full-size driving range, chip and putt course, 18 holes of mini golf, arcade, 600-foot pier, and a variety of water sports available.

Playgrounds

A good place to find activities off the beach lies on Colington Road, the first road south of the Wright Brothers National Monument. Here you'll find the **Outer Banks Chamber of Commerce**, with lots of visitor and relocation information; the **Outer Banks Arboretum**; **Aviation Park**, with a variety of recreation facilities; the **Thomas Baum Senior Center**; the Kill Devil Hills Municipal Center; the First Flight Elementary, Middle, and High Schools;

and the **Dare County Family Recreation Park and Youth Center,** with indoor and outdoor sports. The area is laced with multi-use paths suitable for walking, biking, roller-skating, and skateboarding.

Public playgrounds and recreational facilities in Kill Devil Hills can be found at: **Aviation Park** (Veterans Dr.) with a fitness trail, lighted roller-hockey rink, playground, and restrooms; **Dare County Recreation Park** (252-475-5920; www.co.dare.nc.us; 602 Mustian St.) with a playground, baseball and softball fields, tennis courts, soccer field, volleyball and basketball courts, horseshoe pits, gazebos, and restrooms; **Fresh Pond Park** (off Copley Dr.); and **Meekins Field** (1634 N. Croatan Hwy.) with tennis courts, athletic field, playground, picnic area, and restrooms.

In Kitty Hawk, **Sandy Run Park** on the Woods Road has basketball and shuffleboard courts, a canoe and kayak launch, and a short wetlands boardwalk, plus parking. Farther up Woods Road close to the US 158 intersection, a public park has play equipment for young children, a picnic area, a portable restroom, and parking. Trails through Kitty Hawk Woods begin nearby.

Skate Parks

Maple Skate Park 252-232-3007; www.visitcurrituck.com; Maple Airport Complex, 2826 Caratoke Hwy., US 158, Currituck 27929. Designed by Grindline, a world leader in creating skate parks, this free county park on the mainland receives rave reviews for its 11-foot keyhole and pool coping. Helmets and elbow and knee pads required. The park also has a tot playground, a fitness trail, grills for picnics, and a paved walking trail that circles a fishing lake.

Outer Banks Family YMCA Skatepark 252-449-8897; www.ymcashr.org; 3000 S. Croatan Hwy., MP 11, Bypass, Nags Head 27959. Open to in-line skaters, bikes, and scooters, as well as skateboards, the YMCA's skate park offers daily and weekly passes. Built by Grindline, the 15,000-square-foot park features a concrete bowl and large street course. Open all year. Helmets required, and pads for those under 18.

Fishing

Bridge Fishing

Fish are known to hang out under bridges and around pilings, and several bridges on the Central Beaches are favorite spots for locals to drop a line. Among them: the catwalk on the south side to the Bonner Bridge at Oregon Inlet; the so-called "little bridge" on the eastern end of the Nags Head–Manteo Causeway; and the second bridge on Colington Road, noted for its fine crabbing.

Fishing Charters and Guided Trips

Bodie Island Adventures 252-441-8875, 252-441-6822; www.waterworks.ws; 7649 S. Virginia Dare Trail, Nags Head–Manteo Causeway, Nags Head 27959.

Kayak Fishing Tours 252-441-4124; www.kittyhawk.com. Peaceful paddling combined with fly-fishing is an increasingly popular pastime. Inshore charters in traditional motorized boats also available.

Nags Head Guide Service 252-475-1555, 252-216-7070; www.nagsheadfishing.com. Fish the sounds and backwaters with Captain David Dudley, a winner on the FLW and Bassmaster tours.

★ **Oregon Inlet Fishing Center & Marina** 252-441-6301, 800-272-5199; www.oregon-inlet.com; 98 NC 12, Nags Head 27959. Nearly 50 fishing boats are docked at Oregon Inlet Fishing Center, one of the most famous fishing destinations in the world, thanks to the many big fish brought to its docks. Located at the north end of the Herbert Bonner Bridge, it has the closest access to the Atlantic fishing grounds of any marina on the northern Outer Banks. At the Fishing Center's Web site, you can browse pictures and specs for each boat and visit their individual Web sites, check availability, and book online, or sign up for a makeup charter that will match you with other anglers with similar interests. Prices are standardized and run about $1,500 a day for offshore charters, $900 for nearshore, $600 for inshore and sound fishing in an open boat. Half-day morning or afternoon trips, and shorter evening trips also available.

Fishing Instruction

Cape Hatteras National Seashore 252-473-2111; www.nps.gov/caha. Free introductions to crabbing are offered in summer by the rangers at the Bodie Island Visitor Center.

Jockey's Ridge State Park 252-441-2588; www.jockeysridgestatepark.com. Rangers offer a free Crabby Clinic during the summer months.

Joe Malat's Outer Banks Surf Fishing Schools 252-441-4767; www.joemalat.com; Nags Head. Malat wrote the books, literally, on pier fishing, surf fishing, and crabbing. Three-night surf-fishing schools are held twice a year, with seminars and workshops scheduled year round.

Kitty Hawk Watersports 252-441-2756; www.kittyhawksports.com; 6920 S. Croatan Hwy., MP 16, Bypass, Nags Head 27959. Lessons in kayak fishing available.

Outer Banks Fishing School 252-255-2004; www.obxfishingschool.com; Kitty Hawk. Two-hour, half-day, full-day, and multiple-day indoor and outdoor seminars in saltwater sportfishing taught by top local fishing experts concentrate on subjects specific to the Oregon Inlet region, including rock fishing, speckled trout, flounder, cobia, net casting, inshore trolling, and fishing the towers. Seminars are held at the Hilton Garden Inn, and participants have access to its private fishing pier.

Fishing Piers

Once numerous along the coast, many fishing piers have been lost to storms and development. The threatened Jennette's Pier was recently acquired by the North Carolina Aquarium Society and deeded over to the state to preserve the tradition of pier fishing for future generations.

Avalon Pier 252-441-7494; www.avalonpier.com; 2111 N. Virginia Dare Trail, MP 6.5, Beach Rd., Kill Devil Hills 27948. The 696-foot pier, built in 1958, is open 5 AM–2 AM during the summer, shorter hours in spring and fall. No shark fishing. Live pier cam on the Web site.

Jennette's Pier 252-441-6421; www.jennettespier.net; 7223 S. Virginia Dare Trail, MP 16.5, Nags Head 27959. Originally erected in 1939, the pier is now part of the North Carolina Aquarium system and is being rebuilt with concrete pilings that hopefully will withstand hurricanes. A two-story pier house holds a tackle shop, arcade, gift shop and food service downstairs, and exhibits upstairs.

Kitty Hawk Pier 252-261-1290, 877-629-4586; www.hiltongardeninn.com; 5353 N. Virginia Dare Trail, MP 1, Beach Rd., Kitty Hawk 27949. Now privately operated by the Hilton Garden Inn. Contact the inn for access information.

Nags Head Pier 252-441-5141; www.nagsheadpier.com; 3335 S. Virginia Dare Trail, MP 11.5, Beach Rd., Nags Head 27959. The 750-foot Nags Head Pier has a full-featured tackle shop, rental cottages, and a restaurant where the motto is "You hook 'em, we cook 'em." Open 24 hours a day, with lights for night fishing.

Outer Banks Pier 252-441-5740; www.fishingunlimited.net; 8901 Old Oregon Inlet Rd., MP 18.5, South Nags Head 27959. This 600-foot pier operated by Fishing Unlimited is open 24 hours a day and lit for night fishing. An oceanfront grill serves breakfast and lunch. Senior discount passes available.

Sound Pier, Fishing Unlimited 252-441-5028; www.fishingunlimited.net; 7665 S. Virginia Dare Trail, Nags Head–Manteo Causeway, Nags Head 27959. Fishing Unlimited also operates this 300-foot pier on the Causeway—a great place for crabbing or fishing for speckled trout or other inshore species.

Fishing Supplies and Outfitters

Dock of the Bay Marina 252-255-5578; www.dockofthebay.info; Bob Perry Rd., Kitty Hawk. Located just beyond the public boat launch on Bob Perry Road, this marina with easy access to Albemarle Sound provides diesel, gasoline, and oil, plus groceries, beer, wine, ice, fishing tackle, and bait.

Fishing Unlimited 252-441-5028; www.fishingunlimited.net; 7665 S. Virginia Dare Trail, Nags Head–Manteo Causeway, Nags Head 27959. Complete tackle shop sits next to a 300-foot pier open for fishing and crabbing.

Stop N Shop Convenience & Deli 252-441-6105; www.surffishing.info: MP 8.5, Beach Rd., Kill Devil Hills. Surf-fishing hot spot offers advice and all the equipment you'll need for a successful day of angling.

TW's Bait and Tackle www.twstackle.com; two locations: 252-261-7848, US 158, MP 4, Bypass, Kitty Hawk; 252-441-4807, 2330 S. Croatan Hwy., MP 10.5, Bypass, Nags Head 27959. Custom rods are a specialty at these full-service shops.

Whalebone Tackle 252-441-7413; 7667 S. Virginia Dare Trail, Nags Head–Manteo Causeway, Nags Head 27959. Tackle, ice, and bait at this convenient stop.

Headboats

Miss Oregon Inlet 252-441-6301, 800-272-5199; www.oregon-inlet.com; 98 NC 12, Nags Head 27959. Spend a morning or afternoon on the water, fishing with an experienced crew aboard this 65-foot craft. Family-friendly rates include all the equipment needed to fish. In summer, a twilight sightseeing cruise is offered.

Golf Courses

Limited space and high land values make golf courses rare on the Outer Banks. The ones that do exist are wildly busy during the summer season, with tee times scheduled up to a year in advance. The demand has fueled an explosion of golf courses on the mainland just over the Wright Memorial Bridge in Currituck County, North Carolina's newest golf hot spot.

Packages and specials at several of the region's golf courses can be booked through the Outer Banks Golf Association (800-916-6244; www.golfouterbanks.com).

Courses on the Banks

The Currituck Club 252-453-9400, 888-453-9400; www.thecurrituckgolfclub.com; 620 Currituck Club Dr., Corolla 27927. See listing in the North Beaches chapter.

Pier fishing is a treasured North Carolina tradition.

Duck Woods Country Club 252-261-2609; www.duckwoodscc.com; 50 S. Dogwood Trail, Southern Shores 27949. See listing in the North Beaches chapter.

Nags Head Golf Links 252-441-8073; www.nagsheadgolflinks.com; 5615 S. Seachase Dr., Nags Head 27959. Beautiful Scottish links–style course located in the Village of Nags Head development overlooks Roanoke Sound. The **Links Grille** serves lunch and after-golf libations, as well as Sunday brunch, and is open to the public.

Seascape Golf Links 252-261-2158; www.seascapegolf.com; 300 Eckner St., MP 2.5, Bypass, Kitty Hawk 27949. The windswept dunes and ocean views at this links-style course remind many golfers of Scotland. **Scully's Restaurant** and a pro shop on-site.

Mainland Golf Courses

Carolina Club 252-453-3588; www.thecarolinaclub.com; 127 Carolina Club Dr., Grandy 27939. A local favorite, just 15 minutes north of the bridge, is noted for its fine putting surfaces.

Goose Creek Golf and Country Club 252-453-4008; www.outerbanksgolfgoosecreek.com; 6562 Caratoke Hwy., Grandy 27939.

Holly Ridge Golf Course 252-491-2893; 8818 Caratoke Hwy., Harbinger 27941. 1.5 miles north of the bridge.

Kilmarlic Golf Club 252-491-5465; www.kilmarlicgolfclub.com; 215 West Side Ln., Powells Point 27966. Three miles north of the bridge. Newest course in the area and a beauty.

The Pointe Golf Club 252-491-8388; www.thepointegolfclub.com; 308 Point Golf Club Dr., Powells Point 27966. Located 3.5 miles north of the bridge. Designed by Russell Breeden, this was the first course in the country to use A1 bent grass greens.

The Sound Golf Links 252-426-5555, 800-535-0704; www.albemarleplantation.com; 101 Clubhouse Dr., Hertford 27944. On the shores of Albermarle Sound, this Dan Maples course is worth a drive.

Hang Gliding and Ultralight Instruction

Jockey's Ridge State Park 252-441-7132; www.jockeysridgestatepark.com; Carolista Dr., MP 12, Bypass, Nags Head 27959. People with USHGA Hang 1 or other agency-approved certification may hang glide free of charge on the dunes at Jockey's Ridge. Register with the park office.

Kitty Hawk Kites 252-441-4124, 877-FLY THIS; www.kittyhawk.com; 3933 S. Croatan Hwy., MP 13, Bypass, Nags Head 27959. The world's largest hang-gliding school has been teaching students from ages 8 to 80 how to catch the wind since 1974. Beginner and advanced lessons are held on the soft sand dunes of Jockey's Ridge State Park. For an even more exciting flight, try tandem hang gliding while being towed behind a plane at altitudes up to a mile high. No experience is necessary for tandem gliding, and the activity is handicapped accessible. Ultralight tours and training also available.

Health and Fitness Clubs

Ashtanga Yoga Center 252-202-0345; www.ashtangayogaobx.com; Central Square Shopping Center, 2910 S. Croatan Hwy., MP 11, Bypass, Nags Head 27959. Introductory to advanced classes, special events, and retreats are offered in several disciplines of yoga.

Barrier Island Fitness Center 252-261-0100; www.bistation.com; Cypress Knee Trail, MP 1, Bypass, Kitty Hawk. Day and weekly passes provide access to an indoor pool, hot tub, sauna, steam room, tanning beds, massage therapists, aerobic and free weight equipment, and tennis courts, along with on-site babysitting and a cyber-arcade.

Knuckleup Family Fitness Center 252-255-1662; 3712 N. Croatan Hwy., MP 4.5, Bypass, Kitty Hawk 27949. Work out with kickboxing or jiu jitsu classes. Single classes available.

★ **Outer Banks Family YMCA** 252-449-8897; www.ymcashr.org; 3000 S. Croatan Hwy., MP 11, Bypass, Nags Head 27959. Open daily, this 28,000-square-foot center offers a wide range of equipment, facilities, and classes. Indoor facilities include a lap pool, hot tub, sauna, racquetball courts, cycling studio, and fitness center with FitLinxx strength training. Outdoors is a water park with waterslides, plus a skate park. Massage therapy and free child care are available. Nonmembers can purchase day, week, or monthly passes for individuals or families. Many hotels and vacation cottages also offer free passes to the Y.

Outer Banks Karate Academy & Self Defense Training Studio 252-441-6676; www.obxkarate.com; 4711 S. Croatan Hwy., Croatan Center, MP 17, Bypass, Nags Head 27959. Four-time world champion and Martial Arts Hall of Fame member Master Kym Rock offers classes in Shornji-Ryu, a traditional Japanese-style martial arts, as well as her "Fight Like a Girl" self-defense classes. Children as young as five can participate.

Outer Banks Yoga and Pilates 252-480-3214; www.outerbanksyoga.com; 5200 N. Virginia Dare Trail, MP 1.5, Bypass, Ocean Centre Shops, Kitty Hawk 27949. Single, three-class, and monthly passes available.

Nature Preserves and Eco-attractions

Cape Hatteras National Seashore 252-473-2111; www.nps.gov/caha; NC 12, Nags Head.
Short nature trails lead through the marsh near the Bodie Island Lighthouse. Daily
ranger programs, including bird walks, turtle talks, sound-side seining, and evening
campfires, are offered June through Labor Day. Stop at the Whalebone Junction Information Station for a current schedule.

Jennette's Pier 252-441-6421; www.jennettespier.net; 7223 S. Virginia Dare Trail, MP
16.5, Nags Head 27959. N.C. Aquarium facility preserves the tradition of pier fishing.
Nature exhibits in the pier house include the state's largest collection of mounted trophy
fish.

★ **Jockey's Ridge State Park** 252-441-7132; www.jockeysridgestatepark.com; Carolista
Dr., MP 12, Bypass, Nags Head 27959. Sunset is the most popular time to visit Jockey's
Ridge, when many make the pilgrimage up the 100-foot dune to enjoy a spectacular
360-degree view of the Outer Banks. The Visitor Center Museum provides exhibits and
films explaining the unique ecosystems, and two nature trails explore the maritime
thickets of stunted live oak slowly being buried by the sand. A handicapped-accessible
boardwalk leads out to the dune. Activities available include hang gliding and kite flying,
as well as kayaking, windsurfing, and swimming at the Soundside Road access. Sand-
boarding is permitted during the off-season with a permit. Activity programs, including
birding walks and kayak tours, are offered at the park all year. Admission and all programs are free.

Kitty Hawk Woods Coastal Reserve 252-261-8891; www.ncnerr.org; 983 W. Kitty Hawk
Rd., Kitty Hawk 27949. Nearly 2,000 acres of unspoiled maritime deciduous swamp,
forest, and marsh occupy the center of the town of Kitty Hawk. The Woods Road (NC
1206) runs through the heart of the preserve. Trails through the park can be accessed at
the end of Eckner Street, Amadas Road, and Birch Lane. High Bridge Creek is accessible
by boat from the public boat ramp on Bob Perry Road. **Sandy Run Park** on the Woods
Road has a canoe and kayak launch and a short boardwalk through the wetlands.

★ **Nags Head Woods Ecological Preserve** 252-441-2525; www.nature.org; 701 W. Ocean
Acres Dr., MP 9.5, Bypass, Kill Devil Hills 27948. Over 1,000 acres of maritime forest,
protected by the Nature Conservancy, includes pine and hardwoods, with some trees
over 500 years old, providing a nesting area for over 50 species of birds. Trails and dirt
roads crisscross the preserve, including the **Town Trail**, leading down to the sound.
Maps are available at the Visitor Center.

Outer Banks Arboretum and Teaching Garden 252-473-4290; dare.ces.ncsu.edu; Mustian St., Kill Devil Hills 27948. Located next to the Thomas A. Baum Senior Center, this
pleasant spot has gardens of dune, aquatic, butterfly, and native plants, including many
pest- and salt-resistant species, labeled for identification.

Hunting

The National Park Service allows waterfowl hunting on Bodie Island by registration request
only and limits hunting through a lottery to 20 requests a day. You can get a Reservation
Request Form (RRF) by picking one up at NPS Outer Banks Group Headquarters at Fort
Raleigh National Historic Site in Manteo; by sending a written request to: HUNT, Cape Hatteras National Seashore, 1401 National Park Rd., Manteo, NC 27954; or by printing the form
from the NPS Web site (www.nps.gov/caha) and mailing it to the Manteo address, with a

self-addressed stamped envelope for your notification. Twenty permanent blinds on Bodie Island are assigned to successful lottery applicants.

Lottery winners must be present at the Whalebone Junction Information Station for the hunting blind drawing at 5 AM on the day of the reservation. Any blinds remaining after the day's drawing are assigned on a first-come, first-served basis to walk-in hunters.

To hunt legally at Cape Hatteras National Seashore you must have on your person a valid North Carolina hunting license with North Carolina waterfowl privilege (888-248-6834; www.ncwildlife.org) and a Federal Duck Stamp.

Outer Banks Waterfowl and Fishing Guide Service 252-261-7842; www.outerbankswater fowl.com; 4740 Elm Ct., Kitty Hawk 27949. Captain Vic Berg and his experienced guides take hunters after as many as 27 different species of wildfowl during the hunting seasons (usually scattered from October to January). He also leads fishing trips in the sound and bird-watching excursions.

Spectator Sports

From late May to early August, the **Outer Banks Daredevils** (252-441-0600; www.obxdare devils.com), made up of top-notch college players, play ball against rivals in the Coastal Plain League, the hottest and largest collegiate wood-bat summer baseball league in the nation. Daredevils merchandise is a favorite souvenir. Games are played at the **First Flight Baseball Complex**, 111 Veterans Drive, Kill Devil Hills.

Many tournaments featuring some the top names in surfing, surf kayaking, and kite-boarding are held annually on the Banks. The sound behind Penguin Isle and Windmill Point is a good place to check out the kiteboarding action.

Nags Head Woods, a maritime forest preserve

Tennis Courts

Public courts are located in Kill Devil Hills at MP 6 on the Bypass next to the Kill Devil Hills Fire Department, and at MP 8.5 on Mustian Street next to the Kill Devil Hills library and water plant. In Nags Head, public courts are located at MP 10 behind Kelly's Restaurant.

Water Sports

Kiteboarding and Windsurfing

Steady winds and shallow, protected water stretching for miles create what many boarders consider a paradise for wind-and-water sports. Wind gypsies make their way to the shallow waters of Roanoke and Pamlico Sounds to experience the finest conditions on the East Coast. For the more adventurous, the ocean waves are just a few steps away.

Kiteboarding, sometimes called kitesurfing, has a steep learning curve and requires a great deal of upper-body strength. Equipment for kiteboarding is generally not available for rent, but those interested can take a lesson that includes equipment. Those who complete Professional Air Sports Association–certified training courses may qualify to rent equipment. **Kitty Hawk Kites** also has equipment for sale.

Windsurfing is also sometimes called sailboarding. Equipment for this sport is available for rent from a number of different services, including **Cavalier Surf Shop** (252-441-7349), **Lifesaver Rent Alls** (252-441-6048), **Moneysworth** (252-261-6999), and **Ocean Atlantic Rentals** (252-441-7823).

Windmill Point and the Nags Head Sound Access at MP 16 are considered excellent spots for beginners learning both kiteboarding and windsurfing. More advanced boarders can launch from the Promenade (252-261-4900) at the foot of the Wright Memorial Bridge or from the sound access at Jockey's Ridge. Both are considered prime "bump-and-jump" spots.

Experienced boarders able to handle strong currents, shore break, sandbars, and other hazards can try their skills on the ocean. Popular spots to launch include Jennette's Pier, Coquina Beach, and, for true experts with no fear of sharks, Oregon Inlet.

Kitty Hawk Kites Kite Boarding Center 252-441-0265, 877-FLY-THIS; www.khk kiteboarding.com; 6804 S. Croatan Hwy., MP 15.5, Bypass, Nags Head 27959. PASA-certified instructors offer beginner lessons in kiteboarding that start with mastering the kite on land before heading for the sound. Private lessons and a weekend Fast Track camp are available.

Kitty Hawk Watersports 252-441-2756; www.kittyhawkwatersports.com; 6920 S. Croatan Hwy., MP 16, Bypass, Nags Head 27959. Introductory and private windsurfing lessons are available in shallow waters at this sound-side location. Tandem windsurfing available.

Parasailing

Spectacular views of Jockey's Ridge and the Wright Memorial reward high-flying parasailers.

Kitty Hawk Watersports 252-441-2756; www.kittyhawkwatersports.com; 6920 S. Croatan Hwy., MP 16, Bypass, Nags Head 27959.

The Promenade Watersports 252-261-4400; www.promenadewatersports.com; 105 Promenade Ln., MP 0, Bypass, Kitty Hawk 27949.

Waterworks Sports Center 252-441-8875, 252-441-6822; www.waterworks.ws; 7649 S. Virginia Dare Trail, Nags Head–Manteo Causeway, Nags Head 27959.

Snorkeling and Scuba

The Graveyard of the Atlantic brings divers from around the world to see German U-boats, 18th-century pirate ships, and everything in between on the bottom of the ocean. Warm Gulf Stream waters make diving possible year round.

Dive Shops and Charters

Nags Head Diving 252-473-1356; www.nagsheaddiving.com. NAUI instructors offer a full roster of classes, including a resort course for those who want to try scuba diving for the first time. Beach dives are offered to historic wrecks, including the *Huron*, *Carl Gerhard*, and *Kyzickes*. Equipment rentals also available.

Outer Banks Dive Center 252-449-8349; www.obxdive.com; 3917 S. Croatan Hwy., MP 12.5, Bypass, Nags Head 27959. Located across from Jockey's Ridge, Outer Banks Dive is a full-service shop offering sales, rentals, and repairs, plus instruction for all levels, and guided beach and charter boat dives to historic wrecks.

Shore Snorkeling and Diving

The Outer Banks is the only place on the East Coast where historic wrecks can be reached from the beach. Because they require you to swim on the surface through the surf, beach dives, while shallower than boat dives, are more physically demanding. You need to be in good physical shape and a strong swimmer.

Some of the more popular shore dives along the Central Beaches include the **Triangle Wrecks** (two ships, a freighter and a tanker, now in three pieces) near MP 7, 2nd Street access, Kill Devil Hills, about 150 yards offshore in 20 feet of water; and the *Explorer*, a tugboat that went down in 1919 about 150 yards offshore in 20 feet of water, about 100 yards north of the Nags Head Fishing Pier. The *Huron*, a U.S. gunship that ran aground in 1877, located at MP 11 near the Bladen Street access, 250 yards north of the Nags Head Fishing Pier in 25 feet of water, is marked with buoys during the summer months.

Surfing

The Outer Banks have some of the best breaks on the East Coast, and reports of a storm in the Atlantic set hordes of surfers in motion as they race to catch the big waves. On the Central Beaches, the areas around the piers have some of most consistent surf. You can catch a surf report on the local radio stations or call any of the local surf shops for expert advice. Online, you can see reports direct from the beach twice a day at www.obxsurfinfo.com.

The great surfing has attracted many professional surfboard makers as permanent residents. Called "shapers" in surf lingo, some of these board artists own local surf shops; others work freelance. Their designs push the boundaries of boarding ever outward. Some of the best known local shapers are Murray Ross, Pat McManus, Tim Nolte, Lynn Shells, Steve Hess, Ted Kearns, and Robert "Redman" Manville. Other locally made boards to look for include New Sun, Ability, Avalon, Broken Barriers, Cherry, Future Foils, Hooked, Hot and Nasty, Tropix, Secret Spot, and TK Shapes. Serious surfers can order a board custom crafted by a master just for them.

Surf Shops

The many surf shops along the Central Beaches sell equipment for a variety of board sports. Some also offer rentals and instruction.

Cavalier Surf Shop 252-441-7349; 4324 S. Virginia Dare Trail, MP 13.5, Beach Rd., Nags Head 27959. Family-run shop, in operation since 1960, offers sales and rentals as well as private and group surfing lessons.

Outer Banks Boarding Company 252-441-1939; www.outerbanksboarding.com; 103 E. Morning View Pl., MP 10.5, Bypass, Nags Head 27959. The shop of board-shaping legend Lynn Shell carries his signature Shell Shapes, plus high-tech boards from other top designers. Rentals for every ability and surfing lessons from top pros available.

The Pit Surf Shop 252-480-3128; www.pitsurf.com; 1209 S. Croatan Hwy., MP 9, Bypass, Kill Devil Hills 27948. A great hangout for surfers of all ages, this shop carries its own line of boards made by expert local shapers and is especially friendly to beginning surfers. Boards are available for sale or rent, and lessons and surf camps are offered for beginning and intermediate riders.

Secret Spot Surf Shop 252-441-4030; 2815 S. Croatan Hwy., MP 11, Bypass, Nags Head 27959. Shop owner Steve Hess shapes custom boards and stocks a variety of new and used boards for sale or rent. Beginner and intermediate lessons available.

SOS Enterprises 252-441-1357; 6806 S. Virginia Dare, MP 16, Beach Rd., Nags Head 27959. Rent boards or bikes, or shop for gear and cool threads at the sign of the blue tiki just across from the beach. Upstairs, the **Sandbar** serves hot dogs, sandwiches, and Hawaiian shave ice.

Wave Riding Vehicles 252-261-7952; www.waveridingvehicles.com; 4812 N. Croatan Hwy., MP 2.5, Bypass, Kitty Hawk 27949. The largest surfboard manufacturer on the East Coast is located across the bridge in Currituck County and employs many top shapers. Its retail shop in Kitty Hawk carries the full line of WRV surf, body, skim, snow, and skate boards, plus many hard-to-find brands and cool swim and surf wear with the popular "wave of porpoises" logo, besides offering rentals and repairs.

Whalebone Surf Shop 252-441-6747, 877-855-1975; www.whalebonesurfshop.com; 2214 S. Croatan Hwy., MP 10, Bypass, Nags Head 27959. Open for more than 30 years, Whalebone stocks boards by top shapers for sale and BZ and INT soft-tops for rent. Lessons for beginners never have more than three students per instructor. T-shirts with the shop's skull and crossed surfboards logo are popular even with nonsurfers.

Surfing Instruction and Camps

★ **Hukilau Surf Camp** 252-441-7548; www.surfcampobx.com. Aimed at middle and high school students, these one-day introductions to surfing are a real bargain, offering one-on-one instruction by experienced surfers, all equipment, and a safe environment. Kayak camp is also available.

The Hukilau Surf Camp teaches the essentials of the sport in a single day.

Kitty Hawk Sports Kayak and Surf School 252-261-0145, 866-702-5061;
www.khkss.com; 6150 N. Croatan Hwy., MP 1, Kitty Hawk 27949. Surf clinics, private
lessons, and three-day surf camps include rentals in the rate. Combination surf and
kayak packages available.

Ocean Atlantic Rentals & Surfrider School 252-441-7823, 800-635-9559; www.ocean
atlanticrentals.com; MP 10, Beach Rd., Nags Head 27959. Lessons include surfboard,
wet suit, and wax.

Wildlife Spotting

Bird-watching

With over 400 species documented on the Outer Banks, the area is one of the prime destinations for bird-watching on the East Coast. The annual **Wings Over Water** festival in
November introduces many birding hot spots to newcomers through guided expeditions.

The maritime thickets of Jockey's Ridge State Park are visited by large numbers of
migrating songbirds in late summer and fall, and migrating raptors can be seen along the
Soundside Trail.

The nature trails around **Bodie Island Lighthouse** yield views of wading birds and wintering waterfowl, while **Coquina Beach** across the road is visited by loons in winter, and
other shorebirds during the spring and fall migrations. The world's largest population of
black-capped petrels summers just off this coast.

Nags Head Woods is the nesting spot of over 50 bird species. A list is available in the
Visitor Center. **Kitty Hawk Woods** is equally well populated, and guides are being developed for this area.

Outer Banks Birdwatchers (252-449-0808; 6705 S. Croatan Hwy., MP 15.5 Bypass,
Nags Head 27959) and **Wild Birds Unlimited** (252-261-3155; www.wbu.com; 3832 N.
Croatan Hwy., Kitty Hawk Plaza, MP 4, Bypass, Kitty Hawk 27949) both have a wealth of
information about local bird-watching opportunities, as well as guidebooks and sighting
equipment.

Marine Mammals

Report dead or stranded whales, dolphins, porpoises, or seals as soon as possible to the
National Marine Fisheries Service's **North Carolina Marine Mammal Stranding Network**
at 919-728-8762.

Bodie Island Adventures / Waterworks Sports Center 252-441-8875, 252-441-6822;
www.waterworks.ws; 7649 S. Virginia Dare Trail, Nags Head–Manteo Causeway, Nags
Head 27959. Daily cruises aboard the *Miss Bodie Island* 40-foot pontoon boat offer sightings of dolphins and tours of Wanchese and Manteo harbors.

★ **Nags Head Dolphin Watch** 252-449-8999; www.dolphinwatch.com; 7517 S. Virginia
Dare Trail, Nags Head–Manteo Causeway, Nags Head 27959. This group of independent
researchers studies the Atlantic bottlenose dolphins that make their home in Roanoke
Sound. Two-hour journeys aboard a canopied pontoon boat, offered May through September, are guided by naturalists with a wealth of information about the dolphins, many
of whom have individual names. Reservations are suggested. The boat is handicapped
accessible and has a bathroom onboard.

SHOPPING

The Central Beaches have more shopping options than all the other parts of the Outer Banks combined.

Shopping Centers and Malls

Along the Bypass (US 158), national chains rub elbows with locally-owned shops in a some-times bewildering array of strip malls and shopping centers. A few, usually older, but often very interesting, shops survive over on the Beach Road (NC 12). Here are some of the more notable shopping stops, arranged by town.

KILL DEVIL HILLS

The Dare Centre MP 7, Bypass. Food Lion and Belk, a regional department store favorite, anchor this center.

Lifesaver Shops MP 9, Beach Rd. Small strip of shops on the Beach Road provides many vacation necessities.

Milepost 6 Plaza 252-480-0519; MP 6, Bypass. Small, easy-to-find strip mall houses a coffee shop, a wine and beer shop, plus pottery and beading stores.

Seagate North Shopping Center MP 5.5, Bypass. Locally owned stores and a produce stand make this a good stop.

Seashore Shops MP 9, Beach Rd. Home decor is the specialty here.

KITTY HAWK

Buccaneer's Walk MP 4.5, Bypass. Lots of specialty stores in this nautically themed center.

Kitty Hawk Plaza 252-261-8200; MP 4, Bypass. Specialty stores include an army navy sur-plus store and an excellent thrift store with lots of bargains.

Ocean Centre MP 1, Beach Rd. New strip of shops at the northern end of the Beach Road offers food and shopping options.

Ocean Plaza MP 4.5, Bypass. Trendy boutiques and specialty foods.

Shoreside Center MP 1, Bypass. National chains including Wal-Mart, Radio Shack, and Dollar Tree are found at this large complex, as well as several locally owned shops. RVs may overnight in the lot here.

NAGS HEAD

Central Square MP 11, Bypass. Noted for its group of antiques stores.

Croatan Centre MP 14, Bypass. Located across from the Outer Banks Hospital.

Gallery Row MP 10. Set between the highways, this is the largest concentration of galleries on the beach.

Jockey's Ridge Crossing www.jockeysridgecrossing.com; MP 12.5, Bypass. Located at the site of the original Nags Head Pavilion across from the Jockey's Ridge dunes, this two-story center offers refreshments, shopping, and an indoor climbing wall, plus planned activities most summer evenings.

Outer Banks Mall MP 14, Bypass. Over 30 specialty shops, restaurants, and department stores, including Sears, are located next to the Outer Banks Hospital.

Pirate's Quay Shoppes MP 11.5, Bypass. Sophisticated and fun shops and boutiques next to the YMCA skate park. Look for the huge propeller out front.

Surfside Plaza 252-441-9969; MP 13, Bypass. Located between the highways, Surfside is notable for its proximity to the sands.

Tanger Outlet Mall 252-441-5634; www.tangeroutlet.com/nagshead; MP 16.5, Bypass. Discount shopping for name brands. Check for coupons on the Web site.

Antiques

MeMe's Antique Mall (252-449-6363); **Mystic Antiques & Collectibles** (252-441-1710); **Something Old, Something New** (252-480-30300); 2910 S. Virginia Dare Trail, Central Square, MP 11, Bypass, Nags Head 27959. Three antiques stores located in Central Square present the Central Beaches' largest concentration of vintage collectibles and antiques.

Southern Soldier Antique Mall 252-491-2355; www.southernsoldierantiques.com; 7512 Caratoke Hwy., Jarvisburg 27947. Located 8 miles north of the bridge, this antiques destination has over 10 dealers specializing in Civil War–era and military antiques and hosts monthly auctions and flea markets

Books

Books-N-Things 252-261-4353; 5330 N. Virginia Dare Trail, Ocean Centre, MP 1.5, Beach Rd., Kitty Hawk 27949. Small bookstore opposite the ocean is a great place to pick up a bestseller to read on the beach.

★ **The Island Bookstore** 252-255-5590; www.islandbooksobx.com; 3712 N. Croatan Hwy., MP 4.5, Bypass, Kitty Hawk 27949. With sister stores in Corolla and Duck, the Island Bookstore is a powerhouse on the local literary scene, hosting book signings, author readings, book clubs, and many special events. Staffed by experienced readers, these full-service, independent stores stock thousands of titles and will special order anything they don't have on the shelves. Local subjects are a specialty, as well as large collections of children's titles, audio books, and magazines. *New York Times* best sellers are discounted.

North Carolina Books 252-441-2141; 1500 N. Croatan Hwy., MP 7.5, Bypass, Kill Devil Hills 27948. Located in the building of the Times Printing Co., publisher of the *Coastland Times*, this bookstore offers a big selection of used paperbacks, as well as reduced-price hardcovers. Paperbacks accepted for trade-in credit.

Outer Banks Books 252-441-2682; www.obxbooks.com; 5000 S. Croatan Hwy., Outer Banks Mall, MP 14.5, Bypass, Nags Head 27959. Cookbooks, audio books, children's titles, and coffee table books, among much else, can be found at this store in the Outer Banks Mall, as well as deep discounts on popular fiction and nonfiction and a cyber café where you can get connected.

★ **Roanoke Press and Croatan Bookery Limited** 252-480-1890; 2006 S. Croatan Hwy., MP 10, Bypass, Kill Devil Hills 27948. Another bookshop operated by Times Printing, this one stocks over 100,000 volumes of mostly used and antiquarian books, including many books on North Carolina and Outer Banks topics, some printed by the *Times* itself. Next door, a vintage printing press is sometimes open for viewing.

Clothing

Donna Designs 252-441-6232; Surfside Plaza, MP 13, Bypass, Nags Head. Hand-painted clothing created by a local artist sports fun, beachy designs.

Lil' Grass Shack and Bikini Hut 252-441-2221; 5000 S. Croatan Hwy., Outer Banks Mall, MP 14, Bypass, Nags Head 27959. Try on a new swimsuit or a fun dress for beach or evening in the grass shack dressing rooms.

Lilly's Closet 252-441-2355; www.lillyscloset.net; 3810 N. Croatan Hwy., Buccaneer's Walk, MP 4.5, Bypass, Kitty Hawk 27949. Designer togs for tots from newborn to age 10, plus locally handmade sweaters.

The Mule Shed 252-441-4115; www.themuleshed.com; 5000 N. Croatan Hwy., Outer Banks Mall, MP 14.5, Bypass, Nags Head 27959. An Outer Banks favorite for over 25 years, this shop carries casual fashions from top designers, plus sophisticated jewelry and handbags.

Rock-A-Bye Baby 252-480-2297; www.rockabyebabyobx.com; 4711 S. Croatan Hwy., Croatan Centre, MP 14, Bypass, Nags Head 27959. New and used baby clothes, furniture, and toys, plus maternity and baby shower supplies, and baby equipment rentals for vacationing families.

Shore-Fit Sunwear 252-441-4560; www.obxsunwear.com; 100 E. Helga St., MP 5.5, Bypass, Kill Devil Hills 27948. Swimwear boutique offers fashionable solutions to fit every figure, including many plus-size selections, as well as beach coverups, bags, and sandals.

Consignment and Thrift

A Penny Saved Thrift & Consignment Shop 252-441-8024, Seagate North, MP 5.5, Bypass, Kill Devil Hills 27948.

CHKD Thrift Store 252-255-5437; www.chkd.org; 3838 N. Croatan Hwy., Kitty Hawk Plaza, MP 4.5, Bypass, Kitty Hawk 27949. Thrift store benefits the Children's Hospital of the King's Daughters.

Hotline Pink 252-261-8164; www.ncadvos.com; 4140 N. Croatan Hwy., MP 3.5, Bypass, Kitty Hawk 27949. Proceeds from sales at this hot pink store benefit the local women's shelter and crisis intervention center. Another store with even more good stuff is located in Kill Devil Hills (252-441-1244; 2001 S. Croatan Hwy.).

Crafts

Beach Memories 252-441-7277; www.obxbeachmemories.com; 2236 S. Croatan Hwy., Plaza Del Sol, MP 10, Bypass, Nags Head 27959. Scrapbook supplies.

Cloud Nine 252-441-2992; 3022 S. Croatan Hwy., Pirate's Quay Shoppes, MP 11.5, Bypass, Nags Head 27959. Create your own jewelry with beads from this creative store, or buy a piece of finished jewelry created by locals.

Garden of Beadin' 252-449-5055; www.obxbeads.com; 2200 N. Croatan Hwy., Milepost 6 Plaza, MP 6, Bypass, Kill Devil Hills 27948. Take a beading class or just get a cup of coffee at the Front Porch Café next door and browse the many beads and semiprecious stones available. Children's beading projects and paint-your-own pottery next door make this a great rainy-day stop.

Glazin' Go Nuts Paint Your Own Pottery 252-441-2134; www.obxpottery.com; 2200 N. Croatan Hwy., Milepost 6 Plaza, MP 6, Bypass, Kill Devil Hills 27948.

Island Art Supply & Custom Framing 252-255-5078; www.islandartsupplies.com; 5230 N. Virginia Dare Trail, Ocean Centre, MP 1, Beach Rd., Kitty Hawk 27959.

Outer Banks Bear Factory 252-441-1212; www.obxbearfactory.com; 3941 S. Croatan Hwy., Jockey's Ridge Crossing, MP 12.5, Bypass, Nags Head 27959. A great spot for birthday parties.

The Scrapbook Store and More 252-480-2018; 3105 N. Croatan Hwy., Clark St. Corner, MP 9, Bypass, Kill Devil Hills 27948. Scrapbooking supplies and classes.

Factory Outlet Centers

BrewThru Outlet 252-453-2878; www.brewthru.com; 3101 N. Croatan Hwy., MP 5.5, Bypass, Kill Devil Hills 27948. Licensed beer apparel and memorabilia, plus over 50 different Brew Thru shirts, including annual designs dating back to 1977.

Soundfeet Shoes Outlet 252-441-0715; www.soundfeet.com; 3840 N. Croatan Hwy., Kitty Hawk Plaza, MP 4, Bypass, Kitty Hawk 27949. The Outer Banks' favorite shoe store offers discount prices at this location on sandals, clogs, athletic shoes, and more.

Tanger Outlet Mall 252-441-5634; www.tangeroutlet.com/nagshead; 7100 S. Croatan Hwy., MP 16.5, Bypass, Nags Head 27959. Familiar names with guaranteed discounts. Open all year.

Gifts

Christmas Mouse 252-441-8111; www.christmasmouse.com; 2401 S. Croatan Hwy., MP 10.5, Bypass, Nags Head 27959. It's Christmas all year at this store full of holiday cheer and gift ideas.

The Cotton Gin 252-449-2387; www.cottongin.com; 5151 S. Croatan Hwy., MP 14.5, Bypass, Nags Head 27959. Southern tradition meets coastal charm in room after room of gifts, home and garden decor, dolls, collectibles, and holiday decorations. The original store in Jarvisburg (252-491-2387; Hwy. 158) has an even bigger selection, plus a wine-tasting room.

The Cyber Dog USA 252-449-0331; www.thecyberdogusa.com; 3105 N. Croatan Hwy., Seagate North, MP 5.5, Bypass, Kill Devil Hills 27948. Healthy alternatives and "barking parking" service available by the hour.

Elizabeth Lord 252-261-5859; www.elizabethlordnaturals.com; 3810 N. Croatan Hwy., Buccaneer's Walk, MP 4.5, Bypass, Kitty Hawk 27948. Healthy skin care and bath products are hand made on the Outer Banks with natural ingredients and essential oils.

Puzzles, Pranks & Games 252-261-4323; 3810E N. Croatan Hwy., Buccaneer's Walk, MP 4.5, Bypass, Kitty Hawk 27949. Extensive selection of puzzles, prank gifts, and board games, including "Super Heat Surf" designed by local surfboard shaper Steve Head.

Salty Paws Biscuits 252-480-2284, 888-949-PAWS; www.saltypawsbiscuits.com; 3723 N. Croatan Hwy., Ocean Plaza, MP 4.5, Bypass, Kitty Hawk 27949. Homemade all-natural dog treats in 16 flavors and beach toys for dogs are featured at this dog-friendly store.

Shipwreck 252-441-5739; 7746 S. Virginia Dare Trail, Nags Head–Manteo Causeway, Nags Head 27959. Stop on the causeway for driftwood and shells, plus local crafts and scenic views.

Jewelry

Dare Jewelers 252-441-1112; 5000 S. Croatan Hwy., Outer Banks Mall, MP 14, Bypass, Nags Head 27959. Handcrafted 14K gold sea-life jewelry, and locally created stained-glass designs.

Diamonds 'n Dunes 252-255-0001; www.diamondsanddunes.com; 3708 N. Croatan Hwy., Suite 4, Harbor Bay Shops, MP 4, Bypass, Kitty Hawk 27949. A showroom full of innovative and sophisticated jewelry designs that capture the beauty of the ocean.

Gold-N-Gifts 252-449-2900; 3105 N. Croatan Hwy., Seagate North, MP 5.5, Bypass, Kill Devil Hills 27948. Locally owned store has the largest selection of charms on the beach. Free jewelry cleaning.

Halloran & Company 252-480-3132; www.halloranandco.com; 4711 S. Croatan Hwy., Croatan Centre, MP 14, Bypass, Nags Head 27959. Established in 1996, this is the only jeweler on the Outer Banks licensed to sell official Wright Brothers First Flight Centennial jewelry and ornaments.

Jewelry by Gail 252-441-5387; www.jewelrybygail.com; 207 Driftwood St., Gallery Row, Nags Head 27959. Located on Gallery Row, the shop of nationally recognized jewelry artist Gail Kowalski exhibits "hot off the beach" designs plus a popular line of Outer Banks lighthouse charms in gold and silver.

Lone Wolff Trading Co. 252-449-5111; www.lonewolff.com; 210 E. Gallery Row, Nags Head 27959. Specializing in affordable jewelry made of sterling silver and semiprecious stones.

Natural Creations Fine Jewelry 252-255-2015; www.obxjeweler.com; 5400-H N. Croatan Hwy., Shoreside Center, MP 1, Kitty Hawk 27949. Full-service shop offers loose diamonds and custom-made engagement and wedding bands, plus many pieces of nautical jewelry.

Kitchenware and Home Decor

A Little Added Touch 252-255-5710; www.alittleaddedtouch.com; 2407 N. Croatan Hwy., MP 6, Bypass, Kill Devil Hills 27948. Home accents in bold colors range from clever to sophisticated for every taste and every room.

Nags Head Hammocks 252-441-6115, 800-344-6433; www.nagsheadhammocks.com; 1801 S. Croatan Hwy., MP 9.5, Bypass, Kill Devil Hills 27948. Handcrafted on the Outer Banks since 1974 of materials selected to withstand the harsh weather of the coast, rope hammocks, swings, and chairs are beautifully displayed in a relaxing landscaped setting.

This Is The Life 252-449-5433; www.thisisthelifeonline.com; 3810 N. Croatan Hwy., Buccaneers Walk, MP 4.5, Bypass, Kitty Hawk 27949. Rachel Ashwell Shabby Chic bedding and a complete children's shop.

*Free sails on an authentic shad boat are offered
every summer by the Maritime Museum in Manteo.*

5

ROANOKE ISLAND:
Manteo and Wanchese

Mystery and the Mother Vine

Only 12 miles long and about 3 miles wide, Roanoke Island packs a lot of history into a small, conveniently toured area. Visitors staying elsewhere on the Outer Banks often make a day trip to Roanoke. However, if you are especially interested in history, you'll find a stay on the island rewarding.

This is the location of the famous Lost Colony, the earliest attempt by England to settle men, women, and children in the New World. No one is sure what became of the colony, although speculation and archaeological investigations continue. Visitors have plenty of opportunity to form their own opinions. *The Lost Colony* outdoor drama, Fort Raleigh National Historical Park, and the state-run Roanoke Island Festival Park all present pieces of the puzzle.

The island of Roanoke rose to importance even before Sir Walter Raleigh attempted to place his ill-fated colony here. Its Native American name, unchanged from then till now, indicates that it was a major manufacturing point for *roanoke,* elsewhere called *wampum,* the shell beads used as currency by the natives. The word *roanoke* literally meant "money."

Early settlers thought they were coming to a paradise. Besides the ample fish and shellfish in the surrounding waters, the area was renowned for its grapevines. The colonists all disappeared, but one of the grapevines growing then lives on. The so-called Mother Vine, estimated to be more than 400 years old, continues to thrive in Manteo.

Many landmarks refer to the island's history. The two major towns, Manteo and Wanchese, are named for two Native American chiefs. The youths were taken to England by an early voyage of exploration and returned with Raleigh's expeditions. Their roles in the history of the settlement are part of the mystery, but Manteo is generally believed to have been friendly with the newcomers, while Wanchese proved to be hostile. The story is told in fictionalized form in a film shown daily at Roanoke Island Festival Park.

Oddly, the feelings of the two chiefs are reflected today in the attitudes of the two villages on the island. Manteo, at the northern end of Roanoke, welcomes guests with a wide variety of attractions and accommodations. Wanchese, on the island's southern tip, works hard to maintain its traditions as a fishing village. You'll find few restaurants here, and fewer hotels. But the natives these days are friendly.

The island is easy to navigate. Two causeway bridges link it to the mainland: the old

Business US 64/264 bridge, the William B. Umstead Memorial, at the northern tip of the island, and the newer Bypass US 64/264 bridge, dubbed the Virginia Dare Memorial, the longest bridge in the state at 5.25 miles. The Bypass bisects the island and continues on to Nags Head and the main beaches of the Outer Banks. Traveling east on the Bypass, the two roads meet at a traffic light. Turn north to reach Manteo. Turn south to reach Wanchese.

MANTEO

To outward appearances, Manteo might be any other small fishing village turned to tourism. Narrow streets lead down to the bay. Waterside shops offer practical goods and souvenirs. Boats from far and wide line the docks.

But in most fishing villages, you won't find ladies and gents dressed in the finery of 400 years ago strolling the streets and gardens. In Manteo it's not unusual to encounter Queen Elizabeth I, dressed in her brocades, lace ruffs, and strings of pearls, several times a day.

The northern end of Roanoke Island is virtually a historical park, where the year 1587, when Raleigh's colony is believed to have occupied the site, is celebrated. Here, under hun-

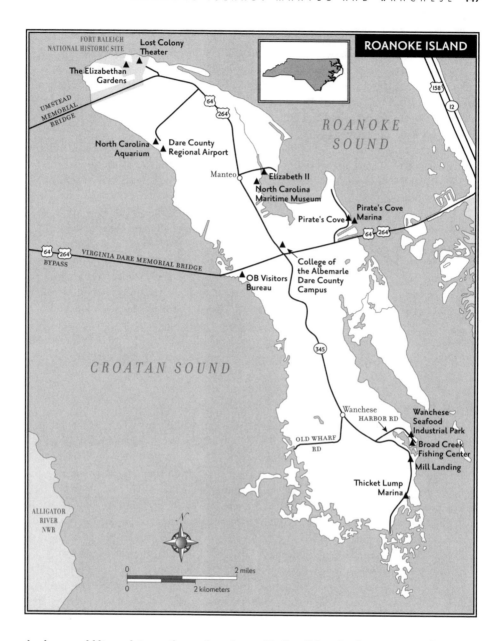

dred-year-old live oak trees, the outdoor drama *The Lost Colony* has been presented nightly every summer for over 70 years. Its **Waterside Theatre** sits adjacent to **Fort Raleigh National Historic Site**, where a visitor center displays the latest archaeological findings, and the **Elizabethan Gardens**, a living tribute to the 16th century.

The main town of Manteo lies a few miles south down a broad avenue. Many of the town's restaurants, motels, and a new complex of government buildings lie along this avenue, US 64/264 Business, which runs along the back of the town's historic downtown.

Stretching from the highway to the waterfront, this historic district, about 10 blocks square, is small, charming, and easily walked. A boardwalk rims the water's edge, with great views any time of day that turn superb at dawn and dusk. Locally owned shops and bed-and-breakfast inns have colonized the historic homes and renovated storefronts.

An ambitious 20-year plan, recently completed under the supervision of Mayor John Wilson, himself an architect and innkeeper, revitalized the historic waterfront of Manteo. Adopted to prepare the town for the 400th anniversary of Raleigh's original colony, the plan resulted in the building of the *Elizabeth II* replica ship, christened at a ceremony attended by Princess Anne of Britain in 1984.

In the years since, many other elements of the plan have come to fulfillment, including a boardwalk and public marina, as well as shops and condominiums along the waterfront. The **Tranquil House Inn**, built to resemble a hotel that welcomed guests in the early 1900s, opened its doors in 1988.

The state of North Carolina has taken an active interest in Manteo and its history, resulting in a cluster of government-subsidized attractions. **Roanoke Island Festival Park,** which completely transformed the environmentally challenged Ice Island, is located directly across Dough Creek from the historic waterfront. It provides the community with a history museum, indoor and outdoor performance venues, plus much else, including a large, free parking lot close to downtown. Other state-funded attractions in Manteo include branches of the **North Carolina Aquarium** and the **North Carolina Maritime Museum.**

Manteo's most precious resource, however, is the people who make this their home. A mix of old boat-building families and newer residents who fell in love with the small town's story, the citizens of Manteo extend a warm welcome to visitors from near and far.

WANCHESE

No one is sure what the word *wanchese* meant in the native Algonquian language, but there's no doubt what the word stands for today. The village of Wanchese is all about fishing, and all about preserving this traditional way of life.

To find Wanchese, head south down the main highway from Manteo to the other end of Roanoke Island. The road, now NC 345 / Mill Landing Road, meanders through marsh before reaching the more populated area at the southern tip of the island. You'll look in vain for a downtown commercial district. All the business of Wanchese takes place on the docks.

A leisurely drive or bicycle ride along the village's winding roads takes you past houses with boats, crab pots, and horses in the back yard. Family homes often have their own docks and piers, with fishing boats tied up alongside. There may be a boat-building shed around back. A recently adopted zoning plan preserves the traditional right of families to both live and work on their land. It also puts some major roadblocks in the way of development, which local residents feared would drive up their property values, a process already witnessed in Manteo.

Many of the roads bear the names of local families, some of whom have been here for centuries, including Etheridge, Daniels, Baum, and Tillett. The Etheridge and Daniels families founded the now international **Wanchese Fish Company,** which remains under family control.

If you find yourself in a long line of slowly moving traffic, be patient. A new boat is likely making its way from boat shed to water. These frequent events turn into impromptu parades as utility teams take down and replace wires to let the big boats pass.

So Wanchese residents continue, as they have for centuries, to harvest the sea. There are only a few restaurants and a couple of bed-and-breakfast inns. The tourists who do find their way here come to board a charter fishing boat, to shop for a boat of their own, or to enjoy a meal snatched fresh from the ocean at the **Fisherman's Wharf Restaurant** (252-473-6004; 3683 Mill Landing Rd., Wanchese 27981). The Daniels family recently reopened this dining destination, closed for several years after a 30-year run. Along with spectacular views of Wanchese harbor, Fisherman's Wharf serves up the freshest seafood, accompanied by locally famous hushpuppies and chocolate pie.

The state has been busy in Wanchese, as in Manteo—but with a different aim. The state-sponsored **Wanchese Seafood Industrial Park,** devoted exclusively to marine-focused industries, opened in 1988. Locals were slow to warm to it, but in recent years the park on Harbor Road has become a beehive of boatbuilding and boat repair, specializing in custom sport fishing boats and commercial trawlers. A large charter fishing fleet makes its home here at **Broad Creek Fishing Center,** and **O'Neal's Sea Harvest** offers fresh seafood at a dockside market.

PIRATE'S COVE

Located between Roanoke Island and the main beaches to the east, Pirate's Cove is clearly visible—some would say all too visible—from the Manteo waterfront.

Today the site of a gated community, a resort, and a marina boasting a large and successful charter fishing fleet, Pirate's Cove was once called Midgett's Hammock, and before that, Ballast Point. Various bars and restaurants were established on the Hammock, and in the late 1980s development began on one of the region's first gated communities. Developer Glenn Futrell remains committed to keeping Pirate's Cove compatible with its unique location in the midst of a salt marsh. Nearly 500 acres here are protected as a bird sanctuary and wildlife preserve.

LODGING

Roanoke Island is a rarity among major vacation destinations. Not even one chain hotel or motel has taken root here. Nearly all accommodations are locally owned and operated, often by families who have lived on the Outer Banks for generations.

Accommodations on Roanoke Island fall into three categories. Three aging motor lodges, all dating from the 1950s and 1960s, are located along the main highway, Business US 64/264. Built nearly 50 years ago to house the early crowds coming to see *The Lost Colony,* these facilities weathered many storms and have the battered appearance to prove it. Amenities are of the most basic kind, although one, the Elizabethan Inn, recently added a full-scale year-round health club. In recent years the money has gone elsewhere, leaving little profit to replace aging rugs, but these family-run enterprises have generally chosen to spend what they have on keeping rooms clean and beds comfortable, rather than investing in a fresh coat of paint. They offer good bargains for travelers who don't demand upscale surroundings.

All other accommodations on Roanoke Island fall into the category of bed-and-breakfast inns of various sizes, from mid-size establishments with up to 30 rooms, to private houses renting out just a room or two. Ranging in price from inexpensive to super pricey, these rooms can provide good value, depending on the amenities and ambience included in the rate.

Other options for accommodations are cottages, apartments, and condominiums available through real estate and rental agencies. Sometimes these can be rented by the week or month.

You may occasionally see Business US 64/264 referred to as Virginia Dare Road. Locals never call it this, however, since NC 12, the Beach Road over on the main beaches, has almost the same name— Virginia Dare Trail.

Seasonal demand can drive up prices to extravagant heights. A room that rents for $59 a night in January may go for $199 in July. Valentine's Day weekend is also a time of high tariffs in Manteo, with its many romantic bed-and-breakfasts, as are May and June, when wedding parties come to town.

Many accommodations require two-night minimum stays on the weekends and three-night minimums on holiday weekends. Some also require notice of cancellations many days in advance in order to retrieve your deposit, up 50 percent of the total price.

Many accommodations on Roanoke Island are now pet-friendly, often with an additional pet fee required.

For last-minute vacations, you can check current vacancies at the official **Outer Banks Visitor Bureau** site: www.outer banks.org. The information is updated weekly from Memorial Day to Labor Day and during holiday periods.

Rate Categories

Inexpensive	up to $80
Moderate	$80 to $150
Expensive	$150 to $200
Very Expensive	$200 and up

These rates are per room, based on double occupancy. They do not include room taxes or any special service fees that may apply. The range is usually due to seasonal changes. Rates during the busy summer season and holiday weekends are often double or more the winter off-season rates.

Properties listed are open year round and are air-conditioned, unless otherwise noted.

Credit Cards

AE—American Express
CB—Carte Blanche
D—Discover Card
DC—Diners Club
J—JCB International Credit Card
MC—Master Card
V—Visa

Hotels and Inns

MANTEO

BURRUS HOUSE INN WATERFRONT SUITES

252-475-1636
www.burrushouseinn.com
509 S. US 64/264 Business, Manteo 27954
Price: Very Expensive
Credit Cards: AE, D, MC, V
Internet Access: Free WiFi

Away from the bustle but within walking distance of the Manteo waterfront, this classic Carolina beach house offers views of Shallowbag Bay from all eight elegantly appointed guest suites located in the main house and waterfront annex. All the suites have both bedrooms and sitting rooms with fireplaces, ceiling fans, refrigerators, microwaves, and coffeemakers. Baths feature Jacuzzi tubs and showers big enough for two. Kitchens are stocked with continental breakfast items, coffee, tea, wine, cheese, and crackers. Third-floor porches offer amazing water views. The tower suites with cathedral ceilings are popular among honeymooners. Private and quiet with few distractions, the Burrus is best suited to couples seeking a romantic getaway.

CAMERON HOUSE INN

252-473-6596, 800-279-8178
www.cameronhouseinn.com
300 Budleigh St., Manteo 27954
Price: Moderate to Expensive

Credit Cards: AE, MC, V
Internet Access: Free WiFi

Just a block from the Manteo waterfront, this restored 1919 arts-and-crafts bungalow features comfortable rooms with period decorations, plus lots of common areas where you can relax and mix with other guests. The six guest rooms and suites have tiled baths, TVs and VCRs, and coffeemakers. Favorite gathering places are the front porch, furnished with wicker furniture and an antique swing, and a large jasmine vine–covered back porch, where rocking chairs surround a fireplace. Breakfasts of muffins, juice, coffee, or tea are served in the dining room, and fresh-baked cookies and other goodies are available around the clock. Guests are free to raid the hospitality refrigerator for drinks and refreshments. The innkeepers are guidebook writers and very helpful in suggesting local activities. Although pets cannot be accommodated, the inn is home to several cats. Children are welcome. Bicycles are included in the room rate. Romance, spa, and sunset cruise packages are available. No smoking is allowed inside.

DUKE OF DARE MOTOR LODGE

252-473-2175
www.ego.net/us/nc/ob/duke/index.htm
100 S. US 64/264 Business, Manteo 27954
Price: Inexpensive
Credit Cards: MC, V

This very basic motel, owned and operated by the local Creef family, offers some of the lowest nightly rates around and is within walking distance of the Manteo waterfront. Built in 1964, the 57 rooms clearly have a few miles on them, but fishermen and bargain hunters will appreciate the inexpensive price. An outdoor pool (open in summer), cable TV, heat and air-conditioning, and in-room phones complete the amenities. Most rooms have two double beds, and some are handicapped accessible.

The friendly staff offers local directions and suggestions. Pets are welcome.

THE ELIZABETHAN INN

252-473-2101, 800-346-2466
www.elizabethaninn.com
814 US 64/264 Business, Manteo 27954
Price: Inexpensive to Expensive
Credit Cards: AE, D, MC, V
Internet: Phones with dataports

Roanoke Island's largest accommodation with 78 units has an attractive Tudor-style, timbered exterior that fits in well with the island's historic theme. Opened in 1954 and renovated in 2003, the motor lodge now has a professionally staffed spa with heated indoor pool, whirlpool, sauna, aerobic and yoga classes, and the latest fitness equipment, as well as a seasonal outdoor pool. Located on wooded property on the island's main drag, the Elizabethan Inn is conveniently situated midway between the *Lost Colony* attractions at the north end of the island and the restaurants and galleries of the Manteo waterfront. Guests can borrow bicycles to explore the bike path that runs in front of the inn. A variety of room types are available, including deluxe rooms with whirlpool bath and king bed, handicapped-accessible rooms, smoking and nonsmoking rooms, pet-friendly rooms, and efficiencies. All rooms have cable TV, and most have refrigerators.

THE INN AT MARSHES LIGHT

252-261-2131, 800-488-0738
www.kittyhawklandcompany.com
201 Fernando St., Manteo 27954

The new 30-room Inn at Marshes Light, opening in 2008, offers upscale overnight accommodations in the newest development on the Manteo waterfront. Looking out across Shallowbag Bay, it is connected by boardwalk to downtown Manteo and offers a swimming pool, plus marina with slips for residents and guest boaters.

ISLAND GUESTHOUSE AND COTTAGES

252-473-2434
www.theislandmotel.com
706 US 64/264 Business, Manteo 27954
Price: Inexpensive to Very Expensive
Credit Cards: AE, D, MC, V
Internet: Free WiFi

The Guesthouse, a cottage located on the main highway through town, offers friendly service and bright, clean accommodations at surprisingly reasonable rates both on and off season. The 14 rooms each have two double beds with fold-out cots available, plus cable TV and air-conditioning. All rooms are nonsmoking, and some are pet-friendly for a small additional fee. The private Tiki bar out back is a favorite place for guests to party. The property is popular for weddings, and an on-site wedding planner is available. A block away, at 708 Wingina Avenue, the same proprietors operate three theme cottages that offer more privacy as well as more upscale amenities. Each cottage has a full kitchen, Dolby surround sound home theater with a flat-screen TV, bath with two-person whirlpool tub, fireplace, and wireless Internet access. The owners are avid surfers and offer guests discounted surfing lessons. Both the guesthouse and cottages are within walking distance of the Manteo waterfront.

ROANOKE ISLAND INN

252-473-5511, 877-473-5511
www.roanokeislandinn.com
305 Fernando St., Manteo 27954
Price: Moderate to Expensive
Credit Cards: AE, MC, V

With an unsurpassed Manteo location and a long tradition of hospitality, the Roanoke Island Inn garners rave reviews from guests. Built in the 1860s for the current innkeeper's great-great-grandmother, the white building is surrounded by distinctive gardens and has grown into a sprawling hostelry looking out over the marsh at Shal-

lowbag Bay. A short stroll down the boardwalk brings you to the waterfront, and complimentary bikes are available to explore the town. The inn also provides dip nets if you want to try your hand at catching crabs. The inn's eight guestrooms each have private entrances, as well as access to a big porch overlooking the water. Two of the rooms are family suites that have small adjoining rooms with twin beds for children. Through the arched carriageway, you'll find a lush garden and koi pond, as well as a two-bedroom bungalow. A continental breakfast is served, and the innkeeper's pantry offers refreshments 24 hours a day. The Roanoke also has a private boat dock and a wedding chapel on the grounds. The inn is open seasonally.

The same innkeeper, who has served several terms as mayor of Manteo, rents other unique properties in the area. The Island Camp is on a private island accessible only by boat and comes complete with crab traps. You must have your own boat and cell phone. Reed Hill, a 1910 historic oceanfront cottage in Nags Head, can be rented by those who crave a stay in an authentic member of the "Unpainted Aristocracy."

THE SCARBOROUGH HOUSE

252-473-3849
www.scarboroughhouseinn.com
323 Fernando St., Manteo 27954
Price: Inexpensive to Moderate
Credit Cards: MC, V

The Scarborough family opens their home in the historic district to guests, offering a unique opportunity to experience life on a local level. Innkeepers Sally and Phil Scarborough, both natives of the Outer Banks, frequently chat with guests in their comfortable living room or while rocking on their porch overlooking the garden. All the guest rooms are furnished with genuine antiques and mementos of Roanoke Island history. The house enjoys a terrific location facing the harbor, just a block from the activity on Queen Elizabeth Avenue.

The Scarborough rents five rooms in the main house, plus two suites in a separate guesthouse and a cottage loft on the grounds. All have a refrigerator, coffeemaker, microwave, and TV, as well as a private bath. A light continental breakfast is offered in your room. The guesthouse suites also have Jacuzzi tubs for two and more complete kitchen facilities.

SCARBOROUGH INN

252-473-3979
www.scarborough-inn.com
524 US 64/264 Business, Manteo 27954
Price: Inexpensive to Moderate
Credit Cards: AE, D, DC, MC, V

The younger generation of the Scarborough family operates this inn on the main highway with the same island hospitality, outstanding cleanliness, and reasonable rates found at the Scarborough House not far away. The cedar-shake main inn has two-story covered porches to catch the island breezes. A total of 12 rooms, each with private bath, cable TV, refrigerator, microwave, and coffeemaker, are distributed among three buildings. One room is handicapped accessible. Complimentary bicycles are available for adult guests, and a light continental breakfast is served.

TRANQUIL HOUSE INN

252-473-1404, 800-458-7069
www.tranquilinn.com
405 Queen Elizabeth Ave., Manteo 27954
Price: Moderate to Very Expensive
Credit Cards: AE, D, MC, V
Internet: In-room broadband and free WiFi

Located directly on the Manteo boardwalk across from the *Elizabeth II*, this elegant inn is top-of-the-line among local hostelries. Richard Gere and Diane Lane stayed here while filming *Nights in Rodanthe,* and other notables seem to find their way here as well. Maybe it's the room service. The hotel's restaurant, **1587**, is one of the finest in the area.

Built of cypress, cedar, and stained glass to resemble historic inns of the past, the Tranquil House is in the heart of downtown Manteo, but its focus is outward toward Shallowbag Bay. The spacious second-floor patio overlooking the harbor is a favorite gathering spot at sunset. Each of the inn's 25 rooms is unique. Two queen suites have separate sitting rooms and two TVs. The three-story hotel does not have an elevator, but a ramp makes the first floor accessible to wheelchairs, with one guest room equipped for the handicapped. Up to two children under 18 may stay free with their parents. Continental breakfast, daily newspaper, bicycle rental, and an afternoon wine and cheese reception are included in the room rate.

THE WHITE DOE INN

252-473-9851, 800-473-6091
www.whitedoeinn.com
319 Sir Walter Raleigh St., Manteo 27954
Price: Expensive to Very Expensive
Credit Cards: MC, V
Internet: Free WiFi

As you walk around the historic district of Manteo, one building in particular is likely to catch your eye. Its turret, wraparound porches, elaborate woodwork, balconies, and extensive gardens make the Queen Anne–style Theodore Meekins house, built in 1910 and on the National Register of Historic Places, stand out. Today it is the White Doe Inn, Manteo's most romantic bed-and-breakfast. Decorated in the Victorian style, its eight uniquely designed bedrooms offer a range of amenities, including private gardens, balconies, canopied beds, stained-glass windows, soaking tubs, and Jacuzzis for two. Both masculine and feminine color schemes are available. All rooms have a CD player with a collection of romantic music, a TV with DVD player, guest bathrobes, and a fireplace. Room rates include a four-course seated breakfast served in the dining room or on the veranda, as well as coffee, dessert, and sherry every afternoon and evening. In-room spa services are available, as are special picnic, wedding, honeymoon, champagne, and chocolate packages, a 24-hour butler's wine pantry, and cappuccino and espresso service. The White Doe received a three-diamond rating from AAA, and the innkeepers, Bob and Bebe Woody, are members of the Professional Association of International Innkeepers.

WANCHESE

ISLAND HOUSE OF WANCHESE BED & BREAKFAST

252-473-5619
www.islandhouse-bb.com
104 Old Wharf Rd., Wanchese 27981
Price: Moderate to Expensive
Credit Cards: MC, V
Internet: Broadband and free WiFi

Located in a rambling historic home in the village of Wanchese, this inn serves a full country-style breakfast buffet with a home-made hot entrée every morning, and sherry and chocolates in each guest room. The three rooms and one suite are decorated with antiques, and each has a private bath, guest robes, clock radio, and cable TV, VCR, or DVD player with a library of films. Guests are welcome to use the freezer to store their catch, or borrow beach chairs, umbrellas, and towels for trips to the beach. They also have access to a 24-hour pantry with refrigerator, microwave, and ice machine. A screened gazebo is available for smokers or just to relax. The inn is adults-only, and pets are not permitted, although the innkeepers will help arrange for boarding. They raise West Highland terriers and bichons.

WANCHESE INN BED AND BREAKFAST

252-475-1166, 252-473-0602
www.wancheseinn.com
85 Jovers Ln., Wanchese 27981
Price: Inexpensive to Moderate
Credit Cards: MV, V
Internet: Free WiFi

Especially popular with anglers, this his-

Wanchese Inn

toric house in Wanchese offers four rooms, including a master suite with king bed and Jacuzzi. A full breakfast is served every morning. After that, you can lounge on the porch or den with a book, take the complimentary beach towels and chairs to the shore, or go fishing. There's a freezer to stash your catch and a 35-foot boat slip where you can dock your boat. Boat and trailer parking is available on-site. Children over 12 are welcome. Pets are not allowed, but the inn will help you arrange boarding nearby. Smoking is not permitted inside the building.

Smaller Inns and Guesthouses

Clemons Cottage 252-473-9870, 252-256-2662; home.earthlink.net/~ncclemons; 406 Budleigh St., Manteo 27954. Quiet cottage in the middle of the historic district offers two bedrooms and a full kitchen, plus a private garden with barbecue grill. Weekly rates are available. Pets are permitted for a fee. Moderate to Expensive.

The Inn at Kimbeeba 252-473-6365, 866-473-6365; www.kimbeeba.com; 102 Grenville St., Manteo 27954. Two guest rooms equipped with cable TV, wireless Internet, refrigerator, and microwave are available in this waterfront island home offering free deepwater dockage; complimentary use of canoes, kayaks, and bicycles; and an ample breakfast with hot entrée. Special dietary requests accommodated. The inn is handicapped accessible with an elevator and has a resident cat and dog. Inexpensive to Moderate.

Manteo Bed and Breakfast 252-473-4952; 306 Ananias Dare St., Manteo 27954. Just one block from the waterfront, this private home offers two guest rooms, with cable TV and WiFi access. A full breakfast is served and special dietary needs can be accommodated. Moderate to Very Expensive.

The Outdoors Inn 252-473-1356; www.theoutdoorsinn.com; 406 Uppowoc Ave., Manteo 27954. Operated by scuba and kayaking instructor Pam Landrum and her boat-building husband Matt, this inn occupies a historic house close to the Manteo waterfront with a swimming pool and hot tub. Two ground-floor rooms have refrigerators and private baths and come with complimentary bicycles and a full breakfast. A no-smoking policy is enforced both inside and on the grounds. Inexpensive to Moderate.

Whispering Bay Waterfront Suites 252-473-5323; www.whisperingbay.com; 103C Fernando St., Manteo 27954. The Serenity Suite, with private entrance and a balcony looking out over Shallowbag Bay, is located over a spa. Very Expensive.

Cottage and Condo Rentals

Pirate's Cove Realty 800-537-7245; www.pirates-cove.com; 1 Sailfish Dr., Manteo 27954. A wide variety of vacation rentals are available in the gated Pirate's Cove community, from seven-bedroom homes to smaller villas and condominiums. Many rental units come complete with bicycles, beach and fishing equipment, and some are equipped for infants. Rentals include linen service and housekeeping. Guests can use the community amenities, including a clubhouse, game room, pool and hot tub, fitness center, playground, volleyball courts, fossil search area, horseshoe pits, putting green, and lighted tennis courts, and receive reduced greens fees at the nearby **Nags Head Golf Links**. A full schedule of activities for children and adults is offered, including the Lil' Pirates Club, a nighttime activity for kids. Massage therapy, babysitting, bike and tennis racquet rentals are also available.

Shallowbag Bay Club 252-475-1617; www.shallowbagbayclub.com; 90 N. Bay Club Dr., Manteo 27954. Several of the fully equipped luxury one- to three-bedroom condos in this sound-front community are available as rentals. Community amenities include a swimming pool and hot tub, fitness center, and game room, as well as the popular **Stripers Bar & Grille.** Slips at the marina are available for transient boaters. Water taxi service is sometimes available to the Manteo waterfront.

RV Resorts

While overnight parking or camping is not permitted there, the **Outer Banks Roanoke Island Welcome Center** (252-473-2138) on the US 64/264 Bypass provides visiting RVers with a free waste dump station.

The Refuge on Roanoke Island 252-473-1096; www.therefuge-roanokeisland.com; NC 345, Wanchese 27981. New camping facility offers full hookups in Wanchese. Amenities include a bathhouse, pavilion with picnic tables and grills, and a dock and boardwalk over the marsh.

DINING

With the exceptions of McDonald's, Subway, and Pizza Hut, Roanoke Island remains free of chain restaurants. Most eateries are family-owned and operated. Often the fresh seafood on the menu comes directly from the family's fishing boat to the table. Keep an eye out for blackboard specials. These change frequently and usually represent what is literally "the catch of the day."

If you are looking for the **Weeping Radish Restaurant and Bavarian Brewery**, a Manteo favorite since 1986, it has moved to an expanded location in Jarvisburg, over the Wright Memorial Bridge in Currituck County. Visit it there to enjoy freshly brewed beer and brewery tours.

Rate Categories

Inexpensive	under $10
Moderate	$10 to $20
Expensive	$20 to $25
Very Expensive	$25 and up

These ratings represent the average cost of an entrée, not including higher-priced specials, that super-size steak or the rack of lamb. They also do not include appetizers, desserts, beverages, taxes, or gratuities.

When a range of ratings is offered, it usually indicates the difference in price between lunch and dinner entrées.

Credit Cards

AE—American Express
CB—Carte Blanche
D—Discover Card
DC—Diners Club
J—JCB International Credit Card
MC—Master Card
V—Visa

Meal abbreviations

B—Breakfast
L—Lunch
D—Dinner
SB—Sunday brunch

Restaurants

MANTEO

★ **1587 RESTAURANT**
252-473-1587
www.1587.com
Tranquil House Inn, 405 Queen Elizabeth Ave., Manteo 27954
Price: Expensive
Children's Menu: Yes
Cuisine: Seafood and chops

ROANOKE ISLAND: MANTEO AND WANCHESE **157**

Liquor: Wine, beer
Serving: D
Credit Cards: AE, MC, V
Handicapped Access: Yes
Reservations: Recommended
Special Features: Full vegetarian menu; reserve wine list

Relax over a glass of wine and watch the moon rise over Shallowbag Bay, then order up a selection of the creative cuisine at 1587, the Tranquil House Inn's signature restaurant. Located directly on the waterfront, 1587 has one of the best views—and some of best food—on the Banks. Executive chef Donny King and his staff exhibit a fine touch with the fresh local ingredients at hand and are constantly designing new, but always delicious, combinations. The menu changes seasonally and features fresh seafood, char-grilled chops, and, often, local game. The salads and desserts here are works of art. If you're just in the mood for something light, stop by the restaurant's copper-top bar, a work of art in itself, for an appetizer or a glass of wine. The cellar selection at 1587 is excellent and received favorable mention in *Wine Spectator*. You'll be favorably surprised by the prices, both for bottles and wines by the glass. One of the Outer Banks's unique fine-dining experiences, this is a don't-miss. You may also want to try the tapas at sister restaurant **Ocean Boulevard** in Kitty Hawk.

BIG AL'S SODA FOUNTAIN & GRILL

252-473-5570
www.themefifty.com
716 S. US 64/264 Business, Manteo 27954
Price: Inexpensive to Moderate
Children's Menu: Yes
Cuisine: All-American and seafood
Liquor: Beer and wine
Serving: B, L, D
Open: Daily, seasonal
Credit Cards: MC, V
Handicapped Access: Yes

Local fishing boat captain Al Foreman, known as Big Al to his friends, grew up around ice cream and always wanted his own old-fashioned soda fountain. He set out to build one on the main road leading to Manteo, and then things got out of hand. He ended up with a complete 1950s-themed restaurant with multiple dining rooms, a big dance floor next to a jukebox full of rock 'n' roll favorites, and a soda fountain counter long enough for a dozen people to spin around on those shiny red stools.

As it turns out, he's needed the room to accommodate the steady stream of families who come in for both the fun atmosphere and the nicely prepared, inexpensive food. Kids can get all their favorites here, for about what you'd pay for a Happy Meal. Meanwhile, adults and teens enjoy a wide selection of burgers, melts, finger food, blue-plate specials, and fresh local seafood, straight off Big Al's *Country Girl* and other local fishing boats. The dessert menu features all the classics, from a banana split to a chocoholic "Wipe Out." You'll have fun here just reading the menu, but there's plenty more to do before and after a meal: Play the jukebox, admire the incredible collection of Coke memorabilia, visit the game arcade, or browse the gift shop full of 1950s-themed souvenirs. Big Al's serves a full breakfast daily from 7 to 11, with a special children's menu. The restaurant has been known to close for a while in the winter. Look for the sign "Gone fishin'."

DARRELL'S RESTAURANT

252-473-5366
523 S. US 64/264 Business, Manteo 27954
Price: Inexpensive to Moderate
Children's Menu: Yes
Cuisine: Seafood
Liquor: Beer and wine
Serving: L, D
Closed: Sunday
Credit Cards: MC, V

The schooner Down East Rover *offers daily cruises from Shallowbag Bay.*

Handicapped Access: Yes
Special Features: Takeout menu

The motto on the menu says it all: "Eat More Fish." This family-owned favorite has been serving local fish and other seafood straight from the boat for over 30 years. The fried oysters are what people rave about, but Darrell's does things like marinated grilled tuna well, too. A wide variety of seafood is prepared both fried and broiled. Available sides branch out beyond the standard fries and slaw to beets, green beans, and baked potatoes. The Surf and Turf is a local favorite, as is the super-budget takeout lunch. Dessert features a legendary hot fudge ice cream cake.

FULL MOON CAFÉ

252-473-6666
www.thefullmooncafe.com
208 Queen Elizabeth Ave., Creef's Corner, Manteo 27954
Price: Inexpensive to Moderate
Children's Menu: Yes
Cuisine: Creative Carolina
Liquor: Beer and wine
Serving: L, D
Credit Cards: MC, V
Handicapped Access: Yes

Catch the laid-back pulse of Manteo at this restaurant located in the heart of it all, under the town clock. Tables on the patio and in the dining room stay busy year round with locals and returning fans from around the country. The eclectic menu brings together cuisines from several continents, ranging from hummus to a shrimp-and-crab enchilada. While offerings change seasonally, some favorites are always available, including the signature Blue Moon Waldorf salad and Low Country Shrimp and Grits. Daily specials include soup, quiche, pasta, and grilled fish *du jour*. The menu includes many creative vegetarian suggestions. The kids' menu offers unusual options, as well.

★ STRIPERS BAR & GRILLE

252-473-3222
www.stripersbarandgrille.com
1100 S. Bay Club Dr., Shallowbag Bay Club, Manteo 27954
Price: Moderate
Children's Menu: Yes
Cuisine: Seafood and steaks
Liquor: Beer and wine
Serving: L, D, SB
Credit Cards: AE, MC, V
Handicapped Access: Yes

Special Features: Happy hour; steamed and raw seafood bar; private club

This restaurant is a little hard to find, tucked away from the road inside the Shallowbag Bay Club. Maybe that's why it's the restaurant most recommended by local folks. The secret to finding it: Turn between McDonald's and Darrell's on the main street through town. Or come by boat. You can tie up at the dock outside.

Stripers is well worth searching out. The three-story building sits right on the waterfront, guaranteeing great views from every seat. Downstairs, the **Bearded Clam Steamer and Raw Bar** is a fun-loving, smoker-friendly hangout where locals gather for happy hour. You can sit inside or out. The second floor is a sophisticated dining room with carpeting, quiet background jazz, and a no-smoking policy. Up top is a private club where liquor by the drink is served. Memberships are available with a modest fee and 72-hour waiting period, as required by North Carolina law.

Signature dishes include the Newport-style clam chowder with cream and dill, Tuna Norfolk topped with crabmeat and wasabi, and the Rockfish Rueben, a tasty take on the classic featuring the restaurant's namesake fish, the rockfish or striped bass, known locally as a striper. Non-seafood dishes range from grilled prime rib to meatloaf, pork loin, and turkey pot pie. Most entrées are available in both small and large portions. The Sunday brunch, voted a favorite by locals, features a variety of eggs Benedict creations, as well as Bananas Foster French Toast, huevos rancheros, and build-your-own omelets. For dessert, try the Blondie, a chocolate butterscotch brownie served à la mode.

PIRATE'S COVE
HURRICANE MO'S
RESTAURANT & RAW BAR
252-473-2266
Pirate's Cove Marina, Nags Head–Manteo Causeway, US 64/264, Manteo 27954
Price: Inexpensive to Moderate
Children's Menu: Yes
Cuisine: Seafood and Caribbean/Cajun
Liquor: Full
Serving: L, D
Open: Seasonal hours
Credit Cards: AE, MC, V
Handicapped Access: Yes
Special Features: Happy hour; early bird prices; full bar service; late-night menu; vegetarian menu

You get great views of the Pirate Cove Marina from both the downstairs dining room and screened porch upstairs at Hurricane Mo's. These docks are home to one of the area's most active charter fishing fleets, and you can check out the catch over one of Mo's Golden Margaritas. Through a quirk in the local liquor laws, this is the only restaurant with a Manteo address allowed to serve mixed drinks. Seafood stars here, raw, steamed, fried, and grilled. Entrées include the CocoMo Mahi, marinated in coconut rum and lime juice, and Pepper Seared Tuna. The kitchen stays open late. You can get a meal until midnight.

Food Purveyors

Bakeries and Coffee Shops

The Coffeehouse on Roanoke Island 252-475-1295; 106-A Sir Walter Raleigh St., Manteo 27954. Located in the heart of historic Manteo, the Coffeehouse uses fresh-ground beans to make an array of coffee drinks both hot and iced, and sells fresh-baked breads, cinnamon rolls, wine, cheese, and handmade chocolates.

Morning Glory Coffee 252-216-5798; 620 Harbor Rd., Wanchese 27981. Located next door to O'Neal's Sea Harvest in the Wanchese Seafood Industrial Park, this little coffee shop serves eye-opening espresso to fisher folk in the predawn hours.

Breakfast and More

Mann's Luncheonette 252-473-3787; NC 345, Wanchese 27981. Friendly staff will fill your orders at the counter located next to **Mann's Grocery and Hardware**. Spencer sausage, a local favorite, is the featured meat in biscuits and breakfast sandwiches, or you can have eggs with your choice of sausage, bacon, "city ham" or country ham. The luncheonette serves rib eyes, barbecue, daily specials, and buckets of fried chicken until 5 PM.

T.L.'s Country Kitchen 252-473-3489; 812 S. US 64/264 Business, Manteo 27954. Breakfast is served anytime at this family-owned local favorite where southern home cooking is the specialty.

Candy and Ice Cream

Island Ice 252-473-2357; Queen Elizabeth Ave., Manteo. Colorful shop next to Carolina Outdoors serves snow cones, old-fashioned and Baltimore style, and ice cream including sugar and fat-free varieties.

The Outer Banks Nut Company 252-473-6771; www.obnuts.com; 105 Budleigh St., Magnolia Market Square, Manteo 27954. The nuttiest place in town, with over 100 varieties of nuts and nut candies, including house flavors such as Crab Shack and Jalapeno, and popular tie-dyed "I got my nuts roasted" logo T-shirts.

Farms, Farmers Markets, and Vegetable Stands

Island Produce 252-473-1303; S. US 64/264 Business, corner of Patty Lane, Manteo. Open seasonally, this roadside stand sells fresh vegetables, herbs, and fruits all summer, then shifts to pumpkins, Christmas trees, and other holiday decor in fall.

Manteo Farmer's Market 252-473-2133; www.townofmanteo.com; George Washington Creef Park, Manteo. Held in the park next to the Maritime Museum on the Manteo waterfront every Saturday morning from mid-June to early September, this market sponsored by the Town of Manteo features local produce, jellies and pickles, home-baked goodies, and crafts.

Sandwich Shops

Great Gut Deli 252-473-4500; www.thicketlumpmarina.com; 219 Thicket Lump Rd., Thicket Lump Marina, Wanchese 27981. The deli upstairs in the Thicket Lump Marina serves sandwiches made of Boar's Head meats and cheese, plus homemade shrimp, chicken, and tuna salads, soups, and daily specials. Eat indoors or out on the shaded deck.

Island Central Grill 252-473-1774; 928 S. US 64/264, Manteo 27954. Colorful, casual spot serves sandwiches and salads on its screened porch, which is enclosed and heated in cooler weather. Shrimp burgers, fish tacos, soft-shell crabs, and seafood baskets, along with crispy Island Fries, beer, homemade limeade, and hand-dipped milkshakes, fill the menu.

Poor Richard's Sandwich Shop 252-473-3333; 303 Queen Elizabeth Ave., Manteo 27954. A presence on the Manteo waterfront since 1984, Poor Richard's is easy to find, with a door opening onto Queen Elizabeth Avenue and another leading directly onto the docks. A full breakfast menu is served until 10:30 AM. Bring your laptop and check your e-mail, thanks to the complimentary WiFi access along the waterfront.

Seafood Markets

Captain Malc's Market 252-473-5525; www.wanchese.com; NC 345, Wanchese 27981. This retail store sits right next to the docks and the newly reopened **Fisherman's Wharf Restaurant**, offering shrimp, scallops, crab, and a variety of fin fish, all fresh off the boat.

O'Neal's Sea Harvest 252-473-4535; www.onealsseaharvest.com; 622 Harbor Rd., Wanchese Seafood Industrial Park, Wanchese 27981. The O'Neal family specializes in fish and crabs caught in local North Carolina waters. Fresh seafood is available according to the season, but most varieties are also available flash frozen year round. The store will pack your cooler full of seafood to take home, or will ship it direct to you.

Takeout and Delivery

China King II 252-473-3868; 309 S. US 64/264 Business, Manteo 27954. Delivers from Mann's Harbor to South Nags Head.

Garden Deli & Pizzeria 252-473-6888; 512 S. US 64/264 Business, Manteo 27954. Free delivery to Roanoke Island and Pirate's Cove, or eat on the shady deck.

Top China 252-473-6660; 218 S. US 64/264 Business, Chesley Mall, Manteo 27954. Delivers to Roanoke Island addresses.

Wines and Spirits

Dare County ABC Store 252-473-3557; www.ncabc.com; US 64/264 Business, Manteo 27954. The only source of bottled hard liquor on Roanoke Island is the state ABC store. It also sells fortified wines. Most state ABC stores are open Monday to Saturday 10 AM to 9 PM and are closed Sunday.

TOURING

The Outer Banks Welcome Center on Roanoke Island (252-473-2138, 877-OBX-4FUN; www.outerbanks.org), located on the US 64/264 Bypass just over the Virginia Dare Memorial Bridge, is the logical first stop as you reach the Banks. Besides an abundance of information on Outer Banks attractions, the expansive complex also offers an accommodation reservation service, a picnic area, and restrooms that are open 24/7. Staffed by friendly natives, the center is open 9–5 every day except Thanksgiving and Christmas. Pick up an **Outer Banks Getaway Card** for local discounts or a **Park and Garden Pass** that will save you 20 percent on visits to Roanoke Island Festival Park and the Elizabethan Gardens.

With the abundance of water all around, most sightseeing tours on Roanoke Island are done by boat. However, several walking tours explore Manteo's historic past and air tours take you up for a bird's eye view of the Banks.

By Air

Aviation companies based at the **Dare County Airport** (252-475-5570; www.darenc.com/Airport) at the northern end of Roanoke Island take you high above dunes and surf, providing a unique view of the fragile environment we call the Outer Banks. Lighthouses, marine wildlife, shipwrecks on the bottom of the ocean—all can be seen best from above.

Barrier Island Aviation 252-473-4247; www.barrierislandaviation.com; 407 Airport Rd., Manteo 27954. Air tours of 30 or 60 minutes are in a high-winged aircraft to make photography easy.

Coast Is Clear Air Tours 252-202-7433; 407 Airport Rd., Manteo 27954. A pilot with 30 years' experience offers air tours in an authentic 1941 open-cockpit biplane.

Kitty Hawk Aero Tours 252-441-8687; www.flyobx.com; 1100 Holly St., Kill Devil Hills 27948. Tours depart from the Dare County Airport in Manteo and cover the whole length of the Banks from Corolla to Ocracoke, depending on your interest. Their flight camp will have you taking off and landing a plane in a single day.

By Boat

Downeast Rover Sailing Cruises 252-473-4866; www.downeastrover.com; Manteo waterfront. If you are visiting Manteo late spring through early fall, you're sure to notice the lovely ship with red sails entering Shallowbag Bay. This is the *Downeast Rover*, a 55-foot topsail schooner, offering three cruises a day, including one at sunset, from the Manteo boardwalk.

Outer Banks Cruises 252-473-1475, 866-473-1475; www.outerbankscruises.com. Dolphin Watches, sunset cruises, bird-watching tours, and fishing trips for shrimp and crab on a covered, pontoon-style boat (complete with restroom) depart from the Manteo waterfront.

Outer Banks Jet Boats 252-441-4124, 877-FLY-THIS; Manteo waterfront. Unique 34-foot jet boat takes up to 32 passengers on high-speed tours in search of dolphins and other wildlife.

★ **Shallowbag Bay Sail About** 252-475-1750; www.obxmaritime.org; 104 Fernando St., Manteo 27954. Every Tuesday, June to October, volunteers from the Maritime Museum take visitors out for a free sunset sail on an authentic shad boat, the official historic boat of North Carolina.

By Canoe or Kayak

Alligator River National Wildlife Refuge Canoe Tours 252-987-2394; www.fws.gov /alligatorriver. The National Wildlife Service offers weekly, three-hour guided canoe tours of the Milltail Paddle Trails, May through October. Proceeds go into a special fund to build a visitor center for Alligator River NWR on Roanoke Island. Reservations required.

Kitty Hawk Kayaks 252-261-0145, 866-702-5061; www.khkss.com. Experienced guides offer paddling tours of the Alligator River National Wildlife Refuge, as well as Roanoke Island tours, full-moon tours, and exclusive tours of the purple marlin roost under the Umstead Bridge.

Kitty Hawk Kites Kayak Tours 252-441-4124, 877-FLY-THIS; www.kittyhawk.com; 307 Queen Elizabeth St., Manteo 27954. Eco-tours with historic themes depart from the Manteo waterfront.

Outdoors Outfitters 252-473-1356; www.theoutdoorsinn.com. Pam Malec Landrum, the author of *Guide to Sea Kayaking in North Carolina*, leads kayak eco-tours and special children's activity tours.

By Bicycle or on Foot

Historic Old Manteo Candle Light Walking Tour 252-441-4124, 877-FLY-THIS; www.manteowalkingtour.com. Knowledgeable guide tells stories of the early years of this historic village with a bit of folklore and a few ghosts thrown in.

Waterside Theatre Tours 252-473-2127, 252-473-3414; www.thelostcolony.org. Evening
tours conducted before each show give a behind-the-scenes look at *The Lost Colony*
theater, prop rooms, and costume shop. Summer only.

CULTURE

Rarely has history played such an important part in the development of a cultural scene as it
has here. The history of the arts in Manteo began in 1937 when local history buffs first presented the outdoor symphonic drama *The Lost Colony* to commemorate the 350th birthday
of Virginia Dare, the first English child born in the New World. Although it was supposed to
run just one summer, the outdoor drama, the first of it kind, gave birth both to a new genre
of theater and an active arts community in the town of Manteo.

The Dare County Arts Council (252-473-5558; www.darearts.org), organized by volunteers in 1975, carries this artistic energy into the community through an active program of
exhibitions, performances, and classes in visual arts, dance, and music. It sponsors an
annual series of exhibits at several venues, including its own Sea and Sounds Gallery in
Manteo's historic district, at the Roanoke Island Festival Park gallery, at artist Glenn Eure's
Ghost Ship Gallery in Nags Head, and elsewhere. During the council's annual studio tour in
March, over 30 artists from Duck to Hatteras open their doors to art lovers.

The area can look forward to an even brighter future in the arts. **The College of the
Albemarle** (www.albemarle.cc.nc.us), part of the state university system, recently initiated
a Professional Crafts program at its Dare County campus in Manteo. Both local residents
and visitors benefit from artists-in-residence programs, continuing-education classes,
short-term workshops, craft fairs, and graduate shows connected with the college.

Both the arts council and the **Roanoke Island Historical Association** (www.thelost
colony.org), producers of *The Lost Colony*, are well supported by the local community. The
annual fund-raisers of these and other associations on the Outer Banks are a great way to
meet local folks. Tickets are often available at the last minute.

Don't miss any of the frequent gallery openings at both the **Sea and Sounds Gallery** and
the gallery across the creek at **Roanoke Island Festival Park**, if you find yourself in the
area. The arts community turns out in force, the art itself is always worth a look, and the
local ladies put out a memorable refreshment table of traditional southern party food.

Check our event listings for specific galas, annual events, and exhibitions.

Architecture

Residents of Manteo have taken a remarkable interest in the community's architectural
character through the years, and the town recently enacted measures to preserve the village's traditional character.

Much of the downtown waterfront was destroyed by a catastrophic fire in 1939. Local
historians used the rebuilding process as an opportunity to rename the streets with more
evocative titles. Water Street became Queen Elizabeth Avenue, with other streets named for
Sir Walter Raleigh, Ananias Dare, and other characters in *The Lost Colony*. Tudor-style
architectural details became popular in the 1940s and can still be found in some commercial structures, such as the Pioneer Theatre.

Several buildings escaped both fire and development. Today, the historic downtown of
Manteo is a mix of architectural styles ranging from late-Victorian to the Western Plains

style popularized by Frank Lloyd Wright. There's even a Sears mail-order arts-and-crafts cottage at 505 Croatan Street.

Two properties are on the National Register of Historic Places: the Queen Anne-style Meekins House at 319 Sir Walter Raleigh Street, today the White Doe Inn; and the George W. Creef Jr. House, at 308 Budleigh Street. The **Manteo Preservation Trust** (MPT) (www.manteopt.com) conducts an annual tour of historic homes in December. Funds raised are used for preservation projects, including the placement of bronze MPT plaques on buildings that predate the 1939 fire.

To protect its historic look and small-town atmosphere, Manteo adopted guidelines that all new construction and renovations must follow. At the town's Web site, www.townof manteo.com, you can download both a sketchbook of historic properties and a manual of the Manteo Way of Building, illustrated with numerous photos. Picket fences are encouraged. Cul-de-sacs are not.

You can see the Manteo Way in action at the new Marshes Light development at the southern end of the Manteo waterfront. Developers hope to blend it seamlessly into the historic village.

Art Museums and Galleries

Manteo's historic waterfront district makes an attractive location for a variety of art studios and galleries. Most are located within a few blocks of each other. The town's monthly First Friday celebrations include a gallery crawl.

Andrus Gallery & Studio 252-305-5411; www.theandrusgallery.com; Waterfront Shops, Queen Elizabeth St., Manteo 27954. Longtime Banks resident and founder of the local high school arts program Steve Andrus displays his light-drenched watercolors of boats, harbors, and other marine subjects.

The Cottage Gallery 252-473-5991; 406 Agona St., Manteo 27954. This is the home and studio of artist George R. Cheeseman. If the artist isn't out front watering the beautiful garden, he's probably inside working on one of his lovely watercolors.

Dare County Arts Council Sea and Sounds Gallery 252-473-5558; www.darearts.org; 104 Sir Walter Raleigh St., Manteo 27954. The arts council sponsors several competitions every year, as well as art classes and monthly exhibitions at its gallery in the heart of historic Manteo. Highlights on the gallery calendar include the October Beach Book Cover Art Competition and the Holiday Small Works Show.

Decoys by Nick Sapone 252-473-3136; 292 The Lane, Wanchese 27981. Call ahead to visit the studio of Sapone, a carver of traditional Outer Banks–style canvas hunting decoys.

Gallery 101 Main Street Studio 252-473-6656; www.gallery-101.com; 101 Budleigh St., Manteo 27954. Fine arts and crafts from some of the area's top artists, including pinhole photography by Gregg Kemp, George Cheeseman's watercolors, and the batik quilts of Ann Harwell.

John Silver Gallery 252-475-9764; www.johnsilvergallery.com; 105 Fernando St., Manteo 27954. Oils by John Silver, including many of local scenes, as well as artwork by other professional artists. Silver also conducts "en plein air" painting workshops.

Nancyware Pottery 252-473-9400; www.nancywarepottery.com; 402 Queen Elizabeth Ave., Magnolia Market, Manteo 27954. Nancy Huse creates high-fired functional pottery in her studio. In the gallery next door, her collectible ornaments and God jar are customer favorites.

Roanoke Heritage Extended 252-475-1442; www.stumpythepirate.com; 109 Sir Walter Raleigh St., Manteo 27954. The home of Stumpy the Pirate Cat, hero of a popular children's book written by Jeremy Bliven, exhibits artwork by its illustrator Herbert Bliven, Jeremy's father. The building is full of fascinating treasure, including seashells, driftwood, duck decoys, and nautically themed gifts.

Roanoke Island Festival Park Art Gallery 252-475-1500; www.roanokeisland.com; 1 Festival Park Blvd., Manteo 27954. Part of the state-operated Festival Park complex, this gallery presents important shows of local and regional art in many media. Annual events include the Quilt Extravaganza in March and the Mollie Fearing Memorial Art Show in May.

Silver Bonsai 252-475-1413; www.silver bonsai.com; 905 S. US 64/264 Business, Manteo 27954. The home gallery of jewelry artists Ben and Kathryn Stewart also exhibits the fine arts and crafts of other

Queen Elizabeth I at the Elizabethan Gardens.

select artists, as well as a large collection of bonsai. Among the art and miniature trees, you'll find Ben Stewart's secret passion: etch-a-sketch art.

Wanchese Pottery 252-473-2099; 107 Fernando St., Manteo 27954. Potters Bonnie and Bob Morrill create handcrafted pottery in this attractive building facing Washington Creef Park on the Manteo waterfront.

Cinema

Pioneer Theatre 252-473-2216; 113 Budleigh St., Manteo 27954. The first and, still, the only movie theater in Manteo, opened in 1918. Today, the Creef family continues to operate the local landmark and keeps prices low to make it affordable for families. One first-run movie plays each week at 8 o'clock nightly. Tickets are $5, and $2 more buys popcorn, candy, and a drink.

Saturday at the Movies 252-475-1500; www.roanokeisland.com; Roanoke Island Festival Park. Part of the North Carolina School of the Arts' Summer Performance Festival, this series screens family features every Saturday from late June to early August at Roanoke Island Festival Park. Admission is free.

Cooking Classes

Outer Banks Epicurean 252-305-0591, 252-473-5558; www.outerbanksepicurean.com; 104B Sir Walter Raleigh St., Manteo 27954. Chef Amy Huggins teaches cooking classes emphasizing local foods at the Dare County Arts Council during the summer. Other projects include wine and food pairing classes and tours to discover the sources of local foods. Sign up for a private cooking lesson and a chef will come to your vacation cottage and teach you to cook a gourmet meal.

Seafood Series, North Carolina Aquarium at Roanoke Island 252-473-3493, 866-332-3475; www.ncaquariums.com; 374 Airport Rd., Manteo 27954. Top chefs from the area share their seafood recipes, after a naturalist from the aquarium talks about the life cycle and natural history of the week's selected seafood.

Historic Homes, Gardens, and Sites

CIVIL WAR TRAIL SITES

www.civilwartraveler.com

Although fortified by Confederate troops, Roanoke Island fell to the Union army in February 1862, after which it was used as a staging site for campaigns farther into North Carolina. Former slaves came to the island to be under the protection of the Federal authorities and built the Freedmen's Colony on a site now lost. A Civil War Trail marker describing the colony is at the base of the William Umstead Bridge, US 64/264 Business, on the Manteo side.

The museum at Roanoke Island Festival Park has an extensive exhibit on Civil War battles and other events of the era.

Several other markers recounting Civil War events are scattered around the island. A sign about the Battle of Roanoke Island is located on the east side of NC 345 just south of the US 64/264 traffic light. One on the Burnside Expedition of 1862, describing the Union capture of the island, is at the Manteo Outer Banks Welcome Center on US 64/264 Bypass. The Gateway to the Albemarle marker, explaining the strategic importance of Roanoke Island, is located on the mainland side of the Umstead Bridge on US 64/264 Business.

★ THE ELIZABETHAN GARDENS

252-473-3234
www.elizabethangardens.org
1411 National Park Dr., Manteo 27954
Open: Monthly hours vary, check Web site
Admission: Adults $8; youths $5; children free; free on Virginia Dare's birthday, Aug. 18

Situated on 10.5 acres next to the Fort Raleigh National Historic Site, the Elizabethan Gardens began as a project of the Garden Club of North Carolina during the 1950s. Over the years, the site on the shores of Roanoke Sound has developed into a rich

This statue representing Virginia Dare as an Indian maiden graces the Elizabethan Gardens.

complex of gardens that delights history lovers, art lovers, and nature lovers alike. The gardens are embellished with many works of sculpture and include a Shakespearean herb garden, and superb collections of camellias and rhododendrons. The Queen's Rose Garden features the Queen Elizabeth rose, a gift from Queen Elizabeth II.

FARMSTEAD PARK

252-473-5440
www.theislandfarm.com
Buzzy Lane, Manteo 27954

The last remaining pre–Civil War farmhouse on Roanoke Island is the area's newest agri-tourism destination. Surrounding farm buildings have been rebuilt, and farm animals of the types raised by Adam Etheridge on the property in the 1850s now live in the barns and pastures. Special exhibits follow the creation of woolen cloth from sheep to loom.

THE FREEDMEN'S COLONY OF ROANOKE ISLAND

252-473-5772, 252-473-2355, 252-473-4275
www.roanokefreedmenscolony.com
Interpretive display located at the northern end of the Manteo Bike Path at the foot of the William Umstead Bridge.
Admission: Free

Recently upgraded with additional informational signs, the small park also has a sandy beach and parking lot on the sound. Another site connected with the Freedmen's Colony established on Roanoke Island from 1862 to 1867 is **Cartwright Park**, on Sir Walter Raleigh Street. The park sits on the grounds of the first church, dated to 1865, of Andrew Cartwright, founder of AME Zion churches in the Albemarle area. Cartwright Park has a picnic shelter, restrooms, grills, and a playground.

FORT RALEIGH NATIONAL HISTORIC SITE

252-473-5772
www.nps.gov/fora
1401 National Park Dr., Manteo 27954
Open: Visitor Center open 9–5 daily year round (except Christmas Day), and grounds are open dawn to dusk. June–Labor Day, the visitor's center stays open until 6 PM, and the grounds remain open until the completion of *The Lost Colony* outdoor drama.
Admission: Free

Located between the Elizabethan Gardens and *The Lost Colony's* Waterside Theatre, the Lindsay Warren Visitor Center exhibits artifacts found on Roanoke Island and tells the story of early explorations and colony attempts. A documentary, *Roanoke: The Lost Colony*, is shown daily. The site contains an earthen fort built in the style used by the adventurers and a nature trail with signs that identify the native plants found in the area in 1585 by naturalist Thomas Hariot. A longer trail leads to an interpretive display on the Freedmen's Colony on the shores of Roanoke Sound. Archaeological investigations are ongoing. In summer a range of free activities are offered, including nature hikes and visits to the park's museum collection building, as well as special programs on the Freedmen's Colony.

LOST COLONY CENTER FOR SCIENCE AND RESEARCH

252-792-3440
www.lost-colony.com
9192 NC 171, Williamston 27892

Dedicated to exploring the mystery of the Roanoke colony, the Lost Colony Center takes a multidisciplinary approach, using geography, geology, history, biology, anthropology, and oceanography to investigate clues. Most recently, the center has embarked on DNA studies aimed at identifying present-day descendants of the colonists. The center runs research field trips to sites under investigation that are thought to be connected with the colonists and other early residents of the coastal region. Call for schedule.

MANTEO WEATHER TOWER

www.townofmanteo.com
Manteo Waterfront

One of the few remaining Coastal Warning Display towers left in the country, and possibly the only one with all its original signal lights intact, the weather tower was recently restored and moved back to the Manteo waterfront. The signal flags warn of wind shifts and approaching storms. An information board at the base of the tower explains the meaning of the various flag combinations.

THE MOTHER VINE

Mother Vineyard Rd., Manteo

Now located on private property, this scuppernong vine still produces fat, white grapes. Experts estimate its age to be at least 400 years old and speculate that it may have been first cultivated by the American Indians in the area before Raleigh's English colonists arrived. The Mother Vine has a central trunk about 2 feet around and covers about half an acre.

THE OUTER BANKS HISTORY CENTER

252-473-2655
www.obhistorycenter.net
1 Festival Park Blvd., Roanoke Island Festival Park, Manteo 27954
Open: Mon.–Fri. 9–5
Admission: Free

This branch of the North Carolina State Archives collects and preserves documentary evidence relevant to Outer Banks history, including books, magazines, newspapers, photographs, maps, and a collection of oral histories. The center is open to all, and most services are free. Permanent and temporary exhibits are on display in the **History Center Gallery.**

PEA ISLAND AFRICAN AMERICAN HERITAGE CENTER AT COLLINS PARK

252-473-1844
www.ecpfc.org
1013 Sir Walter Raleigh St., Manteo 27954
Admission: Free

This new museum preserves the history of the Pea Island Lifesaving Station, the only one to have an all-black crew. Exhibits detail the many daring rescues performed by these brave men. The museum is housed in the station's original cookhouse, moved to this site and restored by descendants of the lifesavers. The **Dellerva Collins Memorial Gardens**, named for an African American woman who served for 26 years on Manteo's Board of Commissioners, surround the museum.

PHOENIX SOCIETY LECTURE SERIES

252-473-2127, 252-472-3414
www.thelostcolony.org
Indoor Film Theatre, Roanoke Island Festival Park
Admission: Free

This lecture and discussion series sponsored by the Roanoke Island Historical Society features researchers, authors, and performers exploring topics relating to the Roanoke Island colonies.

★ ROANOKE ISLAND FESTIVAL PARK AND *ELIZABETH II*

252-475-1500
www.roanokeisland.com
Open: Daily 9–5; until 6 PM April–October. Closed January and first two weeks of February, also Thanksgiving and December 24–26.
Admission: Art gallery and grounds are free; for visits to the *Elizabeth II*, the museum, film, and historical interpretation areas: Adults $8, students (6–17) $5, children (5 and under) free

Located across from the Manteo docks, this state-run facility offers a full roster of activities and amenities to visitors and the Manteo community. Its most visible attraction, the *Elizabeth II*, a replica of a 16th-century sailing vessel like the ones that carried Sir Walter

The Elizabeth II, *an authentic recreation of the ships that brought Sir Walter Raleigh's colonists to the New World, hosts concerts during the summer months.*

Raleigh's colonists, is docked opposite the Manteo waterfront. Her bright colors and jaunty jib advertise the fact that the history interpreted here, the Elizabethan Age, has little in common with the grim groups of Pilgrims and Puritans who later settled farther north. The ship is staffed by costumed characters speaking Elizabethan dialect, who bring those early voyages to life.

The **Settlement Site** explores the daily life of the settlers both at work and play. Nearby at the **American Indian Town**, visitors experience a different way of life, building a log canoe, working a fish trap, and participating in tribal dances.

There's plenty of inside fun at the Festival Park as well, making it a popular rainy-day destination. In the **Roanoke Adventure Museum**, kids can dress in Elizabethan ruffs and bum rolls or American Indian skin tunics, become sailors, pirates, lifesavers, and duck hunters. The excellent docudrama *The Legend of Two Path,* exploring Native American attitudes toward the settlers in their midst, screens several times a day in the film theater.

Admission is charged to visit the interpretive areas, the film, and the museum, but other areas of the park, which covers a small island, are free to the public. These include an excellent museum store with many pirate, Elizabethan, and American Indian–themed gift items, an art gallery with changing exhibits, the Outer Banks History Center, an interpretive boardwalk, and a Fossil Pit. Not least of the free attractions is the spacious parking lot, located across a short bridge from the busy Manteo waterfront, where parking is often hard to find during the summer season.

THE ROANOKE MARSHES LIGHTHOUSE

252-475-1750
www.townofmanteo.com
End of the pier on the Manteo Waterfront
Open: Tue.–Sat. 9–5
Admission: Free

A reproduction of the cottage-style screw-pile lighthouses that once aided navigation in nearby sounds now helps mariners enter Shallowbag Bay. Inside are exhibits on the history of the lighthouse, a wooden hydroplane used in local speedboat races in the 1960s, and an exhibit on local pioneering boatbuilder Warren O'Neal. Visiting boaters can tie up to this pier for complimentary overnight mooring.

SOMERSET PLACE STATE HISTORIC SITE

252-797-4560
www.ah.dcr.state.nc.us/sections/hs/somerset/somerset.htm
2572 Lake Shore Rd., Creswell 27928
Open: Apr.–Oct. Mon.–Sat. 9–5, Sun. 1–5; Nov.–Mar. Tue.–Sat. 10–4, Sun. 1–4, closed Mon.
Admission: Free

One of the largest plantations in the upper South before the Civil War, Somerset Place on the shores of Lake Phelps is today preserved as a state historic site offering a realistic view of the life of all its inhabitants, from the plantation owners to the workers of African descent, both enslaved and free. Seven original buildings as well as the 14-room plantation house have been restored. A number of other buildings and a large formal garden have been reconstructed based on archaeological evidence. In 1986, Somerset was the location

The Roanoke Marshes Lighthouse at the entrance to Shallowbag Bay, a replica of the screwpile lights that once lined the North Carolina sounds

of the first reunion of slave descendants to be held at the original plantation where their ancestors were enslaved, an event credited with starting the national homecoming movement. The plantation is located south of US 64 about an hour's drive west of Manteo.

WANCHESE SEAFOOD INDUSTRIAL PARK

252-473-5867
www.nccommerce.com/wanchese
End of Harbor Rd., off NC 345, Wanchese 27981
Admission: Free

North Carolina's ocean industries are on display in this bustling compound. Fishing boats dock to unload their catch at seafood processing plants, and shipbuilders create and repair everything from custom yachts to seagoing commercial trawlers.

Kids' Culture

Lost Colony Children's Theatre 252-473-3414; www.thelostcolony.org; Waterside Theatre, 1409 National Park Dr., Manteo 27954. Special morning performances of a children's classic, Tuesday and Thursday at 9:30 AM, June–August. Tickets $5 a person.

Summer Children's Performance Series 252-475-1500; www.roanokeisland.com; Roanoke Island Festival Park. Held in the Indoor Film Theater at Roanoke Island Festival Park, this series brings top performers for the younger set to Manteo for a summer of entertainment. Performances held mornings, late June to early August. Free with park admission or to members of Friends of the *Elizabeth II*.

Waterside Theatre Arts & Crafts 252-473-3414; www.thelostcolony.org; Waterside Theatre, 1409 National Park Dr., Manteo 27954. Classes taught by costumed characters from the *Lost Colony* cast teach children ages 7-12 how to create Indian beading and paint watercolors inspired by John White's 1585 drawings.

Museums

DARE COUNTY REGIONAL AIRPORT MUSEUM

252-475-5570
www.darenc.com/Airport/Museum.htm
410 Airport Rd., Manteo 27954
Open: Daily, 8 AM–7 PM
Admission: Free

The aviation history of Dare County may have begun with the Wright brothers, but it didn't end there. Find out the rest of the story at these exhibits housed in the regional airport at the north end of Roanoke Island. The airport, commissioned as a Naval Auxiliary Air Station during World War II, served as a base for Civil Air Patrol antisubmarine searches, and a training facility for many famous navy air squadrons, including the VF-17 "Jolly Rogers." The Ready Room of aviator Dave Driscoll details the history of aviation in the region from the barnstorming days of the 1920s to the dawn of the jet era.

NORTH CAROLINA AQUARIUM AT ROANOKE ISLAND

252-473-3493, 866-332-3475
www.ncaquariums.com
374 Airport Rd., Manteo 27954
Open: 9–5, daily, year round. Closed Thanksgiving, Christmas, and New Year's Day.
Admission: Adults $8, seniors $7, children (6–17) $6, 5 and under free. Free admission on Martin Luther King Day and Veterans Day.

One of three state aquariums located along the coast, this one presents exhibits exploring the waters of the Outer Banks, from the rivers pouring into the sounds to the marine communities offshore in the deep ocean. A number of fish species inhabit the exhibits, from freshwater game fish to sharks, as well as river otters, alligators, and turtles. The highlight of the aquarium is a one-third scale model of the *USS Monitor* in the Graveyard of the Atlantic gallery. A variety of programs go on daily, including films, feedings, and behind-the-scene tours. Fee programs are also offered, including field trips to the salt marsh and ocean, fishing and crabbing lessons, and craft classes.

NORTH CAROLINA MARITIME MUSEUM ON ROANOKE ISLAND

252-475-1750
www.obxmaritime.org
104 Fernando St., Manteo 27954
Open: Tue.–Sat. 9–5
Admission: Free

Housed in the George Washington Creef Boathouse, named for the famous local boatbuilder who created the shad boat, this branch of the North Carolina Maritime Museum exhibits several traditional small watercraft, including an 1883 Creef shad boat, dubbed the "pickup truck of the Banks," spritsail skiffs, and a 1948 Davis runabout. Volunteers and staff repair historic boats and build new ones, take visitors on sailing excursions in a shad boat, and every year teach hundreds of children and adults how to sail. A variety of other classes, from painting to nautical knot-tying, are offered at reasonable prices.

Music and Dance Performances

North Carolina School of the Arts Summer Performance Festival 252-475-1500; www.NCSAsummerfest.org; Roanoke Island Festival Park, Manteo. The state's official college of the arts, located in Winston-Salem, brings its talented students and staff to Manteo each summer for six weeks of concerts, now offered free to the public. Perform-ances by the NCSA Percussion and Jazz Ensembles, as well as the dance and drama departments, are scheduled in the Outdoor Pavilion at 8 PM Tuesday to Friday from late June to early August. No seating is provided, so bring lawn chairs or a blanket along with a picnic to enjoy during the performance. In case of rain, the action moves to the indoor theater, where an afternoon series of performances also takes place.

Outer Banks Forum for the Lively Arts 252-261-4636; www.outerbanksforum.org. Bring-ing top national, international, and regional entertainment to Manteo for more than 25 years, this series sponsors shows each winter from October to April. Tickets are avail-able to the general public. Visit the Web site for information.

Nightlife

With so much performance art in town, and no liquor by the drink, nightclubs have an uphill battle to attract patrons. However, you'll usually find a crowd of locals lifting a beer or glass of wine at **Poor Richard's After Hours** (252-473-3333; 303 Queen Elizabeth Ave., Manteo 27954), the pub located in the front of **Poor Richard's Sandwich Shop** on the Manteo waterfront. Live music is offered several nights a week, and the pub opens at noon on Sunday.

Theater

★ ELIZABETH R & COMPANY

252-475-1500
www.elizabethr.org
Roanoke Island Festival Park. 1 Festival Park
Blvd., Manteo 27954
Tues.-Thurs. in June and August
Admission: Free with park admission; reserva-tions suggested

Of all the actresses who played Queen Elizabeth in *The Lost Colony* through the years, none took to the role more naturally than Barbara Hird. After her stint in the Waterside Theatre ended, Miss Hird went on the road portraying the queen in a one-woman show, *Elizabeth R*, writ-ten and directed by Elizabethan scholar lebame houston. The combination of script and actress

Miss Barbara Hird brings Elizabeth R to life every summer in several theatrical productions.

accurately captures the wit and charisma of the Virgin Queen and has played to critical and audience acclaim. Every summer Hird and houston return to Manteo with *Elizabeth R*, along with *Bloody Mary and the Virgin Queen*, a fun romp through the messy family relations of the Tudors. Recently, Hird and houston added another play to their repertoire, *Shepherd of the Ocean*, exploring the relationship between Sir Walter Raleigh and his queen. The company also presents a new musical, *The Apple Tree*, in July and August at the Elizabethan Gardens. Call 252-473-3761 for reservations.

THE LOST COLONY OUTDOOR DRAMA

252-473-3414, 252-473-2127
www.thelostcolony.org
Waterside Theatre, 1409 National Park Dr., Manteo 27954
Nightly except Sun., June–Aug.
Admission: Adults $16–$20, seniors $15, children 11 and under $8. On some nights children are admitted free or half-price with a paying adult.

Over 4 million visitors have seen the outdoor drama *The Lost Colony* since it debuted in 1937. Commissioned by the residents of Manteo, the symphonic drama scripted by Pulitzer Prize winner Paul Green was the first of its kind. The show has always been lucky in its talent. Andy Griffith started his career playing Sir Walter Raleigh and later returned to film episodes of *Matlock* at the local courthouse. Today he's enjoying his retirement as a Manteo resident. The magnificent costumes are created by William Ivey Long, winner of multiple Tony Awards for production design and himself a local boy who began his theatrical career at the Waterside Theatre.

Six shows a week hardly gets the talent in this show warmed up. The cast and crew of *The Lost Colony* also stage a number of special performances every summer, ranging from Shakespeare to classic musical comedies. The *Reaching for the Stars* cabaret show held toward the end of the season is a much-anticipated annual event. Get your tickets in advance for these shows; you'll save a bundle.

The Lost Colony cast also appears every summer at the popular *Tea with the Queen* events now held at the Waterside Theatre's Backstage Courtyard. Tickets include a sumptuous dessert and tea, an audience with Queen Elizabeth, a backstage tour of the Theatre, and other merriment.

SHORELINE ENTERTAINMENT

252-305-0144
www.shorelineentertainmentobx.com
P.O. Box 1660, Manteo 27954

Lost Colony alum Barbara Dare Hartwig and her husband, Tim, both with extensive theatrical experience, bring Broadway-style musical revues to the stage with their new professional company. Annual shows include Christmas and country music revues.

THEATRE OF DARE

252-261-4064
www.theatreofdare.org

This community theater group has been going strong for nearly two decades. The all-volunteer cast and crew present several musicals and comedies every fall and spring in the company's new home, the auditorium of the College of the Albemarle Roanoke Island campus in Manteo.

RECREATION

Some visitors are under the impression that all the fun on the Outer Banks is on the beach, but Roanoke Island proves them wrong. Air tours, sunset sails, paddling adventures, bike trails, and fishing are just a few of the activities available. The Manteo waterfront is the best place to find the action. Here you can cruise on a sailing schooner or a jet boat, sign up for a dolphin tour, rent a bike or a kayak, or parasail. You can even take a swim. And when it's time to relax, you'll find plenty of dining and shopping just a short walk away.

Beaches and Swimming Holes

While you won't find much surf on the shores of Roanoke Island, you can join the locals at their favorite swimming holes. It's a long-standing community tradition to swim just off the Manteo waterfront, and you'll often see local kids keeping cool next to the Basnight Bridge that arches over Dough Creek to Festival Park.

For a more structured experience, take a dip at the **Old Swimming Hole** (252-475-5910) on Croatan Sound. You'll find it on Airport Road next to the North Carolina Aquarium. Maintained by Dare County, the park has a sandy beach, playground, volleyball court, picnic tables, grills, and restrooms. A lifeguard is on duty daily from Memorial Day to Labor Day, 10 AM to 6 PM.

A small sandy beach, but without a lifeguard, is found at the north end of the multi-use path, next to the Umstead Memorial Bridge.

Bicycling

Best Bike Routes

Manteo is blessed with a wide, paved multi-use path, suitable for walking, jogging, cycling, and rollerblading, that runs along US 64/264 from the Umstead Memorial Bridge to the junction with NC 345. From the light at that intersection it continues as a wide paved shoulder over the Washington Baum Bridge to Whalebone Junction in Nags Head.

More than 8 miles long, the multi-use path joins downtown Manteo with the historic district at the north end of the island, ending at the Freedman's Colony Memorial at the base of the bridge to Manns Harbor. The ride is both cool and colorful, running beneath live oak trees and crape myrtles that bloom all summer.

A nice side trip takes bikers around a loop composed of Scuppernong and Mother Vineyard Roads. Along the way you'll pass the oldest-known grapevine in the country, the so-called Mother Vine, estimated to be more than 400 years old. The vine is now on private property, so take a look from the road.

If you are coming to Manteo to ride the bike path, two good paved parking areas are located at Roanoke Island Festival Park and at the end of the path at the Umstead Bridge.

Bike Rental Shops

Carolina Outdoors 252-473-2357; 307 Queen Elizabeth St., Manteo 27954. Single, tandem, and children's bikes, plus infant seats and trailers, are available at this shop on the Manteo waterfront. Helmets and locks are free. Best deal is the three-hour special.

Boats and Boating

Roanoke Island has a rich history of boatbuilding, and that tradition continues today. Manteo's early residents included famous boatbuilding names such as Davis, O'Neal, and Creef. George Washington Creef, patriarch of the clan, invented the shad boat, named the official state boat of North Carolina. Boats custom-built in Carolina are considered the best available by many anglers and mariners around the world. The *Elizabeth II* was built by local craftsmen on the waterfront at Manteo next to the Maritime Museum.

Boatbuilders

If you're in the market for a boat of your own, you've come to the right place. Contact local professional boatbuilders to see their prebuilt models, or design your own custom yacht. Several companies are located in Wanchese's Seafood Industrial Park, including Croswait, Sculley, Briggs, Bayliss, and Bluewater Yachts. Another group operates in Manns Harbor on the mainland. Or contact the Maritime Museum and sign up to build your own small craft.

Mann Custom Boats Inc. 252-473-1716; www.paulmanncustomboats.com; 6300 US 64/264 Business, Manns Harbor 27953. Mann-built boats are proven winners in fishing tournaments.

North Carolina Maritime Museum at Roanoke Island 252-475-1750; www.obxmaritime.org; 104 Fernando St., Manteo 27954. Classes offered include Build a Boat in a Day and Build a Kayak.

Spencer Yachts Inc. 252-473-6567; www.spenceryachtsinc.com; 31 Beverly Dr., Wanchese 27981. Producers of high-performance sport fishing yachts.

Canoeing and Kayaking

Alligator River Wildlife Refuge Paddle Trails 252-473-1131; www.fws.gov/alligatorriver; Buffalo City Rd. off US 64. The 15 miles of canoe and kayak trails on Milltail Creek provide one of the best ways to see this wilderness. The trailhead is about a 20-minute drive from Roanoke Island. More paddling trails are located at the **Palmetto-Peartree Preserve, Mattamuskeet NWR**, and **Pettigrew State Park** (see listings under Nature Preserves).

Carolina Outdoors 252-473-2357; 307 Queen Elizabeth St., Manteo Waterfront. Rent single or tandem kayaks right on the waterfront to explore Shallowbag Bay and surrounding waters. You can launch from a floating dock behind the shop.

College of the Albemarle 252-473-2264, ext. 221, Manteo. One-day, six-hour classes in kayak paddling and safety include practice in Roanoke Sound.

Marinas

Several marinas on Roanoke Island welcome transients who want to cruise in and stay aboard their boats, or just stop by for dinner on the docks. Most host excursion boats or charter fishing vessels, so a marina can be an exciting place to hang out, even if you don't have a boat.

Broad Creek Fishing Center and Marina 252-473-9991; www.broadcreekfishingcenter.com; 708 Harbor Dr., Wanchese Seafood Industrial Park, Wanchese 27981. This fully equipped marina offers new floating dock slips for boats from 28 to 70 feet, and smaller transient slips with all the amenities, plus a 70-ton travel lift, engine, electronic and welding services, canvas repair, and a dry stack facility. The headboat *Miss Broad Creek*

The Lake Mattamuskeet Pumping Station is being restored by the state of North Carolina.

calls the marina home, as does a big charter fishing fleet.

Manteo Waterfront Marina 252-473-3320; 207 Queen Elizabeth Ave., Manteo 27954. Numerous transient berths with full hookups are available in this attractive location on the waterfront in downtown Manteo. Showers, laundromat, ship's store, and numerous onshore amenities are nearby. The town hosts free wireless Internet access along the entire waterfront.

Marshes Light Marina 252-475-9863; 201 Fernando St., Manteo 27954. New marina with full-service transient slips is connected to downtown Manteo by a boardwalk.

Pirate's Cove Yacht Club 252-473-3906, 800-367-4728; www.fishpiratescove.com; US 64 at the west end of the Washington Baum Bridge, Nags Head–Manteo Causeway. Transient slips include electric, water, and cable TV in the dockage rate, with access to the gated community's pool and hot tub, fitness center, sauna, and tennis courts, plus laundry facilities, showers, private fish-cleaning house, and a courtesy van. Internet access is available in the ship's store.

Shallowbag Bay Marina 252-473-4946, 252-202-8505; www.shallowbagbayclub.com; 100 Bay Club Dr., Manteo 27954. Boat slips come with all club amenities, including a pool, fitness center, bicycles, cable and phone hookups, and a courtesy car. A ship's store and excellent seafood restaurant are located on-site, with slip space available for customers.

Thicket Lump Marina 252-473-4500; www.thicketlumpmarina.com; 219 Thicket Lump
Rd., Wanchese 27981. Located just 5 miles from Oregon Inlet, Thicket Lump is full-
service with fuel, a ship's store, and private slips. Dolphin tours, charter fishing, and
headboat trips are available from the docks. The shaded patio of the **Great Gut Deli** is a
favorite lunch stop.

Public Boat Ramps and Docks

North Carolina Fish and Wildlife maintains public boat ramps at the west end of Bowser-
town Road, Manteo; on Mashoes Road, Manns Harbor; and on Buffalo City Road and East
Lake in the Alligator River Wildlife Refuge. A boat ramp at the base of the Washington Baum
Bridge on the Nags Head–Manteo Causeway, opposite Pirate's Cove, is equipped with parking for boat trailers and restroom facilities.

Dare County maintains public boat ramps in Manteo on Queen Elizabeth Avenue at the
foot of the Basnight Bridge; in Wanchese, between the Fisherman's Wharf Restaurant and
Moon Tillett's Fish Company; and on the mainland in Manns Harbor, on Old Ferry Dock
Road. Thicket Lump Marina in Wanchese also offers a public boat ramp.

Public docks are available for daytime use on the Manteo waterfront along the boardwalks leading to the Roanoke Marshes Lighthouse and the town gazebo.

Sailing Lessons

North Carolina Maritime Museum on Roanoke Island 252-475-1750; www.obxmaritime
.org; 104 Fernando St., Manteo 27954. Staffed by people who love to get out on the water,
the museum offers private and class sailing instruction for children and adults. The
tremendously popular Outer Banks Community Sailing Program gives school-age
sailors five days of sailing experience with special classes in racing. Applications can be
submitted as early as January 1 and can be found online.

Family Fun

Public playgrounds are located in Manteo next to the Old Fishing Hole on Airport Road; at
Manteo Elementary School at 701 N. US 64/264 Business; at Cartwright Park on Sir Walter
Raleigh Street; and on the Manteo waterfront. In Wanchese, a playground can be found at
"Pigum" Walker Park (252-473-6638) on Pond Road.

The **Manteo Skateboard Park** behind the College of the Albemarle's Roanoke Island
campus (US 64/264 Business) is open to the public. Wanchese is the home of skate-park
builder Matt Corbett and his legendary 10-foot-deep Wanchese Bowl.

Fishing

The wide variety of offshore, inshore, and sound fishing available, as well as the fighting
reputation of the local fish, makes this region one of the great fishing destinations of the
world. Two of the area's largest charter fishing fleets dock in Wanchese and at Pirate's Cove.
Wanchese also is home to a large commercial fishing fleet that ships its catch around the
world.

Fishing Charters and Outfitters

Broad Creek Fishing Center 252-473-9991; www.broadcreekfishingcenter.com; Wanchese Seafood Industrial Park. The large charter fleet based here offers light-tackle sound
fishing, shrimping, and shark trips, as well as inshore, offshore, and fishing at deep-

water ocean wrecks. A two-for-one special includes both Gulf Stream fishing and wreck fishing on the same trip. The marina has a full-service ship's store and a professional fish-cleaning station.

The Country Girl 252-473-5577; www.themefifty.com; Pirate's Cove Marina. The 57-foot *Country Girl*, operated by the folks that run Big Al's Grill, heads out for a day of wreck fishing Memorial Day through Labor Day, then goes after rockfish in the winter. Tuna trips are available year round. All bait and tackle furnished. Families with children welcome.

Grandpa Shrimp and Crab Charters 252-473-1475; www.grandpafishncharters.com; Manteo Waterfront Marina. Experience the life of a professional fisherman with Captain Russell Firth, as he drags a commercial-style shrimp net behind the boat, then takes you to check a line of crab pots. You sort the catch and keep everything of legal size—a favorite with families. Sunset cruises, tower trips, and nighttime shark fishing also available.

Mainland Charters 252-473-0953, 252-473-8332; Manns Harbor. Captain Ralph Craddock has a couple of boats working out of Manns Harbor on the mainland offering inshore, nearshore, offshore, and open-boat fishing. For families, he offers the Sunset Combo, leaving at 4 PM. It starts off with some fishing, runs down a line of crab pots, and ends with a scenic sunset tow with a shrimp net. Rods and tackle provided.

Pirate's Cove Yacht Club 252-473-3906; www.fishpiratescove.com; west end of the Washington Baum Bridge on the Nags Head–Manteo Causeway. The 20 or so charter fishing boats based here head for the Gulf Stream for tuna, dolphin, wahoo, and marlin, nearshore for cobia or Spanish mackerel, or fish the inlet for trout, flounder, bluefish, and striped bass. Makeup charters available.

Thicket Lump Marina 252-473-4500; www.thicketlumpmarina.com; 219 Thicket Lump Rd., Wanchese 27981. Charter excursions offered include everything from half-day trips with light tackle to 11-hour offshore marathons.

Fishing Piers

Causeway Dock and Pier The public dock and pier under the Washington Baum Bridge on the south side of the Nags Head–Manteo Causeway, just opposite Pirate's Cove, is a popular spot for crabbing and fishing. Large parking lot, restrooms, and public boat ramp available.

Headboats

Headboats or party boats typically provide all the bait and fishing tackle you'll need to have a good time. Rates are charged per person and are reasonable, usually $30–$35 for adults, less for children under 10. Bathrooms and refreshments are available onboard, and gear and licenses are provided. It's a great introduction to fishing for all ages.

The Crystal Dawn 252-473-5577; www.themefifty.com; Pirate's Cove Marina. A 65-foot party boat, operated by the family that owns **Big Al's Soda Fountain and Grill**, takes anglers out for half-day fishing trips in inlet and sound. Sunset cruises are also available at reasonable rates.

The Miss Broad Creek 252-473-9991; broadcreekfishingcenter.com; 708 Harbor Rd., Wanchese 27981. Sailing out of Broad Creek Fishing Center in Wanchese Seafood Industrial Park, this 61-foot boat takes up to 46 people on morning and afternoon half-day fishing trips, and sunset cruises.

The Roseanne 252-216-5273; Thicket Lump Marina, Wanchese. This 40-foot boat takes up to 16 passengers out for half-days of sound fishing. Bait and tackle are included, plus a first mate who will help bait your hook.

Health and Fitness Clubs

Island Wellness 252-473-1504, 252-256-0112; 105 Budleigh St., Manteo 27954. Personal fitness coaching by Deb Taylor includes nutritional and wellness counseling.

Nautics Hall Health & Fitness Complex 252-473-1191; www.elizabethaninn.com; 814 US 64/264 Business, Manteo 27954. The Elizabethan Inn's fitness center offers aerobic classes, water aerobics in the indoor pool, and a free weight room, plus a whirlpool and sauna. Passes available for those not staying at the inn.

Outer Banks Yoga and Pilates 252-480-3214; www.outerbanksyoga.com; Elizabethan Inn, Manteo. Classes are offered in Manteo at the Elizabethan Inn's health club. Drop in rates and three-class passes available.

Hunting and Shooting

Hunting is permitted in the region's National Wildlife Refuges under strict national and state regulation. Seasons vary greatly even year to year, and each refuge and species has its own set of regulations. White-tailed deer are the most numerous, and most frequently hunted, species. Waterfowl hunting is allowed on a very limited basis, with permits awarded by lottery. A special Youth Waterfowl Hunt is held annually. Visit the North Carolina Wildlife Resources Commission Web site, www.ncwildlife.org, for seasons, regulations, license locations, and lottery details.

AJ's Sea Duck and Trophy Swan Hunts 252-925-9903, 866-UNC-SWAN; P.O. Box 578, Englehard 27824. Adam Jones guides hunts for sea duck, swan, and bear.

DPlace LLC 252-542-0342; www.dplacellc.com; P.O. Box 194, Englehard 27824. Jim Stevens leads bow and gun hunts for trophy bucks and black bear, featuring state-of-the-art game retrieval and processing facilities.

Jennette's Guide Service 252-925-1521; www.ncduckhunts.com; 11281 North Lake Rd., Englehard 27824. Teddy "Tadpole" Gibbs will take you out for sea ducks and swans on Pamlico Sound and Lake Mattamuskeet.

Outer Banks Gun Club 252-473-6655, 252-449-6540; www.outerbanksgunclub.com; Link Rd., US 264, Manns Harbor 27953. Public shooting facility has archery, pistol and rifle ranges, plus trap house sporting clays. Handicapped accessible.

Nature Preserves

ALLIGATOR RIVER NATIONAL WILDLIFE REFUGE
252-473-1131
www.fws.gov/alligatorriver
Located along US 64 west of Roanoke Island
Admission: Free

Alligator River is one of the most accessible of the area's refuges, thanks to its location just west of Roanoke Island and the Outer Banks. Several public-use areas and programs are located on US 64, including the **Red Wolf Howling Safaris**, held weekly in the summer months and less frequently the rest of the year. Call 252-796-5600 or visit www.redwolves

Alligator River and Swan Quarter

Just over the bridges on the mainland, a network of wildlife refuges, state parks, conservation and game lands preserves a wilderness of brackish marsh, freshwater lakes, and wooded wetlands. US 64 and US 264, which run together through Roanoke Island, divide as they reach the mainland and sweep out north and south to embrace this immense area of undeveloped land called the Albemarle Peninsula.

Man has made few inroads into this wilderness, although not for lack of trying. Numerous land development companies over the years have sought to drain Lake Mattamuskeet and convert the rich bottomland into farms, and a great pumping station still stands as a monument to the endeavor. But the water always comes creeping back.

Today, a few farms grow cotton, sweet potatoes, and onions as sweet as Vidalias. Along the marshy coast, US 264 passes the little fishing villages of Stumpy Point and Englehard and Swan Quarter, largely untouched by tourism. The towns along US 64, Columbia and Plymouth, once important seaports along Albemarle Sound, quietly dream of their historic pasts.

Most of the vast interior is managed by a patchwork of federal and state agencies. Wildlife, including black bear, deer, and American alligator, is found here in abundance. The U.S. Fish and Wildlife Service is reintroducing the endangered red wolf into the area.

Every winter, the lakes in the region host huge flocks of migrating tundra swans, ducks, and snow geese, making this one of the best bird-watching areas on the East Coast. Bald eagles, ospreys, and wading birds live here all year. Spring and fall, migrating songbirds stop here on their journeys, filling the forests and swamps with their music.

.com to register; Howlings cost $5 per person. The Howlings meet at the **Creef Cut Wildlife Trail**, a paved, half-mile, universally accessible trail that leads to a freshwater marsh. **Refuge Wildlife Drive**, where sightings of black bear are very frequent, also begins here. The 5-mile unpaved drive is appropriate for cars or mountain bikes. Creef Cut is about a 20-minute drive from Manteo.

Another cluster of public-use areas is located at the end of unpaved Buffalo City Road, which turns off to the south a few miles farther west on US 64. Here you'll find a boat ramp for the refuge's 15 miles of paddling trails on Milltail Creek. Small motorboats are also permitted. The refuge offers guided canoe tours weekly from May to October. Call 252-987-2394 for reservations.

Nearby is another handicapped-accessible trail, the **Sandy Ridge Wildlife Trail**, a half-mile earth path and boardwalk through a cypress swamp. Both trails have handicapped priority fishing docks. A North Carolina fishing license is required.

GULL ROCK GAME LAND

252-482-7701
www.ncwildlife.org
Outfall Canal Rd. (NC 1164), east of Swan Quarter
Admission: Free

Roads cross these game lands, allowing wildlife viewing from your car. A short loop road leads to a managed waterfowl impoundment, but the gate is closed March to September, when you'll have to walk. A public boat ramp is located at the end of Outfall Canal Road.

★ MATTAMUSKEET NATIONAL WILDLIFE REFUGE

252-926-4021
www.fws.gov/mattamuskeet
38 Mattamuskeet Rd. off US 264, Swan Quarter 27885
Admission: Free

Lake Mattamuskeet, North Carolina's largest natural lake, is the winter home of huge flocks of tundra swans, snow geese, Canada geese, and ducks. A paved road (NC 94) runs on a causeway across the center of the refuge. A 5-mile unpaved wildlife drive leads to park headquarters, next to the historic **Lake Mattamuskeet Pumping Station**, an impressive, if ineffective, structure, now being renovated as an environmental education center. A short nature trail begins in this area. Other refuge amenities include three boat ramps and several observation decks and towers. The lake is very shallow and appropriate only for small boats, including canoes and kayaks. A paddle trail leads along the lake's southern shore. Fishing is permitted March through October.

PALMETTO-PEARTREE PRESERVE

252-796-0723, 919-967-2223
www.palmettopeartree.org
Pot Licker Rd., northeast of Columbia
Admission: Free

The Conservation Fund manages this preserve, known locally as P3. It's a top birding site and contains one of the last large populations of the endangered red-cockaded woodpecker. Several trails and boardwalks lead through the preserve, as well as a paddling trail.

PETTIGREW STATE PARK

252-797-4475
www.ncparks.gov
2252 Lake Shore Rd., Creswell 27928
Admission: Fees for camping

Centered on 5-mile-wide Lake Phelps, one of the cleanest lakes in North Carolina, Pettigrew State Park is a paradise for paddling, bass fishing, and hiking through sweet gum and cypress forests. Wilderness camping, a boat ramp, fishing pier, and numerous hiking trails are available. The area has a rich human history as well. Native American dugout canoes dated to nearly 5,000 years ago are on display in the park's information center. In the days before the Civil War, **Somerset Place** (252-797-4560), on the shores of Lake Phelps, was one of the largest plantations in the area. Today it is a state historic site with tours offered all year. Admission is free.

POCOSIN LAKES NATIONAL WILDLIFE REFUGE

252-796-3004
www.fws.gov/pocosinlakes
205 South Ludington Dr., Columbia 27925
Admission: Free

This 110,000-acre refuge is home to black bear and a variety of birds. Tundra swans, snow geese, and ducks winter here in great numbers. Fishing for black crappie, sunfish, and catfish is popular in the refuge's canals. The park's welcome center in Columbia offers interpretive exhibits and a boardwalk along the Scuppernong River.

SWAN QUARTER NATIONAL WILDLIFE REFUGE
www.fws.gov/swanquarter

The extensive coastal marsh included in this refuge harbors large populations of diving ducks, wading birds, and shorebirds, as well as osprey nesting sites. It also provides habitat for American alligators and bald eagles. Located west of the village of Swan Quarter, it is accessible only by boat. Several boat ramps and a fishing pier at Bell Island are the only amenities. The refuge is run by the staff at **Mattamuskeet National Wildlife Refuge**.

Racquet Sports and Tennis
Tennis and basketball courts located at Manteo Middle School on US 64/264 Business are open for public use after school hours. More tennis courts are available at Walker Park, 260 Pond Road, in Wanchese.

Spas and Bodywork
Bodywork for Balanced Health 252-216-8072; 102 Old Tom St., Suite 203, Evans Bldg., Manteo 27954. Shaena Hollomon, a licensed massage therapist, offers Thai, Swedish, deep-tissue, and sports massage.

Waterfront Salon & Day Spa 252-473-5323; www.thewaterfrontsalonandspa.com; 103B Fernando St., Manteo 27954. This spa, with a view of Shallowbag Bay, has a tempting array of treatments for body and soul. Try the Elizabethan Garden, an aromatherapy massage combined with guided imagery. The salon specializes in braids and updos for brides.

Trails and Eco-attractions
Trails at Fort Raleigh National Historic Site 252-473-5772; www.nps.gov/fora; 1401 National Park Dr., Manteo 27954. The 1.25-mile **Freedom Trail** leads from the parking lot in front of the Elizabethan Gardens to the Freedman's Colony exhibit at the foot of the Umstead Bridge. Along the way, signs identify plants used in the native Algonquian culture. The shorter **Thomas Heriot Nature Trail** winds on sandy paths under old live oaks down to the shore. Signs here hold quotes from Heriot's journals on the local flora he found in the New World, and the ways colonists used them.

Manteo Waterfront & Roanoke Island Festival Park www.townofmanteo.com; www .roanokeisland.com. Take a stroll along the Manteo waterfront for relaxing views of marsh and sound. The boardwalk stretches all the way to the **Marshes Light Marina**, curves around a bit of marsh, and passes in front of the Maritime Museum. Continuing along the town docks, you pass a pirate-themed playground, the **Roanoke Marshes Light**, and the town gazebo.

Next walk over the Cora Mae Daniels Basnight Bridge, pausing to enjoy the close-up view of the *Elizabeth II*. The sidewalk will take you to another boardwalk, this one along the shores of the island, that houses Festival Park with a view of the high white dunes of Jockey's Ridge across the sound. Interpretive signs tell of the environmental restoration of this once badly damaged shoreline.

Public restrooms and parking are located at Roanoke Island Festival Park and next to the Maritime Museum on Fernando Street.

Roanoke Island Marsh Game Land 252-482-7701; www.ncwildlife.org; NC 345, south of Manteo. Short walking trail leads to views of a 40-acre waterfowl impoundment and a black needlerush marsh.

Watersports

Parasailing

Fly the Wolf 252-441-4124, 877-FLY-THIS; www.kittyhawk.com; Manteo waterfront. Fly solo or with your best bud high above Shallowbag Bay. Prices rise with the altitude. Observers can ride along for $20. Discounts on weekends and mornings.

Scuba Shops and Charters

Ghost Fleet Dive Charters 252-423-045; www.ghostfleetdivecharters.com; 212 Thicket Lump Rd., Wanchese 27981. Captain Crocket and his dive boat *The Poppy* take charters on voyages of discovery to some of the most famous wrecks in the Graveyard of the Atlantic, including the steamer *Oriental* and several German U-boats. Top-notch rental equipment, air and nitrox fills, instruction, and lodging packages available.

Nags Head Diving 252-473-1356; www.nagsheaddiving.com; 406 Uppowoc Ave., Manteo 27954. Pam Malec Landrum teaches a wide variety of scuba courses, and will take you on shore dives to historic wrecks. Rental scuba gear is available.

Wildlife Spotting

Bird-watching

Roanoke Island and the adjacent Albemarle Peninsula contain exceptional opportunities for birding year round. The **North Carolina Birding Trail** (919-604-5183; www.ncbirding trail.org) identifies 11 places to look for birds in the area. Trail guides, including detailed maps and directions, can be downloaded from the Birding Trail Web site. Guided trips to many of these areas are offered during the Wings Over Water festival every November.

Other popular spots to look for birds on Roanoke Island include the area around Dare County Airport (swallows, martins, upland sandpipers); the freshwater pond at the foot of Umstead Memorial Bridge (warblers); and Sunnyside Lane (hummingbirds).

The Umstead Memorial Bridge has gained fame as a roosting location for huge flocks of purple martins in July and August. Over 100,000 birds can be observed returning to roost under the bridge at dusk. Informational signs are located at the base of the bridge on the northwest side in Manns Harbor, where the viewing is best. The **Coastal Carolina Purple Martin Society** (252-394-6205; www.purplemartinroost.com) coordinates educational programs. **Kitty Hawk Kayaks** (252-261-0145, 866-702-5061; www.khkss.com) offers paddle trips to the bridge to see the incoming birds.

Outer Banks Cruises (252-473-1475, 866-473-1475; www.outerbankscruises.com) takes bird-watchers to Pelican Island, where over 4,000 of the big birds roost.

Marine Mammals

The waters around Roanoke Island abound in bottlenose dolphin during the summer months. These outfitters offer tours that guarantee sightings:

Outer Banks Cruises 252-473-1475, 866-473-1475; www.outerbankscruises.com; Manteo waterfront. Guarantees sightings on Dolphin Watch cruises June to October. Dolphin mating and births are often observed.

Paradise Dolphin Cruises 252-441-6800, www.ghostfleetdivecharters.com. Set sail from Thicket Lump Marina in Wanchese aboard the 40-foot *Kokomo*.

Wildlife Tours

Red Wolf Howlings 252-796-5600; www.redwolves.com; Alligator River NWR, Creef Cut Wildlife Trail parking lot. Wildlife staff lead an evening trip into the woods to hear the red wolves howl every week during the summer, and occasionally at other times of the year. The cost of the program is $5. Summer howlings frequently fill up, so make reservations in advance. Bug spray and flashlights are a must.

SHOPPING

Manteo has no malls and only one strip shopping center. Wanchese can say the same. Most of the shopping options are located in downtown Manteo close to the historic waterfront. There you'll find numerous shops offering a variety of practical and gift items.

Shopping Centers and Malls

Chesley Mall 210 S. US 64/264 Business, Manteo 27954. All the stores you simply have to find—grocery, post office, video store—are conveniently centralized in this strip mall on the main highway.

Mann's Sentry Hardware and Mann's Red and White 252-473-5664; 2991 NC 345/Mill Landing Rd., Wanchese 27981. Owned and operated by the Mann family, Wanchese's version of a shopping center includes a grocery store, old-fashioned hardware, and a luncheonette, all connected by interior doors. You can fill up on gas out front.

Old Town Manteo shopdowntownmanteo.tripod.com. Numerous new and restored buildings dedicated to eclectic shops, galleries, and restaurants are located within just a few blocks, making Old Town an excellent shopping destination.

White's Shopping Center, Manns Harbor 252-473-2256; 7395 US 64/264, Manns Harbor 27953. General store and grill on the mainland offers fishing supplies, souvenirs, burgers, and beach equipment at prices usually less than you'll find on the beach.

Antiques

400 Budleigh Street Antique Mall 252-473-9339; 400 Budleigh St., Manteo 27954. The 25 rooms here are filled with all sorts of antiques.

Clemons on Budleigh 252-473-9870; www.home.earthlink.net/~ncclemons; 406 Budleigh St., Manteo 27954. This historic house is filled with antique furniture, glass, china, and linens, plus other unique items.

Outer Banks Quilts and Antiques 252-473-4183; 108 Sir Walter Raleigh St., Manteo 27954. An antiques mall with a dozen different dealers shares space with quilting fabrics and supplies. Antique quilts are on display.

Books and Music

Burnside Books 252-473-3311; 610 US 64/264 Business, Manteo 27954. New and used books, many of them titles on local history and lore issued by Penny Books, a local imprint, published by Burnside's parent company, Times Printing, which also puts out the *Coastland Sentinel* three times a week.

★ **Manteo Booksellers** 252-473-1221; www.manteobooksellers.com; 101 Sir Walter
Raleigh St., Manteo 27954. A refuge for book lovers for over 20 years, this store welcomes browsers to sit and read awhile. Owner Steve Brumfield stocks a huge selection of
regional titles and local authors, cookbooks, mysteries, classical literature, and everything in between. A special area is devoted to young readers. The shop hosts a busy
schedule of signings and special events, including an annual Herbert Hoover Birthday
Party in August.

Mother's Money 252-473-6901; 207 Queen Elizabeth Ave., Waterfront Shops, Manteo
27954. Refresh with a soda or ice cream cone while you browse books on local subjects,
including lots of children's titles, or check your e-mail on their computer.

Clothing

Georgie's Place 252-475-9895; 107 Budleigh St., Phoenix Shops, Manteo 27954. Go girlie
at Georgie's, where you'll find ruffles and lace galore, stained glass, baby gifts, smocked
dresses, garden hats, and robes.

Lady Banks 252-475-1212; www.ladybanks.com; 107F Budleigh St., Phoenix Shops, Manteo
27954. Fun handbags, sandals, hats, and other accessories. The only Pandora jewelry
dealer on Roanoke Island.

Waterstreet Station 252-473-5323; 103A Fernando St., Manteo 27954. Colorful island
print resort wear, linen clothing, and brand-name accessories.

Crafts

Art, Glass n' Fire 252-473-6734; www.artglassnfire.com; 200 Sir Walter Raleigh St., Manteo
27954. Paint-your-own pottery gallery also offers mosaic and glass fusion projects for
all ages. Popular spot for parties; summer kids' camp and kids' night out also available.

Christmas Shop and Island Gallery 252-473-2838; www.outerbankschristmas.com; 621 S.
US 64 Business, Manteo 27954. One of Manteo's most popular shops has reopened, now
housing an array of local craft shops and boutiques, as well as the famous Christmas displays.

★ **Endless Possibilities** 252-475-1575; www.ragweavers.com; 105 Budleigh St., Manteo
27954. Unique handwoven and handcrafted items made from recycled clothing are produced and sold here to benefit the Outer Banks Hotline and Crisis Intervention and Pre-
vention Center. Pick up a diva boa, a purse made of men's cast-off ties, or a
one-of-a-kind wall hanging. You can watch the weavers at work on the looms or get
behind the shuttle yourself. They'll teach you how to weave, and the items you produce
will be sold for this good cause.

Fine Yarns at Kimbeeba 252-473-6330; www.kimbeeba.com; 107D Budleigh St., Phoenix
Shops, Manteo 27954. Fine yarns and fibers, knitting, crocheting, spinning, and weav-
ing supplies, plus a gallery of fiber artworks by local artists.

Gifts

The Cumberland House 252-473-6689; www.cumberlandhouseobx.com; 105 Budleigh
St., Magnolia Market, Manteo 27954. Gifts for weddings are the specialty at the only
Southern Living at Home bridal registry on the Outer Banks.

My Secret Garden 252-473-6880; 101 Sir Walter Raleigh St., Manteo 27954. A favorite stop
for residents and visitors alike displays a wealth of ornaments for your garden, plus gift
items, stuffed animals, mermaids, and fairies.

Puparazzi! Pet Bow-tique 252-473-2094; puparazzi.tripod.com; 107E Budleigh St., Manteo 27954. Find gifts and treats for your pet at this fun shop that hosts a pet party on the First Friday of every month.

Home Decor

Inspired by the Sea 252-473-9955; www.furnitureinspiredbythesea.com; 107 Budleigh St., Phoenix Shops, Manteo 27954. Hand-painted scenes of lighthouses, shells, and seascapes grace functional furniture items.

Manteo Furniture Company 252-473-2131, 800-682-1944; www.manteofurnitureobx .com; 209 Sir Walter Raleigh St., Manteo 27954. This locally owned company established in 1945 has the area's largest selection of brand-name appliances and furniture. They deliver from Corolla to Ocracoke and will haul off the old stuff, for free.

Jewelry

Modern Heirloom 252-475-1413; www.modernheirloom.com; 905 US 64/264 Business, Manteo 27954. Husband-and-wife team Ben and Kathryn Stewart create timeless masterpieces from precious metals and gemstones.

Muzzie's Antiques 252-473-4505; www.muzziesantiquesobx.com; 101A Fernando St., Manteo 27954. Vintage, estate, and antique jewelry is Muzzie's specialty, along with vintage clothing, garden statuary, and unique engagement rings.

Something Special 252-475-1594; 107A Budleigh St., Phoenix Shops, Manteo 27954. Browse gifts for all ages, including watches and silver jewelry, while you enjoy complimentary coffee, tea, or wine.

Sporting Goods and Clothing

Manteo Marine Inc. 252-473-2197; www.manteomarine.com; 411 S. US 64/264 Business, Manteo 27954. A family of Coast Guard veterans runs this leading dealer in boats and outboard motors. Their "test drive" policy lets you try out a boat before you buy.

Mike Keller Ltd. 252-473-5007, 800-683-8464; www.mikekellerltd.com; 416 Russell Twiford Rd., Manteo 27954. Foul-weather gear, crabbing supplies, cast nets, fishing accessories, and Grundens' "Eat Fish" line of clothing.

The broad ponds of Pea Island National Wildlife Refuge are a favorite stop for waterfowl and photographers.

6

Hatteras Island

One Road On, One Road Off

Hatteras Island is the most fragile section of the Outer Banks, and the heart of the Cape Hatteras National Seashore. Here you can see nature at work, as wind and water compete to build land, and to wash it away.

In the past, one continuous strip of sand stretched from Bodie Island to the tip of Ocracoke. A great unnamed storm opened both the Oregon and Hatteras inlets in 1846, creating the Hatteras Island we know today.

Experts say that within not too many years, Hatteras will break into separate islands, as new inlets open across the sandy barrier, which at some points is less than a quarter-mile wide.

In fact, this process is already in motion. Dare County has identified several hot spots where new inlets are most likely to open and has installed webcams so people can watch the progress and check on road conditions (www.co.dare.nc.us/webcam).

PEA ISLAND

As you come across the Herbert Bonner Bridge from Bodie Island, the abandoned Oregon Inlet Life-Saving Station sits awash in sand. Just beyond, dunes crowd close to the narrow pavement of NC 12, frequently blowing over the road. Waves often wash across this area during storms.

The first 13 miles south of the bridge are part of the 6,000-acre **Pea Island National Wildlife Refuge,** the wintering grounds of more than a dozen waterfowl species. Large fresh and brackish water impoundments and natural ponds take up most of the width of the island.

Biologists studying the ecosystem have determined that periodic overwash is a natural process and an essential part of maintaining the habitat. NC 12, running between the ponds and the dunes, is in the way.

Controversy continues as the Department of Transportation considers various short- and long-term solutions to the problem. But in the meantime, this stretch of NC 12 is a fascinating showcase of nature in motion and brings the rich wealth of waterfowl close to the road for convenient viewing.

The **Pea Island Visitor Center** is the best place to stop. Here you can pick up a map of the very easy walking trails in the refuge and get help identifying the species you will see. If

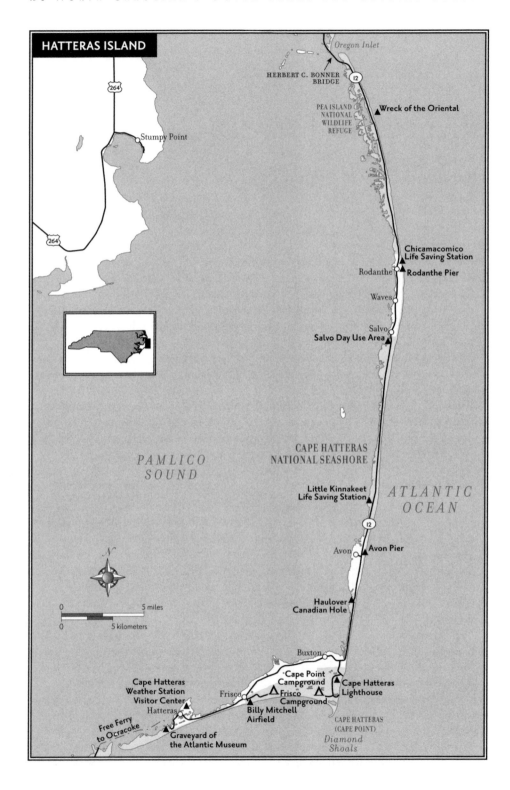

HATTERAS ISLAND

Oregon Inlet

HERBERT C. BONNER
BRIDGE

Stumpy Point

PEA ISLAND
NATIONAL
WILDLIFE
REFUGE

▲ Wreck of the Oriental

Chicamacomico
Life Saving Station

Rodanthe   ▲ Rodanthe Pier

Waves

Salvo
Salvo Day Use Area ▲

PAMLICO
SOUND

CAPE HATTERAS
NATIONAL SEASHORE

Little Kinnakeet
Life Saving Station ▲

ATLANTIC
OCEAN

Avon ○ ▲ Avon Pier

Haulover
Canadian Hole ▲

Buxton

Cape Point
Campground
Cape Hatteras
Weather Station   Frisco
Visitor Center Frisco   Campground
Hatteras   ▲ Billy Mitchell
                    Airfield

▲ Cape Hatteras
Lighthouse

CAPE HATTERAS
(CAPE POINT)

Free Ferry
to Ocracoke

Graveyard of
the Atlantic Museum

Diamond
Shoals

0   5 miles
0   5 kilometers

you cross the dunes here to walk along the ocean, you may see the boiler of a steamer that wrecked in 1862, the *Oriental*, above the waves. Continuing south from Pea Island you come to the famed "S Curves," a section of beach noted for its exceptional surfing and its tendency to wash over.

THE TRI-VILLAGES (RODANTHE, WAVES, SALVO)

Towering above the wild dunes, the tall cottages of Mirlo Beach are the first signs of human habitation on Hatteras. Named for a torpedoed ship that sank close by, and a famous rescue, Mirlo is the most quickly eroding stretch of beach on Hatteras.

Once the northern half of Hatteras was the Chicamacomico (chik-a-ma-CO-mee-ko) Banks, taking its name from an Algonquian word meaning sinking or subsiding sands. Villages formed around lifesaving stations established by the federal government in the late 1800s, when numerous shipwrecks gave this coast the well-deserved name, Graveyard of the Atlantic. With no reliable means of summoning help, lifesavers patrolled every foot of coast, 24 hours a day, on the watch for ships in distress.

In the shadow of the Mirlo Beach cottages, the **Chicamacomico Life Saving Station** sits facing the ocean, as it has since 1874. The restored buildings are filled with memories of heroic rescues, violent storms, daily drills, and the harsh life along these shores in years past.

Across the street from the lifesaving station, a road leads down to Rodanthe Harbor, site of a Civil War battle. The village of Chicamacomico was renamed Rodanthe (roe-DAN-thee) when the U.S. Postal Service arrived in 1874. Over time, South Rodanthe and Clark received new postal service names as well, becoming Waves and Salvo. Today you have to look closely to see boundaries between these villages.

In fact, there is a growing trend to refer to this section of Hatteras as the Tri-Villages. It's noted for its many campgrounds and great king mackerel fishing from the pier.

One name you're sure to encounter is Midgett. Descended from a man who purchased land in this area as early as 1717, members of the family today run stores and restaurants, operate one of the area's largest real estate firms, and continue the family's long tradition of serving in the Coast Guard. At the time of the *Mirlo* rescue, five of the six lifesavers on duty were named Midgett. The sixth was married to a Midgett girl.

As you leave the Tri-Villages and enter the National Seashore, the **Salvo Day Use Area** along Pamlico Sound is a great rest stop where you can check out the shallow waters, sunbathe, or windsurf. There's an old cemetery here as well, with many local names on the headstones.

AVON (KINNAKEET)

Ten miles farther down NC 12, Avon is another village that received a name change from the U.S. Postal Service. Many residents still refer to it by its earlier name, Kinnakeet, a village that grew up between the Little Kinnakeet and Big Kinnakeet Life Saving Stations.

The **Avon Fishing Pier** is the town's most notable landmark, famed as a spot to catch drum. The main part of the town lies west of NC 12 along the sound.

Just south of Avon, back in the National Seashore, you'll pass Canadian Hole, famous among windsurfers worldwide. The National Park Service calls it the **Haulover Day Use**

Area and provides restrooms and showers here. The name refers to a pre-windsurfing use of the area, when locals would haul their boats across this narrow stretch of island to avoid the long sail around.

BUXTON

Traveling farther south, you often see kiteboarders' foils above the sound, and up ahead the Banks's most famous landmark, the spiral-striped **Cape Hatteras Light**, comes into view. A climb up the lighthouse offers a staggering view of the cape. To the west and south stretch **Buxton Woods**, one of the largest remaining maritime forests on the East Coast. To the east the treacherous Diamond Shoals stretch 8 miles out to sea, a constant menace to navigation.

Most commercial development in Buxton lies along NC 12 and the Buxton Back Road. Before the post office renamed it for a Fayetteville judge, this area was called simply the Cape. Buxton has a reputation as a casual family-oriented resort, popular for surf fishing, surfing, and—on the sound side—windsurfing and kiteboarding. Buxton was also the location of an immense Indian town, perhaps Croatan, the home of Manteo, friend of the Lost Colony. The site is being excavated in sections by East Carolina University teams.

FRISCO

Formerly the town of Trent (in pre–post office days), Frisco is a quiet family resort town with a lovely fishing pier on the ocean. Back in the 1920s, locals had front-row seats as General Billy Mitchell, a World War I flying ace and early supporter of airpower, tried to build an airfield in the sand. A squad of airplanes soon arrived, then bombed and sank two former battleships just offshore. This early demonstration of airpower is credited with sparking the development of the U.S. Air Force as well as naval aviation. Mitchell was later court-martialed for his outspoken statements, but his views were vindicated by events. Frisco's airport, not far from the fishing pier, is named for Mitchell, as was the famous B-25 Mitchell bomber, a key to victory in World War II.

HATTERAS VILLAGE

Soon after Hatteras Inlet opened in 1846, watermen began moving to the area to enjoy easy access to the rich fishing grounds offshore. In 1935 the Hatteras Development Co. installed an electric generator and ice plant where Oden's Dock now stands, bringing Hatteras into the modern age. Two years later Captain Ernal Foster began taking anglers out after blue marlin aboard his boat the *Albatross*, founding the charter fishing industry in North Carolina.

Despite booming tourism and lots of new construction, the village of Hatteras is actively seeking to preserve its traditional commercial and sport-fishing culture. Life here still revolves around the town's marinas and docks, and many of the inhabitants are members of old island families. The Hatteras watermen share their heritage every September at the annual Day at the Docks and Blessing of the Fleet.

In September 2003, Hurricane Isabel cut the village off from the rest of the island, throwing a new inlet across NC 12 north of town and causing widespread devastation. The Army Corps of Engineers filled the new inlet in record time, but this section of the island is

The 1874 Chicamacomico Life Saving Station displays a unique version of Carpenter Gothic architecture.

still considered unstable. A webcam atop the Hatteras Village water tower keeps an eye on NC 12 toward Frisco.

At the southern end of NC 12 sit the ferry docks where a free state ferry leaves for Ocracoke Island every day, year round. On the far side of the ferry landing, the **Graveyard of the Atlantic Museum** presents the dramatic tales of many ships and sailors, brought to grief.

GETTING AROUND

Without taking a boat or airplane, there is only one way on and off Hatteras Island: the Herbert C. Bonner Bridge. Built in 1962, it replaced the state ferry service that began in 1935.

At the other end of the island, free ferries still run to Ocracoke Island, where NC 12 continues south. The ferries run every day on a regular schedule that changes with season and demand. Ferry service will, however, occasionally be canceled in times of storm or high seas. Check the ferry Web site at www.ncferry.org for the schedule. You can call 252-986-2353 or toll free 800-368-8949 for current conditions. The crossing takes about 40 minutes.

Although NC 12 is frequently over-washed by storm waters and covered with sand, the state's Department of Transportation remains committed to keeping the road open and invests considerable manpower and equipment in this ongoing project.

The aging Bonner Bridge is being replaced but should remain open during construction. If storm or other accident should render the bridge impassable, the state plans to immediately begin ferry service across Oregon Inlet. You can check on the progress of roadwork along this coast by visiting www.obtf.org.

LODGING

As Hatteras Island is the part of the Outer Banks most affected when big storms blow through, its properties may be either battered or brand new. Most of the motels along the "skinny" part of the island above Buxton fall into the former category and show their age. On the other hand, many of the motels in Hatteras Village were newly constructed after Hurricane Isabel washed many of the former structures into the sea in 2003. The motels of Buxton and Frisco fall in between. Many of them are older properties, but well kept and updated. You'll also find a few nice bed-and-breakfast inns along this part of the island.

Hatteras has also seen a great surge in new vacation homes in recent years, most of them large, multi-bedroom structures with many amenities. However, some of the more modest beach houses of an earlier day can still be found, especially in Buxton and on the sound side of the island.

Hatteras Island is the last refuge on the North Carolina coast for camping, with numerous campgrounds, both large and small, welcoming big RVs as well as tents. Several are directly on the ocean or sound, offering a great vacation experience for modest prices.

For last-minute vacations you can check current vacancies at the official **Outer Banks Visitor Bureau** site, www.outer banks.org. The information is updated weekly from Memorial Day to Labor Day and during holiday periods.

Rate Categories

Inexpensive	up to $80
Moderate	$80 to $150
Expensive	$150 to $200
Very Expensive	$200 and up

These rates are per room, based on double occupancy. They do not include room taxes or any special service fees that may apply. The range is usually due to seasonal changes. Rates during the busy summer season and holiday weekends are often double or more the winter off-season rates.

Properties listed are open year round and are air-conditioned, unless otherwise noted. Minimum stays may apply.

Credit Cards

AE—American Express
CB—Carte Blanche
D—Discover Card
DC—Diners Club
J—JCB International Credit Card
MC—Master Card
V—Visa

Resorts and Hotels

BUXTON
CAPE HATTERAS BED AND BREAKFAST
252-995-6004, 800-252-3316
www.surforsound.com/main/capehatteras
46223 Old Lighthouse Rd., Buxton 27920
Price: Moderate
Credit Cards: MC, V
Internet Access: Free WiFi

Enjoy a stay at one of this inn's nine guest rooms, each named for a famous hurricane.

Located a short walk from the beach, the inn is smoke-free and received three diamonds from AAA. All rooms have cable TV, a small refrigerator, a coffeemaker with complimentary coffee and tea, and some have microwaves. You can watch the Cape Hatteras Lighthouse from the Great Room or the large sundeck furnished with comfortable tables and chairs and a gas grill. Guests have the use of bicycles, beach chairs, and coolers, as well as lockable surfboard and sailboard storage. Gourmet breakfasts are a highlight of a stay here, with menus that change daily. Special dietary needs can be accommodated.

CAPE PINES MOTEL
252-995-5666, 866-456-9983
www.capepinesmotel.com
47497 NC 12, Buxton 27920
Price: Inexpensive to Moderate
Credit Cards: MC, V
Internet Access: Free WiFi

Located just a half-mile from the Cape Hatteras Lighthouse, the Cape Pines is an older property but is immaculately maintained and professionally run. It offers clean, comfortable, freshly renovated rooms in a two-story main building and cottages set amid lush landscaping. All rooms have cable TV, and deluxe rooms come equipped with refrigerator, microwave, and coffee pot. One- and two-bedroom suites have a living room and fully equipped kitchen. Guests enjoy a large pool, gas and charcoal grills in the picnic area, a fish cleaning station, and a playground with swings, horseshoe pit, and croquet. Smoking and nonsmoking rooms are available, as are pet-friendly rooms for an additional fee.

THE INN ON PAMLICO SOUND
252-995-7030, 866-PAMLICO
www.innonpamlicosound.com
49684 NC 12, Buxton 27920
Price: Moderate to Very Expensive
Credit Cards: D, MC, V
Internet Access: Free WiFi

A favorite for honeymoons and romantic getaways, this quiet inn enjoys a lovely setting along the sound where stunning sunsets are nightly events. Innkeeper Steve Nelson has created a retreat that manages to be both casual and elegant. The inn's 12 rooms range from modest queens to new king rooms, with whirlpool tubs and private porches. All rooms have TVs with DVD and VCR. The daily rate includes a gourmet three-course breakfast with menus that change daily; afternoon cookie breaks; complimentary beverages and snacks; use of the inn's kayaks, bicycles, beach chairs, and towels; and all the chocolate you can eat. Other amenities include a pool, a 14-seat HD theater with 1,600 DVD titles, and a lending library of books to enjoy on the many porches and decks where hammocks and lounge chairs overlook the sound. Windsurfing, kiteboarding, and fishing can be enjoyed from the inn's docks, and lessons and charters can be arranged, as can in-room massage services. The property is handicapped accessible.

The inn is locally renowned for its cuisine, and dinner here, served in the dining room or on the deck, is open to the public. Reservations are required. Chef Billy Kelly and his staff prepare everything from elegant picnics to breakfast in bed for guests. They'll also cook the fish or ducks you catch. The inn excels at special events, hosting weddings, private film festivals, and corporate retreats with equal ease.

LIGHTHOUSE VIEW MOTEL
252-995-5680, 800-225-7651
www.lighthouseview.com
46677 NC 12, Buxton 27920
Price: Inexpensive to Expensive
Credit Cards: MC, V
Internet Access: Free WiFi

Located directly on the oceanfront with no

road to cross to get to the beach, the Lighthouse View has been operated by the Hooper family since the 1950s. Over the years, the property has grown to include 85 diverse units, ranging from standard rooms and efficiencies to one- and two-bedroom villas and cottages. The largest, the Shell Castle Cottage, accommodates up to 10 people. All units have refrigerators, microwaves, coffeemakers, cable TVs, and phones. A heated pool and hot tub are located on the oceanfront. Other amenities include a playground, barbecue grills, and lighted fish-cleaning tables. Most units require guests to climb at least one flight of stairs. No pets, although a number of cats make their homes here. You can walk down the beach to the Cape Hatteras Lighthouse.

Hatteras Village
BREAKWATER INN
252-986-2565, 877-986-2565
www.breakwaterhatteras.com
57896 NC 12, Hatteras 27943
Price: Inexpensive to Moderate
Credit Cards: MC, V
Internet Access: Free WiFi (some rooms)

The former Hatteras Harbor Motel continues its tradition of welcoming fishermen and hunters. A new sound-front building houses 21 nonsmoking rooms with two queen beds, a kitchenette, high-speed Internet access, and private decks with fabulous sunset views. Two king-bed suites have full kitchens, sofas, and Jacuzzi tubs. The older Fisherman's Quarters building offers standard rooms with two beds, a microwave, and refrigerator, plus an efficiency with living room area and full kitchen. These rooms can accommodate pets, and some are smoker friendly. All units have cable TV. Guests enjoy a continental breakfast and a pool in season. The **Breakwater Restaurant** and Oden's Dock and Marina Store are next door.

HATTERAS LANDING ROOFTOP RESIDENCES
252-986-2841, 800-527-2903
www.hatteraslanding.com
58848 Marina Way, Hatteras 27943
Price: Expensive to Very Expensive
Credit Cards: MC, V
Internet Access: Free WiFi

Upscale lodgings atop the Hatteras Landing shopping complex have two or three bedrooms, 2.5 baths, a kitchen equipped with GE appliances and granite countertops, several cable TVs with DVD players, stereos with CD players, washer/dryers, Internet access, private balconies, and up to 2,200 square feet of space. Boardwalks to the sound and beach, and marina slips are available, along with elevator access to on-site shopping and dining. No smoking or pets.

SEA GULL MOTEL
252-986-2550
www.seagullhatteras.com
56883 NC 12, Hatteras 27943
Price: Moderate
Credit Cards: MC, V
Internet Access: Free WiFi

Completely refurbished after Hurricane Isabel in 2003, the Sea Gull sits on the oceanfront with its own beach. The 15 rooms all have microwave, refrigerator, cable TV, and phone. Efficiencies, a two-bedroom apartment, and larger cottages that sleep six are also available. Amenities include morning coffee, a swimming pool, a picnic area with grills, and a fish-cleaning table. The Sea Gull is closed during the winter.

SEA SIDE INN
252-986-2700, 800-635-7007
www.coverealty.com
57321 NC 12, Hatteras 27943
Price: Inexpensive to Moderate

The top of the Cape Hatteras Lighthouse is the best vantage point to view the island.

Credit Cards: MC, V
Internet Access: Free WiFi

Originally named the Atlantic View Hotel, this was the first hostelry to receive guests in Hatteras Village. The historic 1928 inn was completely renovated with modern amenities after Hurricane Isabel, but retains its cedar-shingle charm. Six suites and four standard rooms, each with private bath and cable TV, are richly paneled and furnished in antiques and wicker. Several, including a honeymoon suite, have Jacuzzi tubs. Spacious decks with grills and common rooms with fireplaces make this a pop-ular place for special events, including weddings. Meal options are available. The inn is a block from the ocean. No pets or smoking permitted. Handicapped-accessible rooms available.

THE VILLAS AT HATTERAS LANDING

252-986-1110, 800-527-2903
www.villasofhatteras.com
58822 Marina Way, Hatteras 27943
Price: Moderate to Expensive
Credit Cards: MC, V
Internet Access: Free WiFi in office area

This complex next to the Hatteras ferry dock, a former Holiday Inn Express, has 53 one-bedroom units available for nightly or weekly rental. Each condominium has a king bed and sleeper sofa, microwave, cable TV, telephone, fully equipped kitchen, and a private balcony or patio. Free guest laundry, swimming pool, sundeck, and boardwalk to the beach are available in the complex. No smoking or pets.

RODANTHE

SEA SOUND MOTEL

252-987-2224
seasound.home.mindspring.com
24224 Sea Sound Rd., Rodanthe 27968
Price: Inexpensive to Moderate
Credit Cards: MC, V

Just a short walk from the beach, this family favorite is noted for its hospitality, and many guests return every year. Standard rooms have one queen bed and refrigerator. Deluxe rooms have two queens, a refrigerator, microwave, and coffeemaker. Efficiencies with full kitchens are also available, as is one pet-friendly unit. Guests can enjoy an outdoor pool, fish-cleaning table, and picnic area with grills. The Sea Sound is closed during the winter.

Cottage Courts

Avon Cottages 252-995-4123; www.avoncottages.com; 40279 Younce Rd., Avon 27915. Modern cottages with two to four bedrooms rent mostly by the week, but a few efficiencies are available by the night.

Dillon's Corner Cottages and Village Homes at the Outer Banks Motel 252-995-5601, 800-995-1233; www.outerbanksmotel.com; 46577 NC 12, Buxton 27920. Located in Buxton just north of the lighthouse, this complex offers a wide range of accommodations, from motel rooms and oceanfront cottages to homes in the village, at great prices. All guests can use the pools, hot tub, rowboats with crab nets, and WiFi at the motel.

Hatteras Cabanas 252-986-2562, 800-338-4775; www.dolphin-realty.com; Hatteras Village. Each efficiency condo has a kitchen, two sundecks, and is topped by a "crow's nest."

Vacation Home and Condo Rentals

For additional rentals on Hatteras Island, check the real estate listings in the North and Central Beaches sections.

Colony Realty 252-995-5891, 800-962-5256; www.hatterasvacations.com; 40197 Bonito Rd., NC 12, Avon 27915. Specializing in smaller, affordable homes suitable for one or two families, Colony also has longer rentals available on Hatteras Island.

Dolphin Realty 252-986-2241, 800-338-4775; www.dolphin-realty.com; 56821 NC 12, Hatteras 27943. Smaller rental company handles properties exclusively on Hatteras Island, including the Hatteras Cabanas.

★ **Hatteras Realty** 252-995-5466, 800-HATTERAS; www.hatterasrealty.com; 1156 NC 12, Avon 27915. The more than 500 vacation homes of every description represented by Hatteras come with member privileges at Club Hatteras, the company's private clubhouse in Avon, with a large heated pool, tennis courts, putting green, playground, snack bar, and changing rooms with showers. Renters can participate in the company's fee-based activities, including a children's day camp. Last-minute three-night stays available.

Midgett Realty 800-527-2903; www.midgettrealty.com; three office locations: 252-995-5333, Island Shops, Avon; 252-986-2841, Hatteras Village; 252-987-2350, Rodanthe. One of the oldest families on the Banks represents nearly 600 rental properties on Hatteras Island, including the condominiums at Hatteras Landing.

Outer Beaches Realty 800-627-3150; www.outerbeaches.com; three office locations: 252-995-4477, Avon; 252-986-2900, Hatteras Village; 252-987-2771, Waves. Operating exclusively on Hatteras Island, Outer Beaches lists over 550 properties, including cottages especially suited to windsurfers, and handicapped-accessible properties. New program eliminates most extra fees.

Surf or Sound Realty 800-237-1138; www.surforsound.com; two office locations: 252-995-5801, Avon; 252-987-1444, Salvo. Over 400 premium homes on Hatteras Island, many with luxurious amenities.

RV Resorts and Campgrounds

★ **Camp Hatteras RV Resort & Campground** 252-987-2777; www.camphatteras.com; 24798 NC 12, Rodanthe 27968. Located on both sides of NC 12, this camping resort offers paved full-hookup sites with cable TV, plus three swimming pools, a hot tub,

The beach in the Tri-Villages gets crowded during the summer months.

clubhouse, tennis courts, miniature golf, a sound-side marina and boat ramp, stocked
fishing ponds, and free WiFi access. WaveRunner and kayak rentals are located on-site.
Open all year.

Cape Hatteras KOA 252-987-2307, 800-562-5268; www.capehatteraskoa.com; NC 12,
Waves. Large campground on the oceanside of NC 12 has over 300 campsites for RVs and
tents, plus one- and two-bedroom Kamping Kabins, which are not air-conditioned or
heated. Amenities include two pools, a hot tub, café, game room, playground, and
planned activities. A kids' train, jumping pillow, mini-golf, kayak rentals, WiFi access,
cable TV hookups, pancake breakfasts, and mechanical bull and surfboard rides are on-
site, all for additional fees. Canine campers enjoy a fenced dog park where they can run
free. Open all year.

Cape Woods Campground 252-995-5850; www.capewoods.com; 47649 Buxton Back Rd.,
Buxton 27920. Occupying a shady pond-side location in Buxton Woods, this family-run
campground has a variety of sites for RVs and tents, plus cabin rentals, pool, heated
bathhouse, laundry, playground, and fish-cleaning stations. Fifty-amp service available.

Frisco Woods Campground 252-995-5208, 800-948-3942; www.outer-banks.com
/friscowoods; NC 12, Frisco 27936. Large, shady campground with 150 RV sites, 100 tent
sites, and air-conditioned cabins, is popular with windsurfers and kayakers, thanks to
its easy launch on Pamlico Sound. Full hookups with cable, pool, laundry, LP gas sales,
fish-cleaning station, and a camp store are available, plus free WiFi.

Hatteras Sands RV Resort 252-986-2422, 888-987-2225; www.hatterassands.com; 57316
Eagle Pass Rd., Hatteras 27943. Highly rated Good Sam campground has over 100 full-
hookup and tent sites, as well as six two-story air-conditioned cabins that look like doll-
houses. Resort-style amenities include a large pool area with kids' pool and spa, fitness

room, a bathhouse that is both heated and air-conditioned, laundry, adult lounge, and a
game room with pool tables. Paddleboats and pedal cars are available for rent.

Island Hide-A-Way Campground 252-995-6628; Buxton Back Rd., Buxton 27920. Small
campground accommodates 30 RVs and 15 tents, with hookups and a bathhouse.

National Park Service Cape Point Campground 252-473-2111; www.nps.gov/caha; 46700
Lighthouse Rd., Buxton 27920. Located within walking distance of the lighthouse and
the beach, 202 sites for RVs and tents are paved, with picnic tables and grills, but no
hookups. No reservations; stays limited to 14 days. Restrooms, cold-water showers,
drinking water, dump station, and pay phone provided. Open summer only.

National Park Service Frisco Campground 252-473-2111; www.nps.gov/caha; 53415 Billy
Mitchell Rd., Frisco 27936. Located amid sand dunes on the oceanfront, the 127 sites
here have no hookups. Restrooms, cold-water showers, and drinking water are available. No reservations; 14-day maximum stays. Open April to October.

Ocean Waves Campground 252-987-2556; www.oceanwavescampground.com; 25313 NC
12, Waves 27982. Quiet campground has over 60 sites with full hookups, cable TV, game
room, camp store, swimming pool, hot showers, laundry, and free WiFi, plus direct
access to the ocean. Tent sites available. Open all year.

Rodanthe Watersports and Campground 252-987-1431; www.watersportsandcampground
.com; 24170 NC 12, Rodanthe 27968. This small campground on Pamlico Sound is a
favorite with windsurfers, kiteboarders, and kayakers. Water and electric hookups for 15
RVs under 25 feet, and 20 tents; full bathhouse. Campers get discounts on watersport
rentals on-site.

Sands of Time Campground 252-995-5596; www.sandsoftimecampground.com; 125
North End Rd., Avon 27915. Quiet park set in a fishing village has full hookups with
cable TV for 57 RVs, plus 15 shady tent sites with water and electric. Bathhouse, laundry,
lighted fish-cleaning table, and a fish freezer.

DINING

Like the island itself, restaurants on Hatteras have a more temporary nature than in
other parts of the Banks. Hurricanes may come through and change the lay of the
land, as Isabel did in 2003, and establishments may rebuild, or they may not. Since
many restaurants make most of their money in the summer months, then take the winter
off, eateries tend to change hands frequently. Your favorite hangout one summer
may have a new owner or a different cuisine by the next.

Dining on Hatteras is relentlessly casual, with very few white-tablecloth establishments. Several very well-known spots are
paper-plate and plastic-fork casual. Restaurants here aren't as geared to large
groups as places you find farther north on the Banks, and service can sometimes get
spotty when the kitchen and wait staff are overextended.

One local specialty, which you'll find under varying names up and down this
coast, is Hatteras clam chowder. It's a whole different take on the genre, having a clear
broth with neither cream nor tomatoes. The clam's own juices are used along with potatoes and onions sautéed in bacon drippings;
it is seasoned with cracked pepper, and salted to taste. Locals often add a splash of
Texas Pete, a hot sauce that—despite its name—is made in North Carolina.

Hatteras Island remains the last place on the outer islands where liquor by the drink
is not available, and since a special referendum to change this regulation failed to pass
in the fall of 2007, it will probably remain

that way for the foreseeable future. Some establishments have brown-bagging licenses, a convoluted custom where you bring your own bottle and pay for set-ups. The local **North Carolina ABC store** (252-995-5532; www.ncabc.com; 47355 NC 12) is at the Osprey Shopping Center in Buxton.

Most restaurants on Hatteras Island close for at least part of the winter, so it's always a good idea to call ahead.

Rate Categories

Inexpensive	under $10
Moderate	$10 to $20
Expensive	$20 to $25
Very Expensive	$25 and up

These ratings represent the average cost of an entrée, not including higher-priced specials, that super-size steak or the rack of lamb. They also do not include appetizers, desserts, beverages, taxes, or gratuities. When a range of ratings is offered, it usually indicates the difference in price between lunch and dinner entrées.

Credit Cards

AE—American Express
D—Discover
DC—Diners Club
MC—Master Card
V—Visa

Meal Abbreviations

B—Breakfast
L—Lunch
D—Dinner
SB—Sunday brunch

Restaurants

AVON
DIRTY DICK'S CRAB HOUSE

252-995-3708
www.dirtydickscrabs.com
39449 NC 12, Avon 27915
Price: Moderate to Expensive
Children's Menu: Yes
Cuisine: Seafood
Liquor: Beer and wine
Serving: L, D
Closed: Winter
Credit Cards: MC, V
Handicapped Access: Yes
Special Features: On-site store; free WiFi access; second location at Hatteras Landing

Crabs every which way, from a crab martini to crab lasagna, are the name of the game here. The menu offers lots of different kinds of crabs, from local blue crabs and soft-shells to king, snow, and Dungeness brought in from the Pacific. The fresh fish catch of the day is prepared several delicious ways, including cedar-planked. Steaks and ribs, plus a number of Louisiana specialties, fill out the menu. Soups, dressings, and sauces are made fresh in-house. Sides range from sweet-potato fries to grits. Other locations on the Banks are at MP 10 on the Bypass in Kill Devil Hills (252-449-CRAB), and at Hatteras Landing (252-995-3425) next to the ferry dock. Their "I Got My Crabs at Dirty Dick's" logo attire is world famous.

DOLPHIN DEN

252-995-7717
40126 NC 12, Avon 27915
Price: Inexpensive to Moderate
Children's Menu: Yes
Cuisine: Seafood
Liquor: Beer and wine
Serving: L, D
Credit Cards: D, MC, V
Handicapped Access: Yes
Special Features: Early-bird specials

Broiled and fried seafood, plus several Italian pasta dishes, are joined by the obligatory rib eye at this family favorite. The Coconut Shrimp is one of the most popular dishes. On the lunch menu you'll find lots of sandwiches and salads, including a tasty shrimp-and-mango combination. Desserts are homemade, and the key lime pie is award-winning.

THE FROGGY DOG
RESTAURANT & PIRATE PUB

252-995-5550
www.froggydog.com
40050 NC 12, Avon 27915
Price: Inexpensive to Expensive
Children's Menu: Yes
Cuisine: Seafood
Liquor: Beer and wine
Serving: B, L, D
Closed: Winter
Credit Cards: MC, V
Handicapped Access: Yes
Special Features: Senior menu; Tadpole
Corner play area; Ribbit's Gifts; TVs in
lounge; live entertainment; daily happy
hour crab and shrimp specials; late-night
menu

A landmark in Avon, the Froggy Dog provides food early to late, plus entertainment and some great souvenirs. Big breakfasts feature pancakes and omelets, but the crowds really pick up in the afternoon when Froggy's serves crab legs and boiled shrimp at special prices, as well as an inexpensive lounge menu of sandwiches and burgers. Everything here is prepared in-house. Come hungry to dinner if you plan on ordering the Surf & Turf or Seafood Medley.

THE MAD CRABBER

252-995-5959
40369 NC 12, Avon 27915
Price: Expensive
Children's Menu: Yes
Cuisine: Seafood
Liquor: Beer and wine
Serving: D
Closed: Winter
Credit Cards: MC, V
Handicapped Access: Yes
Special Features: Pool table

New location of this longtime favorite has a cool log-cabin vibe accented with homespun quilts. The food that made it popular remains the same—huge piles of fresh seafood. To get a taste of everything, order the Mad Platter, a pizza pan heaped high with steamed crab legs or blue crabs, mussels, clams, oysters, crawdads, shrimp, and scallops. The spicy steamed shrimp and scallops are local favorites. Nice list of beers on tap and wines complements the menu.

★ OCEANA'S BISTRO

252-995-4991
www.oceanasbistro.com
41008 NC 12, Avon 27915
Price: Inexpensive to Moderate
Children's Menu: Yes
Cuisine: American
Liquor: Beer and wine
Serving: L, D.
Credit Cards: MC, V
Handicapped Access: Yes
Special Features: Live entertainment; sushi night; daily specials; plasma TV at bar

Bright pink building opposite the Avon Pier serves a pleasing mix of favorites in a relaxed atmosphere. The menu features lots of sandwiches and salads, plus quesadillas and stuffed potatoes. Prime rib is offered at dinner, along with pasta and seafood specialties. Desserts and soups are homemade.

BUXTON
THE CAPTAIN'S TABLE

252-995-3117
47048 NC 12, Buxton 27920
Price: Moderate
Children's Menu: Yes
Cuisine: Seafood
Liquor: Beer and wine
Serving: L, D
Closed: Winter
Credit Cards: MC, V
Handicapped Access: Yes
Special Features: Senior menu; covered deck; smoke-free dining room

Locally owned restaurant receives high marks for both its fresh seafood and its friendly service. Donna Scarborough, the owner, is married to a commercial fisher-man, so the Fresh Catch is always a good bet here. A Mediterranean Seafood Platter sautés North Carolina shrimp, clams, and scallops in white wine and olive oil. At lunch you can get a soup-and-salad combo, or visit the salad bar. Baby back ribs are another specialty, along with pastas, home-style sides, and homemade desserts and milkshakes.

DIAMOND SHOALS RESTAURANT

252-995-5217
46843 NC 12, Buxton 27920
Price: Inexpensive to Moderate
Children's Menu: Yes
Cuisine: Seafood
Liquor: Beer and wine
Serving: B, L, D
Closed: Winter
Credit Cards: MC, V
Handicapped Access: Yes
Special Features: Gift shop; seafood market

Reliable local spot serves satisfying meals at reasonable prices. A breakfast buffet is offered on weekends in season, and the regular breakfast platters are varied and ample. At lunch you can order burgers, sal-ads, sandwiches, and fried seafood baskets. Dinner adds several more elaborate seafood dishes, plus steaks and pork chops, as well as all-you-can-eat specials. Diamond Shoals has numerous aquariums filled with tropical fish—the largest collection on the island—making it a favorite with kids.

THE INN ON PAMLICO SOUND RESTAURANT

252-995-7030, 800-PAMLICO
www.innonpamlicosound.com
49684 NC 12, Buxton 27920
Price: Expensive
Children's Menu: Yes
Cuisine: Locavore
Liquor: Beer and wine
Serving: D

Credit Cards: D, MC, V
Handicapped Access: Yes
Special Features: Dining on deck

Definitely the class act when it comes to dining on Hatteras Island, the restaurant of this elegant inn accepts a limited number of outside reservations for dinner. Menus change nightly as the talented chefs create gourmet dishes based on the freshest local produce and seafood available, as well as organic grain-fed beef and vegetable-fed chicken. Vegetarian and vegan choices are also available. Soups and desserts are homemade and outstanding. You can dine on the deck overlooking Pamlico Sound or in the white-tablecloth dining room. Extensive wine list.

POP'S RAW BAR

252-995-7734
48967 NC 12, Buxton 27920
Price: Inexpensive
Children's Menu: Yes
Cuisine: Seafood
Liquor: Beer and wine
Serving: L, D
Closed: Sunday
Credit Cards: MC, V
Handicapped Access: Yes
Special Features: Bar; darts; TV

Pop's is open all year, and most evenings find it crowded with locals, enjoying fresh steamed seafood, bowls of Hatteras chow-der, burgers, barbecue, and a menu of bar favorites. The atmosphere here is some-times smoky but always casual, and the food is top-notch. Locally made crab cakes and fish cakes, spicy steamed shrimp, really cold beer, and lots of local gossip make this place an experience.

HATTERAS VILLAGE
BREAKWATER RESTAURANT & BAR

252-986-2733
www.breakwaterhatteras.com
NC 12, Oden's Dock, Hatteras 27943

Price: Expensive
Children's Menu: Yes
Cuisine: Seafood
Liquor: Beer and wine; brown bagging
Serving: D
Closed: Winter
Credit Cards: MC, V
Special Features: Bar; deck; live entertainment at sunset

Enjoy the fabulous sunset views from this restaurant on the second floor at Oden's marina. The menu is creative, offering unusual appetizers and specials, including a highly praised dish of mussels simmered in a blue cheese sauce. Entrées range from a Hatteras Seafood Stew to Filet Oscar topped with crabmeat. Fresh seafood comes fried or broiled in white wine and butter. You can eat in the white-tablecloth dining room or in more casual surroundings on the large covered deck, where you'll often encounter a band playing music to end the day in style.

DINKY'S WATERFRONT RESTAURANT

252-986-2020
www.dinkysrestaurant.com
57980 NC 12, Village Marina, Hatteras
Price: Moderate
Children's Menu: Yes
Cuisine: American
Liquor: Beer and wine; brown bagging
Serving: D
Credit Cards: MC, V
Handicapped Access: Yes
Special Features: Bar; smoke-free; takeout available

Open all year, this is hot spot for locals who gather around the mahogany bar after the fishing fleet comes in. Steaks and seafood fresh off the boat dominate the menu, along with daily specials. Regulars recommend the crab cakes and soups. The restaurant is small, with just 48 seats, but offers great sunset views over the water. If you were lucky on your fishing trip, ask Dinky's to cook up your catch.

THE TRI-VILLAGES
(RODANTHE, WAVES, SALVO)
ATLANTIC COAST CAFÉ

252-987-1200
www.atlanticcoastcafe.com
25150 NC 12, Waves 27982
Price: Inexpensive to Moderate
Children's Menu: Yes
Cuisine: American
Liquor: Beer and wine
Serving: B, L, D
Closed: Winter
Credit Cards: AE, D, MC, V
Special Features: Takeout available; free WiFi access; burger happy hour

This Internet hot spot is a favorite with campers from the KOA located just across NC 12. In the morning the café serves breakfast sandwiches, French toast and pancakes, wraps and classic breakfast plates. Later in the day, you can have a crab cake or shrimp Reuben "Hatteras style" with slaw, or classic corned beef with kraut. Burgers are made of tuna, chicken, or beef, and are half-price from 4 to 6 PM. Eat inside or on the deck with a view of Pamlico Sound, especially nice at sunset. The café also prepares boards loaded with their most popular menu items, perfect for groups or parties.

BOARDWOK SOUTH

252-987-1080
24267 NC 12, Pamlico Station, Rodanthe 27968
Price: Moderate
Children's Menu: Yes
Cuisine: Asian, Seafood
Liquor: Beer and wine
Serving: L, D
Closed: Winter
Credit Cards: MC, V
Special Features: Bar; takeout available

Located on the second floor of Pamlico Station, the Boardwok has a terrific view of sunsets over the sound, a somewhat sophisticated atmosphere, and prices to match. The specialties here are Asian stir-fried dishes made with rice, lo mein, or rice noodles with your choice of vegetables, meat, or seafood. There are surf-and-turf entrées as well, including an excellent crab cake, fresh tuna steak, a super-rich Crabmeat and Butter dish, rib eyes, and filet mignon. The menu also offers a nice list of sandwiches, salads, and appetizers, and tasty crab bisque.

Food Purveyors

Bakeries and Coffee Shops

The Dancing Turtle Coffee Shop 252-986-4004; 58079 NC 12, Hatteras 27943. Dog-friendly Internet hot spot serves a full menu of coffee drinks, plus iced tea and coffee, organic teas, and tasty muffins.

Island Coffee & Gifts 252-987-1500; 26657 NC 12, Salvo 27982. Located next to Island Dyes' collection of tie-dyed clothing and tobacco products, this shop lets you get both your caffeine and shopping fix.

Island Perks Coffee Shop two locations: 252-986-1111, 46618 NC 12, Buxton 27920; 252-995-7977, 50840 NC 12, Indian Town Gallery Shops, Frisco 27936. Coffee made of beans roasted on the Outer Banks, fresh baked goods, and free WiFi are available at both these local favorites. The Buxton location serves a full breakfast and home-style lunch all year.

Orange Blossom Bakery & Café 252-995-4109; www.orangeblossombakery.com; 47208 NC 12, Buxton 27920. Famous for its huge Apple Uglies, this café located near the entrance to Cape Hatteras Lighthouse also serves breakfast sandwiches, organic coffees, cinnamon rolls, hand-glazed doughnuts, and the soon-to-be-famous Chocolate Ugly.

Uglie Mugs Coffeehouse 252-995-5590; 40534 NC 12, Kinnakeet Shoppes, Avon 27915. Internet hot spot has a computer you can use, plus great coffee and cinnamon buns.

Breakfast

Endless Summer 252-986-2205; www.hatteraslanding.com; 58848 Marina Way, Hatteras Landing, Hatteras 27943. Located next to the ferry docks, the deli here is a great place to pick up breakfast before the ferry ride to Ocracoke.

Gingerbread House Bakery 252-995-5204; 52715 NC 12, Frisco 27936. Hansel and Gretel–style cottage offers inside and outside seating, as well as delicious baked goods, breakfast biscuits, French toast, and waffles. A favorite with kids.

The Shrimp Shack 252-986-4003; 56870 NC 12, Hatteras 27943. Casual spot serves a full breakfast menu and can handle large groups. Try the shrimp burger for lunch.

Sonny's Restaurant 252-986-2922; 57947 NC 12, Hatteras 27943. After more than three decades serving Hatteras diners, Sonny's has breakfast figured out: homemade biscuits and home fries, big servings, friendly service.

Candy and Ice Cream

Topping off the evening with an ice cream binge is an honored summer tradition for many vacationing families. Look for the local "Hatteras style" cone: a scoop of ice cream topped with a layer of shaved ice and the syrup of your choice. Vanilla ice cream topped with root beer ice is a popular favorite.

Cool Wave Ice Cream Shoppe 252-995-6366; 47237 NC 12, Buxton 27920. Hand-scooped ice cream is served at this shop next to the mini-golf course.

Hatteras Island Snowballs 252-986-2064, NC 12, Frisco. Hatteras-style snowballs are a specialty.

Ocean Gourmet and Gifts 252-987-1166; 24753 NC 12, Rodanthe 27968. Homemade fudge, ice cream, and candy shop is within walking distance of Camp Hatteras.

Scotch Bonnet Candies and Gifts 252-995-4242, 1-888-354-4242; www.scotchbonnet fudges.com; 51684 NC 12, Frisco 27936. This shop, making outstanding homemade fudge, 24 flavors of saltwater taffy, and doggie treats, has been featured on the *Food Network*.

★ **Uncle Eddy's Frozen Custard and Coffeehouse** 252-995-4059; 46860 NC 12, Buxton 27920. Homemade frozen custard in an ever-expanding list of flavors including fig (a local favorite), sorbet smoothies, coffee drinks, and open-air seating, plus unlimited mini-golf next door.

Village Conery 26204 Monitor Lane, Salvo 27982. Soft-serve and hand-dipped ice cream and frozen yogurt come in your choice of shakes, sundaes, splits, or cones.

Groceries and Specialty Foods

Lines can be outrageously long at the Food Lion in Avon on the weekends, as everyone checks into their vacation cottages and shops for the week ahead. Avoid the crowds by shopping at one of the local groceries that have served the islanders for generations, at a local seafood market, or at one of the many gourmet food shops that flourish on Hatteras. You can always visit the Food Lion later; it's open 24/7 during the summer season.

AVON

Breeze Thru Avon 252-995-3347; 40374 NC 12, Avon 27915. No need to get out of your car to score beer and soft drinks at this drive-through convenience store.

★ **Island Spice & Wine** 252-995-7750; 40246 NC 12, Avon 27915. The over 200 wines and champagnes, microbrews, and imports stocked here include many North Carolina brands. Lots of supplies for gourmet cottage meals. Check the schedule for wine tastings.

Kinnakeet Corner 252-995-7011; NC 12 and Harbor Dr., Avon 27915. Located at the road that will take you down to Avon's fishing harbor, this little store and gas station stocks groceries and serves hot breakfast and lunch.

The Village Grocery 252-995-4402; 40618 NC 12, Avon 27915. Upscale grocery in the heart of Avon.

BUXTON

Conner's Supermarket 252-995-5711, 47468 NC 12, Buxton 27920. Locally owned and operated grocery, serving locals and visitors for half a century.

HATTERAS

★ **Burrus Red & White Supermarket** 252-986-2333; 57196 Kohler Rd., Hatteras 27943. Located in the heart of Hatteras Village, this family-run grocery has been serving locals since 1866. Excellent deli items, fresh meat, seafood, and produce, plus all the necessities and a friendly staff. Open all year.

Lee Robinson's General Store 252-986-2381; 58372 NC 12. Hatteras 27943. An island classic that has weathered many hurricanes.

The Salty Gourmet 252-986-9944; 57204 NC 12, Beacon Shops, Hatteras 27943. Super selection of gourmet goodies, from sushi-making supplies to organic foods, microbrews and wine, plus lots of free samples. Sponsors wine tastings and cooking demos.

TRI-VILLAGES (RODANTHE, WAVES, SALVO)

The Blue Whale 252-987-2335; 27307 NC 12, Salvo 27972. Fun stop sells groceries and gas, beer and wine, plus a popular logo tee.

Big Waves Market and Deli 252-987-2352, 26006 NC 12, St. Waves Plaza, Waves 27982. Small grocery has beer, wine, and seafood, plus hot foods, sandwiches, and daily specials.

JoBob's Trading Post 252-987-2201; 23202 NC 12, Rodanthe 27968. JoBob's stocks a great selection of fresh seafood and sauces, in addition to beer, wine, bait and tackle.

Mac's Market at Island Convenience 252-987-2239; 23532 NC 12, Rodanthe 27968. Mac Midgett's store has some of everything, including groceries, bait and tackle, and a popular deli counter.

Pizza

Angelo's Pizza 252-995-6364; 46903 NC 12, Buxton 27920. Nice eat-in spot has good pizza, plus other pasta favorites, and a mean Philly cheesesteak sub. Kids like the arcade room. Open all year.

Gingerbread House Bakery 252-995-5204; 52715 NC 12, Frisco 27936. Specialty pizzas with regular and whole-wheat crusts get the real bakery treatment.

Lisa's Pizzeria 252-987-2525; 24158 NC 12, Rodanthe 27968. Hand-tossed pizza heads the menu. Eat in, take out, or get free delivery (after 4 PM).

Mona Lisa's Pizzeria and Bakery 252-986-1587; 58848 NC 12, Hatteras Landing, Hatteras 27943. Pizza slices, breakfast sandwiches, boxed lunches for the ferry, and seagull biscuits, next to the ferry dock. Delivery available.

Nino's Pizza 252-995-5358; 41188 Palazzolo Rd., Avon 27915. Hand-tossed pizzas and pasta dishes, plus burgers, subs, and salads. Beer available. Free delivery in Avon.

Rocco's Pizza and Italian Restaurant 252-986-2150; www.obxroccos.com; 57331 NC 12, Hatteras 27943. A full menu ranging through Italian dishes, salads, seafood, and home-made desserts is served all year.

Topper's Pizza and Pasta 252-995-3109; 41934 NC 12, Hatteras Island Plaza, Avon 27915. This local favorite serves specialty pizzas and oven-baked subs, plus daily specials made from family recipes. Beer and wine available on-site. Free WiFi access. Delivery from Avon to Frisco. Open all year.

Sandwiches and Takeout

Bubba's Original Bar-B-Q 252-995-5421; www.bubbasbbque.com, 53060 NC 12, Frisco 27936; **Bubba's Too BBQ & Chicken** 252-995-4385; Hatteras Island Plaza, NC 12, Avon. Both locations serve hickory-smoked pork, beef, turkey, and chicken barbecue basted in Bubba's original sauce, clams, and chili con carne, as well as homemade desserts such as sweet potato pie. A country breakfast is served every morning. Delivery available from Rodanthe to Hatteras Village.

Buxton Munch Company 252-995-5502; 47355 NC 12, Osprey Shoppes, Buxton 27920. Small sandwich shop serves great wraps, quesadillas, and vegetarian dishes for lunch on weekdays all year, amid '60s music and memorabilia.

Hatteras Harbor Deli 252-986-2552; www.hatterasharbor.com; 58058 NC 12, Hatteras Harbor Marina, Hatteras 27943. Enjoy breakfast and lunch sandwiches at dockside tables, or pick up a bag lunch before your fishing charter. Opens early.

Hot Tuna Grub & Pub 252-987-2266; 23500 NC 12, Rodanthe 27968. This casual spot with a cool vibe serves steamed and fried seafood, Chicago-style pizza, and sandwiches to take out or to enjoy in the bar or dining room. Delivery available in the Tri-Villages.

Marilyn's Deli 252-987-2239; 23532 NC 12, Island Convenience, Rodanthe 27968. Popular stop with surfers and locals for the home-cooked specials at breakfast and lunch.

★ **Martha Jane's Kitchen and Chocolate Bar** 252-986-2024; 56910 NC 12, Stowe on Twelve, Hatteras 27943. Gourmet sandwiches, homemade chicken and pasta salads, and desserts are great at this sweet little spot.

Cafe 12 252-995-3602; 41934 NC 12, Hatteras Island Plaza, Avon 27915. A creative, Mediterranean-tinged menu of "flat top" tortillas, seafood, and vegetarian items, and extensive by-the-glass wine list, make this a favorite gathering spot among locals.

Sooey's BBQ & Rib Shack 252-986-1227; www.sooeysbbq.com; 53674 NC 12, Frisco 27936. Eastern N.C. pork barbecue, ribs, beef brisket, and family-style sides, to eat in or take out.

Teach's Island Bar & Grill 252-986-2139; www.teachslair.com; Teach's Lair Marina, Hatteras. Great views team with a menu of sandwiches, plus baby back ribs, fish taco salads, and seafood dim sum. Children and senior menus available.

Top Dog Café 252-987-1272; 27982 NC 12, Waves 27982. Dine on huge burgers, seafood, hot dogs, beer and wine, on the deck or screened porch of this casual, family-friendly spot.

Seafood Markets

A few pounds of steamed shrimp make an inexpensive and delicious meal. Most seafood markets will steam shrimp or crabs for you at no additional charge.

Austin's South Island Seafood and Produce 252-987-1352; 23325 NC 12, Rodanthe 27968. Fresh local seafood, available raw or cooked to order, plus fruits and produce, deli meats, and steaks and pork chops cut to order.

Buxton Seafood 252-995-5085; 49799 NC 12, Buxton 27920. Fresh local seafood, plus steaks, wine, produce, and other groceries.

★ **Risky Business Seafood Markets** www.riskybseafood.com; Avon location: 252-995-7003, 40658 NC 12; Hatteras Village location: 252-986-2117, Oden's Dock, NC 12. These markets, where the quality of the seafood is anything but risky, offer steamed or raw crabs, famous secret-recipe crab cakes, and a variety of other local seafood. They will also clean, vacuum pack, and freeze your catch, then pack it for travel when you leave, or ship it to you.

Surf's Up Seafood Market 252-995-3432; 41838 NC 12, Hatteras Island Plaza, Avon 27915. Local and imported seafood includes live lobsters, king and snow crab legs, salmon, and red snapper, plus clam bakes with all the fixings to cook at home.

TOURING

In 2007 the Outer Banks Visitors Bureau opened its new **Hatteras Welcome Center** (252-986-2203, 877-629-4386; www.outerbanks.org) in the recently restored 1901 U.S. Weather Bureau Station. Here you'll find information on attractions and events and can view exhibits on the history of weather forecasting. The welcome center is located next to the Burrus Red & White grocery in the heart of Hatteras Village, at 57190 Kohler Road, and is open 9–5 all year.

You can take a virtual tour of Hatteras Village at the Web site of the **Hatteras Village**

Civic Association, www.hatterasonmymind.com, where links show pictures of some of the storms that have hit the island, as well as historic sites, some still standing, some washed away. The Web site has many interviews with local people discussing everything from the history of sport fishing to famous shipwrecks and German sub attacks.

By Bus or Minivan

Hatteras Tours 252-475-4477; www.hatterastours.com. Native historian Danny Couch
conducts tours of Hatteras Island that combine old-time stories he heard as a boy with
plenty of real scholarship. Tours aboard Couch's 25-passenger, air-conditioned bus are
a great way to get up to speed on island issues. He also takes his bus over to Ocracoke
several times a week, telling stories laced with pirates and ponies.

By Air

Burrus Flightseeing Tours 252-986-2679; www.hatterasislandflightseeing.com; Billy
Mitchell Airport, Frisco. Local pilot Dwight Burrus offers air tours that provide fabulous
views of the Cape Hatteras Lighthouse, shipwrecks, Ocracoke ponies, and more.

CULTURE

Although overgrown by the profitable tourist industry, the traditional villages of Hatteras
Island continue to function, grouped around fishing piers now, instead of lifesaving stations. In the winter months, community association, church, and fire company events
dominate the event calendar.

Architecture

In 1874 the U.S. Life Saving Service began building stations along the East Coast. The earliest stations were designed by architect Frances W. Chandler in an eclectic style with
medieval and Renaissance influences. The stations' architecture, called carpenter Gothic,
used a board-and-batten style put together with wooden pegs that reminds many people of
Scandinavian ski lodges. Most of these stations have been lost to fire or flood, or altered
over the years, but Hatteras Island has two of the best-preserved of all the 1874 stations,
plus one very authentic replica of this unique architectural style.

The best, most completely restored station is the very first one built along this coast,
now part of the **Chicamacomico Historic Site** (252-987-1552; www.chicamacomico.net).
The National Park Service is restoring the Little Kinnakeet station, also built in the 1870s,
located just north of Avon. The **Pea Island Art Gallery** (252-987-2879), the last building on
the sound side as you leave Salvo heading south, authentically reproduces much of the
intricate woodwork that is the hallmark of carpenter Gothic style.

Art Galleries and Museums

The beauties of storm and sun have attracted a large colony of artists to Hatteras, including
many fine photographers specializing in wildlife, sunsets, and surfscapes.

Blue Pelican Gallery 252-986-2244; www.bluepelicangallery.com, www.photosfromthe
porch.com; 57762 NC 12, Hatteras 27943. Hatteras Island native Jenn Johnson displays
her photography and unique jewelry, along with the work of other local artists, at this
gallery next to the Burrus Red & White.

The Barnett Graveyard provides a stark contrast to the large vacation homes and upscale shopping of Hatteras Landing.

Gaskins Gallery 252-995-6617; 40462 North End Rd., Avon 27915. This gallery in a traditional cedar-shake cottage displays paintings and pottery by local artists, as well as photography and prints, and offers a framing service. Collectors of Fenton art glass and
Annalee dolls will enjoy shopping here.

Indian Town Gallery 252-995-5181; www.indiantowngallery.com; 50840 NC 12, Frisco
27936. One-of-a-kind artworks by Outer Banks artists in a variety of mediums are displayed at this gallery, where you can watch artist Wayne Fulcher, grandson of a Cape Hatteras lightkeeper, at work.

★ **Karen Rhodes Billfish Art** 252-986-4096; www.reelfishart.com; 56910 NC 12, Stowe
on Twelve, Hatteras 27943. Artist Karen Rhodes' artworks take a humorous look at the
life of a billfish. The images also adorn a wide range of products from clothing to home
décor, lip gloss to candles.

★ **Pea Island Art Gallery** 252-987-2879; www.peaislandartgallery.com; 27766 NC 12,
Salvo 27982. Housed in a replica of one of the lifesaving stations, a work of art in itself,
Kim Robertson's gallery exhibits her own artwork as well as the work of some 100 other
talented artists. A portion of sales benefits the Pea Island Wildlife Refuge and the Chicamacomico Life Saving Station.

Red Drum Pottery 252-995-5757; www.reddrumpottery.com; 51976 NC 12, Frisco 27936.
The studio of potters Rhonda Bates and Wes Lassiter displays their original pieces,
including a collection of beach and nautical-theme Christmas ornaments. Wes, familiar

to Molasses Creek fans as "Banjo Wes," is often at work in the studio. During the summer the gallery hosts the **Frisco Jubilee**, evenings of original bluegrass tunes.

Sandy Bay Gallery 252-986-1338; 57204 NC 12, Beacon Shops, Hatteras 27943. Lovely selection of art, blown glass, sculpture, and jewelry includes many local works.

Woods Oceanic Arts 252-995-6165; 47188 NC 12, Buxton 27920. Check out the local talent at this gallery featuring a wide variety of arts and crafts, next to the Orange Blossom Bakery.

Historic Homes and Sites

BARNETT GRAVEYARD
Hatteras Landing
NC 12, Hatteras Village

An evocative graveyard dating to 1859 can be reached by a boardwalk over the marsh north of Hatteras Landing. Buried amid the twisted cedars are Stephen and Rebecca Barnett, lost when their schooner broke up on the Ocracoke shoals.

★ CAPE HATTERAS LIGHTHOUSE
252-995-4474
www.nps.gov/caha
Lighthouse Rd., Buxton 27920
Hours: Visitor Center and museum open all year, 9–6, mid-June to Labor Day; 9–5 the rest of the year. The lighthouse is open for climbing from mid-April to Columbus Day. Tours begin at 9 AM and run every 10 minutes until 5:30 PM in summer, 4:30 in spring and fall. Admission: Climbing tour tickets are $7 for adults; $3.50 for seniors 62 or older and children 12 and under. Admission to the park and museum is free.

The iconic landmark of Hatteras Island continues to flash its warning out to sea as it has since 1870. The 208-foot tower, the tallest lighthouse in the nation, is painted with a distinctive black and white spiral pattern and flashes every 7.5 seconds. Visitors at least 42 inches tall can climb the 268 steps to the walkway at the top of the light for great views over Hatteras Island and Diamond Shoals. Next to the lighthouse, the two-story Double Keepers Quarters has been restored and houses a visitor center, bookstore, and the **Museum of the Sea**, with exhibits on the history and ecology of the Outer Banks and information on the lighthouse and its dramatic move inland in 1999. A video on "The Move of the Century" is shown daily at the museum. During the summer months, park rangers offer a variety of free programs on the history of the lighthouse and the cape, including talks on shipwrecks, lifesavers, and pirates.

★ CHICAMACOMICO LIFE SAVING STATION HISTORIC SITE
252-987-1552
www.chicamacomico.net
23645 NC 12, Rodanthe 27968
Hours: Mid-Apr. to Nov., Mon.–Fri. 12–5 PM
Admission: Adults $6; seniors 65 and up and students $4; family groups, including all children under 17, $15

This historic site is dedicated to the amazing history and valiant heritage of the U.S. Life

Saving Service, which gave birth to the U.S. Coast Guard in 1915. The service achieved many daring rescues along this coast in the days when the area was earning its title as Graveyard of the Atlantic. The complex of buildings in Rodanthe is the most complete lifesaving station complex remaining on the East Coast. It includes the 1874 station, the first to be built on the Outer Banks, and the 1911 Life-Saving Station, now restored as a gift store and museum. Exhibits detail the daily drills of the lifesavers, as well as the many rescues and wrecks that took place along this coast. Other buildings on the site include the 1907 Midgett House, with original furnishings. Volunteer crews from nearby Coast Guard stations reenact the breeches buoy drill every week during the summer season.

CIVIL WAR TRAILS

www.civilwartraveler.com

Markers in the parking lot of the Graveyard of the Atlantic Museum describe the capture of Forts Hatteras and Clark in 1861, the sinking of the *USS Monitor* in 1862, and other wartime shipwrecks. A marker in the parking lot of the Hatteras Village Civic Center on NC 12 describes the amphibious assault on Forts Hatteras and Clark. Nearby, a marker located on the grounds of Eastern Carolina Bank (57197 Koehler Rd., a block west of NC 12), describes islanders' attempt to reconstitute a Union-oriented government.

A marker across NC 12 from the Chicamacomico Life Saving Station in Rodanthe tells the tale of the infamous Chicamacomico Races, during which Confederates and Federals chased each other up and down the island in October 1861. A marker in a picnic area on the sound nearby describes the capture of the *Fanny*, a Union supply ship, on October 1, 1861.

LITTLE KINNAKEET LIFE SAVING STATION

252-995-4474
www.nps.gov/caha
NC 12, Cape Hatteras National Seashore
Not open to the public

Located down a short road on the sound side of NC 12, just north of the town of Avon, the Little Kinnakeet Station is being restored by the National Park Service, which moved it away from the ocean. The station complex, currently surrounded by a high fence, includes an 1870s building and a 1904 building, both similar to the already restored buildings at Chicamacomico, and offers an interesting perspective on the challenges faced by preservationists. The National Park Service is also restoring stations at Bodie Island and Creeds Hill, near Frisco.

MONITOR NATIONAL MARINE SANCTUARY

757-599-3122
www.monitor.noaa.gov
Open to divers by permit only

Located in 230 feet of water, about 16 miles south-southeast of Cape Hatteras Lighthouse, the wreck of the most famous Civil War ship was discovered in 1973. Because of its depth and the extreme currents present in the area, only the most technically proficient divers receive permits to visit the sanctuary. The National Oceanic and Atmospheric Administration (NOAA), which administers the sanctuary, successfully raised the *Monitor*'s gun turret in 2002. Most recovered *Monitor* artifacts are at the **Mariners' Museum** (757-596-2222,

The 1901 U.S. Weather Station, now a welcome center for Hatteras Island

800-581-7245; www.monitorcenter.org) in Newport News, Virginia; however, some artifacts can be seen at the Graveyard of the Atlantic Museum in Hatteras Village.

THE OLD GRAY HOUSE
252-995-6098
www.outerbanksshells.com
Light Plant Rd., Buxton 27920
Open: Daily; closed in winter
Admission: Free

Take a step back in time with a visit to this traditional homestead owned by a family that has been on the island since the 1600s. Built largely from salvaged ship timbers, the house today is filled with local crafts. Outside, a big collection of shells occupies several shacks, and the old chicken coop displays bird models and coconut art. Nearby are the old outhouse and a garden full of native plants such as the yaupon. A path leading through the woods to the **Cape Pines Motel** is posted with signs about island lore.

SALVO POST OFFICE
NC 12, Salvo

Famous as the country's smallest post office until it was decommissioned in 1992, the tiny white building with blue and white trim is now listed on the National Register of Historic Places. It sits along the west side of NC 12 just south of the Park Road junction. The nearest operating U.S. Post Office is in Waves.

SERENDIPITY BEACH COTTAGE
22847 NC 12, Rodanthe 27968
Not open to the public

Mirlo Beach's most northern oceanside house, Serendipity, served as a location in the movie *Nights in Rodanthe*, starring Richard Gere and Diane Lane. Waves frequently wash over this section of NC 12.

U.S. WEATHER BUREAU

252-986-2203, 877-629-4386
www.outerbanks.org
57190 Kohler Rd., Hatteras 27943
Open: 9 AM–5 PM, all year
Admission: Free

Built in 1901, this first U.S. Weather Bureau Station played a key role in the nation's developing meteorological network and in the lives of local residents, giving warning of oncoming storms. The building in Hatteras Village, now on the National Register of Historic Places, has been restored to its original appearance, with a cedar-shingled widow's walk. Today, it houses an Outer Banks Visitor Center.

Museums and Exhibits

★ FRISCO NATIVE AMERICAN MUSEUM & NATURAL HISTORY CENTER

252-995-4440
www.nativeamericanmuseum.org
53536 NC 12, Frisco 27936
Open: 11–5, Tue.–Sun.
Admission: $5 per person; $15 per family; $3 seniors

Built close to the site of an early Indian village, this museum displays an amazing collection of Native American artifacts from pre-colonial to modern times. Of special interest are the dugout canoe found on museum property and items from the archaeological dig nearby. The museum also contains galleries of art and antiques, a natural history room, bookstore, and a gift shop offering the work of over 30 Native American artists. Outside, a bird garden and nature trails connect with the natural world.

★ GRAVEYARD OF THE ATLANTIC MUSEUM

252-986-2995, 252-986-2996
www.graveyardoftheatlantic.com
59200 Museum Dr., Hatteras 27943
Open: 10–4, Tue.–Sat.
Admission: Free

This fascinating museum, now a part of the North Carolina state history museum system, is dedicated to conserving the maritime heritage of the area and memories of the hundreds of shipwrecks that line the coast. On display are shipwreck artifacts from the age of pirates through World War II, including some recovered from the wreck of the ironclad *Monitor*, and an Enigma machine from a German submarine. The star of the collection is the 1854 Fresnel lens from the first Cape Hatteras Lighthouse; the lens disappeared during the Civil War and was only recently recovered and restored. The dramatic building, with a sweeping design resembling the bones of a shipwreck, sits at the end of NC 12, on the far side of the state ferry docks.

WORLD RECORD BLUE MARLIN
Hatteras Village Library and Community Center
57960 NC 12, Hatteras 27943
Admission: Free

This open-air exhibit displays what was once the world-record blue marlin, an 810-pound monster caught June 11, 1962, by Captain Bill Foster of the Albatross Fleet. The catch established Hatteras as one of the top sport-fishing capitals of the world.

Music and Nightlife
Restaurants and bars on Hatteras Island are allowed to serve only beer and wine. Entertainment is sparse during the winter, when many spots close or cut back their hours. The nightlife scene gathers steam during the summer months, when you'll find live entertain-

The Graveyard of the Atlantic Museum houses a restored Fresnel lens.

ment at the Froggy Dog, the Mad Crabber, and Oceana's Bistro in Avon. **Avon Café** (252-995-7866; 40774 NC 12, Avon 27915) is a popular hangout for the boarding crowd, with a big bar menu and vegetarian offerings.

The Breakwater Restaurant (252-986-2733) in Hatteras Village sponsors sundown music on its deck overlooking Oden's Dock in season.

The Sandbar Grille (252-995-3411; www.sandbarandgrille.com; 49250 NC 12) in Buxton is popular with the bar crowd, thanks to its late-night menu, sushi, game room, and schedule of live entertainment and karaoke.

Uncle Pauly's at the East Coast Surf Shop (252-987-1623; 24394 NC 12) has the hottest nightlife scene in Rodanthe, with live music, a dance floor, and karaoke some nights. The grill here serves breakfast, lunch, and dinner, with Caribbean and Asian touches.

During the summer months, the **Red Drum Pottery** (252-995-5757; www.reddrumpottery .com) hosts the Frisco Jubilee (www.friscojubilee.com), weekly evenings of original bluegrass tunes by the Diamond Shoals Band.

RECREATION

Fishing is the traditional recreational activity on Hatteras Island, from inexpensive angling from the beach or piers to high-end trips after big-game fish in the Gulf Stream. Recent years, however, have seen a huge increase in the popularity of board-based water sports, as surfers, then windsurfers, and most recently kiteboarders, flock to take advantage of Hatteras Island's unique combination of wind, water, and waves.

Beaches

Hatteras Island faces the Atlantic with a long, unspoiled beach for some 50 miles, from the Bonner Bridge to the spit south of Hatteras Village. The island bends to the west after Cape Hatteras, and the water and waves along the southern shore are often warmer and less wild than the eastern-facing beaches farther north.

Most of the beach is under the management of the National Park Service, which maintains several spots along NC 12 where you can park and cross the dunes. It's not advisable to pull off on the shoulders of NC 12, as the sand there can be deceptively deep. There are no lifeguards along this beach.

If your car has four-wheel drive, you can drive onto the beach at off-road vehicle ramps located along the island. The beaches in front of the island villages are generally closed to vehicle traffic from March 15 to September 15. Several sand roads lace the area of Cape Point near the lighthouse, and the Old Sand Road beyond the Graveyard of the Atlantic Museum leads down to the shore of the inlet. Pick up a current off-road driving map at one of the visitor centers on the island.

All beaches are subject to closure for resource protection during the nesting and pre-nesting seasons of piping plovers and other rare shorebirds, as well as loggerhead and green turtles. Weekly access reports are issued March through November, and closures are strictly enforced. No driving on the national seashore beaches is allowed after dark during most of the year. When after-dark driving is permitted, you must get a free permit from the National Park Service before setting out.

As the result of a recent court case, a settlement between the National Park Service and conservation groups now provides greatly increased protection for shorebirds and sea-turtles, resulting in much more of the shoreline being closed or inaccessible to Off-Road Vehicles (ORVs) and pedestrians. Several very popular surf fishing areas, including Bodie Island Spit, Cape Point, and Hatteras Spit, are occasionally closed, taking some visitors by surprise. You can get up-to-date information on closures from the NPS visitor centers located in the seashore or on the NPS Web site at www.nps.gov/caha. Local tackle shops are ready with advice about alternate spots to cast your line.

A bathhouse with showers and changing rooms is maintained by the National Park Service at Sandy Bay, between Frisco and Hatteras Village. The beach next to the old lighthouse site is handicapped-accessible and also has a lifeguard during the summer.

In Hatteras Village a public beach ramp is located across from the Graveyard of the Atlantic parking lot. Another wooden ramp crosses over to the beach at the end of Flambeau Lane off Eagle Pass Road in the village. On the beach there you may be able to see the wreck of a coastal schooner, depending on sand and tides.

Sound Access

There are many places to access the typically quiet waters of Pamlico Sound along the west side of Hatteras Island. Most are reached via sand roads suitable for four-wheel-drive vehicles. Two day-use areas have paved parking, restrooms, and showers. The **Salvo Day Use Area,** formerly a national park campground, is just south of the village of Salvo and has a nice, shallow beach for children. The **Haulover Day Use Area,** otherwise known as Canadian Hole, is famous for its popularity with windsurfers. An additional public sound access is located at **Sandy Bay,** south of Frisco.

Beach Buggy and Jeep Rentals
Island Cruisers 252-987-2097; www.hatterasjack.com; 23902 NC 12, Rodanthe 27968 27968. Several models of classic VW buggies and Suzuki Samurai 4x4s are available for on-road or off-road cruising.

Bicycling

Best Bike Routes
Biking down NC 12 on Hatteras is not for the inexperienced, although it's an exhilarating ride, especially in the off-season when traffic is light. The road is very narrow through the Pea Island Wildlife Refuge, and often over-washed with sand and water. South of the refuge, a 4-foot shoulder runs along the road all the way to the ferry docks in Hatteras Village.

Paved off-road multi-use paths paralleling the west side of NC 12 are under way through the Tri-Villages, Avon, and Buxton. The northernmost path will run from the Rodanthe Waves Salvo Community Building (252-987-1303; www.rwscivic.org; 23186 Myrna Peters Rd., Rodanthe 27968) to the Salvo Day Use Area. Additional paths will join Avon with national seashore ramps to the north and south, and the Cape Hatteras Lighthouse with the park service bathhouse in Frisco.

Bike and Beach Equipment Rentals
Hatteras Landing Activity Rentals 252-986-2077, 800-551-8478; www.hatteraslanding.com. Road-legal mopeds, gas-powered scooter boards, men's and women's beach cruisers and mountain bikes, BMX and chopper bikes for kids, and bikes

with training wheels, are rented by the hour, day, or week. Bic surfboards, Morey boogie boards, ZAP skim boards, plus fins and car racks, are available by the day or week.

Island Cycles & Sports 800-229-7810; www.islandcycles.com; Avon location: 252-995-4336; 41934 NC 12, Hatteras Island Plaza; Hatteras location: 252-986-2233; 57698 NC 12. Sales and rentals of bikes and scooters in a wide variety of makes and models, Repairs and accessories available, as well as kayak, surfboard rentals, kiteboarding lessons, and skateboard sales.

Ocean Atlantic 252-995-5868; www.oceanatlanticrentals.com; NC 12, Avon. Adult and children's bikes available by the day or week, plus surfboards, kayaks, and much more. Free delivery.

Boats and Boating

It is easy to launch kayaks and other shallow-bottom craft at any sound-side access point. Jet Skis and power boats are allowed only in the waters off the island's villages, as the National Park Service does not allow you to launch or operate power craft within park boundaries.

Kayak Rentals and Tours

Hatteras Island Boardsports 252-995-6160, 866-442-9283; www.hiboardsports.com; 41074 NC 12, Avon 27915. Kayak rentals with free delivery.

Hatteras Island Sail Shop 252-987-2292; www.hiss-waves.com; 25410 NC 12, Waves 27982. On-site launch and eco-tours available.

Hatteras Parasail & Kayak 252-986-2627, 252-986-2243; www.hatterasparasail.com; Oden's Dock, Hatteras Village. Morning and evening eco-tours explore the waterways and marshes on the sound side of Hatteras Village. Single and double kayaks available, along with child booster seats.

Hatteras Watersports 252-987-2306; 27130 NC 12, Salvo 27982. Ocean and touring kayaks for rent; on-site launch with showers and restrooms; eco-tours available.

Island Cycles 252-995-4336, 800-229-7810; www.islandcycles.com; two locations: 41934 NC 12, Hatteras Island Plaza, Avon 27915; 57698 NC 12, Hatteras 27943.

Kitty Hawk Kites 877-FLY-THIS; www.kittyhawk.com; Avon location: 252-995-6060, Island Shops; Hatteras location: 252-986-1446, Hatteras Landing; Rodanthe location: 252-984-1044, Camp Hatteras; Waves location: 252-987-1100, St. Waves Plaza. Ocean and sound kayaks available for rent. You can launch into the sound from the Camp Hatteras, Avon, and Hatteras Landing locations. Eco-tours of Pea Island, Graveyard of the Atlantic, and sunset paddles available.

Rodanthe Watersports and Campground 252-987-1431; www.watersportsandcamp ground.com; 24170 NC 12, Rodanthe 27968. On-site launch, restrooms, and showers.

Marinas

Albatross Fleet at Foster's Quay 252-986-2515; www.albatrossfleet.com; 57976 NC 12, Hatteras 27943. The Outer Banks' very first charter fishing fleet originated here in 1937 and still takes anglers to the Gulf Stream after the big ones. Stop by to see the unique Hatteras-style boats with sharp, flared prows and rounded sterns, designed to help boats safely run the breaking waves of the inlet.

Hatteras Harbor Marina 252-986-2166; www.hatterasharbor.com; Hatteras Village. Protected, full-service marina, home to the area's largest charter fishing fleet, offers deep-

The charter fleet heads back to the marinas of Hatteras Village at the close of another day of offshore fishing.

water slips with water and electric for transients up to 60 feet. Showers and a coin laundry are available for visiting boaters, or you can rent an efficiency apartment over the marina. The **Harbor Deli** specializes in bag lunches for charters.

Hatteras Landing Marina 252-986-2077; www.hatteraslanding.com/marina; Hatteras Village. Located in the Hatteras Landing Resort, immediately adjacent to the ferry docks, this marina has a 9-foot-deep basin and more than three dozen slips that can accommodate boats up to 75 feet. Hookups include cable TV and telephone. Showers, laundry, and a huge ship's store and deli are available for boaters. Inshore and offshore charters, sightseeing cruises, and on-site rental apartments.

Oden's Dock 252-986-2555, 888-544-8115; www.odensdock.com; Hatteras Village. Oden's is a center of activity in Hatteras Village, as the home of a charter fishing and duck hunting fleet, kayak tours, and parasailing, the **Breakwater Inn and Restaurant**, **Risky Business Seafood Market,** and two headboats offering fishing and sightseeing cruises. Transient boat slips with hookups are available by the night or month.

Scotch Bonnet Marina 252-995-3052, 252-995-4242; Frisco. Twenty slips with water and electric are available for transients up to 30 feet long. Showers, ice, and marina store available.

Teach's Lair Marina 252-986-2460, 888-868-2460; www.teachslair.com; 58646 NC 12, Hatteras 27943. Transient boaters can dock at this 87-slip marina by the day, week, or month. Dry storage, boat ramp, ship's store, bait and tackle shop, and restaurant are on-site. A dozen charter fishing and dive boats dock here.

Village Marina 252-986-2522; www.villagemarinahatteras.com; Hatteras Village. This full-service marina offers slip rentals, dry storage, a ship's store, and a motel, plus **Dinky's Restaurant**.

Personal Watercraft and Boat Rentals

Hatteras Island Sail Shop 252-987-2292; www.hiss-waves.com; 25410 NC 12, Waves 27982. Sailboats for rent.

Hatteras Watersports 252-987-2306; 27130 NC 12, Salvo 27982. Personal watercraft and Hobie Cat sailboats for rent.

★ **Kitty Hawk Kites at Camp Hatteras** 252-984-1044, 877-FLY-THIS; www.kittyhawk.com, 24798 NC 12, Camp Hatteras, Rodanthe 27968. WaveRunner rentals.

Ocean Air Sports 252-995-5000; www.oceanairsports.com; 39450 NC 12, Avon 27915. Personal watercraft rentals and test drives of multi-sport craft.

Ride Hatteras 252-995-6755; www.ridehatteras.com; 40168 NC 12, Avon 27915. Catamaran rentals and lessons.

Rodanthe Watersports and Campground 252-987-1431; www.watersportsandcampground .com; 24170 NC 12, Rodanthe 27968. Personal watercraft and sailboat rentals.

Saint Clair Landing Campground 252-987-2850; NC 12, Rodanthe. Small campground offers boat rentals.

Public Boat Ramps

The New Inlet Boat Ramp, a free public ramp located in the Pea Island National Wildlife Refuge, can accommodate small boats only.

Both Rodanthe and Avon have boat ramps, but they can be hard to find. Ask for directions at one of the local bait and tackle stores.

Several hotels and campgrounds have ramps where you can launch for free if you are a guest or for a fee if you aren't. Camp Hatteras is one with a good location on the sound.

In Hatteras Village you can launch at either Teach's Lair Marina or the Village Marina for a fee, or in Frisco at the Scotch Bonnet Marina.

Family Fun

Dare County's Fessenden Center (252-475-5650; www.dare.nc.com; 46830 NC 12, Buxton 27920) boasts a new, state-of-the-art skateboard park with street course and a reportedly gnarly bowl. For other skateboard opportunities, check in with the folks at the **Avon Skate & Surf Shop** (252-995-4783; www.avonsurfshop.com; 40136 NC 12, Avon 27915).

The Junior Ranger and Seashore Ranger programs at the Cape Hatteras National Seashore (252-995-4474; www.nps.gov/caha) include a variety of free, family-friendly activities during the summer months at the Cape Hatteras Lighthouse Visitor Center.

The area near the lighthouse has several family activities. **Uncle Eddy's Frozen Custard** (252-995-4059; 46860 NC 12. Buxton), next to the Falcon Hotel in Buxton, has 18 holes of mini-golf with unlimited play and 50 flavors of homemade custard. Just down the road, **Cool Wave Ice Cream Shoppe** (252-995-6366; 47237 NC 12, Buxton) also offers the popular ice cream and mini-golf combination.

At Buxton's **Double L Bird Ranch and Petting Zoo** (252-996-0412; 47051 Buxton Back Rd.), kids can meet and feed more than 200 birds of many different species.

Frisco Mini-Golf and Go-Karts (252-995-6325; NC 12, Frisco) has 18 holes of mini-golf where kids under six play free, a game room with pool table and video games, a snack bar, karts, and bumper cars. The nicely landscaped property has a deck and goldfish pond and stays open until late in the evening.

Large game arcades with pool tables and video games can be found in Buxton at **Angelo's Pizza** (252-995-6364) and in Avon at **Mack Daddy's Crab Shack** (252-995-5060). In Hatteras, **Kitty Hawk Kites** (252-986-1446) supervises a 32-foot outdoor climbing wall at Hatteras Landing. There's also a playground at this location.

Families enjoy watching the fishing fleet come in at the several marinas in Hatteras Village. Prime time is between 3:30 and 5 PM.

The **Graveyard of the Atlantic Museum** (252-986-2995; www.graveyardoftheatlantic .com) offers a weeklong Shipwreck Archaeological Workshop every June, giving students in grades 8–12 a hands-on experience in excavating shipwrecks, including a trip to the *Monitor* National Marine Sanctuary. Apply in advance.

The evening **Pirate Adventure Cruise** aboard the *Cap'n Clam* out of Oden's Dock (252-986-2365; www.odensdock.com) in Hatteras Village is a must for Jack Sparrow fans. The fee includes free swords, eye patches, root beer grog, and plenty of swashbuckling.

In Avon, Hatteras Realty (252-995-5466l; 41156 NC 12) offers **Club Hatteras Kids programs** including the Kinnakeet Sound Safari day camp and Kids' Night Out. Families also enjoy hitting a few balls at **Avon Golf** (252-995-5480; NC 12), an 18-hole putting course in front of the Avon Fishing Pier, where you can play until midnight.

In Avon's Kinnakeet Shoppes, **Studio 12—Paint Our Pottery** (252-995-7899; www .studio12hatteras.com; 40534 NC 12) is a popular spot on rainy days and for parties. Next door, the **Hatteras Toy Store** (252-995-7171; www.hatterastoystore.com) offers daily children's activities during the summer, including Paint with Thomas Play Day, and hermit crab races. **Uglie Mugs** (252-995-5590), also in this plaza, has beading supplies.

Avon has the only movie theater on Hatteras Island. **R/C Theatres Hatteras Movies 4** (252-995-9060) is in the Hatteras Island (Food Lion) Plaza on NC 12.

In Rodanthe, **Waterfall Action Park** (252-987-2213) has waterslides and seven racetracks, including speedboats, dune buggies, and sprint cars, plus kiddie rides, miniature golf, bumper boats, and bungie jumping.

Fishing

Just 12 miles from the docks in Hatteras Village is the Gulf Stream, the highway used by the big-game fish. Because this is the southernmost range of some species and the northernmost of others, the waters off Cape Hatteras earned the name "Gamefish Junction," with more types of fish caught here than any other destination on the East Coast. Billfish anglers from around the world come to attempt the rare Grand Slam, by catching a blue marlin, a white marlin, and a sailfish. Tarpon, renowned for their fighting spirit, swim these waters as well.

The fishing is equally good for "meat fish" in the area, with numerous bass, bluefish, king mackerel, tuna, and dolphin (mahi mahi) brought to boat. Something is biting here year round. January to March brings striped bass, yellowfin and giant bluefin tuna. Summer is the high time for dolphin and the billfish, with king mackerel peaking in the fall. Many world-record fish have been caught off Hatteras.

Each of the marinas in Hatteras Village (see our Marinas listings) hosts its own charter fleet. Charter boats typically accommodate groups of up to six. If your group is smaller, ask about a makeup charter.

Fishing Instruction

Every June, **North Carolina State University** (919-515-2261; continuingeducation.ncsu .edu/fishing) sponsors an annual sport-fishing school in Hatteras, with two days of classroom instruction and two offshore excursions hunting big-game fish.

Ryan White, a master long-distance tournament caster, offers beach fishing and casting lessons through the **Hatteras Jack Tackle Shop** (252-987-2428; www.hatterasjack.com) in Rodanthe.

During the summer, members of the **Cape Hatteras Anglers Club** (252-995-4253; www.capehatterasanglersclub.org) give free lessons in surf casting and fishing through the **Cape Hatteras National Seashore** (www.nps.gov/caha). Poles are provided, but you must bring your own bait. Free lessons in cast netting are also offered.

Fishing Piers and Bridges

The three fishing piers on Hatteras Island offer some of the best pier fishing anywhere. You do not need a fishing license to fish from a pier, as they carry blanket licenses. Pier houses at each location sell bait, tackle, gifts and snacks, and rent rods, reels, and other equipment. Sightseers can walk out on any of the piers for a dollar or so. The piers are closed during the winter months.

Avon Fishing Pier 252-995-5480; www.avonpier.com; 41001 NC 12, Avon 27915. This 600-foot pier is a hot spot for red drum and stays open all night during the fall run.

Bonner Bridge, NC 12. A catwalk from the southern end of the Bonner lets you fish around the pilings out in Oregon Inlet. There's a large paved parking lot at the base of the bridge. When the Bonner is replaced in the next few years, the old bridge may be adapted as fishing piers. It is free to fish here, but you do need a saltwater license.

Cape Hatteras Fishing Pier (Frisco Pier) 252-986-2533; 54221 Cape Hatteras Pier Dr., Frisco 27936. Located on the south coast below Cape Hatteras, the Frisco Pier is noted for the great quantity of fish caught here, including many king mackerel.

Hatteras Island Resort Fishing Pier (Rodanthe Pier) 252-987-2323; www.hatterasisland resort.com; 24251 Atlantic Ave., Rodanthe 27968. At 850 feet, the Rodanthe pier is the island's longest. The large pier house has an air-conditioned game room with pool table, air hockey, arcade games, and a jukebox.

Headboats

Cap'n Clam 252-986-2365; www.odensdock.com; Oden's Dock, Hatteras Village. The 68 foot *Cap'n Clam* makes two trips a day around Hatteras Inlet fishing for flounder, sea bass, trout, and other inshore and sound fish. In the evening the headboat offers a Pirate Adventure Cruise, great for kids.

Miss Hatteras 252-986-2365; www.odensdock.com; Oden's Dock, Hatteras Village. To experience fishing on the Gulf Stream, sign up for this headboat's 10-hour trip and bottom fish for snapper, triggerfish, grouper, and sea bass. A shorter 4-hour trip is offered to nearshore waters or try the **Dolphin and Wildlife Sunset Cruise**. In the fall, *Miss Hatteras* goes after king mackerel.

Stormy Petrel II 252-986-1363, 252-473-9163; www.thestormypetrel.com; Hatteras Landing Marina, Hatteras Village. This 61-foot boat is able to handle larger groups, up to 24 people, for bottom or inshore fishing or trolling in the Gulf Stream. It also offers party boat cruises for sightseeing or pelagic bird watching.

Tackle Shops

Hatteras Island has a lot of tackle shops, but it also has a lot of fish. Stop by any of these for excellent advice and personal service. All of the shops listed are official fish-weighing stations.

Dillon's Corner 252-995-5083; www.dillonscorner.com; 47692 NC 12, Buxton 27920. Downstairs you'll find a complete selection of fishing gear, upstairs a gallery of gifts, apparel, and art. Fishing cottages available.

★ **Frank and Fran's Fisherman's Friend** 252-995-4171; www.hatteras-island.com; 40210 NC 12, Avon 27915. Frank and Fran's is small, friendly, family run, a gathering spot for anglers, and home of the world-record red drum. Fishing advice, weather reports, and coffee are all complimentary.

Frisco Rod and Gun 252-995-5366; www.friscorodgun.com; 53610 NC 12, Frisco 27936. Bryan Perry, chief of the Frisco Volunteer Fire Department, owns and operates this tackle and gun shop, along with the Frisco Market, at the junction of NC 12 and Billy Mitchell Road.

Hatteras Jack 252-987-2428; www.hatterasjack.com; 23902 NC 12, Rodanthe 27968. Master caster Ryan White's shop will build you a custom rod and reel, rent you a beach buggy, fix you up with a box lunch, or feed you a hearty meal from 6 AM to 10 PM.

Mac's Tackle & Island Convenience 252-987-2239; 23532 NC 12, Rodanthe 27968. This tackle shop also has a wrecker service if you get stuck in the sand.

The Red Drum 252-995-5414; www.reddrumtackle.com; NC 12, Buxton. Serving the fishing public since 1954, the Red Drum occupies a legendary position on the local scene. The strip of shops also has a market, gas station, and auto repair.

The Roost Bait & Tackle 252-986-2213; www.teachslair.com; Teach's Lair Marina, Hatteras Village. The Hissey brothers, well known locally for their expertise, offer advice and top-notch equipment at this store.

Golf

Avon Golf 252-995-5480; www.avonpier.com; 41001 NC. 12, Avon Fishing Pier, Avon 27915. This 18-hole putting range with well-kept greens makes a good spot to practice your short game. Play all day and night for one price.

Ocean Edge Golf Course 252-995-4100; 53725 NC 12, Frisco 27936. Public 1,400-yard, par 30, nine-hole executive-style course covers 23 acres of dunes and is open all year.

Hiking

Buxton Woods 252-261-8891; www.ncnerr.org; NC 12, Buxton. A number of trails and multi-use paths run through this maritime forest. The **National Park Service Nature Trail** (252-995-4474; www.nps.gov/caha) begins at a picnic area just beyond the Cape Hatteras Lighthouse. The shady three-quarter-mile loop runs along pine needle–covered paths where interpretive signs explain the ecosystem of the area, along the way passing Jennette's Sedge, a freshwater marsh caught between dunes. Many creatures are seen along this trail, including cottonmouth snakes, so be wary. The **Open Ponds Trail** begins farther down the road near an old British cemetery and connects with other trails that enter the woods from roads off NC 12. The **Buxton Woods Off-Road Trail** begins on Old Doctor's Road. Other access roads are Flowers Ridge Road and Water Association Road. Look for kiosks containing trail maps in these locations.

Frisco Native American Museum 252-995-4440; www.nativeamericanmuseum.org; 53536 NC 12, Frisco 27936. A pleasant nature trail begins in the back of the parking lot and winds through 3 acres of maritime forest.

Pea Island National Wildlife Refuge 252-987-2394; www.fws.gov/peaisland; NC 12. The refuge has two handicapped-accessible trails, where bird watching is good all year and

Horseback riding along the Hatteras Island beach

spectacular in the winter months when the migratory waterfowl are in residence. **The North Pond Trail** leads along the south side of the pond to a dual-level observation tower. The shorter **Salt Flats Wildlife Trail** leads along the north side of the pond to an observation deck. A service road connects these two trails along the west side of the pond, and many people walk the entire loop. The final leg of the loop, however, runs along the shoulder of NC 12, a sometimes dangerous proposition. Instead, cross over the dunes and return along the beach, where you'll see the boiler of the *Oriental*, which sank in 1862, about 100 yards offshore. The Pea Island trails are open during daylight hours all year.

Horseback Riding

Horses are allowed on the beaches of the National Seashore but must follow the same rules and use the same access ramps as off-road vehicles.

Equine Adventures 252-995-4897; www.equineadventures.com; Piney Ridge Rd., Frisco 27936. The only stable offering horseback rides on the Outer Banks takes groups through the maritime forest and onto the beach, where you can trot or canter, depending upon your riding ability. Rides are offered all year. You can also board your horse here.

Hunting

No hunting is permitted in the Pea Island National Wildlife Refuge or in the Hatteras Island sections of the National Seashore.

Ken Dempsey's Guide Service 252 986-2102; www.kendempseyguide.com; 56192 Cedar Ave., Hatteras 27943. Dempsey takes hunters to blinds located in Pamlico Sound. Charters include use of Dempsey's handcrafted decoys.

Nature Preserves and Eco-attractions

Buxton Woods Coastal Reserve 252-261-8891; www.ncnerr.org; NC 12, Buxton. Over 2,000 acres of maritime forest, the largest remaining on the Banks, occupies the southeast coast of Hatteras Island from Cape Point to Hatteras Village. Rare plants and animals make their homes here, and the woods are noted for bird watching, and rare butterflies, including the giant swallowtail and gossamer-winged northern hairstreak.

Cape Hatteras National Seashore 252-995-4474; www.nps.gov/caha; Lighthouse Rd., Buxton 27920. The park's visitor center is located in the **Double Keepers House** at the foot of the Cape Hatteras Lighthouse. The beach next to the lighthouse is the only one on Hatteras with a lifeguard, on duty mid-June to mid-August. The park service offers a busy schedule of free activities on Hatteras every summer, ranging from bird walks to snorkeling trips on the sound. A bathhouse with showers and changing rooms and a fully wheelchair-accessible beach access boardwalk is located at Frisco. Beach wheelchairs can be borrowed from the park service by calling 252-995-4474 or 252-473-2111.

★ **Pea Island National Wildlife Refuge** 252-987-2394; www.fws.gov/peaisland; NC 12. Occupying the northern 13 miles of Hatteras Island, this refuge offers superb bird watching and handicapped-accessible hiking trails, as well as a pristine stretch of beach, where endangered shorebirds and loggerhead sea turtles nest. Paved parking areas are located at the base of the Bonner Bridge next to Oregon Inlet, and at the visitor center, about 4 miles south of the bridge. The refuge trails and beach are open during daylight hours. The visitor center is open 9–5 during the summer, and 9–4 the rest of the year. No vehicles are allowed on the beach in the refuge, and fires and camping are prohibited.

Racquet Sports and Tennis

On Hatteras Island, tennis courts are located in Buxton at the **Fessenden Center** (252-475-5650; 46830 NC 12) and at the **Cape Hatteras School** (47500 Middle Ridge Trail, Buxton 27920). Courts at the school are available for public use after school hours. The Fessenden is a Dare County community activity center with a full roster of classes and activities for all ages.

Spas and Fitness

In Touch Massage & Wellness Center 252-995-4067; 50840 NC 12, Frisco 27936. Spa treatments here use only natural and organic products. Acupuncture, massage, and a boutique of organic beauty products available.

Outer Banks Jazzercise 252-995-3144, 252-216-9181; Hatteras Community Center, NC 12, Hatteras Village. Changing rooms, weights, and mats available.

★ **Pam Bailey Massage & Body Work** 252-305-8822; www.pambailey.biz; 40246 NC 12, Avon 27915. Pam, a gifted healer and licensed massage therapist, offers treatments in cranio-sacral, polarity, cranial rolfing, and other therapies. She also teaches yoga classes at several locations around the Banks.

Spa Koru 252-995-3125; www.spakoru.com; 40920 NC 12, Avon 27915. Salon and spa offers a full menu of beauty and body treatments based on South Pacific island rituals. A complete fitness center with state-of-the-art equipment is located on-site.

Spectator Sports

Kiteboarding and windsurfing make exciting watching, and the sound-side coast between Avon and Buxton is the best spot to watch. You can pull off into the paved parking area at the Haulover Day Use Area, otherwise known, and internationally famous, as Canadian Hole.

The **East Coast Surfing Championships,** held annually in September near Cape Hatteras Lighthouse, attract top surfers from around the world, and surfing fans who come to watch the action.

Fishing is something of a spectator sport on Hatteras as well. The docks in Hatteras Village are especially crowded during tournaments, when top anglers bring in the big ones.

Water Sports

Among the numerous water-sports shops on Hatteras Island, several offer good destinations for a day-long excursion, with rentals of several different watercraft, plus showers, restrooms, and picnic facilities. All are located on Pamlico Sound.

Hatteras Watersports 252-987-2306; 27130 NC 12, Salvo 27982. Rent WaveRunners, kayaks, and sailboats at this family-operated water-sports mecca located in the former Pea Island Life Saving Station. A large lawn with picnic tables and volleyball court, restrooms with hot showers, plus a beach on the sound, make this a great place to spend an afternoon.

Kitty Hawk Kites Camp Hatteras 252-984-1044, 877-FLY-THIS; www.kittyhawk.com; NC 12, Rodanthe. The Camp Hatteras location offers a nice dock, kayak and WaveRunner rentals, a fish-cleaning table, and friendly staff.

Rodanthe Watersports and Campground 252-987-1431; www.watersportsandcampground .com; 24170 NC 12, Rodanthe 27968. Rent Jet Skis, kayaks, and sailboats, and enjoy their sound-side beach and hot showers.

Kiteboarding and Windsurfing

The combination of steady winds and shallow water makes Hatteras Island the best destination in the East for windsurfing and kiteboarding. Pamlico Sound, with its 35-mile-wide expanse of waist-deep water, provides some of the best flat-water riding in the world. Located just south of Avon, **Canadian Hole,** officially named the Haulover Day Use Area, is a favorite with windsurfers. Just across NC 12 and over the dunes lies **Ego Beach,** a hot spot for wave sailing. Kiteboarders congregate just south of Canadian Hole at **Kite Point.** The Salvo Day Use Area, south of the Tri-Villages, is a great alternative to the crowds at Canadian Hole.

Rentals and Lessons

Fox Watersports 252-995-4372; www.foxwatersports.com; 47108 NC 12, Buxton 27920.
Hatteras Island Sail Shop 252-987-2292; www.hiss-waves.com; 25410 NC 12, Waves 27982. Free sailing site with grass rigging.
Island Cycles & Sports 800-229-7810; www.islandcycles.com; Avon location: 252-995-

4336; 41934 NC 12, Hatteras Island Plaza; Hatteras location: 252-986-2233; 57698 NC 12. Lessons for all abilities using Flexifoil kites.

Kite Hatteras 252-305-5290; www.kitehatteras.net; Buxton. Ty Luckett's custom kite boats and tower apparatus let you develop boarding skills in a controlled environment. Kite camps and wake-boarding also available.

Ocean Air Sports 252-995-5000; www.oceanairsports.com; 39450 NC 12, Avon 27915. Formerly Windsurfing Hatteras. You can launch on-site. Special windsurfing lessons are offered for children.

Outer Banks Kiting 252-305-6839; www.outerbankskiting.com; Avon. Kiteboarding lessons for all abilities, kite cruise, kite camp, wake-boarding instruction, and sunset cruises.

REAL Kiteboarding Center 252-995-6596, 866-REAL-KITE; www.realkiteboarding.com; two locations: 47170 NC 12, Bilbo's Plaza, Buxton 27920; 25676 NC 12, Waves 27982. Dedicated completely to the sport of kiteboarding, REAL has two locations on Hatteras Island. The original shop in Buxton offers gear sales and free WiFi near the popular KP (Kite Point) riding venue. The Waves location includes the **Lesson Center,** plus shopping, on-site lodging, and dining. REAL offers a wide variety of lessons, including the three-day "Zero to Hero" camp and special lessons for women riders.

Ride Hatteras 252-995-6755; www.ridehatteras.com; 40168 NC 12, Avon 27915. Lessons and rentals for windsurfing and kiteboarding.

Sail World 252-995-5441; www.hatteras.ws; 41074 NC 12, Avon 27915. Also sells skateboards and board accessories.

Parasailing

Hatteras Parasail & Kayak 252-986-2627, 252-986-2243; www.hatterasparasail.com; Oden's Dock, Hatteras Village. Single or tandem rides.

Snorkeling and Scuba

The many ships that lie in the Graveyard of the Atlantic make for some of the best, and most challenging, open-water wreck diving anywhere. The remains of blockade runners and Federal gunboats from the Civil War era mingle on the bottom with German U-boats and their prey. The Web site www.uwex.us/ncwrecks has a listing of wrecks in these waters, some with GPS coordinates.

Dive Shops and Charters

Captain Art's Atlantic Wreck Diving 252 986-2835l; home.att.net/~CaptArt; Teach's Lair Marina, Hatteras Village. Veteran diver Captain Art Kirchner takes divers to some of the less-visited wrecks in the region.

Dive Hatteras 703-818-1850, 703-517-3724; www.divehatteras.com, Teach's Lair Marina, Hatteras Village. Specializing in the shipwrecks of Diamond Shoals, dive masters Ann and Dave Sommers take small groups to some of the deeper, more challenging sites.

Outer Banks Diving 252-986-1056; www.outerbanksdiving.com; 57540 NC 12, Hatteras 27943. Experienced NAUI dive master John Pieno offers recreational and deeper technical dives, as well as trips to shallow-water wrecks suitable for snorkeling. Underwater photography, treasure hunting, and spearfishing trips can be arranged. The dive shop offers gear sales, repairs, and rentals, including underwater cameras and computers.

Shore Snorkeling and Diving

Strong swimmers can reach a few of the wrecks along the Hatteras Island coast. The *LST 471*, which sank in 1949, is about 100 yards offshore, a mile north of the Rodanthe Fishing Pier, in 15 feet of water. The *Oriental,* also called the Boiler Wreck, a Federal transport that sank in 1862, lies off the beach opposite the Pea Island National Wildlife Refuge visitor center in 20 feet of water. The boiler is visible above the waves.

Snorkeling in Pamlico Sound is far safer, and an interesting experience, with small fish, shrimp, and crabs to be seen. The **Cape Hatteras National Seashore** (252-995-4474; www.nps.gov/caha) offers sound snorkeling adventures during the summer months. **Ocean Atlantic** (252-995-5868; www.oceanatlanticrentals.com) rents fins, snorkels, and masks.

Surfing

Known among surfers as a "wave magnet," Hatteras Island is acknowledged as the top surfing destination on the East Coast. The Eastern Surfing Association (www.surfesa.org) holds its championships at the breaks off the Cape Hatteras Lighthouse every September. The island's 50 miles of uncrowded beach breaks and its consistent and nicely shaped waves attract surfers, and more than a few surfboard makers (called "shapers"), from around the world. The biggest swells are usually late in the hurricane season, from August to November. You can check current surf conditions at www.obxsurfinfo.com.

Most Hatteras surf shops are closed during the winter months when the surf's up in Hawaii.

Surf Shops

Avon Surf Shop 252-995-4783; www.avonsurfshop.com; 40136 NC 12, Avon 27915. Run by Jennifer and Eric Harmon, a couple who are passionate about surfing and skateboarding, this shop offers surfboard rentals and lessons, plus a full-service skate shop. Formula Surfboards, shaped by local Eric Holmes, are available here.

Fox Watersports 252-995-4372; www.foxwatersports.com; 47108 NC 12, Buxton 27920. Founded by the late surfboard shaper and sailboard pioneer Ted James, Fox is still run by his family and carries custom boards based on his best designs, as well other top brands.

Hatteras Island Boardsports 252-995-6160, 866-442-9283; www.hiboardsports.com; 41074 NC 12, Avon 27915. Boards shaped by top competitor Mark Newton are for sale.

Hatteras Island Surf Shop 252-987-2296; www.hiss-waves.com; 25410 NC 12, Waves 27982. New and used boards, plus rentals and lessons.

Natural Art Surf Shop 252-995-5682; www.surfintheeye.com; 47331 NC 12, Buxton 27920. Owner Scott Busbey shapes his custom In the Eye boards at this shop in Buxton.

Rodanthe Surf Shop 252-987-2412, NC 12, Rodanthe. Run by hard-core surfers, this shop sells Hatteras Glass Surfboards, shaped on-site and a longtime local favorite.

Surf Camps and Lessons

Good Times Surf School and Water Sports Camp 252-987-2245; www.goodtimessurf.com; 23282 NC 12, Rodanthe 27968. Surf lessons and camps for all ages, as well as board rentals.

Ocean Atlantic Surfrider School 252-995-5868; www.oceanatlanticrentals.com; NC 12, Avon. Group, private, and semiprivate lessons, as well as rentals in a variety of lengths.

Wildlife Spotting

Bird-Watching

The **Pea Island National Wildlife Refuge** (252-473-1131; www.fws.gov/peaisland) is considered one of the finest birding destinations in North Carolina, with habitats ranging from salt marsh, to freshwater impoundments, to beach and dune. The land around the Cape Hatteras Lighthouse is also a noted birding area, especially during the spring and fall migrations, when the British Cemetery has visiting songbirds. The waters off Hatteras Island, where the warm Gulf Stream waters meet the cooler Labrador Current, are some of the most productive in the western North Atlantic for viewing pelagic birds, including many rare species.

Wildlife Tours and Charters

Miss Hatteras 252-986-2365; www.odensdock.com; Oden's Dock, Hatteras Village. This headboat offers a Dolphin and Wildlife Sunset Cruise.

Pea Island Bird Walks & Canoe Tours (252-473-1131; www.fws.gov/peaisland) Free bird walks are offered year round from the visitor center. Special programs focus on raptors and sea turtles during the summer months. Canoe tours in Pamlico Sound led by a naturalist are offered for a fee. Call 252-987-2394 to register.

Pea Island Eco Kayak Tours 252-261-6262; www.outerbankskayaktours.com. Kayak tours led by experienced naturalists explore this birding paradise and the clear waters around it.

Seabirding Pelagic Trips 252-986-1363; www.seabirding.com; Hatteras Landing Marina, Hatteras Village. Full-day trips to view pelagic birds, including the yellow-nosed albatross and white-faced storm petrel, on the Gulf Stream, are offered all year and are not recommended for children. Captain Patteson also offers a three-hour Coastal Nature Cruise and Dolphin Watch suitable for families.

The abandoned Oregon Inlet Coast Guard Station lies nearly buried in dunes.

SHOPPING

While the majority of shopping options on Hatteras Island are locally owned enterprises, some chain stores have come here and tend to attract the largest crowds, thanks to their national reputations. The local stores cluster around these nationals, and the shopping centers in which they are located are usually referred to by the chain's name, no matter what the actual name of the center may be. In Hatteras Village, many restaurants and shops are located in the marinas that line NC 12.

Shopping Centers and Malls

AVON

Dairy Queen Shopping Center 252-995-5624; 39774 NC 12, Avon 27915. Besides the frozen treats that make Dairy Queen famous, you'll find several art shops, and an Internet café.

Hatteras Island Plaza 41934 NC 12, Avon 27915. Universally known as the Food Lion shopping center, this is the island's largest "strip" mall and home to more than a dozen shops, restaurants, and a cinema. Look for the **Beach Pharmacy** (252-995-3811), which carries craft supplies, and **Sweet & Simple Pleasures** (252-995-0012), where you can sample some excellent fudge.

Kinnakeet Shoppes 40534 NC 12, Avon 27915. This cedar-shingled row of shops is a great stop for families, with toys, pottery, beading, coffee and WiFi.

BUXTON

Osprey Shopping Center 47355 NC 12, Buxton 27920. This strip of shops houses the island's ABC liquor store (252-995-5532), and a retro-themed sandwich shop. Out front there's a picnic area, and **Buoy's** (252-995-6575), a popular seafood restaurant.

FRISCO

Indian Town Gallery Shops 252-995-5474; www.indiantowngallery.com; 50840 NC 12, Frisco 27936. Art-oriented group of shops about 4 miles south of the lighthouse.

HATTERAS VILLAGE

Beacon Shops 57204 NC 12, Hatteras 27943. Upscale stores offer clothing, specialty foods, and art.

Hatteras Landing 252-986-2205; www.hatteraslanding.com; 58848 Marina Way, Hatteras 27943. Located next to the ferry docks, this large, modern shopping center contains a number of shopping, dining, and activity options.

Stowe on Twelve Shops 56910 NC 12, Hatteras 27943. Fun shops are run by some of the island's coolest ladies. You can rent the apartment over the shops for your getaway.

TRI-VILLAGES

Island Convenience Store 252-987-2239; 23532 NC 12, Rodanthe 27968. Midgett family complex sells about everything from auto repair to delicious deli. There's a campground out back, with LP gas sales.

Pamlico Station Shops 252-987-1288; 24267 NC 12, Rodanthe 27968. Two-story building houses a wealth of shopping options, including gift and clothing stores, a T-shirt outlet, and restaurants.

St. Waves Plaza 252-207-7916, 252-491-9999; www.stwavesplaza.com; 26006 NC 12, Waves 27982. New strip of shops on the ocean side of NC 12.

Books and Music

★ **Buxton Village Books** 252-995-4240; www.buxtonvillagebooks.com; 47918 NC 12, Buxton 27920. Located in a Civil War-era cottage, this charming store carries an amazing range of new and used books for all ages. Specialties include sea stories, fishing guidebooks, southern fiction, and books on Hatteras history. Owner Gee Gee Rosell hosts frequent book signings and stocks note cards by local artists.

Clothing

Envy Boutique 252-986-1116; 56910 NC 12, Stowe on Twelve, Hatteras 27943. Owner Jody Stowe selects hot West Coast fashions designed for "heartbreakers."

Hotline Thrift Shops www.obhotline.org; 252-986-1332, Buxton; 252-473-5121, Rodanthe. These are great spots to pick up some gently used beachwear, and all the proceeds benefit the Hotline's 24-hour crisis-intervention programs.

Izabelle's Closet 252-986-6575; www.izabellescloset.com; 57204 NC 12, Beacon Shops, Hatteras 27943. Specialty boutique offers a variety of casual and easy-to-wear clothing, many in natural fibers, including the popular Flax label.

Surfside Casuals five locations on Hatteras Island: 252-995-5577, Hatteras Island Plaza, Avon; 252-995-3352, NC 12, Buxton; 252-995-4408, NC 12, Frisco; 252-986-2727, Hatteras Landing, Hatteras; 252-987-1414, Pamlico Station, Rodanthe. Locally owned and operated chain is noted for its friendly staff and wide selection of beachwear. The Rodanthe location is an outlet store with all swimsuits on sale.

Gifts

Family Jewels 252-986-2323; 56882 NC 12, Stowe on Twelve, Hatteras 27943. Wendy Stowe Sisler designs jewelry of glass beads, freshwater pearls, and semiprecious stones.

Hatteras Island Toy Store 252-995-7171; www.hatterastoystore.com; 40530 NC 12, Avon 27915. This store devoted to kids has an playroom dedicated to Thomas the Tank Engine. Daily activities during the summer.

Hatteras Trading Company 252-995-9990; 51858 NC 12, Frisco 27936. Useful beach wind blocks, for sale or rent, plus locally made fish replicas, and the Salty Parrot Room, full of island fun.

Mad Mad Hatteras 252-995-6873; 41076 NC 12, Avon 27915. Zany purple shop offers art-to-wear, cottage decor, and whatnots galore.

Home Decor

All Decked Out 252-995-4319, 800-321-2392; www.obxoutdoorfurniture.com; 53392 NC 12, Frisco 27936. Comfortable, durable outdoor furniture is handcrafted from Atlantic white cedar.

Dockside Hatteras 252-995-5445; 40220 NC 12, Avon 27915. Furniture and beach accessories crowd this eclectic shop. Free delivery.

This Little Cottage 252-995-3320; 53430 NC 12, Southside Center, Frisco 27936. Top brand names in home decor, linens, and dinnerware, plus hip clothing and unique gifts.

Bicycles are the best way to get around in Ocracoke Village.

7

OCRACOKE ISLAND

Off the Grid

> *"If once you have slept on an island*
> *You'll never be quite the same...."*
> —Rachel Field

Ocracoke is a true island. No bridge links it to the mainland, so to get here you must take a boat or plane. The state of North Carolina obligingly provides three different ferries to Ocracoke. The one from Hatteras is free, while the other two cost money; but however you arrive, the trip lends a sense of isolation to the island. You cannot easily leave this place. Someone must ferry you away. Although, locals say, once the sand gets between your toes, you may not ever want to leave.

ISLAND TIME

For eons, the island belonged to the birds and the waves. Later, the ponies arrived and flourished, survivors perhaps of Spanish attempts to establish colonies along the Carolina coast.

The local natives, the Woccon tribe, used to come to the island for oyster roasts, a tradition that has changed little over the years. Their name for the island, "Wococon," appears on John White's 1585 map. The island's name had morphed into Occocok by Blackbeard's day. No one is sure how the "r" sneaked into the present-day name of Ocracoke. Locals today will tell you: "Pronounce it like the vegetable and the soft drink."

The island's location, next to an inlet that gives access to the great Pamlico and Albemarle Sounds, gave Ocracoke a unique prominence during the age of sail. In colonial days, two-thirds of all North Carolina shipping passed through Ocracoke Inlet, the only gap in the northern Outer Banks that has remained open continuously since the 1500s.

The first to take advantage of this position were the pirates. Blackbeard and his cohorts would lurk here, waiting for rich ships to pass. Between raids they came ashore to drink rum and roast pigs. The island became a known gathering spot for pirates, and it was here that Lieutenant Maynard of the British Navy hunted Blackbeard down. The fateful battle, which ended with the pirate's head hanging from the bowsprit of Maynard's ship, took place just offshore at a place known today as Teach's Hole.

The constantly shifting sands of the inlet made passage dangerous for ships, and in 1715

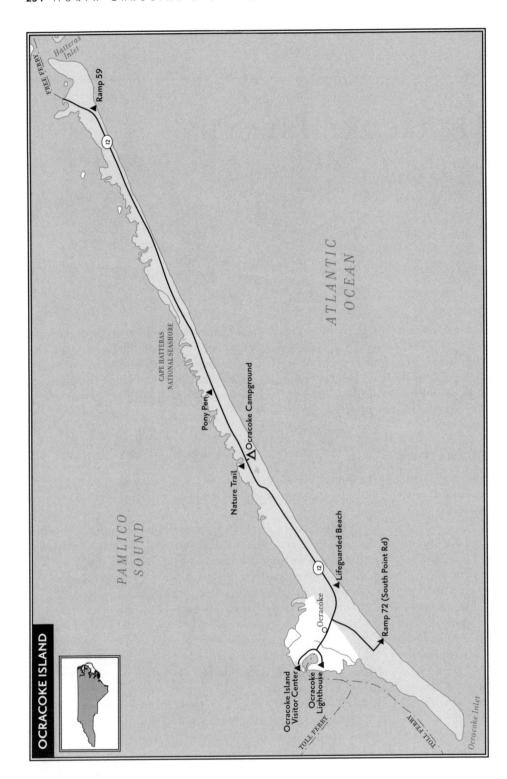

OCRACOKE ISLAND

Hatteras Inlet

FREE FERRY

Ramp 59

12

CAPE HATTERAS
NATIONAL SEASHORE

Pony Pen

Ocracoke Campground

Nature Trail

PAMLICO
SOUND

ATLANTIC
OCEAN

12

Lifeguarded Beach

Ramp 72 (South Point Rd)

Ocracoke

Ocracoke Island
Visitor Center

Ocracoke
Lighthouse

TOLL FERRY

TOLL FERRY

Ocracoke Inlet

the North Carolina colonial government sought to establish a community of pilots on Ocracoke to guide ships through. By the 1730s, Pilot Town was well established at what is today Springer's Point.

Many of the families that live on the island are descendants of those early pilots. The names of Howard, Williams, Garrish, Balance, O'Neal, Gaskill, Stryon, and Wahab all appear on census records from the 1700s, and you'll meet people with the same names running the shops, charter boats, and restaurants of Ocracoke today.

Perhaps most notable among these are the Howards, descended from a William Howard, who bought the island in 1759. Legend connects him with Blackbeard's quartermaster, also a William Howard, the only member of the pirate crew to escape hanging. Look for the **Village Craftsmen** shop on Howard Street, established by the eighth generation of the family to live on Ocracoke.

The first lighthouse built in the area, a wooden structure on Shell Castle Island in 1798, was replaced in 1823 by the current white tower of the Ocracoke Light. It's the oldest operating lighthouse in North Carolina, and the second-oldest continuously operating in the United States.

In 1846, a great storm opened Hatteras and Oregon Inlets, and from that date the importance of Ocracoke Inlet began to decline. Shipwrecks along this coast did not, however, and many local families joined the Life Saving Service, or turned to commercial fishing and hunting.

During World War II, the U.S. Navy established a base on Ocracoke to chase the German subs that were decimating shipping along the coast. The 500 men stationed there complained it was "the Siberia of the East Coast" due to the lack of amusements navy men typically enjoyed, but more than one ended up marrying a local girl and staying on after the war.

The navy base has disappeared except for a large cistern, but the military left a lasting legacy on the island's footprint. Cockle Creek, until then just a swampy inlet in the marsh, was dredged for the navy boats, becoming **Silver Lake Harbor,** today the centerpiece of Ocracoke Village. This lone village occupies less than a third of the island on the southwest Pamlico Sound side. The 16 or so miles of oceanfront beach remain completely undeveloped, part of the **Cape Hatteras National Seashore** established in 1953. This is one of the last places on the East Coast of the United States where you can look both ways, up and down the shore, and not see a single structure built by man.

Until the 1950s, when North Carolina began regular ferry service, Ocracoke remained largely isolated from the rest of the world. Through the centuries, the local residents developed their own unique style of speech, known to linguists as the Ocracoke brogue. Visit the docks around Silver Lake and you may hear the boat captains and mates still using terms you won't hear elsewhere and commenting on the "hoi toide."

The ferries brought a steadily increasing tide of visitors to Ocracoke, and tourism is now the major industry. The village of 800 year-round residents swells to over 7,000 during the summer season. Tourism reached storm force after Dr. Beach named Ocracoke the best beach in America in 2007. Ferry operators reported an immediate jump in number of visitors to the island.

Locals, feeling the glare of the spotlight, hope that all the publicity doesn't attract a new breed of pirates to their island. It's hard to imagine waterslides or mini-golf courses on Ocracoke. But the year-round residents also welcome the increase in tourism—and the income it brings. Villagers, both the descendants of the old residents, who call themselves

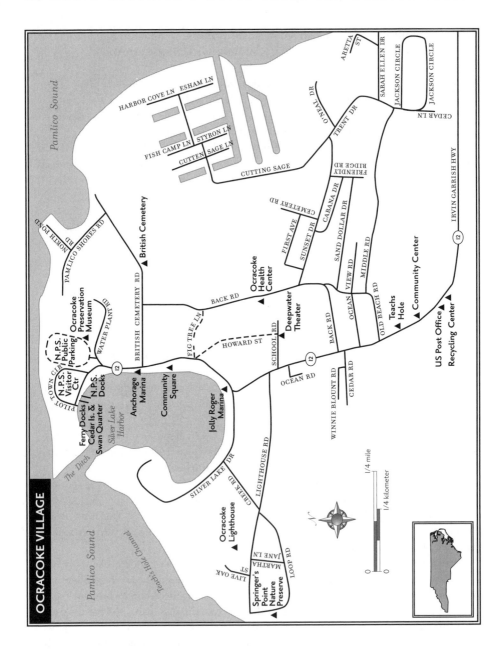

the O'Cockers, and newer settlers, are determined to preserve the family traditions, laid-back lifestyle, and close-knit community that make Ocracoke special.

Many visitors catch just the briefest glimpse of Ocracoke and its unique qualities as they drive from one ferry landing to the other. To them, the island is just a traffic jam around the harbor and another two-lane stretch of road through the dunes. However, for those who park their vehicles in the large lot behind the **National Park Service Visitor's Center** next to the docks and wander out into the village on foot, Ocracoke often becomes a favorite vacation memory.

Visit the dockside watering holes. Wander the old lanes paved with oyster shells. Look for galleries hidden amid the gnarled live oaks. Listen to some local music. Stroll the beach looking for shells or shipwrecks. Take time to watch the sun set. Relax. You're on island time.

GETTING THERE

Several times a day Ocracoke Village looks like New York City at rush hour. But the similarity lasts only for about 15 minutes. The ferry has come in.

A typical Outer Banks island, about 16 miles long and just 5 miles acoss at its widest point, Ocracoke lies about 20 miles off the mainland. State-operated ferries arrive at both the north and south ends. NC 12 runs between the ferry docks.

The free ferry at the north end connects with Hatteras Village, a trip that takes about 40 minutes.

Two ferries come to the docks in the south, at the far side of Ocracoke Village. From here you can go to Cedar Island, where a short drive brings you to Beaufort and the Crystal Coast; or to Swan Quarter, the Hyde County seat, on the Albemarle peninsula. Both trips take about 1.5 hours. Reservations are recommended for these ferries, especially in the summer, and a fee is charged. Contact the North Carolina Ferry Division (800-BYFERRY; www.ncferry.org) for prices and schedules.

A note on hours: As the tourist trade increases into the spring, fall, and winter seasons, hotels, restaurants, and other establishments are expanding their hours to meet demand. Although a listing may say that the place you'd like to go is closed seasonally, a telephone call will often reveal that the welcome mat is out.

A note on addresses: Who was Irvin Garrish anyway? Many of the addresses listed here are on Irvin Garrish Highway, named for the first Hyde County commissioner from Ocracoke and one of the first captains of the Cedar Island Ferry. This is the official name of NC 12, which runs from the Hatteras ferry dock down the length of the island until it reaches the waterfront. There, it makes a sharp right turn to the west, running along the water to the ferry docks that will take you to Cedar Island or Swan Quarter. At this T intersection

Portsmouth: Ghost Town of the Outer Banks

The green lawn behind the picket fence is perfectly manicured. The church door stands open. At the graveyard, fresh flowers adorn several graves. To outward appearances, Portsmouth is a thriving village. But there are no people here, only the wind.

Once, Portsmouth was the region's primary port, a larger town than Ocracoke, on the other side of the inlet. The town's main industry was "lightering," transferring cargo to small, shallow-draft boats to make the run through the inlet. But times changed, other inlets opened, and the population slowly drifted away or died off. The last two residents moved to the mainland in 1971.

It's easy to see ghosts here, to imagine a figure in a long skirt and bonnet closing a cottage door, or to catch a glimpse of a grizzled lifesaver, peering out to sea from his high tower.

Today part of Cape Lookout National Seashore, Portsmouth Island and its village are preserved by the National Park Service. The descendants of former residents continue to treasure the village and make frequent visits. A Portsmouth homecoming, open to the public, is held on alternate years.

(sometimes referred to as Kayak Corner), Silver Lake Drive is to your left, running around the eastern edge of the harbor.

Ocracoke Village is the only town on Ocracoke Island, and all establishments listed here, except the National Park Service campground, are located within its boundaries. The zip code for the entire island is 27960.

LODGING

Like the village itself, Ocracoke inns generally have a little more character than those elsewhere on the Banks. You may find yourself passing a family of cats in the hall, or renting a room from a published author. What you won't find is cookie-cutter resorts or chain hostelries. Lodgings in Ocracoke Village are eclectic, no two the same. Mostly the inns are owned by local families, some of whom have returned to their roots to open inns after successful careers off island.

The vast majority of rentals on Ocracoke are cottages handled by local real estate companies. While a few of the newer ones are large multi-room constructions, the majority are small, neat houses crouched among gnarled live oaks that protect them from the weather. Some have waterfront locations on canals leading to Pamlico Sound, but none is on the beach. The Atlantic side of the island remains totally undeveloped, under the care of the National Park Service.

While more innkeepers are staying open all year, Ocracoke Island is still a very seasonal place, quiet in the winter months, but welcoming to visitors. In fact, for many regular guests, this is their favorite time of year, when the traffic dies down and the beach is deserted.

In season and out, rental fees tend to be a bit less than in other areas of the Banks—one of the advantages of an island that can't be reached by bridge.

Rate Categories

Inexpensive	up to $80
Moderate	$80 to $150
Expensive	$150 to $200
Very Expensive	$200 and up

These rates are per room, based on double occupancy. They do not include room taxes, the 7 percent state sales tax, and the 3 percent Hyde County occupancy tax, or any special service fees that may apply. The range is usually due to seasonal changes. Rates during the busy summer season and holiday weekends are often double or more the winter off-season rates.

Credit Cards

AE—American Express
D—Discover
DC—Diners Club
MC—Master Card
V—Visa

Hotels and Inns

OCRACOKE VILLAGE
THE ANCHORAGE INN & MARINA
252-928-1101
www.theanchorageinn.com
180 Irvin Garrish Hwy., NC 12
Price: Moderate to Very Expensive
Credit Cards: D, MC, V

Located on Ocracoke's harbor, the Anchorage Inn has its own marina, a private pool, a sundeck, a raw bar and grill, plus terrific views of the harbor at sunset. The five-story brick inn contains 35 modern rooms and two suites, served by an elevator. Both smoking and nonsmoking rooms are available, and the fourth floor is smoke-free. Continental breakfast is included. Two suites are located on the fifth floor and have private balconies. Pets are allowed in some rooms on the first floor for an extra fee.

Charter fishing excursions can be arranged, and the inn offers fishing and accommodation packages. Small boats, bikes, and scooters are available for rent. Open from March to November, the inn accepts reservations only by phone.

BEACH HOUSE BED AND BREAKFAST
252-928-1411
www.ocracokebeachhouse.com
1111 Irvin Garrish Hwy., NC 12
Price: Inexpensive to Moderate
Credit Cards: D, MC, V

Built in 1918 as a hunting lodge, this cottage has wide oak plank floors and a cypress beaded ceiling that evoke the Ocracoke of an earlier time. The four guest rooms are totally modernized however, with central heat and air-conditioning, private baths, queen beds, small refrigerators, and cable TV. All are upstairs and can accommodate a maximum of two people. The favorite activity here is rocking on the covered porch adjusting to "island time." Innkeepers Carol and Warren Ritchie serve a full breakfast in the dining room in summer and a continental breakfast upstairs in winter. Open all year, the property is nonsmoking and pets are not allowed. Although it's set well back from the busy harbor area, the action at Howard's Pub is close by.

BLACKBEARD'S LODGE
252-928-3421, 800-892-5314
www.blackbeardslodge.com
111 Back Rd.
Price: Inexpensive to Expensive
Credit Cards: AE, D, MC, V
Internet Access: Free WiFi in common areas

The hotel that started Ocracoke's tourism industry in 1936 has been completely refurbished and is now back in the family of the original owner. Stanley "Chip" Stevens, who bought the hotel in 2007, is the great grand-nephew of the man who built the hotel,

The 1823 Ocracoke Lighthouse dominates views on the island.

Robert Stanley Wahab. Stevens seeks to reestablish his uncle's vision of the lodge as the most welcoming on the island. Today, a statue of Blackbeard the pirate greets guests as they enter the spacious lobby. Comfortable couches and a wood-burning stove invite both hotel guests and day-trippers to sit and relax awhile. The yellow frame lodge has 38 air-conditioned units with a wide variety of sleeping arrangements, from regular doubles to full-kitchen efficiency apartments that sleep eight. The decor of the rooms is equally varied, from sleek modern to cozy quilted to romantic pastels. All rooms have satellite color TV, private baths, and refrigerators. A few smoking and pet-friendly rooms are available. The lodge has a heated pool, wide porches furnished with rocking chairs and swings, and a game room with pool table, foosball, and video and board games. Bicycles are available for rent, and a free shuttle takes guests to the harbor or airport. The property is open all year. Rates are higher if you stay only one night during the peak season or on weekends. Romance and honeymoon packages are available.

CAPTAIN'S LANDING

252-928-1999
www.thecaptainslanding.com
324 Irvin Garrish Hwy., NC 12
Price: Expensive to Very Expensive
Credit Cards: MC, V
Internet Access: Free WiFi

Located directly on the waterfront of Silver Lake, Captain's Landing lets guests put the traffic literally behind them. Owner Betty Chamberlin, a descendant of some to the island's oldest families, designed this inn on the old Howard property to maximize views of the harbor and the island's renowned sunsets. Eight spacious suites each sleep four and have a full kitchen and 1.5 baths, as well as a private deck equipped with lounge chairs. A penthouse with all the comforts of home sleeps eight.

The Captain's Cottage, formerly a 1950s post office building, sits next to the inn, offering modern amenities, including a big-screen LCD television and gourmet kitchen, in a private setting. All guests enjoy access to a DVD library, bicycles for exploring the island, and complimentary boat dockage with hookups just outside their doors. All accommodations are nonsmoking, and pets are not allowed.

THE CASTLE ON SILVER LAKE BED AND BREAKFAST AND CASTLE VILLAS

252-928-3505, 800-471-8848
www.thecastlebb.com
www.thecastlevillas.com
155 Silver Lake Dr.
Price: Moderate to Expensive in the B&B. Expensive to Very Expensive in the suites

Credit Cards: MC, V
Internet Access: Free WiFi

Once the domain of the legendary Sam Jones, this house built by local craftsmen in the mid-1900s soon earned the nickname of "The Castle," thanks to its many-gabled roof and lofty cupola. After many years of neglect, the landmark building has been completely refurbished as a bed-and-breakfast inn with 11 elegant rooms, all paneled with beautiful wood. Each has a private bath with shower. A hot breakfast buffet is served daily. High atop the inn occupying the entire third floor, the Lighthouse Suite is the inn's most requested accommodation. Guests here enjoy a queen bed, a sitting room, and an extra-large shower with a window looking out on the Ocracoke lighthouse. They also have use of the private Cupola Room, equipped with satellite TV and stereo, and a large deck. The bed-and-breakfast does not allow children under 12.

Behind the inn, 10 villas, ranging from studios to three-bedroom suites, are available for larger parties or families with children. All guests can enjoy the Castle's amenities, which include an on-site spa, outdoor heated pool, pool house with sauna and steam shower, bicycles, and complimentary dockage at the inn's dock. Be sure to climb the outside stairs up to the widow's walk around the inn's cupola for a spectacular view.

THE COVE BED & BREAKFAST

252-928-4192
www.thecovebb.com
21 Loop Rd.
Price: Expensive to Very Expensive
Credit Cards: MC, V
Internet Access: Free WiFi

The Cove's location at the far end of Lighthouse Road guarantees a peaceful experience but is only a short walk from village attractions. The rambling building houses suites and regular rooms in two wings, named Sunrise and Sunset. Suites designed for romantic getaways, with queen beds, two-person Jacuzzis, and private decks, occupy the top floor of each wing. Several rooms can accommodate three guests, but all must be at least age 15. All rooms have private baths and balconies, plus cable TV. Innkeepers John and Kati Wharton serve a full breakfast and welcome guests with a wine reception. The inn is pet- and smoke-free, but smoking is allowed on balconies. A shuttle will pick guests up from the airport or docks. A number of special packages are available, including murder mystery weekends.

CREWS INN BED & BREAKFAST

252-928-7011
www.ocracokers.com
503 Back Rd.
Price: Inexpensive
Credit Cards: MC, V

Step into the lives of old-time Ocracokers at this historic 1908 inn, once the home of the O'Neal and Garrish families. It sits in the midst of mature red cedars and live oaks at the end of an oyster shell driveway, not far from Silver Lake. Rooms are furnished with iron bedsteads, quilts, and the simple antiques typical of island homes. They do not have TVs or phones. Two rooms on the first floor have private baths, while the two on the second share a bath. Up top is the Captain's Quarters, with private deck and clawfoot tub. A continental breakfast is served every morning and warm hospitality all day. The wraparound porch, partially screened and furnished with rockers and swings, is a great place to read *Ocracokers*, a book on local history written by the inn's owner, Alton Ballance. He grew up next door and can frequently be seen around the property. Proceeds from the sale of the book benefit the Ocracoke School, where Ballance once taught English and journalism.

HARBORSIDE MOTEL

252-928-3111
www.ocracokeharborside.com
244 Irvin Garrish Hwy., NC 12
Price: Moderate
Credit Cards: AE, D, MC, V

Located just across the street from the waterfront, Harborside has been a popular destination since 1965. Family-owned and -operated, the motel offers 14 rooms with two double beds, refrigerator, television, and private bath. The four efficiencies, which require a minimum stay of six days, add a kitchen with microwave and dining area. Room rates include breakfast, making this a good bargain. The serve-yourself menu includes a wide variety of pastries, bagels, cheese biscuits, coffee and tea, juice, and fig cake, a local specialty made from the fruit that grows abundantly in the village. A sundeck, boat dock, and boat ramp are available across the street. Guests share the motel with a colony of cats. AAA and senior discounts are available. Harborside closes from mid-November to Easter.

THE ISLAND INN AND VILLAS

252-928-4351, 877-456-3466
www.ocracokeislandinn.com
25 Lighthouse Rd.
Price: Inexpensive to Very Expensive
Credit Cards: MC, V

Built of shipwrecked wood in 1901, the part of the inn fronting on Silver Lake is the island's oldest commercial building, originally built as an Oddfellows Lodge. Today the building houses 16 rooms furnished with antiques, including the unique Crow's Nest rooms with soaring ceilings and lofty balconies under the eaves. Some of the inn rooms have TV, and all include a full breakfast. The 12 villas are new one- and two-bedroom condo units with balconies overlooking the inn's heated pool. All have Jacuzzi tubs, washers and dryers, and full kitchens. The inn closes in winter, but the villas stay open all year.

OSCAR'S HOUSE

252-928-1311
www.oscarsbb.com
660 Irvin Garrish Hwy., NC 12
Price: Inexpensive
Credit Cards: MC, V

Built by one of the island's last lighthouse keepers in 1940, Oscar's has four charming guest rooms with original bead-board walls and a laid-back, creative vibe nourished by innkeeper Ann Ehringhaus, a photographer, massage therapist, and interfaith minister. Guests share the two baths and a private outdoor shower under a cedar tree. Ann serves a healthy breakfast daily and can accommodate special diets. A deck with barbecue grill and bicycles are free for guests to use. Closed in winter.

PELICAN LODGE

252-928-1661, 888-7PELICAN
www.bbonline.com/nc/pelican
1021 Irvin Garrish Hwy., NC 12
Price: Inexpensive to Moderate
Credit Cards: MC, V

Operated by the same folks who run Pelican Airways, this inn located close to the airport has four rooms plus the Skylark Suite. All have private baths and include a healthy breakfast prepared by innkeeper Nancy Carlson, a registered dietitian. Guests can relax on the deck on top of the building or in a shady gazebo. The Pelican is open all year and offers free pickup from the airport.

Cottage and Condo Rentals

Blue Heron Realty 252-928-7117, 866-576-7117; www.blueheronvacations.com; 161 Back Rd. This new company started by an island native, Jennifer Esham, offers friendly, personal service and a variety of houses all over the village, including several historic cottages. You can browse and book online.

Ocracoke Island Realty 252-928-6261; www.ocracokeislandrealty.com; 1075 Irvin Garrish Hwy., NC 12. The island's premiere real estate company handles the rental of over 300 privately owned properties that run the gamut from small but historic cottages to luxurious sound-front properties with private docks and swimming pools, at an equally wide variety of prices. Condominium properties represented include the Horizon—fronting on Teach's Hole—and, on the Silver Lake waterfront, Down Creek and Pirate's Quay, both with their own docks. Most rent by the week, but some shorter getaway packages are available, especially off-season. Most properties come without linens, but you can rent them and other vacation essentials from Beach Outfitters on Ocracoke Island Realty's Web site, where you'll also find extensive pictures of all rental properties.

Cottages Courts and Apartments

A number of cottages, apartments, and guest rooms are for rent in Ocracoke Village, often at rates less than the more luxurious hotels and rental houses.

Corinne's Studio Apartments 252-928-5851; 59 Silver Lake Dr. Two studios on the waterfront. Pets welcome.

Edwards of Ocracoke 252-928-4801, 800-254-1359; www.edwardsofocracoke.com; 226 Old Beach Rd. Laid-back motel rooms, efficiencies and private cottages.

Lightkeeper's Guest House 252-928-1821; www.islandpath.com; 61 Creek Rd.

Pony Island Motel & Cottages 252-928-4411, 866-928-4411; www.ponyislandmotel.com; 785 Irvin Garrish Hwy., NC 12. One of the largest inns on the island, with 50 guest rooms and efficiencies, 4 cottages, a swimming pool, and a popular family restaurant on-site.

Wagon Wheel Cottages 252-928-5321; Silver Lake Dr. Small cottages with a great location are popular with hunters and fishermen, as well as families on a budget.

RV Resorts

Because it takes a boat trip to reach the island, it's a good idea always to make advance reservations to camp, especially in the busy summer season. Even the National Park Service takes reservations for its campground here, unlike its other facilities on the Banks.

Beachcomber Campground 252-928-4031; 990 Irvin Garrish Hwy., NC 12. This campground situated behind Ocracoke Station, a busy gas station and convenience store at the north end of the village, has water and electric sites for 29 RVs, plus a few tent sites, a bathhouse with hot showers, dump station, picnic tables, and grills. Cable TV at some sites. Leashed pets allowed for a small fee. Open all year.

Ocracoke Campground 252-928-5111, 800-365-CAMP, 877-444-6777; NC 12. The National Park Service operates this 136-site campground on the oceanfront about 4 miles from the village ferry docks. Paved sites can be used by either tents or RVs. No slideouts. An unspoiled beach is just over the dunes. Amenities are basic: cold showers, running water, flush toilets, dump station, picnic tables, and grills. Rangers lead evening programs and campfires during the summer months. Handicapped-accessible sites available. Maximum stay is 14 days. Closed in the winter. Reservations and mosquito repellent recommended.

Teeter's Campground 252-928-3135; 200 British Cemetery Rd. Located in the historic district, Teeter's has the island's only full hookups (two sites), plus a dozen more with water and electric, and 10 for tents. Hot showers, picnic tables, grills, and cable TV are available. Open March to the end of November.

Most rental cottages on Ocracoke sit amid twisted live oaks.

Pet Accommodations

Sandy Paws Bed & Biscuit Inn 252-928-3093; 136 West End Rd. Hotels and rental cottages that don't allow pets recommend you board your family friend at Sandy Paws. Doggie day care is also available.

DINING

Cuisine in Ocracoke used to begin and end with fried fish, but those days are long gone. Today, fish is still the main event on many menus, but creative chefs have found a host of new and delicious ways to prepare it. Restaurants also offer a wide variety of choices for those who don't eat seafood, including steak and prime rib, poultry, and vegetarian selections.

To see what's biting in local waters, visit the historic Ocracoke Seafood Company on the waterfront. Here local fishing trawlers land their catches. Some seafood is available for retail sale; some makes its way to local restaurants. The friendly staff here will help you identify what you see. You may want to check out some of the more unusual local fish, such as sheepshead or spadefish, said to taste much like grouper and red snapper. Shrimp and blue crab are plentiful in these waters.

Many, if not most, of the restaurants in town offer takeout or have self-serve windows. This reflects the big need for bag lunches and picnics experienced by both locals and visitors. People stock up on provisions before heading to the beach, boarding a charter fishing boat, or taking the shuttle to Portsmouth Island. Getting a bag lunch to take on the state-run ferries is also a good idea, as they offer very limited food options—vending machines and coffee. If you have a ferry to catch or other time constraint, call ahead to order.

If you plan on doing a lot of cooking in your vacation rental, consider shopping on your way to the island to pick up your favorite foods and essential items. Groceries are limited on Ocracoke, although improving, and a specialty store now offers many gourmet-cooking items. The one thing you won't need to bring is fish; the Ocracoke Seafood Company should be able to meet your needs with its fresh catch.

A major change came to the Ocracoke dining scene in 2007 when liquor by the drink came to Hyde County. While a few restaurants immediately added a full cocktail menu, many are taking a go-slow approach to the change. However, mixed drinks will undoubtedly become more common as time goes on.

Rate Categories

Inexpensive	under $10
Moderate	$10 to $20
Expensive	$20 to $25
Very Expensive	$25 and up

These ratings represent the average cost of an entrée, not including higher-priced specials, that super-size steak or the rack of lamb. They also do not include appetizers, desserts, beverages, taxes, or gratuities. When a range of ratings is offered, it usually indicates the difference in price between lunch and dinner entrées.

Credit Cards

AE—American Express
D—Discover
DC—Diners Club
MC—Master Card
V—Visa

Meal Abbreviations

B—Breakfast
L—Lunch
D—Dinner
SB—Sunday brunch

Restaurants

THE BACK PORCH
RESTAURANT AND WINE BAR

252-928-6401
110 Back Rd.
Price: Moderate to Expensive
Cuisine: Seafood and steaks
Liquor: Full bar
Serving: D
Open: Daily; call for off-season hours
Credit Cards: MC, V
Handicapped Access: Yes
Special Features: Wine bar; no smoking

A favorite with local Ocracokers, the Back
Porch has a warm, inviting atmosphere,
with low lights and white tablecloths.
Twisted trees and a fence of cacti shield the
outside of the old building, increasing the
intimacy. Dine inside in the air-conditioning or on the large, screened porch. The
menu changes here seasonally but always
features fresh fish caught locally. Many of
the preparations, such as the Vietnamese
lime sauce available on the fresh catch, have
an Asian fusion slant. Big appetites will
enjoy the seafood platter, a local favorite
loaded with baked fish, sautéed shrimp, and
crab beignets. Half-portions of some dishes
are available for the smaller appetite.
Steaks, poultry, and pork dishes, plus a vegetarian black bean casserole, round out the
menu. A full cocktail menu now supplements the extensive wine list.

★ CAFÉ ATLANTIC

252-928-4861
1129 Irvin Garrish Hwy., NC 12
Price: Moderate
Children's Menu: Yes
Cuisine: Seafood
Liquor: Beer and wine
Serving: D, SB
Closed: Seasonally
Credit Cards: AE, D, MC, V
Handicapped Access: Yes
Special Features: Senior menu; no smoking

Seafood comes in interesting combinations
at this tall beach house on the northern
edge of town. Try the Pesto Scallops or the
Tomatillo Shrimp for something a little different. The crab cakes and clams casino are
popular favorites. Purists will enjoy the
broiled or fried seafood platters or the surf-
and-turf selections. Pasta, spinach lasagna,
seafood salads, homemade soups, veal pic-
cata, and a tender Cuban-grilled chicken
make the menu user-friendly for all. For a
local treat, sample the rosemary chèvre and
fig preserve appetizer. Sunday brunch, a
favorite with locals, includes breakfast specials and mimosas, as well as seafood platters, wraps, burgers, and salads. Desserts
here are fabulous and homemade. Take
time over a glass of wine to enjoy the views
out over marsh and dunes, and the artwork
by local artists on the walls.

CAPTAIN BEN'S RESTAURANT

252-928-4741
875 Irvin Garrish Hwy., NC 12
Price: Inexpensive to Moderate
Children's Menu: Yes
Cuisine: Seafood
Liquor: Beer and wine
Serving: L, D
Closed: Seasonally
Credit Cards: MC, V
Handicapped Access: Yes
Special Features: Senior menu; lounge and
porch

A favorite with locals and families since
1970, this casual spot decorated with nautical memorabilia seats 100 in the main dining room. Owner/chef Ben Mugford
prepares seafood every which way—fried,
broiled, baked, sautéed, and smoked. He's
especially known for his Caesar salads, his
crab ball appetizers, and his prime rib,
served daily. Sides include fried green
tomatoes, and the pies and cakes are baked
on premises. Lunch, served until 4 PM, adds
burgers and a big menu of sandwiches.

THE FLYING MELON

252-928-2533
804 Irvin Garrish Hwy., NC 12
Price: Inexpensive to Moderate
Children's Menu: Yes
Cuisine: Seafood, Creole, Asian fusion
Liquor: Beer and wine
Serving: B, D, SB
Closed: Sunday evening and Monday, seasonal
Credit Cards: MC, V
Handicapped Access: Yes
Special Features: Brunch served daily 9 AM–2 PM; takeout available

To say it's eclectic doesn't really do the menu here justice, but whatever you order you will likely come away singing the praises of the chefs at the Flying Melon. The tiny, bright, even funky dining room is the scene of daily brunch, where the specialties are *pain perdu* (New Orleans–style French toast), an oyster po' boy, and pork barbecue smoked on-site. Come dinnertime, the kitchen switches continents, serving up dim sum and satay, spicy Thai beef salad, and curries, in addition to a variety of fresh seafood, shrimp creole, pork loin with mango chutney, steaks, and chicken. Every dish has creative flair, and the homemade desserts are to die for. Beverages run from sweet or unsweet tea to a nice selection of import beers.

HOWARD'S PUB & RAW BAR

252-928-4441
www.howardspub.com
1175 Irvin Garrish Hwy., NC 12
Price: Inexpensive to Moderate
Children's Menu: Yes
Cuisine: American
Liquor: Full bar
Serving: L, D, SB
Credit Cards: D, MC, V
Handicapped Access: Yes
Special Features: Live bands; bar; big-screen TV; darts, foosball and pool tables; lunch specials; on-site store; takeout available

For lots of Outer Banks visitors, a trip to Howard's is an annual pilgrimage. Some of them ride over on the free ferry and never make it any further than this restaurant and bar that sits at the northern limit of Ocracoke Village. An on-site store sells Howard's famous T-shirts, license plates, and other collectibles. Barbecued ribs, char-grilled rib eyes, steamed shrimp, chili, and the Ocracoke oyster shooter (with hot sauce and beer) are the specialties here, but everyone will find something to like on the extensive eight-page menu that ranges from pizza to live Maine lobster. After a day of fishing or beachcombing, relax with a cold one from Howard's list of 200 beers on the big screened porch or up on the rooftop deck with a view over the dunes to the ocean. This is entertainment central, with live bands, bar games, and sports on the numerous TVs. Kids' meals come served on a Frisbee. This is one place on Ocracoke guaranteed to be open when you stop by; they serve every day of the year, including holidays. When hurricanes roll in, they just crank up the generator.

JASON'S RESTAURANT

252-928-3434
1110 Irvin Garrish Hwy., NC 12
Price: Inexpensive to Moderate
Children's Menu: Yes
Cuisine: Seafood
Liquor: Beer and wine
Serving: L, D
Closed: Seasonally
Credit Cards: MC, V
Handicapped Access: Yes
Special Features: Bar; takeout available

Casual low-key spot is a favorite hangout for locals and visitors alike. The big bar here offers several beers on tap, including Bass, Guinness, and Hefeweizen, by the glass or pitcher, plus a complete selection of all the

The ghost village of Portsmouth lies just across the inlet from Ocracoke.

most popular bar food. Take a seat on the screened porch and choose among pasta with marinara and meatballs, pesto, or Alfredo sauce, vegetarian lasagna, pizzas, steaks, jerk chicken, sandwiches, and fresh local seafood. The same menu is served all day. Tuesday is sushi day. Prices are some of the most reasonable on the island.

JOLLY ROGER PUB & MARINA

252-928-3703
www.silverlakemotelandinn.com
396 Irvin Garrish Hwy., NC 12
Price: Moderate
Children's Menu: Yes
Cuisine: Seafood, Mexican
Liquor: Beer and wine
Serving: L, D
Closed: Seasonally

Credit Cards: MC, V
Handicapped Access: Yes
Special Features: Live music; bar; marina

A casual, open-air spot that sits right on the docks in front of the Silver Lake Motel serves food mostly of the fried variety—sandwiches and baskets of fried fish, shrimp, and oysters, plus a few Mexican offerings. The best bet is the catch of the day. All tables are outside, on a deck or under umbrellas and awnings; some are in the full sun. Food comes in plastic baskets with throw-away utensils. The main attraction here, however, is the location directly on the waterfront. In fair weather, a crowd gathers at cocktail hour to see what the charter fleet brings in and to watch the sun set. Live music adds to the sunset vibe. A great place to develop that Ocracoma.

THE PELICAN RESTAURANT AND PATIO BAR

252-928-7431
305 Irvin Garrish Hwy., NC 12
Price: Inexpensive to Moderate
Children's Menu: Yes
Cuisine: Seafood
Liquor: Beer and wine
Serving: B, L, D
Open: Daily; call for off-season hours
Credit Cards: MC, V
Handicapped Access: Yes
Special Features: Happy hour specials; live music; bar

The Pelican occupies a historic house just across the street from the waterfront, and its shady, dog-friendly patio set amid live oaks makes a great retreat after a day on the water. Best known and loved for happy hour shrimp, 3–5 PM, and the live music that follows, this laid-back spot also serves breakfast, lunch, and dinner daily. The eggs Benedict, Pelican style, with lump crabmeat, and omelets of every variety are the specialties at breakfast. At dinner, try the jalapeño shrimp.

★ SMACNALLY'S RAW BAR AND GRILL
252-928-9999
180 Irvin Garrish Hwy., NC 12, Anchorage
Inn Marina
Price: Inexpensive to Moderate
Children's Menu: Yes
Cuisine: Seafood
Liquor: Beer and wine
Serving: L, D
Closed: Seasonally
Credit Cards: MC, V
Handicapped Access: Yes
Special Features: Clambake delivery

Located on the docks at the Anchorage Inn Marina, this is a great place to kick back with a cold one while you check out the catch of the charter fishing boats. sMacNally's keeps its beer on ice and claims it's the coldest in town. Raw and steamed local seafood is the specialty, but the juicy Angus burgers come highly recommended as well. You can also get your seafood fried or grilled. Best bets for groups are the Beach Buckets, filled with clams, shrimp, oysters, crawfish, or crab legs, based on availability, plus corn on the cob and red potatoes.

Food Purveyors

Bakeries and Coffee Shops
The Fig Tree Bakery and Deli 252-928-3481; 1015 Irvin Garrish Hwy., NC 12. The Fig Tree has what it takes to assemble a great picnic or bag lunch for ferry or beach. Try a deli sub or the pimiento cheese sandwich, a Southern favorite. Baked goods and breakfast sandwiches also available.

★ **Ocracoke Coffee Co. & Island Smoothie** 252-928-7473; www.ocracokecoffee.com; 226 Back Rd. With a wide porch, a shady yard, more than 30 varieties of fresh-roasted beans, fruit smoothies, and free wireless Internet access, this coffee shop is a favorite hangout for many residents and visitors.

Breakfast and More
Other popular stops for breakfast are the **Pelican**, the **Flying Melon**, and the **Fig Tree Bakery**.

Ocracoke Station Deli 252-928-4031; 990 Irvin Garrish Hwy., NC 12. Locals drop by for breakfast biscuits and the latest news. Deli sandwiches, pizza slices, hot dogs, lunch specials, and a salad bar are offered all day.

Pony Island Restaurant 252-928-5701; www.ponyislandmotel.com; 51 Ocean View Rd. Big breakfasts at reasonable prices make this place a favorite with families. Try the famous Pony Potatoes, topped with sour cream and salsa.

Candy and Ice Cream
Candyland: The Candy Store 252-928-4387; ocracokehammocks.catalog.com; 201 British Cemetery Rd. Sample more than a dozen varieties of fudge in this shop sharing space with Ocracoke Hammocks.

The Slushy Stand 252-928-1878; 473 Irvin Garrish Hwy., NC 12. Located at the three-way junction where NC 12 meets the water, this landmark serves ice cream, frozen yogurt, homemade Italian gelato, cold drinks, and coffee. You can also rent a bike.

Sunset Sweets 252-928-2500; Community Square Shops, 272 Irvin Garrish Hwy., NC 12. Frozen yogurt, fudge, sundaes, and milkshakes are available at this convenient harborside stop.

The Sweet Tooth 252-928-3481; sweettooth.catalog.com; 1015 Irvin Garrish Hwy., NC 12. The pink building on the main road into town carries a variety of fine chocolates, truffles, and homemade fudge, ice cream, milkshakes, and coffee drinks, plus a selection of desserts from brownies to pies.

Delis and Specialty Foods

ABC Store 252-928-3281; www.ncabc.com; 950 Irvin Garrish Hwy., NC 12, at the Variety Store Shops. The state-run liquor store here has some unusual hours, especially off-season. Check for the latest.

The Community Store 252-928-9956; www.ocracokescommunitystore.com; 294 Irvin Garrish Hwy., NC 12. The heart of the community once again, the newly reopened landmark offers groceries and general store merchandise, plus organic, natural, and dairy-free items. Delivery available.

Island Natural Health Store 252-928-6211; 170 Back Rd. This shop within the Sunflower Center stocks supplements, teas, gluten-free breads, soy products, and organic foods, including fresh organic produce in season.

Ocracoke Variety Store and True Value Hardware 252-928-4911; 950 Irvin Garrish Hwy., NC 12. A one-stop store where you'll find groceries, fresh meats, beer, wine, ice, plus souvenirs and beach, boating, and camping gear. Check the bulletin board for local events.

The Vegetable Man 782 Irvin Garrish Hwy., NC 12. Look for fresh produce being sold on the lawn of the East Carolina Bank, several days a week.

Zillie's Island Pantry 252-928-9036; www.zilliespantry.com; Spencer's Market, 585 Irvin Garrish Hwy., NC 12. A godsend to gourmet cooks on the island, Zillie's stocks items from around the world, including pâtés, smoked salmon, cheeses, and much, much more. The shop also has a huge selection of wine and the island's best stock of imported beers and microbrews. Weekly wine tastings are community events.

Takeout

Back Porch Lunchbox 252-928-3651; 747 Irvin Garrish Hwy., NC 12. Pick up a gourmet bag lunch for the ferry at this to-go window. Unique sandwiches, cold steamed shrimp, tasty side salads, plus fruit, drinks, ice cream, smoothies, and home-baked cookies are available.

Creek Side Café 252-928-3606; 621 Irvin Garrish Hwy., NC 12. Now a self-service café, the Creek Side continues to serve its popular blackened shrimp, chicken, and fish, as well as burgers, seafood baskets, and the locally famous key lime pie, all at reasonable prices. Beer and wine is available to drink at tables on the patio.

Thai Moon 252-928-5100; Spencer's Market, 589 Irvin Garrish Hwy., NC 12. Authentic Thai food is available for takeout only. Tom Yum soup, curries, pad thai, plus terrific takes on local seafood and vegetarian choices.

Seafood Markets

★ **Ocracoke Seafood** 252-928-5601; www.ocracokeseafood.com; 416 Irvin Garrish Hwy., NC 12. Seafood arrives fresh off the boats that dock just behind this market. Offerings vary by day and season, but you'll often find shrimp, crabs, clams, flounder, and mahi mahi (dolphin) harvested in local waters, as well as two island favorites, spadefish and sheepshead, not often seen on menus.

TOURING

A good place to begin a tour of the island is the **National Park Service Ocracoke Island Visitor's Center** (252-928-4531; 38 Irvin Garrish Hwy., NC 12) located next to the ferry docks in Ocracoke Village. Here you'll find information on both the national seashore and the town, and a bookshop full of local-interest books. Rangers lead programs during the summer at various locations around the park, including history and ecology talks, bird walks, and excursions that teach crabbing and seining techniques.

There's a large parking lot behind the visitor's center. Leave your vehicle there and set off on foot to explore the town. Walking tour maps are available at the visitor's center and at the **Ocracoke Preservation Society Museum** on the other side of the parking lot.

By Air

Pelican Airways 252-928-1661, 888-773-5422; Ocracoke Airstrip, Irvin Garrish Hwy., NC 12. Sightseeing flights, charter flights, flying lessons, and service to regional airports from Norfolk to New Bern.

By All Terrain Vehicle and Beach Buggy

Portsmouth Island ATV Excursions 252-928-4484; www.portsmouthislandatvs.com; Jolly Roger Marina. Wade and Gwen Austin take groups to Portsmouth Island for a four-hour tour of the deserted village April through November. ATV riders must be 16 years of age and have a valid driver's license. Helmets are provided. For families, the Austins have Kawasaki Mules, which accommodate four.

By Boat or Kayak

★ **Portsmouth Island Boat Tours** 252-928-4361; www.austinboattours.com; Community Square Docks. Captains Rudy and Donald Austin run a shuttle service from the Ocracoke

Activity on Ocracoke centers on Silver Lake Harbor.

waterfront to the ghost village of Portsmouth. You have time for a self-guided tour of the
town, now under the care of the National Park Service, a swim, and some beachcombing
on the unspoiled beach, before your pickup, four hours later. Bring insect repellent,
drinking water, suntan lotion, a hat, and good walking shoes. The beach is 1.5 miles
from the village. The shuttle costs $20 round-trip.

The Austins also operate a narrated sightseeing tour of Pamlico Sound, visiting the
sites of Fort Ocracoke, Shell Castle Island, Pelican Island, and other local landmarks.
During the tour Rudy Austin tells local tales in the fast-disappearing Ocracoke brogue.

Ocracoke Adventures 252-928-7873; 460 Irvin Garrish Hwy., NC 12. Kayak eco-tours.

Ride the Wind Surf Shop 252-928-6311; www.surfocracoke.com; 486 Irvin Garrish Hwy.,
NC 12. Kayak eco-tours explore the history and ecology of Ocracoke. Sunrise, sunset,
and full-moon tours are offered all summer, as well as a history tour to Springer's Point
and Teach's Hole. The shop also rents kayaks by the hour, day, or week.

★ *The Windfall* 252-928-7245; www.schoonerwindfall.com; Community Square Docks.
Captain Rob Temple takes his 57-foot gaff-rigged schooner on daily sails from the Ocracoke waterfront, May through October. She's hard to miss with the Jolly Roger flying
from her mast. During the hour-long sails, Temple tells tales about Ocracoke's most
infamous resident, Blackbeard, including many little-known facts. Prices are reasonable, $20 a person, $10 for children ages 4–11, for the hour cruise; $25 for the slightly
longer sunset sail. Temple also offers a special Pirate Cruise. No credit cards are
accepted.

On Foot

Ocracoke Ghost and History Walk 252-928-6300; www.villagecraftsmen.com; Village
Craftsmen, 170 Howard St. Eighth-generation Ocracoker Philip Howard and his trained
staff lead two different walking tours of Ocracoke Village, and both have plenty of ghosts
stories. Tours last about 90 minutes and cover 1.5 miles. Cost is $12 for adults, $6 for
ages 12 and under. Self-guided MP3 tours also available.

CULTURE

Thanks to their centuries of isolation, the islanders developed a unique culture, creating
their own forms of entertainment and creativity. Sea chanteys blended with folk music
around winter fires, decoy carving developed into fine art, and always there was—and is—
the inspiration of sea, wind, and sand.

Architecture

Some 200 acres of the village (about half the total area) is officially identified as the Ocracoke Historic District. Concentrated around Silver Lake, the district includes 232 historic
buildings, 15 cemeteries, plus the lighthouse, cisterns, picket fences, and docks dating
from 1823 to 1959, when Ocracoke is considered to have entered the modern era. Many of
the older houses are traditional story-and-a-jump cottages with steep gable roofs, front
porches, chimneys on the end, tongue-and-groove interior walls, and rooms in the attic.
The outside is usually covered with cedar shakes, and there may still be a cistern to catch
the rain, the island's only source of freshwater in the early days. Many of the homes in the
historic district display wooden plaques giving the construction date and name of the original occupant.

The Ocracoke Preservation Society (252-928-7375; www.ocracokepreservation.org) has developed a booklet documenting the historic district and its special architectural features. It's available at the society's museum bookstore or through its Web site, for those wishing to know more about the Ocracoke style.

Sam Jones, a Norfolk industrialist, was another major influence on Ocracoke architecture. During the 1950s Jones engaged local craftsmen in a variety of construction projects, most of his own fanciful design. Two significant examples survive along the waterfront: the many-gabled Castle, now a bed-and-breakfast inn, and Berkley Manor, formerly an inn, recently purchased by a developer.

Galleries

The funky personality, natural beauty, and relative isolation of the island have led many creative folk to settle here. Information on Ocracoke's galleries and artists, plus gallery openings, the annual Artwalk, and other events, can be found at www.art-on-ocracoke.com.

Bella Fiore Pottery 252-928-2826; 80 Back Rd. Sarah Fiore's microwave- and oven-safe stoneware pottery reflects the beauty of the island environment.

Deepwater Pottery 252-928-3936; www.deepwaterpottery.com; 34 School Rd. Dedicated to artful living, Deepwater is a focus of Ocracoke culture. The pottery shares the historic 1898 Dezzie Bragg house with **Books to be Red**, and the **Deepwater Theater** is next door.

Down Creek Gallery 252-928-4400; www.downcreekgallery.com; 260 Irvin Garrish Hwy., NC 12. This gallery on the waterfront represents over 125 local and regional artists and craftspeople. Weekly art openings during the summer season.

Downpoint Decoys 252-928-3269; www.thecaptainslanding.com; 324 Irvin Garrish Hwy., NC 12. In a building formerly part of the legendary Green Island Duck Hunting Club, David O'Neal, a noted carver and collector of decoys, carries on the historic traditions.

The Gathering Place 252-928-7180; www.ocracokegatheringplace.com; 587B Irvin Garrish Hwy., NC 12, Spencer's Market. Mermaid and lighthouse art mixes with Ocracoke pottery and works by local and regional artists.

Island Artworks 252-928-3892; www.islandartworks.com; 89 British Cemetery Rd. Artist Kathleen O'Neal's original jewelry, made of precious metals, gemstones, and beachcombed treasures, forms the heart of a collection of works by local and regional artists.

Over the Moon 252-928-3555; 64 British Cemetery Rd. Lots of handcrafted items crowd this old island house, including pottery and ceramics, blown glass, pewter and wooden kitchenware, plus jewelry, cards, and recycled art.

Secret Garden Gallery 252-928-2598; www.art-on-ocracoke.com; 72 Back Rd. Jewelry designer Barbara Hardy and her husband, Ray, a painter and collage artist, present their own art, plus works by more than 50 other artists. An upstairs gallery hosts rotating exhibits.

Sunflower Center for the Arts 252-921-0188; 170 Back Rd. Carol and Jim O'Brien present their original handcrafted jewelry as well as a large collection of estate pieces. The upstairs gallery is devoted to art and glass by local artists. Classes in arts and crafts are also offered.

Tree Top Studio 252-928-9997; 402 Back Rd. Featuring paintings by local artists, this little studio also does professional framing.

★ **Village Craftsmen** 252-928-5541; www.villagecraftsmen.com; 170 Howard St. Stocks a wide variety of crafts by over 300 American crafters, including many from the Outer Banks. Gallery founder Philip Howard, an eighth-generation Ocracoker, is a wealth of information on the island, past, present, and future, and admits he just may be descended from one of Blackbeard's pirate crew.

Historic Homes and Sites

British Cemetery British Cemetery Rd. The bodies of four British sailors who lost their lives when a German submarine torpedoed *HMS Bedfordshire* on May 11, 1942, are buried here under a British flag. The U.S. Coast Guard performs an honor guard ceremony every year on the anniversary of the ship's sinking.

Fort Ocracoke Historical Marker Irvin Garrish Hwy., NC 12. Located at the back of the parking lot behind the National Park Service Visitor's Center, this marker gives information about Fort Ocracoke, once located just offshore. The site of the fort is now underwater but has been excavated by divers, and some of the artifacts are on display in the Ocracoke Preservation Museum.

Howard Street www.ocracokevillage.com. Shaded with live oak, yaupon, and myrtle trees, this street paved with oyster shells was once one of the village's main streets. The houses still belong to the island's oldest families, and the live oaks here are the most ancient on the island.

North Carolina Center for the Advancement of Teaching Campus at Ocracoke Island www.nccat.org. The 1940 U.S. Coast Guard Station, located beyond the ferry docks at the mouth of Silver Lake Harbor, has been restored for use as a campus offering enrichment programs for North Carolina teachers. A historic bell, on loan from the Coast Guard, sits on the harbor side of the facility.

Ocracoke Lighthouse 252-928-4531; www.nps.gov/caha; Lighthouse Rd. Most visitors to the island make their way to its most prominent landmark, the 70-foot lighthouse that continues to help guide ships today as it has since 1823. It is North Carolina's oldest operating lighthouse and the second-oldest continuously operating one in the country. A short boardwalk leads to the base of the lighthouse, past the old keeper's cottage surrounded by twisted trees. The lighthouse is not open for climbing, but during the summer you can have a look inside the base if a docent is on duty.

★ **Ocracoke Preservation Society Museum** 252-928-7375; www.ocracokepreservation .org; 49 Water Plant Rd. Located in a historic 1900 house next to the National Park Service Visitor's Center, this museum is a community-based effort with strong support from native families. The rooms are furnished with donated antiques, decoys, model boats, and exquisite quilts. Special exhibits explore the island's hunting and fishing traditions, Civil War history, and the distinctive Ocracoke Island brogue. Outside, the yard, enclosed in a rose-twined picket fence, contains an original cistern, a life car used by the U.S. Life Saving Service, and a traditional 1934 fishing boat. During the summer, local residents, many of them cultural treasures themselves, give talks on the porch. The museum's gift shop is an excellent source of books on local history and culture. Admission to the museum is free.

Ocracoke Seafood Company 252-928-5601; www.ocracokeseafood.com; 416 Irvin Garrish Hwy., NC 12. The last surviving fish house on Ocracoke remains in its historic spot on the waterfront due to an intense community effort led by the nonprofit Ocracoke Working Watermen's Association (www.ocracokewatermen.org). Visitors are welcome.

Portsmouth Island 252-728-2250; www.nps.gov/calo. Once larger and more prosperous

The Ocracoke Preservation Society Museum

than Ocracoke on the other side of the inlet, today Portsmouth is a ghost town, maintained in pristine yet lonely splendor by the National Park Service as part of Cape Lookout National Seashore. The NPS offers guided tours of the village, or you can take a self-guided tour. Maps, restrooms, and history exhibits can be found at the visitor's center, close to the dock where boat shuttles drop off day-trippers. Several buildings are open to the public, including the general store and post office, the Methodist church, and the lifesaving station.

Teach's Hole Blackbeard Exhibit 252-928-1718; www.teachshole.com; 935 Irvin Garrish Hwy., NC 12. This pirate store with over 1,000 pirate-related items offers educational exhibits, including weapon and pirate flag displays, old bottles, and a documentary film on Ocracoke's most famous resident and his pirate associates.

Music and Nightlife

For a small island, Ocracoke makes a lot of music. The island traditions of impromptu back-porch jam sessions, potluck dinners, and community square dances have morphed into something the locals call Ocrafolk, a unique form of Americana music melded from old and new musical styles. The members of **Molasses Creek** (www.molassescreek.com), Gary and Kitty Mitchell and Fiddler Dave, are at the heart of the movement. The trio plays a fusion of folk, bluegrass, and humorous ballads, writing songs inspired by their location on Pamlico Sound. They began performing weekly at the Deepwater Theater and inviting local talents, such as native musician Martin Garrish and Roy Parsons, a local boy who toured with the Barnum & Bailey Circus band way back when, to sit in.

In 1996 Gary Mitchell recorded a compilation album of songs by local musicians, called

Ocrafolk. Its popularity led to recurring performances by the Ocrafolk Opry and the ever-growing **Ocrafolk Festival of Music and Storytelling** (www.ocrafolkfestival.org), held every year in June.

Soundside Records (www.soundsiderecords.com), a label run by Molasses Creek members, offers an impressive list of discs by local and regional artists, including the popular series of Ocrafolk samplers.

To see the future of music on the island, watch for announcements of the Flat Cat Café, an open-mike night featuring members of the Ocracoke School Music Club. The school is attended by grades K–12, and performers at the Flat Cat may range from first-graders to rising seniors, some of whom have already recorded albums.

During the summer you'll have several choices for live music most nights of the week, a result of the many talented performers based here and the community support they enjoy. In addition to the Deepwater Theater's nightly shows, you can regularly find music at Howard's Pub, the Jolly Roger, Creekside Cafe, and the Pelican.

The laws allowing mixed drinks in the village are leading to new nightlife options. **Mango Loco Restaurant and Lounge** (928-2874; 1050 Irvin Garrish Hwy., NC 12) is one of the first of this new breed of nightspot, scheduling local and regional bands and open-mike nights, in addition to serving a mix of Caribbean and Mexican food with full cocktail service.

★ **Deepwater Theater** 252-928-3411, 252-928-4280; www.molassescreek.com; School Rd. From June to September, you can catch some of the brightest stars of the local music scene at the Deepwater Theater, an intimate space that regulars compare to an overgrown screen porch. While schedules vary every year, performers usually include **Captain Ron Temple** and his Rumgagger Pirate Show (www.schoonerwindfall.com), Noah Paley and songwriting duo **Coyote** (www.coyotemusic.net), *Prairie Home Companion* award-winners Molasses Creek, and the ever-evolving **Ocrafolk Opry.** Classes in yoga and tai chi are also held at the theater.

Ocrafolk School 252-928-4280; www.ocrafolkschool.org. Weeklong seminars by island experts offer classes ranging from basketry, cooking, and sea chanteys, to Ocracoke history, ecology, and sailing. Students participate in community events including evening sings, square dances, and storytelling.

Outer Banks Murder Mystery 252-928-6300; www.villagecraftsmen.com. Professional storyteller Lou Ann Homan conducts murder mystery evenings tailored for your group. Costumes and props are included. She will also come to your vacation cottage for an evening of ghost or pirate tales.

RECREATION

If you want to play golf on vacation, or have young ones that need to ride roller coasters, Ocracoke is not the destination for you. The attractions here are walking and swimming on one of the best beaches in the country, exploring the historic village, slowing down, reading a book, or just relaxing. You can find more action out on the water, but even there you'll encounter the island's laid-back vibe, locally referred to as the Ocracoma.

Beaches

The island's more than 16 miles of undeveloped beach, managed by the National Park Service as part of the Cape Hatteras National Seashore, are its greatest asset and in recent years brought Ocracoke to international prominence. After ranking Ocracoke for four years among his top three, in 2007 Dr. Beach named Ocracoke's **Lifeguarded Beach** the best in the country.

The shoreline's wide, non-crowded, and unpolluted sands, plus the warm Gulf Stream waters that allow swimming into the late fall, attracted Dr. Beach's attention. Surfing, shelling, surf fishing, bird-watching, and just plain old loafing are the favorite activities on this beach, where no highrises block the sun.

Beach Access

Parts of the 16.5 miles of beach on Ocracoke Island are open to both off-road vehicles (ORVs in park parlance) and pedestrians. There are six places where you can park and walk over the dunes to the beach, and several beach access ramps for four-wheel-drive vehicles.

The boardwalk opposite the pony pens is a popular spot to cross to the beach. Ramp 70, also called the Airport Road, is the beach access most used by locals.

The parking lot for the award-winning Lifeguarded Beach can be found about a half mile north of ramp 70, about 1.5 miles north of the village, on NC 12. This beach also has changing rooms and showers. Look for the brown swimmer sign. Lifeguards are on duty Memorial Day to Labor Day.

The northern end of the island, accessed via ramp 59, and the southern end, accessed by ramp 72, also known as South Point Road, are popular spots for surf fishing, although subject to closures to protect nesting birds and sea turtles.

Current information on beach closures, activities, and regulations can be found on the Cape Hatteras National Seashore Web site, www.nps.gov/caha, or by calling 252-473-2111.

Named the Best Beach in the U.S. in 2007, the sands of Ocracoke Island are the perfect place to relax.

Beach Buggy and Jeep Rentals

Beach Ride 4x4 Rentals 252-916-0133; www.ocracoke4x4rentals.com; 1070 Irvin Garrish
Hwy., NC 12. Automatic four-wheel-drive SUVs for rent by the day.

Nor'easter Charters 201-401-8610, 877-8BUNKER; www.noreastercharters.com. Rent an
OBX-style fishing jeep, by the day or week, completely equipped for surf fishing.

Bicycling

Best Bike Routes

The best way to see Ocracoke Village is by bike. Ride the Loop Road to the lighthouse, visit
Springer Point and the British Cemetery, and gallery hop along the Back Road. Especially
seek out the old lanes paved with crushed oyster shell such as Howard Street and Fig Tree
Lane.

A new paved, multi-use path connects the village with the National Park Service campground and the Lifeguarded Beach.

Bike Rental Shops

Most hotels and inns rent bicycles if they aren't included for free in the room rate. Shacks
and stands along the main street also offer convenient daily rentals.

Beach Outfitters 252-928-6261; www.ocracokeislandrealty.com; 1053 Irvin Garrish Hwy.,
NC 12. Large bike stand outside the Ocracoke Island Realty office at the north end of the
village.

Island Rentals 252-928-5680, 252-928-8058; 144 Silver Lake Rd., Ocracoke Harbor Inn.
Rents bikes as well as motorboats. Daily, weekly, and three-day rates available.

The Slushy Stand 252-928-1878; 473 Irvin Garrish Hwy., NC 12. Rents adult, kid, and tandem bikes, adult tricycles, and baby seats, by the hour, day, or week. Locks are included.

Wheelie Fun Scooter Rentals 252-928-6661; www.theanchorageinn.com; Anchorage
Marina, 180 Irvin Garrish Hwy., NC 12. The marina rents both bikes and scooters, by the
hour or day. Helmets provided.

Boats and Boating

All the boating action centers on Silver Lake, the harbor that provides a focal point for
Ocracoke Village.

Jet Skis and Personal Watercraft

Ocracoke Wave Runners 252-928-2600, 252-921-0314; 460 Irvin Garrish Hwy., NC 12,
Gun Barrel Point Marina. Half-hour and hour-long rentals let you explore Silver Lake
and the waters of Ocracoke Inlet on your own. Tours also available.

Kayaking and Canoeing

Ocracoke Village is an ideal location for kayaking. The calm waters of Silver Lake, with the
lighthouse visible in the background, make a safe and scenic spot for a family paddle. Just
stay clear of the ferry docks. The sound side of the island is covered in marsh where many
wading birds can be seen, especially at dawn and dusk. Another favorite paddle is southeast
along the coast toward Springer's Point.

More-experienced paddlers may want to cross Ocracoke Inlet to Portsmouth but should
get local advice on winds, tides, and weather before setting out.

Marinas

Most of the recreation on the island, beyond the beach, is found at the docks along Silver Lake. Several fun establishments have sprung up on the waterfront, where you can kick back with a cold beverage and watch the nautical action.

Those who arrive by boat will find consistent depths of 8 feet in Silver Lake Harbor and in the well-maintained channels leading to it.

Anchorage Marina 252-928-6661; www.theanchorageinn.com; 180 Irvin Garrish Hwy., NC 12. Full hookups including cable, fuel, and pump-out service are available for transient boaters, with access to showers and a swimming pool. Vessels up to 100 feet can dock. **sMacNalley's Raw Bar** serves local seafood and cold ones on the dock in season. Bikes and scooters for rent by the hour, day, or week.

Community Square Docks 324 Irving Garrish Hwy., NC 12. Sign up here for boat tours and ferry service to historic Portsmouth or sunset sails aboard the *Windfall*. Fuel for boats is available, as are occasional slips for transients and a dinghy dock.

Gun Barrel Point Marina, located at the "T" where NC 12 meets the water, sometimes referred to as Kayak Corner. The *Miss Ocracoke* party boat, Ocracoke Wave Runners, and Ride the Wind kayaks operate from here.

Jolly Roger Pub & Marina 252-928-3703; www.silverlakemotelandinn.com; 396 Irvin Garrish Hwy., NC 12, across the street from the Silver Lake Motel. Parasail Ocracoke and several charter-fishing boats dock here, convenient to the refreshments and fun served up daily by the pub.

National Park Service Docks 252-473-2111; www.nps.gov/caha. Located next to the ferry docks at the far end of Silver Lake, these government-run docks host boats up to 80 feet at low rates. Dockage is first come, first served, and there is a 14-day limit on stays during the summer. Services include electric hookup, available in summer only, low-pressure water connections, and bathrooms across the street.

Powerboat Rentals

Island Rentals 252-928-5680, 252-928-8058; 144 Silver Lake Rd., Ocracoke Harbor Inn. If you have some boating experience, you can rent a motorboat or flat-bottom skiff at the Ocracoke Harbor Inn.

Restless Native Small Boat Rentals 252-921-0011, 252-928-1421; Anchorage Marina, 180 Irvin Garrish Hwy., NC 12. Be your own captain in a flat-bottom skiff with outboard motor. After a brief orientation, explore the harbor and sound on your own, go fishing, or clamming. Daily and package rates available.

Public Boat Ramps

Several boat ramps are available in the village. The National Park Service maintains a free boat ramp at the back of the large parking lot next to the visitor's center, but you cannot launch personal watercraft such as Jet Skis from here—they are not allowed in the waters of the national seashore. Boat ramps charging a fee are located at the Anchorage Marina and at the Harborside Motel.

Sailboat Charters

Schooner *Windfall* 252-928-SAIL; www.schoonerwindfall.com; Community Square Docks. The 57-foot gaff-rigged schooner can be chartered for up to 30 passengers by the

Surf fishing on the beaches around Ocracoke

hour. The captain is an ordained minister, if you choose to exchange vows onboard. Regular sailing tours, sunset tours, and pirate tours are available daily from May to October.

Fishing

Docked less than 20 miles from the Gulf Stream, Ocracoke's charter-fishing fleet conducts some of the most successful, and reasonably priced, offshore trips on the coast, and the rich waters of Pamlico Sound are just outside the harbor.

Many of Ocracoke's charter fleet captains are descendants of families who have fished this region for generations, and will take you to productive spots that the out-of-town fisherman will never find.

Although Ocracoke has no fishing piers, surf fishing is tremendously popular along the unspoiled beaches of the island. A four-wheel-drive vehicle is a must.

Fishing Charters and Outfitters

Devereux II 252-921-0120, 252-928-5331; thedevereux.tripod.com; Anchorage Marina. Captain Reid Robinson takes special interest in the serious angler who wants to go after trophy fish. Available for tournaments.

Drum Stick 252-928-5351, 252-473-0106, 800-825-5351; Anchorage Marina. Captain David Nagel's charter boat has the distinction of catching the state-record king mackerel, an 82-pound, 66-inch monster. A wide variety of excursions are possible, including makeup trips, night drum fishing, shark fishing, Gulf Stream trolling, and winter fishing for giant bluefin tuna.

Fish Tale 252-921-0224, 252-928-3403; Jolly Roger Marina. Educational family trips use light tackle for calm-water fishing on Pamlico Sound and include lessons in fish identification, perfect for first time anglers. The Catch Your Dinner special offers a quick two-hour trip after good "eating" fish. Tackle, bait, ice, and fish filleting are included.

Nor'easter Charters 201-401-8610, 877-8BUNKER; www.noreastercharters.com. If you want to try surf fishing but don't have a clue about how to get started, Captain Scott Hampton and his team will take you to the best surf fishing locales in their fleet of four-wheel-drive vehicles, completely equipped with rods and reels, bait, tackle, and cooler. Off-shore charters also available.

Ocracoke Sportfishing 252-928-4841, 800-305-1472; www.ocracokesportfishing.com; Community Square Docks. The O'Neals, father and son, belong to a native Ocracoker family with a fishing heritage that dates back to the 1600s. Join Captain Ronnie O'Neal for a full or half day of sport fishing aboard the *Miss Kathleen*. Or set out with Ronnie's son, Captain Ryan O'Neal, in the 24-foot *Tarheel*, for a day of inshore light-tackle fishing, clamming, or a night trip to gig flounder.

Osprey Charter Fishing 252-928-4020, 252-995-2626; www.ospreycharterfishing.com. Captain Jette Carr, one of the few female charter-boat captains on the coast, offers trolling, bottom, and wreck fishing aboard the 36-foot *Osprey*. Carr will also take you surf fishing, gill netting, or clamming, if you prefer.

Rascal 252-928-6111, 252-921-0180; Ocracoke Harbor Inn, 144 Silver Lake Rd. Captain Norman Miller offers special rates for families on inshore and offshore fishing, and lodging discount packages at the Ocracoke Harbor Inn. Red drum runs are a specialty.

Many local buildings are constructed from wood salvaged from the ocean.

Headboats

Miss Ocracoke 252-928-6060; Gun Shot Marina, Silver Lake. A native Ocracoke captain pilots the local headboat out twice a day for a half day of inshore drift fishing or offshore wreck fishing—wherever they're biting. Walk-ups are welcome. All bait and tackle, plus fish cleaning, are provided. Sunset dolphin cruises are offered in season.

Horseback Riding

Morning Star Stables 252-921-0383; www.morningstarstablesonline.com. Horseback rides on the beach available all year.

Tackle Shops

Anchorage Marina 252-928-6661; www.theanchorageinn.com; 180 Irvin Garrish Hwy., NC 12. Ship's store here carries ice, bait, and tackle.

O'Neal's Dockside II Tackleshop 252-928-1111; 800 Irvin Garrish Hwy., NC 12. A huge variety of fishing gear is available for sale or rent, plus free fishing advice from members of one of the oldest families on the island. Hunting, camping, and marine supplies also in stock.

Ocracoke Variety Store 252-928-4911; 950 Irvin Garrish Hwy., NC 12. This one-stop shop offers groceries and microbrews, as well as bait and tackle, beach supplies, and much more. Open all year.

Tradewinds Bait & Tackle 252-928-5491; www.fishtradewinds.com; 1094 Irvin Garrish Hwy., NC 12. Rod, reel, and clam rake rentals, tackle sales and repairs, camping and beach supplies, ice, snacks, and advice can all be found here. Surf fishing is the passion of the owners, and they have an official weigh station where you can register your citation fish.

Hunting

Shooting waterfowl is a treasured winter tradition in many Ocracoke families. Some native Ocracokers now offer guide services, taking visiting hunters after the red heads, blue bills, black ducks, pintails, brants, widgeons, and geese that winter in Pamlico Sound. You'll find a unique kind of blind in use here: the curtain blind, a kind of sink box developed in the area.

Curtain Box Hunting 252-928-4408. Native guide Russell Williams specializes in curtain blind trips. Packages including accommodations can be arranged through the Pony Island Motel.

Island Guide Services 252-928-2504, 252-928-2509. Ken Tillett and Earl Gaskins continue the hunting traditions of their forefathers, who were guides at the legendary Green Island Hunting Club. Trips include stake and pit blinds, decoys, and transport.

Mason's Guide Service 252-928-7308, 252-921-0100. Native Rodney Mason offers waterfowl hunting, plus inshore and offshore fishing.

Ocracoke Sportfishing 252-928-4841, 800-305-1472; www.ocracokesportfishing.com. The O'Neals, father and son, also lead hunting trips during the winter season.

Ocracoke Waterfowl Hunting 252-928-5751. Native Monroe Gaskill provides bush blinds, transport, a resting area for dogs, and deploys more than 100 decoys at each blind.

Open Water Duck Hunting 252-928-7170; www.ocracokeduckhunting.com. Wade Austin is the fourth generation of his family to guide hunters. Curtain boxes, boat, bush, and layout blinds available.

Nature Preserves and Eco-attractions

Hammock Hills Nature Trail, Cape Hatteras National Seashore 252-473-2111; www.nps.gov/caha; Irvin Garrish Hwy., NC 12, 3 miles north of Ocracoke Village. This 30-minute hike over remnant dunes covered with maritime forest and through salt marsh leads to an overlook on Pamlico Sound. Located across NC 12 from the National Park Service campground; there is ample parking and good birding here. Park rangers conduct numerous free programs during the summer months, introducing the ecology and wildlife of the island, including the native ponies.

★ **Springer's Point** 252-449-8289; www.coastallandtrust.org; Loop Rd. The North Carolina Coastal Land Trust protects 121 acres of maritime forest overlooking Ocracoke Inlet and Teach's Hole. In fact, the property was once known as Teach's Plantation, and legend says the infamous Edward Teach, aka Blackbeard, had an island outpost here where he roasted pigs and drank rum with his fellow pirates. Today, the property is heavily wooded with gnarled live oaks, ivy, and red cedars. A short trail leads down to a beach on the sound with a view of a heron rookery. Along the way is an old cemetery where entrepreneur Sam Jones is buried next to his favorite horse. Locals claim the cemetery, in fact the entire point, is haunted. No parking is available, so walk or bike to the site.

Windmill Point 252-928-7375; www.ocracokepreservation.org; end of Silver Lake Rd. This conservation easement protects the area on the far side of Silver Lake from future development. Once the site of a windmill used to grind grain, the area is now heavily wooded. Locals recommend taking Robbie's Lane, a sandy path found at the end of Silver Lake Road, out to an uninhabited beach along Pamlico Sound to catch a spectacular sunset.

Shelling

Some of the best shelling in the state is found along the Atlantic side of Ocracoke. Lucky beachcombers may collect a variety of different whelks, sand dollars, and possibly a rare Scotch bonnet, the North Carolina state shell. The best time to search for shells is right after high tide or after a storm. The northern end of the island has a gentle slope, good for finding unbroken shells.

Spas and Wellness

Ann Ehringhaus Massage Therapy 252-928-1311; www.annehringhaus.com, www.oscars bb.com; 660 Irvin Garrish Hwy., NC 12. Treatments and classes in a variety of energy modalities including Reiki, Chinese acupressure, and the Rosen Method of Emotional Healing.

Deep Blue Day Spa & Massage Therapy 252-921-0182; www.deepbluedayspa.com; 155 Silver Lake Dr. Thalassotherapy, using seawater, sea salts, seaweed, and other products from the sea, plus a full menu of massage therapy, facials, and body treatments, is featured at the day spa located in the pool house of the Castle bed-and-breakfast.

Island Path 252-928-1821, 877-708-7284; www.islandpath.com. Ruth Fordon and Ken DeBarth offer life coaching, personal path retreats, and creativity camps.

Water Sports

Although the water-sports industry here is not yet as organized as you'll find farther north on the Banks, the area has a lot of excellent opportunities for extreme water fun.

The church at Portsmouth Village

Surfing experts say Ocracoke has some of the best, and least crowded, waves on the East Coast. Locals here consider surfing an important part of island life. Ocracoke's high school was the first east of the Mississippi to offer a surfing class.

Parasailing Ocracoke 252-928-2606; Jolly Roger Marina, Irvin Garrish Hwy., NC 12. Get the big picture as you fly high with this locally owned outfitter. A kiosk outside the Jolly Roger takes reservations.

Ride the Wind Surf Shop 252-928-6311; www.surfocracoke.com; 486 Irvin Garrish Hwy., NC 12. Kayak and surf specialists offer kayak ecotours and rentals by the hour, day, or week, as well as surfing lessons and board rentals. From May to August, students ages 9–17 can attend a three-day Surf Camp to learn both technique and safety procedures on surf, skim, and boogie boards. Members of the staff surf every morning of the year and invite island visitors to join them.

Wildlife Spotting

Ocracoke, like other Banks islands both north and south, has its own herd of wild ponies. No one has ever been sure where they came from, but they played an important role in island life for several centuries, serving as mounts for local residents and pulling lifesaving equipment to wreck sites.

In the late 1950s, when the road, now NC 12, was paved down the length of the island, collisions between cars and ponies, which then numbered in the hundreds, became a problem. The National Park Service initially wanted to remove all the ponies from Ocracoke, but at the request of island residents agreed to keep a small herd in a 180-acre pasture. A boardwalk leads from a parking area along NC 12 to a viewing deck where the ponies, now numbering between 25 and 30, can be observed. National Park Service rangers present a program on the ponies during the summer months.

The pony pens are located on the sound side of NC 12, about 6 miles south of the Hatteras Ferry docks and 7 miles north of Ocracoke Village.

Bird-Watching

The sections of the Cape Hatteras National Seashore located on Ocracoke are some of the most isolated and undisturbed on the East Coast and are popular nesting sites for a variety of shorebirds, including the endangered piping plover. Sections of the national seashore are frequently posted during the summer to protect nesting shorebirds and sea turtles. On offshore islands, brown pelicans, black skimmers, and terns can be seen during nesting season.

Popular birding spots on Ocracoke Island include the oceanside pond just south of the Hatteras Ferry terminal, where waterfowl gather during late fall and winter. The surf zone all along the Atlantic side of the island is rich in red knots, sanderlings, plovers, and other shorebirds. South Point Road, at beach access ramp 72, offers especially good birding prospects.

Wading and marsh birds, as well as migrating songbirds, are often seen along the **Hammock Hills Nature Trail**, across NC 12 from the National Park Service campground.

Marine Mammals

The waters of Pamlico Sound and offshore on the ocean side are rich in sea life year round. Boats making their way through Ocracoke Inlet often encounter groups of bottlenose dolphin. More rare are whale sightings. Whale hunting was once a lucrative pursuit in these parts. Today, more different species of whales migrate along the coast of North Carolina than any other stretch of the East Coast. While no organized whale-watching tours are taking place at this time, the experienced captains of Ocracoke know where to look, if asked. Sperm whales and the extremely rare northern right whales migrate past the coast in springtime; humpback and fin whales pass in fall. Pilot whales can be seen all year. Some

The last of Ocracoke's native ponies can be seen at the NPS pony pens.

whales, such as the orcas, stay far from shore in deep water, but juvenile humpbacks can sometimes be seen from the Ocracoke beaches, breaching and forming bubble nets in the rich waters.

Wildlife Tours and Charters

The Miss Ocracoke (252-928-6060; Anchorage Marina) goes out on two-hour dolphin cruises at sunset during the summer season. Captains Rudy and Donald Austin (252-928-4361, 252-928-5431; www.austinboattours.com; Community Square docks) take visitors out to see the dolphins and a brown pelican rookery in Pamlico Sound. In spring and fall **Portsmouth Island ATV Excursions** (252-928-4484; www.portsmouthislandatvs.com; Jolly Roger Marina) offers bird-watching trips aboard ATVs through Portsmouth Island's tidal flats to see shorebirds such as rare curlew sandpipers and bar-tailed godwits.

SHOPPING

Most shops on Ocracoke Island are small and eclectic, mixing practical items with souvenirs for visiting tourists. The "necessities" can be found in general store–type shops, which carry a large variety of different and useful groceries and goods, but perhaps not the selection of brands that people are used to at home. Locals make regular runs "up the beach" across the Hatteras Ferry to get items unavailable on Ocracoke, returning as quickly as possible with full trunks and sighs of relief.

Shopping Centers and Destinations

Back Road Loop British Cemetery and Back Roads. Over a dozen interesting shops and galleries line these shady lanes, and traffic is generally light, making it ideal for a stroll or a bike ride. Here you'll find a gourmet restaurant, a neat coffeehouse and bookstore, and the Ocracoke Library with Internet access and a porch full of rocking chairs.

Captain's Landing Shops Irvin Garrish Hwy. (NC 12) and Silver Lake. Clustered around Captain's Landing Hotel are several shops, most in historic buildings that once housed the post office, which has since moved to the north end of town.

Community Square Shops and Dock Irvin Garrish Hwy. (NC 12) and Silver Lake. Centered on the beloved Community Store, the shops and dock at this location have been the center of Ocracoke life since the days when mail boats, once the island's only contact with the outside world, tied up here.

The Shops at Spencer's Market Irvin Garrish Hwy. (NC 12) and School Rd. Ocracoke's newest shopping destination consists of a complex of shops set a bit back from the harbor.

Books and Music

★ **Books to Be Red** 252-928-3936; 34 School Rd. Sharing a historic building with the Deepwater Pottery, this small bookstore has an excellent selection of local and regional titles. Red-headed owner Leslie Ann Lanier stocks her shelves with titles ranging from light beach reading to historical research, with a special section of books and puzzles for children. If you prefer to write your own story, you'll find a nice selection of journals here, as well.

Java Books 252-928-3937; 226 Back Rd. The sister store of **Books to Be Red** is conveniently located inside the **Ocracoke Coffee Company** and stocks local and regional books, fiction and nonfiction, for both adults and kids. Enjoy a latte while you browse.

Ocracoke Preservation Society Museum Gift Shop 252-928-7375; www.ocracokepreser
vation.org; 49 Water Plant Rd. The museum's gift shop stocks a range of books relating
to Ocracoke for all ages, plus cookbooks published by local churches and restaurants,
DVDs of local storytellers, and music CDs by local musicians. Sales benefit the society.

Clothing

Harborside Gift Shop 252-928-3111; www.ocracokeharborside.com; 229 Irvin Garrish
Hwy., NC 12. Carries top-label resort wear, batik dresses, the original line of popular Sea
Dog T-shirts, and the island art of Douglas Hoover and Teressa Williams.

Mermaid's Folly 252-928-RAGS; www.mermaidsfolly.com; Irvin Garrish Hwy., NC 12. The
former owners of **Island Ragpicker** present a selection of their best selling "sea-spir-
ited" clothing, including Hawaiian shirts, sarongs, and tees.

Natural Selections Hemp Shop 252-928-4367; www.ocracokeislandhemp.com; 35 School
Rd. Environmentally conscious shop carries a wide range of clothing, handbags, hats,
even snacks, made of hemp and other natural fibers, plus Andromeda Soaps, an all-natural line made on Ocracoke.

Gifts

Albert's Styron Store 252-928-2609; 300 Lighthouse Rd. This 1920 landmark on Lighthouse Road lives on, run by Albert's granddaughter, thanks to its initials, offering T-
shirts with the popular ASS and Fat Boys Fish Company logos.

Annabelle's Florist and Antiques 252-928-4541; 278 Irvin Garrish Hwy., NC 12, Community Square Shops. Cute historic building on the pier is filled with the creations of local
floral designer Chester Lynn, plus antiques and gifts.

The Barefoot Bohemian 252-928-9090; www.barefootbohemians.com; 216 Irvin Garrish
Hwy., NC 12, Anchorage Marina. Funktacular gifts from blown glass to sarongs, plus
popular logo Bare Wear.

Captain's Cargo 252-928-9991; www.thecaptainslanding.com; 326 Irvin Garrish Hwy., NC
12. Former post office on the **Captain's Landing** property displays an eclectic collection
of nautical gifts, shells, bath products, and island arts and crafts, tucked into the old
postal boxes.

Island Ragpicker 252-928-7571; 515 Irvin Garrish Hwy., NC 12. Seemingly assembled from
driftwood, the ten rooms of this shop near the **Slushy Stand** contain original hand-
loomed Ragpicker rugs, crafts, apparel, wind chimes, and the Title Wave Room, filled
with cards and books of local interest.

Pamlico Gifts 252-928-6561; www.ocracokeisland.com/pamlico_gifts.htm; Lighthouse Rd.
In her cute shop at the end of a path next to the lighthouse, Elizabeth Parsons sells shell
art, primitive paintings, birdhouses, and hand-etched glass created by herself and her
late husband Roy, plus much more. Roy, a much-loved local treasure known for his
model boats and yodeling singing style, passed in September 2007.

Teach's Hole Pirate Specialty Shop 252-928-1718; www.teachshole.com; 935 Irvin Garrish
Hwy., NC 12 at West End Rd. All things pirate are on sale at this shop stocking over 1,000
items of "piratical piratephernalia."

Home Decor

Ocracoke Island Hammock Co. 252-928-4387; ocracokehammocks.catalog.com; 201
British Cemetery Rd. Hammocks, swings, and chairs are made on-site.

Ocracoke Island Woodworks 252-928-7001; www.ocracokeislandwoodworks.com; Ocean
View Rd. Comfortable Adirondack chairs, swings, and other outdoor furniture are
handcrafted by local Ocracokers from white cedar, the same wood used to build boats. It
doesn't splinter and looks better the longer is sits out in the weather.

Ocracoke Restoration 252-928-2669; www.ocracokerestoration.com; 585 Irvin Garrish
Hwy., NC 12, Spencer's Market. Shop stocks some 200 pieces of new and antique
stained-glass windows, lamps, and smaller pieces, plus English antiques, estate jewelry,
and decorative accents, including wrought-iron gates.

Brown pelicans, at the northern end of their range, nest at an island rookery just off Ocracoke.

Wine shops are part of the Beaufort scene.

8

THE SOUTH BANKS:
Cape Lookout and the Crystal Coast

Legacy of the High Seas

The Crystal Coast, also known as the Southern Outer Banks or SBX, is a place of contrasts. Recorded history here stretches back over 300 years, and has always had a close relationship with the sea. Beaufort, North Carolina's third oldest town, was an early seaport of vital importance to the state during the Age of Sail. Pirates and privateers made cameo appearances throughout the region's history, including the infamous Blackbeard, who wrecked his flagship, *Queen Anne's Revenge,* on the shoals off Bogue Banks. Commercial fishing and boatbuilding have been the backbone of the economy here for centuries.

In 1858, the railroad arrived when former North Carolina governor John Motley Morehead extended the rails to the deepwater port he built across the inlet from Beaufort. The community that grew up around the port took its name from the visionary governor, becoming Morehead City. The area's first beach resort, Atlantic Beach, was established on Bogue Banks across from Morehead City to serve travelers arriving by rail.

Atlantic Beach and Emerald Isle, communities at either end of Bogue Banks, evolved into popular vacation destinations for families and servicemen from the Marine Corps at nearby Camp Lejeune and Cherry Point air station. Today, Bogue Banks is home to a string of increasingly upscale resort communities catering to vacationers attracted by the area's largely undiscovered white sand beaches and family-friendly activities.

However, the South Banks have another face. The area north of Beaufort, called Down East by locals, has been among the last along the coast to be caught up in development. Here families still carve decoys, build boats, and sew quilts as their ancestors have done for generations.

Just offshore lie the islands of Core and Shackleford Banks, areas once home to thriving communities that were swept away by storms in the 1890s. Today, National Park Service caretakers and herds of wild ponies are the only year-round inhabitants of these lonely isles.

CAPE LOOKOUT AND THE CORE BANKS

The five uninhabited islands stretching from Ocracoke Inlet to Beaufort Inlet, making up the Cape Lookout National Seashore, have more than 55 miles of pristine ocean beach wiped nearly clean of all traces of human occupation. Originally used as hunting and fishing

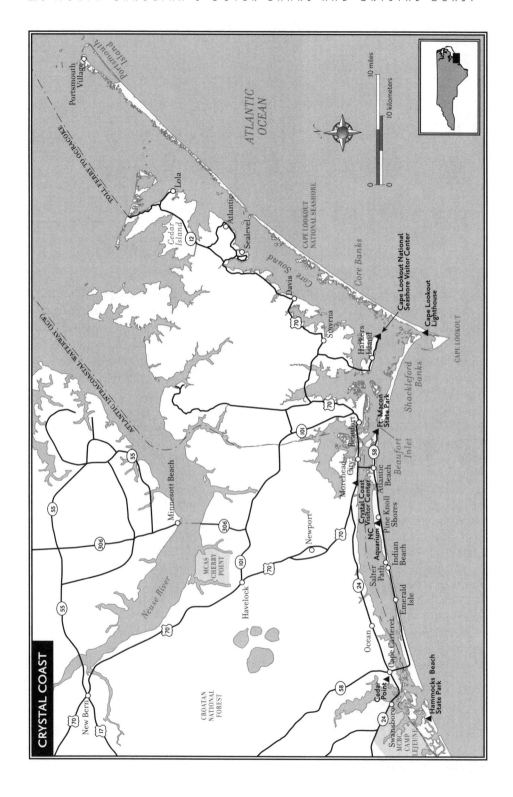

CRYSTAL COAST

grounds by the Coree Indians, from whom they take their name, the Core Banks remain today, as then, a rich ecological treasure, one of the most significant undeveloped barrier island systems in the world.

At the north end of Core Banks, once prosperous **Portsmouth Village**, now a ghost town administered by the National Park Service, is most easily reached from Ocracoke Island. See our coverage in that chapter.

Cape Lookout Lighthouse is located near the southern hook of South Core. Nearby lie the remnants of **Cape Lookout Village**, including an old Coast Guard Station. The area is reached via private passenger ferries from Harkers Island, where the **Cape Lookout National Seashore Visitor Center** is located, and from Beaufort's waterfront. Private watercraft can also land on the Banks at designated spots.

From Cape Lookout, the **Shackleford Banks** stretch west to a point opposite Fort Macon. Once the location of the whaling village of **Diamond City,** the island was abandoned by its inhabitants after a hurricane in 1899 sent a storm surge over the island. Today, the island's sole residents are about 150 ponies of Spanish descent who have adapted to the harsh conditions.

Down East

> ...*A Downeaster is best defined as one who prefers salt fish (notably spots) for breakfast. But mostly it is a state of mind, where the people like wooden boats and build them in back yards beneath big live oak trees....*
>
> —from When the Water Smokes *by Bob Simpson*

The marshes and forests north of Beaufort are dotted with small communities where generations of Down East families continue their traditions of boatbuilding, decoy carving, hunting, fishing, and farming. The people here retain an exceptional sense of place and are actively involved in preserving their way of life. There is no better place to discover these traditions than the **Core Sound Waterfowl Museum and Heritage Center** on Harkers Island. Here frequent events bring residents together to meet with visitors for authentic Down East celebrations. Next door, the recently expanded **Cape Lookout National Seashore Visitor Center** offers exhibits on the ecology, history, and culture of the region.

Beaufort

The charming village that is today the seat of Carteret County began life as Beaufort-by-the-Sea back in 1709, making it the state's third oldest town. Pronounced in the French manner with a long "o" (in contrast to the South Carolina Beaufort, pronounced "byoo-furt"), the town is a favorite stop for yachts cruising the Atlantic Intracoastal Waterway (ICW) as well as visitors seeking history, water-based recreation, and fine cuisine.

The pedestrian-friendly historic district centers on Front Street, facing the town docks. Here you'll find a variety of restaurants, bed-and-breakfasts, historic houses, and boat tours and water taxis to nearby islands. The wild ponies on Carrot Island can often be seen just across the water.

Shops along the waterfront offer an eclectic blend of nautical items, antiques, and local artwork. **The Beaufort Historic Site** and the **North Carolina Maritime Museum** provide context on the area's rich background of pirates, merchants, and commercial fisheries.

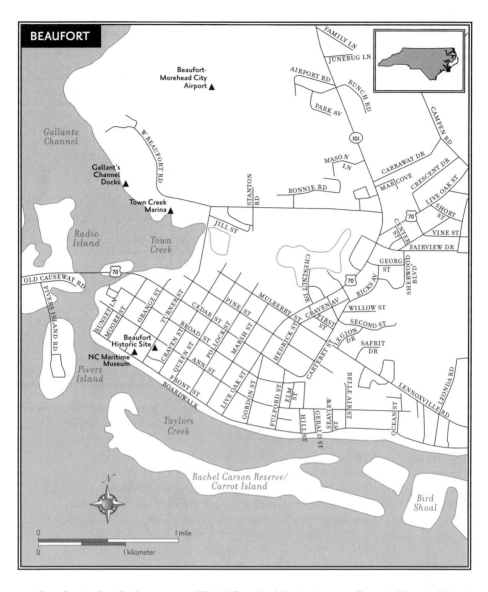

Beaufort is also the home port of North Carolina's last privateer, Captain Horatio Sinbad. His ship, the brigantine *Meka II*, can often be found at the Gallant's Channel docks, and the captain himself frequents the establishments along Front Street.

MOREHEAD CITY AND THE MAINLAND

Just across the bridge from Beaufort lies the commercial center of Morehead City, one of North Carolina's two deepwater state ports. The adjacent waterfront area is home to an active charter fishing fleet, as well as seafood restaurants and markets featuring fish fresh from the sea. Several of these, including the **Sanitary Fish Market** and **Captain Bill's**, have been in operation since before World War II, and are landmarks along the coast. The town is a center for marine research, as well, with several government and university facilities.

The tracks of **Governor Morehead's railroad** run right down the center of the town's main drag, Arendell Street, US 70. Many of the Morehead City's attractions, restaurants, and shops lie along either side.

BOGUE BANKS: ATLANTIC BEACH TO EMERALD ISLE

Uniquely situated along the Carolina coast, Bogue Banks runs east to west, so both sunrise and sunset can be enjoyed from your oceanfront balcony. The long white sand beaches that gave the area its Crystal Coast nickname face south, bringing warmer water and different surf than ocean beaches farther north. On the north side of Bogue, quiet sound waters make this a great destination for paddling and boating, and provide a breeding ground for many birds, as well as the seafood that has made this coast famous.

Accessible for many years only by ferry and toll bridges, the communities of Bogue Banks are today served by high rise bridges at both east and west ends. NC 58 runs the length of the island between the bridges, some 25 miles, and is dotted with public ocean- and sound-access points along its length. Mile markers, with signs marked MM, are in use at half-mile intervals, starting at the east end near Fort Macon.

Atlantic Beach

The original resort on Bogue Banks, located opposite Morehead City, had its first beach pavilion back in the 1880s. However, military forts have occupied the eastern tip of the island since before the Revolutionary War. Today's **Fort Macon,** an impressive pentagon-shaped masonry structure, is also North Carolina's most popular state park, thanks to its fine public beach.

The heart of Atlantic Beach lies at the end of the causeway from Morehead City. On the oceanfront lies the area once famous as **The Circle,** a collection of rides, dance halls, taverns, and hotels. Today, renamed The Grove, it's being transformed by a mixed-use project, which will include several condominium towers. Some of the local color, including an ice cream shop, a few taverns, and the area's best diner, remain, however, as does the public boardwalk and the wide, white sand beach adjacent to public parking.

Pine Knoll Shores

Just west of Atlantic Beach, dense growths of twisted live oaks shield most of Pine Knoll Shores (PKS) from passing eyes. This was once the private estate of heiress Alice Hoffman, who willed the land to her cousins, the children of President Theodore Roosevelt. The kids of the National Parks founder followed in their father's footsteps, setting aside much maritime forest as the **Theodore Roosevelt Natural Area**, now the home of the **North Carolina Aquarium**, and developing the rest with an eye on ecology. The island's only golf course is located on stunning terrain here.

Indian Beach/Salter Path

If there was ever a heaven on earth, it was here. There was wild country on each side of us. We had a church. We had a school. If anybody got sick, they helped out. They had a feeling for each other, a love for one another....

—*Lillian Smith Golden, 1901–1985, Native of Salter Path*

In these two towns located in the middle of the island, the past and future of Bogue Banks meet. Salter Path, one of the oldest villages on the island, is home to descendants of the original settlers, some of whom floated their houses over from Diamond City, the lost town of Shackleford Banks. Officially part of the Hoffman estate, the land was awarded to the established families through a series of court cases. Today, the residents continue their traditional lifestyle as commercial fishermen, selling their catch at local markets. To take advantage of the increasing tourist trade, they've also branched out into Jet Ski and kayak rentals, and offer a variety of watersport adventures.

The modern world crept up on the fishing port, however, with several large condominium projects built on either side. In 1973, these areas incorporated as the town of Indian Beach, wrapping unincorporated Salter Path in a doughnut of upscale development. Together, the two towns offer a range of accommodation and dining options from down-home to world-class.

Emerald Isle

Developed as a resort in the 1950s, Emerald Isle recently celebrated its 50th anniversary. Named for the dense maritime forest that dominated the area, today Emerald Isle is a family-oriented destination with many kid-friendly activities, and a large selection of beach cottages in every size and price range. The town has several public parks along both the ocean and sound, all the way down to the western tip of island, and a new system of multi-use paths. NC 58 crosses back to the mainland on the scenic Cameron Langston Bridge, intersecting with NC 24 at a busy shopping corner of big box stores.

Many homes in Beaufort Village have elaborate woodwork.

SWANSBORO

From its junction with NC 58, NC 24 continues west over the White Oak River to Swansboro, another historic fishing village with an eclectic downtown. A statue of Captain Otway Burns, a privateer captain in the War of 1812 and native son, stands in the waterfront park. Just to the west of town, **Hammocks Beach State Park** offers daily boat trips to Bear Island, site of some of the most impressive and unspoiled natural dunes on the East Coast.

Swansboro sits at the eastern edge of Onslow County, home of the Marine training base **Camp Lejeune**. The camp itself has many historic sites; however, NC 172 across the base is generally closed due to security concerns. The impressive and moving **Beirut, Vietnam, and World Trade Center monuments** in Jacksonville, however, are open to all.

LODGING

Visitors have a wide range of lodging to choose from on the Crystal Coast, from elegant "condotels" and timeshares to wilderness campsites and houseboats.

In historic Beaufort, most of the accommodations are of the bed-and-breakfast variety, with a few larger inns. Morehead City is the home of numerous national chain hostelries, including an Econo Lodge, Comfort Inn, and Holiday Inn and Suites. The Sheraton on Atlantic Beach is the only national chain hotel located directly on the oceanfront.

Many hotels on Bogue Banks are converting into condominiums, with a concurrent upgrade in décor and price. However, some smaller family motels still offer deals for those on a budget. Marinas and dive shops throughout the region often have discounted motel, cottage, or bunk accommodations available. Bare bones cottages are available on Core Banks, within the National Seashore.

Bogue Banks, especially the communities of Emerald Isle and Salter Path, used to have a number of campgrounds. Today, most have disappeared under the wave of development washing across the island. However, a number of RV resorts on the mainland front on Bogue Sound. The Down East region also has several smaller campgrounds, most with boat ramps.

The majority of families arriving for their annual vacation week rent cottages from the many real estate companies on the Crystal Coast. Available accommodations range from houses in Beaufort's historic district, to oceanfront condo units, to multi-bedroom "sandcastles" at a wide range of price points.

Another option is to rent a houseboat and park your floating condo across from the Beaufort waterfront, off Cape Lookout, or inside Shackleford Banks for the ultimate getaway. It's an easy way to join the boating set.

Rate Categories

Inexpensive	up to $80
Moderate	$80 to $150
Expensive	$150 to $200
Very Expensive	$200 and up

These rates are per room based on double occupancy. They do not include room taxes or any special service fees that may apply. The range is usually due to seasonal changes. Rates during the busy summer season and holiday weekends are often double or more the winter off-season rates. All properties are air-conditioned and open all year unless otherwise noted. Minimum stay may be required, especially on holidays when rates may be higher.

Credit Cards

AE—American Express
CB—Carte Blanche
D—Discover
DC—Diners Club
MC—Master Card
V—Visa

Resorts, Hotels, and Inns

ATLANTIC BEACH/PINE KNOLL SHORES
★ **ATLANTIS LODGE**
252-726-5168, 800-682-7057
www.atlantislodge.com
123 Salter Path Rd., Pine Knoll Shores 28512
Price: Inexpensive to Expensive
Credit Cards: MC, V
Internet Access: Free WiFi

A. C. and Dot Hall operate this retro retreat with a friendly vibe set amid the live oaks along the oceanfront. Pets of all kinds are welcome here as long as they are well behaved, and many guests return every year, so reservations should be made far in advance. Standard rooms with two doubles or a king bed, and completely equipped efficiencies, open onto balconies or a peaceful, grassy courtyard, where feeders attract many birds. A wooden boardwalk leads to a wide beach where beach attendants provide complimentary lounges, chairs, and umbrellas during the summer months. Lovely landscaping surrounds a quiet pool, where a little waterfall leads to a baby pool. High atop the three-floor building, a sun deck and lounge with pool table, Ping-Pong, library, and big-screen TV provides a gathering spot where guests can socialize. Non-pet rooms are also available, and all rooms have coffeemakers and cable TV.

CARIBBE INN

252-726-0051
www.caribbe-inn.com
309 E. Fort Macon Rd., Atlantic Beach 28512
Price: Inexpensive
Credit Cards: MC, V

Brightly painted and immaculately clean, the Caribbe Inn is a favorite among bargain hunters, with prices half of what you'd pay in a chain hotel. The inn is located across the street and a short walk from the beach, but backs up to Bogue Sound with its own boat dock and slips. If you fish, you can use the fish-cleaning station, then store your catch in the deep freezer or cook it up on the grill in the waterfront BBQ area. Rooms here are cheerfully decorated with murals of sea life, a hit with kids. All have cable TV, refrigerators, microwaves, telephones with free local calls and voice mail, and ceiling fans. Two children under 12 stay free. Efficiencies and pet-friendly rooms are available, as are special weekday, weekend, golf, and fishing packages.

BEAUFORT
ANCHORAGE HOUSE

252-728-9908
www.anchoragehouse.net
211 Turner St., Beaufort 28516
Price: Moderate to Expensive
Credit Cards: AE, D, MC, V
Internet Access: Free WiFi

The historic 1866 Gothic-Revival cottage with heart pine floors, mahogany woodwork, and a wide porch for rocking, offers five bed-and-breakfast rooms, several with simulated woodstoves and Jacuzzis. All rooms have cable TV, down comforters, and Egyptian cotton sheets. Breakfasts feature homemade baked goods, and a gift shop on premises sells pie and coffee you can enjoy on the porch. Picnic lunches and breakfast in bed can be special ordered. The Anchorage also rents several cottages and duplexes in the area, including the 1920 Hughes bungalow on the Anchorage grounds and a pet- and family-friendly duplex at Atlantic Beach. The inn itself doesn't allow pets or smoking.

CEDARS BY THE SEA

252-728-7036
www.cedarsinn.com
301 & 305 Front St., Beaufort 28516
Price: Moderate to Expensive
Credit Cards: AD, MC, V
Internet Access: Free WiFi

Located directly on Front Street facing the water, the Cedars occupies two of Beaufort's most historic houses, the 1768 William Borden House and the 1858 Belcher Fuller House, plus a honeymoon cottage with separate entrance and whirlpool bath. Set amid cedars and lush landscaping, the buildings today house 11 guestrooms and suites, furnished with claw-foot tubs, canopied beds, and other antiques. All rooms have cable TV and hair dryers, but no telephones. Guests enjoy a full breakfast served in the formal dining room, use of bicycles to explore the town, and a wine bar on premises. The Cedars has won many awards and is recommended by *Conde Nast Johansens*.

COUNTY HOME BED & BREAKFAST

252-728-4611
www.countyhomeb-b.com
299 NC 101, Beaufort 28516

Price: Moderate
Credit Cards: MC, V
Internet Access: Free WiFi

A bed-and-breakfast like no other, this inn was once the county home housing the local poor, beginning in 1914. Abandoned for many years, the sturdy tin-roofed structure, now listed on the National Register of Historic Places, survived to be completely renovated into 10 spacious two-room suites, each with its own bath, kitchenette, TV, VCR, and telephone. Each suite has two private entrances: one opening onto a veranda with rocking chairs and a second giving access to a back deck with barbecue grills, overlooking the landscaped grounds dotted with hammocks and swings. Each suite has a refrigerator stocked with juices, fruit, yogurt, bottled water, and complimentary wine. A basket of warm muffins and bagels along with a local paper is delivered to each room every morning. The County Home is located on the edge of town, with plenty of parking for boats. Bikes are available for guests. Children and pets are welcome.

★ INLET INN
252-728-3600; 800-554-5466
www.inlet-inn.com
601 Front St., Beaufort 28516

Price: Moderate
Credit Cards: AE, D, MC, V
Internet Access: Free WiFi in office

Located at the corner of Front and Queen Streets, the 36-room Inlet Inn enjoys the best location in town. Several fine restaurants are just across Queen Street, the boat tour docks lie directly across Front Street, and all the town's dining and shopping action is just steps away. The three-story building has an elevator and a top-floor lounge where a widow's walk balcony overlooks the waterfront. All rooms are spacious, and have private, but no-frill baths. Rooms on the first two floors have king beds and private balconies. Third-floor rooms have two queens and a window seat overlooking the inlet. All rooms have refrigerators, cable TV, hair dryers, telephones, and coffeemakers, and many of the first floor rooms have gas fireplaces. A call in the morning brings a complimentary tray of fresh baked muffins, bagels, and juice, plus a newspaper, to your door. Boat slips are available. No pets.

★ PECAN TREE INN
252-728-6733, 800-728-7871
www.pecantree.com
116 Queen St., Beaufort 28516

Distinctive white picket fences line yards in Beaufort.

Price: Moderate
Credit Cards: AE, D, MC, V
Internet Access: Free WiFi

Innkeepers Dave and Allison DuBuisson make relaxation and charm the norm at the Pecan Tree, housed in a Victorian building that started life as the town's Masonic Lodge back in 1866. Rock the morning away on the upstairs balcony, have a cup of tea on the wraparound front porch amid wicker and gingerbread woodwork, or just chill out next to the lily pond with the neighborhood cats. The nine guestrooms are elegantly appointed with antiques, and equipped with cable TV, telephones, and hair dryers. Two suites have king beds and double Jacuzzis. A downstairs parlor is stocked with books of local interest, and an ample breakfast buffet with fresh fruit and baked goods is served in the dining room next door. A refrigerator with ice maker is available for all guests. Beyond the parking lot a large flower and herb garden includes many unusual species. The garden is open to the public. Complimentary bikes are available for guests, and the location is just a few steps from Front Street. Children under 10 and pets cannot be accommodated.

CAPE CARTERET/CEDAR POINT/SWANSBORO
★ BEST WESTERN SILVER CREEK INN
252-393-9015, 877-459-1448
www.bestwestern.com
801 Cedar Point Blvd., Swansboro 28584
Price: Moderate
Credit Cards: AE, CB, D, DC, MC, V
Internet Access: Free WiFi

Conveniently located to both Swansboro and Emerald Isle, this hotel has all the amenities, plus a friendly staff of locals. Each of the 65 guest rooms has a refrigerator, microwave, cable TV, coffeemaker, hair dryer, and iron with ironing board. The AAA three-diamond hotel has an elevator, an outdoor pool and whirlpool, and serves free continental breakfast daily. Local calls and parking are free. Handicapped accessible rooms, nonsmoking rooms, golf packages, and suites are available. No pets. Children ages 17 and under stay free.

HARBORLIGHT GUEST HOUSE
252-393-6969, 800-624-8439
www.harborlightnc.com
332 Live Oak Dr., Cape Carteret 28584
Price: Expensive to Very Expensive
Credit Cards: AE, MC, V
Internet Access: Free WiFi

Selected as one of the best undiscovered bed-and-breakfasts in the country, the Harborlight sits slightly off the beaten track on a peninsula jutting into Bogue Sound. The isolation and gracious amenities make this a favorite for romantic getaways. Six elegantly appointed suites offer two-person whirlpool tubs, fireplaces, cable TV with DVD players, waterfront decks, and awesome views. Gourmet breakfasts, served in your suite or on the deck, include creative dishes such as baked grapefruit, peach glazed French toast, and sausage stuffed mushrooms. One ground floor suite is handicapped accessible. Guest may use the inn's beach chairs and umbrellas, kayaks, and fishing tackle. Romance packages with in-room massage available.

DOWN EAST
CALICO JACK'S INN AND MARINA
252-728-3575
www.capelookoutferry.com
1698 Island Rd., Harkers Island 28531
Price: Inexpensive
Credit Cards: MC, V

Calico Jack's has 21 rooms and efficiencies next to the water on Harkers Island. A 52-slip marina offers a discount rate to guests who bring their boats, and has a boat ramp as well. A passenger ferry runs daily across the sound to the docks closest to the Cape Lookout Lighthouse and over to Shackleford Banks, where the wild ponies roam. Rooms are comfortable and well kept and all have cable TV. For an extra $10 you can get a picture window with a great view of the light-house. Weekly rates available.

OTWAY HOUSE BED & BREAKFAST

252-728-5636
www.otwayhouse.com
68 US 70 East, Otway 28516
Price: Moderate
Credit Cards: AE, D, MC, V

Located on six acres in the quiet little town of Otway, this dog-friendly inn rents four elegantly furnished rooms with private baths, ceiling fans, and cable TV. The canine members of the party enjoy quality dog food, indoor and outdoor kennels, and a doggy play area. Human guests can indulge in a full breakfast, often including the inn's signature whole-wheat pancakes with bananas and pecans, before an active morning of rocking on the porch. Several free boat ramps are located close by, and the property has plenty of room for boat trailers.

INDIAN BEACH/SALTER PATH

★ THE OCEAN CLUB

252-247-2035, 888-237-2035
www.theoceanclubnc.com
1700 Salter Path Rd., Indian Beach 28575
Price: Expensive to Very Expensive
Credit Cards: MC, V
Internet Access: Free WiFi

Stretching across Bogue Banks with both oceanfront and sound front units, the Ocean Club rents villas with one to three bedrooms in mostly three-story buildings with elevators and covered parking. The property employs ecologically advanced technology to cause the least impact on the local environment. Each unit is cleverly decorated and fully equipped, with two baths, full kitchens, washer/dryers, large screen TVs, and covered decks with water views. Linens are provided. Many units also have video game players, answering machines, and wireless Internet access. Outdoor amenities include pool complexes on both the beach and sound, with a heated pool and whirlpool, a children's pool and cabana, an activity pavilion and bocce ball play area, a golf putting course, lighted clay tennis courts, and a fishing pier great for sunset views. Beach attendants are on duty during the summer season with chairs and umbrellas. Guests can use the state-of-the-art fitness center with its full menu of classes, and receive discounts at the Ocean Club's luxurious spa. Most rentals are weekly, but some nightly rates are available in the off-season.

WILLIAM AND GARLAND MOTEL

252-247-3733
www.williamandgarlandmotel.com
1185 Salter Path Rd., Salter Path 28575
Price: Inexpensive
Credit Cards: D, MC, V

This small family-owned and operated hotel offers simple, clean lodgings, personal service, and great rates and location. Basic rooms have one double bed, refrigerator, coffeemaker, and cable TV. Single efficiencies add a full kitchen; double efficiencies have two double beds. A mobile home with two bedrooms can also be rented. Direct access to the beach is via a lovely nature trail. The property is pet-friendly.

Small Bed-and-Breakfast Inns and Guest Houses

Ann Street Inn 877-266-7814; www.annstreetinn.com; 707 Ann Street, Beaufort 28516. Beautifully restored 1832 house has porches lined with wicker and rocking chairs, a full hot breakfast, and an award-winning water garden.

Captain's Quarters Bed & Biscuit 252-728-7711, 800-659-7111; www.captainsquarters.us; 315 Ann St., Beaufort 28516. Victorian beauty in the historic district features Ms. Ruby's famous "Riz" biscuits, and a daily sunset toast.

Chinaberry Inn 252-225-0875; www.chinaberryinn.com; 876 Seashore Dr., Atlantic 28511. 1930's-era Dutch Colonial in the tiny town of Atlantic, located Down East, offers one elegant suite, with Jacuzzi, and a balcony overlooking Core Sound.

Cousin Martha's Bed and Breakfast 252-728-3917, 877-464-7487; www.cousinsbedand breakfast.com; 305 Turner St., Beaufort 28516. Two upstairs rooms of the 1820s Jarvis Brown House are for rent. Downstairs, Chef Elmo whips up goodies in the kitchen, making for memorable breakfasts.

Langdon House 252-728-5499; www.langdonhouse.com; 135 Craven St., Beaufort 28516. Historic 1730s house rents a large master guest suite with second-floor porch access and large jetted tub.

Old Seaport Inn 252-728-4300, 800-349-5823; www.oldseaportinn.com; 217 Turner St., Beaufort 28516. Four elegantly appointed rooms furnished with antiques and flanked by spacious porches overlook an English courtyard garden.

The Red Dog Inn 252-728-5954; www.thereddoginnbb.com; 113 Pollock St., Beaufort 28516. Historic house just a half-block from the waterfront offers three luxurious, dog-friendly rooms.

The Swashbuckler Inn 252-838-1047; www.swashbucklerinn.com; 1333 Island Rd., Harkers Island 28531. Pirate-themed bed-and-breakfast has wireless Internet, two-person whirlpool tubs, and bountiful breakfasts.

Cape Lookout National Seashore/Core Banks Cabins

Great Island Cabins 877-956-6568; www.capelookoutconcessions.com; 142 Willis Rd., Davis 28524. Cabins on the South Core Banks sleep from four to 12 people. Accommodations are basic, with screened porches, bunk beds, hot water, full baths with showers, and gas stoves, but no electricity. They are wired for generators, which can be rented separately, as can air-conditioning units.

Morris Marina Kabin Kamp 252-225-4261, 877-956-6568; www.capelookoutconcessions .com; 1000 Morris Marina Rd., Atlantic 28511. Cabins on the North Core Banks are reached by ferry from Atlantic. Air-conditioning is available in some cabins for an extra charge. One cabin is handicapped accessible. Vehicle fuel is available on-site.

Houseboat Rentals

Both these companies provide an experienced captain to take your houseboat to your preferred mooring place.

Endless Summer Houseboat Rentals 252-241-9718; www.endlesssummerhouseboat rentals.com; 167 C St., Newport 28570. Houseboats sleep eight, and rent by the weekend or week. No pets.

Outer Banks Houseboats 252-728-4129; www.outerbankshouseboats.com; 324 Front St., Beaufort 28516. Houseboats for weekend, weekday, or full-week rentals come with a Carolina skiff for getting around. Pets okay with deposit.

Vacation Cottage and Condo Rentals

Atlantic Beach Realty 252-240-7368, 800-786-7368; www.atlanticbeachrealty.net; 14 Causeway Shopping Center, Atlantic Beach 28512. Voted Best Beach Cottage & Condo Company on the Crystal Coast, Atlantic handles over 200 properties.

Beaufort Realty 252-728-5462, 800-548-2961; www.beaufortrlty.com; 325 Front St.,

Beaufort 28516. Lists cottages and condos in Beaufort, including many on the waterfront and in the historic district.

Cape Lookout Realty 252-728-2375; www.capelookoutrealty.com; 834 Island Rd., Harkers Island 28531. Quiet cottages, many with private docks and boat ramps, in the Down East communities.

Emerald Isle Realty 252-354-3315, 800-849-3315; www.emeraldislerealty.com; 7501 Emerald Dr., Emerald Isle 28594. Representing 750 cottages and luxury "sandcastles," this company has a "no worries" policy that minimizes extra fees, and adds free perks such as continental breakfast and concierge services.

Foster Rentals Realty 252-247-2048; www.jimfosterrealty.com; Carriage Crossing Townes, Morehead City 28557. Specializes in oceanfront condo rentals in Atlantic Beach.

Shorewood Real Estate 888-557-0172; www.shorewoodrealestate.net; 7703 Emerald Dr., Emerald Isle 28594. Specializes in Emerald Isle rental properties.

Campgrounds and RV Resorts

Cedar Creek Campground & Marina 252-225-9571; 111 Canal Dr., Sealevel 28577. Family run Good Sam park has swimming pool, boat ramp, saltwater fishing dock, and game room.

Coastal Riverside Campground 252-728-5155; www.coastalriverside.com; 216 Clark Ln., Beaufort 28516. Shady campground just north of the village has a 320-foot pier and a boat ramp.

Croatan National Forest 252-638-5628; www.cs.unca.edu/nfsnc; 141 E. Fisher Ave., New Bern 28560. Two of the forest's campgrounds are developed for RVs. The **Neuse River Campground**, located next to a popular swimming beach, has 42 sites, nine with electric hookups, flush toilets, warm showers, drinking water, a dump station, and hiking trails. The **Cedar Point Campground**, near Swansboro, has 42 sites, all with electric hookups, a bathhouse with warm showers and flush toilets, drinking water, a boardwalk trail, and a boat ramp for kayaks or other shallow-bottomed boats. Both campgrounds are open all year and are handicapped accessible.

Driftwood Motel, Restaurant, and Campground 252-225-4861; www.clis.com/deg; 3575 Cedar Island Rd., Cedar Island 28520. Located next to the Cedar Island Ferry, this campground has full hookups, a dock and boat ramp, and the **Driftwood Restaurant** across the street.

Goose Creek Resort 252-393-2628, 866-839-2628; www.goosecreekcamping.com; 350 Red Barn Rd., Newport 28570. A favorite with families and fishers, thanks to a large swimming pool, 135-foot waterslide, beach area, Jet Skis, boat ramp, and a 250-foot fishing pier. Open all year.

Holiday Trav-L Park Resort 252-354-2250; www.htpresort.com; 9102 Coast Guard Rd., Emerald Isle 28594. Oceanfront resort offers 325 sites with full hookups, WiFi, and cable TV. Planned activities, a pool, raceway, beach concessions, and modern bathhouse are on-site.

Water's Edge RV Park 252-247-0494, 252-247-0709; www.watersedge-rvpark.com; 1463 NC 24, Newport 28570. Campers enjoy full hookups, a pier on Bogue Sound, paddleboats, kayaks, and planned activities.

Whispering Pines RV Park and Campground 252-726-4902; www.ncpines.com; 25 Whispering Pines Rd., Newport 28570. Situated amid tall pines, full hookup RV and tent sites include access to a large pool. Open all year.

Dining

In this land of fishing and farming, Carteret County chefs rely on fresh seafood and produce as the basis for their menus. Local specialties include soft-shell crabs, collard greens, shrimp burgers, and the ever-popular hush puppy. Beaufort enjoys a reputation as one of the top towns for fine dining in the state, and, as an extra bonus, most of the restaurants are located in the historic district within walking distance of each other.

The Culinary program at Carteret Community College in Morehead City is turning out talented chefs, and raising the standard of dining all over the county. Increasingly, interesting and eclectic dining venues can be found tucked in amid the pizza takeouts and ice cream parlors typical of beach culture. You can enjoy lunch created by the CCC culinary students on Wednesdays when classes are in session. Call 252-222-6036 for reservations and details.

Rate Categories

Inexpensive	under $10
Moderate	$10 to $20
Expensive	$20 to $25
Very Expensive	$25 and up

These ratings represent the average cost of an entrée, not including higher priced specials, that super-sized steak, or the rack of lamb. It also does not include appetizers, desserts, beverages, taxes, or gratuities. When a range of ratings is offered, it usually indicates the difference in price between lunch and dinner entrées.

Credit Cards

AE—American Express
CB—Carte Blanche
D—Discover Card
DC—Diners Club
J—JCB International Credit Card
MC—Master Card
V—Visa

Dining on a deck overlooking the ocean in Atlantic Beach

Meal abbreviations
B—Breakfast
L—Lunch
D—Dinner
SB—Sunday Brunch

ATLANTIC BEACH/PINE KNOLL SHORES
AMOS MOSQUITO'S
RESTAURANT & BAR
252-247-6222
www.amosmosquitos.com
703 E. Fort Macon Rd., Atlantic Beach 28512
Price: Moderate
Children's Menu: Yes
Cuisine: Seafood
Liquor: Full bar
Serving: D, weekend brunch in summer
Closed: Winter
Credit Cards: AE, D, MC, V
Handicapped Access: Yes
Special Features: Sushi and karaoke on
Thursday nights; nightly specials; outdoor
dining

Cleverly decorated, fun restaurant has great
views over the sound. The menu features
fresh seafood and vegetables, but also offers
brown sugar glazed meatloaf, pork ribs, and
a New York strip. Seafood is available
steamed or broiled, as well as fried. Kids
have a great time at "Skeeters," ordering
Slimewiches (grilled cheese) and Snake
Skins (buttered noodles) off the children's
menu. For dessert, s'mores, cooked over a
brazier at the table, are another kid favorite.
Adults without children in tow may want to
dine in the bar or on the patio, as the dining
room is often packed with family groups.

★ CRAB'S CLAW
RESTAURANT & OYSTER BAR
252-247-4155
www.crabsclaw.com
201 W. Atlantic Blvd., Atlantic Beach 28512
Price: Moderate to Expensive
Children's Menu: Yes
Cuisine: Caribbean, seafood

Liquor: Full bar
Serving: L, D
Closed: Wednesdays, sometimes Tuesdays
Credit Cards: AE, D, MC, V
Special Features: Outside dining on ocean-
front deck; raw and steam bar; Jammin'
Jamaican habanero sauce for sale; non-
smoking dining room.

Executive Chef Antoinette Oberci, a Johnson & Wales graduate, selects the fresh local
seafood served here each morning and
grows her own herbs. Dishes tend to
Caribbean treatments with some Mediterranean accents, and include several spicy
offerings. Appetizers range from local lit-
tleneck clams from Harkers Island to a
spicy crab dip praised by *Southern Living*.
Steamer pots with seafood and vegetables
are a specialty, with oysters available in season, and a special steamed veggie pot for
vegetarians. Fire-grilled salmon, St. Louis-
style ribs, jalapeno cornbread, and key lime
pie are local favorites.

BEAUFORT
★ AQUA
252-728-7777
www.aquaexperience.com
114 Middle Ln., Beaufort 28516
Price: Inexpensive to Expensive
Children's Menu: No
Cuisine: Seasonal tapas
Liquor: Full bar
Serving: D
Closed: Sundays and Mondays
Credit Cards: AE, D, MC, V
Handicapped Access: Yes
Special Features: Wine specials; Friday
martini night; monthly wine-pairing din-
ners; nonsmoking dining room; outdoor
dining

Seasonal menus at Aqua showcase fresh
local seafood and produce in creative combinations. The menu is divided into small
plate and large plate dishes. Small plates
may range from a Japanese Bento box with

seared yellow fin tuna and seaweed salad to a Mozzarella Napoleon layered with local eggplant and tomatoes. Large plates are sturdier fare, but still creative: a filet of choice beef rubbed with coffee, or fresh triggerfish crusted with wild mushrooms. Aqua's signature Caesar salad is justly famous, as are the house-made desserts. The wine menu is extensive and a nightly "wine discovery" is available by the glass at a special price. You can dine in the stylishly decorated contemporary dining room or outside on the roofed patio. The whole place is quite a contrast to the company's other restaurant, **Clawson's**, around the corner.

BEAUFORT GROCERY CO.

252-728-3899
www.beaufortgrocery.com
117 Queen St., Beaufort 28516
Price: Inexpensive to Very Expensive
Cuisine: American
Liquor: Full bar
Serving: L, D, SB
Closed: Tuesdays
Credit Cards: AE, D, MC, V
Handicapped Access: Yes
Special Features: Picnic baskets; deli counter; bakery; charge for sharing

A casual spot for lunch, this local favorite becomes a sophisticated fine dining experience every evening. Executive chef Charles Park gives a creative twist to everything on the menu. Lunch features homemade soups, a wide selection of salads made from local produce, puff pastries stuffed with shrimp or chicken salad, and sandwiches on home baked bread. Dinner entrées range from rib-eyes rubbed with blackened huckleberries to pork chops stuffed with fresh mozzarella. Vegetarian selections are equally creative. All desserts, including a variety of cheesecakes and a great pecan pie, are homemade.

CLAWSON'S 1905 RESTAURANT & PUB

252-728-2133
www.clawsonsrestaurant.com
425 Front St., Beaufort 28516
Price: Moderate
Children's Menu: Yes
Cuisine: Seafood
Liquor: Full bar
Serving: L, D
Closed: Sundays, except in summer
Credit Cards: AE, D, MC, V
Handicapped Access: Yes
Special Features: Beer samplers; bar with big-screen TVs

This landmark on the Beaufort waterfront occupies a series of historic buildings over 100 years old. Decorated with memorabilia from the town's history and other period items, the restaurant is often crowded with tourists during the summer months. The menu ranges from the standard list of appetizers, salads, and burgers, to some excellent seafood bisque and the famous potato "dirigibles" stuffed with your choice of seafood, deli meats, or veggies. Entrées feature many seafood and pasta combinations, fried and grilled seafood plates, plus ribs and a few steaks. The mud pie, made with Oreos and Rocky Road ice cream, is another local favorite and well worth the calories. The cozy bar is a favorite retreat among locals who know they can find the best beer selection in town here, including many North Carolina microbrews.

FRONT STREET GRILL AT STILLWATER CAFE

252-728-4956
www.frontstreetgrillatstillwater.com
300 Front St., Beaufort 28516
Price: Inexpensive to Expensive
Children's Menu: No
Cuisine: Regional Southern
Liquor: Full bar
Serving: L, D, SB
Closed: Winter

Credit Cards: MC, V
Handicapped Access: Yes
Special Features: Outdoor rum bar; dining on the deck; daily dinner and drink specials; dock space for diners arriving by boat

Casual waterfront setting meets creative cuisine in the best possible combination. The unpretentious street front belies an elegant interior dining room, where you dine on white linen. Or have your meal beneath an umbrella on the casual Afterdeck with unexcelled views of the harbor. Sunsets here are spectacular, and after dark the deck is romantically lit by hurricane lamps. The menu, featuring signature dishes from the kitchen of brother and sister team Bryan and Tracey Carithers, incorporates Old South recipes with Caribbean, Asian, and other changing influences. Typical lunch offerings include a Seafood Cobb among a wide selection of creative salads and sandwiches, including Pimento Cheese made with Vermont cheddar. The dinner menu features fresh seafood, such as pan roasted flounder topped with a smoked bacon, asparagus, and crab sauté. Breads and desserts are made in house. The extensive wine list, with many Pinot Noirs, regularly qualifies for the *Wine Spectator*'s Award of Excellence. The outdoor bar stocks a great selection of imported rums.

THE NET HOUSE

252-728-2002
113 Turner St., Beaufort 28516
Price: Moderate
Children's Menu: Yes
Cuisine: Seafood
Liquor: Full bar
Serving: D
Credit Cards: MC, V
Handicapped Access: Yes
Special Features: Nightly specials; no reservations

Conveniently located across the street from the Beaufort Historic Site, this casual, family-run restaurant is just what seafood lovers are looking for—abundant portions simply prepared—and crowds line up in summer to get a seat. Shellfish, flounder, and the daily catch are available steamed, broiled, panned in butter, or lightly breaded and fried. Cold salad plates and seafood cocktails are available as well. Softshell crabs stuffed with crabmeat and Grouper Dijon are often on special, and worth looking for. Outstanding crab soup, excellent appetizers, and homemade key lime pie bracket the meal at either end.

ROYAL JAMES CAFE

252-728-4573
117 Turner St., Beaufort 28516
Price: Inexpensive
Children's Menu: Yes
Cuisine: Seafood
Liquor: Full bar
Serving: B, L, D
Open: Daily
Credit Cards: AE, D, MC, V
Handicapped Access: Yes
Special Features: Counter service; antique Brunswick pool tables; late-night hours

Beaufort's oldest business in continuous operation is this casual spot named after a pirate ship. Take a seat at the counter or at a table for a Southern breakfast with grits, or one of the café's signature cheeseburgers, topped with secret chili sauce. The menu features Beaufort's version of fast food: shrimp burgers, local steamed shrimp, and Down East clam chowder, all washed down by your choice from a lengthy list of beers. The bar is a local hangout, so expect to meet some characters if you visit late in the evening.

THE SANDBAR AND TIKI BAR AT TOWN CREEK MARINA

252-504-7263
www.thesandbar.org
232 W. Beaufort Rd., Beaufort 28516

Price: Moderate to Expensive
Children's Menu: Yes
Cuisine: Seafood
Liquor: Full bar
Serving: L, D, weekend brunch
Credit Cards: MC, V
Special Features: Daily specials; outdoor seating; marina with dock for diners arriving by boat; waterfront Tiki bar; drink menu; live entertainment

Beautifully decorated with copper sculptures and murals of mermaids, this restaurant located above the Town Creek Marina is a great place to eat or meet for a cocktail as the sun sets. The creative, upscale menu specializes in local seafood, steamed and broiled, although you'll also find interesting takes on steaks, chicken, lamb, and duck, and a variety of pasta dishes, amid the daily specials. The crab-stuffed lobster, pistachio crusted triggerfish, flash-fried calamari, and sesame seared ahi tuna are all highly recommended.

★ THE SPOUTER INN
252-728-5190
www.thespouterinn.com
218 Front St., Beaufort 28516
Price: Inexpensive to Expensive
Children's Menu: Yes
Cuisine: Seafood
Liquor: Full bar
Serving: L, D, SB
Closed: January–mid-February
Credit Cards: MC, V
Handicapped Access: Yes
Special Features: Nightly fresh fish specials; retail bakery counter; outdoor waterfront dining; dock; reservations recommended

Superb waterfront views and friendly service make this a winner for lunch or dinner. You can dine inside or out on the partially covered deck where you may spot porpoises or the Carrot Island horses. During the day, the menu features a wide range of salads, pastas, and sandwiches, including a terrific

shrimp salad. Dinner entrées include a mixed grill of fresh catch with scallops and shrimp, and a Down East version of Bouillabaisse, as well as Black Angus prime rib and maple bourbon BBQ pork ribs. On Sunday, a special brunch menu offers Eggs Orleans, sitting atop crab cakes, seafood omelets, and crab-stuffed portabellas. Desserts prepared in the on-site bakery are fabulous, as is the Banana Crème Crepe, a house specialty for over 25 years.

DOWN EAST
DRIFTWOOD MOTEL'S PIRATE'S CHEST RESTAURANT
252-225-4861
www.clis.com/deg
3575 Cedar Island Rd., Cedar Island 28520
Price: Moderate
Children's Menu: Yes
Cuisine: Seafood
Liquor: Beer, wine, brown bag permit
Serving: L (summer), D
Credit Cards: AE, D, MC, V
Handicapped Access: Yes
Special Features: Salad bar; early bird specials; vegetarian entrées available

Located next to the ferry docks, the Driftwood is a convenient stop before or after a trip to Ocracoke. Seafood, fried, broiled, steamed, boiled, or panned in butter, makes up most of the menu, with fried combination platters, cold plates, and pasta dishes available. A cup of cream of crab soup or Core Sound chowder is a good way to warm up on a blustery day, or select a grilled chicken or BBQ pork plate, or a veggie burger for a lighter meal. Locals come here for the prime rib special on the weekends. A salad bar is available during the summer, and the homemade lemon meringue pie is much praised.

EMERALD ISLE
★ KATHRYN'S BISTRO & MARTINI BAR
252-354-6200
8002 Emerald Dr., Emerald Isle 28594

*Hand-carved decoys, a traditional art form
Down East*

Price: Expensive
Children's Menu: No
Cuisine: Steaks and seafood
Liquor: Full bar
Serving: D
Credit Cards: AE, D, MC, V
Handicapped Access: Yes
Special Features: Martini menu; cocktail
bar; nightly specials

A favored destination for date nights or
special occasions, Kathryn's wood-fired
grill turns out delicious Black Angus steaks,
fresh local seafood, pork tenderloin, and
roast chicken. The Maryland-style crab
cakes are considered the best on Bogue
Banks, and the Carolina Classic provides a
unique take on the shrimp and grits standard. If you're just looking for something
light, sit at the elegant mahogany and granite bar and enjoy your choice of 30 martinis,
plus a lengthy list of excellent appetizers
ranging from baked stuffed oysters to Beef
Carpaccio.

RUCKERJOHN'S RESTAURANT AND MORE

252-354-2413
www.ruckerjohns.com
8700 Emerald Dr., Emerald Isle 28594
Price: Moderate
Children's Menu: Yes
Cuisine: American
Liquor: Full bar
Serving: L, D
Credit Cards: AE, MC, V
Handicapped Access: Yes
Special Features: Outdoor dining; lounge;
daily specials; entertainment

Overlooking the lake behind Emerald Plantation Shopping Center, RuckerJohn's has a
huge menu of popular favorites from pizza
to baby back ribs, including many dishes
prepared on a charcoal grill. Pastas,
steamed and fried fresh seafood, salads and
sandwiches, burgers, steaks, chicken, and
pork chops ensure that everyone in the
group will find something they like. RJ's
skewered shrimp, wrapped in bacon and
grilled, is recommended.

MOREHEAD CITY
CAFE ZITO

252-726-6676
www.cafezito.com
105 11th St., Morehead City 28557
Price: Inexpensive to Expensive
Cuisine: Mediterranean
Liquor: Beer and wine
Serving: D
Closed: Tuesday
Credit Cards: MC, V
Handicapped Access: Yes
Special Features: Wine dinners; tapas
nights; outdoor dining

Musician-turned-chef Baptist Knaven uses
the freshest locally grown produce, seafood,
and meats in his innovative, Mediterranean-inspired menus. Sunday and Monday are Tapas nights, with selections
starting at $4. A more traditional dinner
menu is served Thursday–Saturday, featuring duck, pork, steaks, and seafood, all
from local providers. The restored 1898
house decorated with local artwork provides

a relaxed and lovely setting. You can eat inside or outdoors on the porch.

CAPTAIN BILL'S WATERFRONT RESTAURANT

252-726-2166
www.captbills.com
701 Evans St., Morehead City 28557
Price: Inexpensive to Moderate
Children's Menu: Yes
Cuisine: Seafood
Liquor: Beer and wine
Serving: L, D
Credit Cards: MC, V
Handicapped Access: Yes
Special Features: Daily specials; all-you-can-eat lunch buffet; ice cream and candy counter

Fresh local seafood, available fried, broiled, panned in butter, or topped with an au gratin cheese sauce, has been the specialty here for over 60 years. Many of the dishes are from old family recipes, and a country cooking special with fresh vegetables is served for lunch daily. Arrive on a Wednesday or Saturday to sample the famous Conch Stew. Hand cut Black Angus steaks and a few chicken dishes satisfy people who don't like seafood. This is a family favorite with large tables in the dining room, and a deck overlooking the harbor where kids can visit the seagulls and the family of otters that make their home here. All desserts are homemade and include a wide variety of pies, ice cream, and fudge.

SANITARY FISH MARKET & RESTAURANT

252-247-3111
www.sanitaryfishmarket.com
501 Evans St., Morehead City 28557
Price: Inexpensive to Moderate
Children's Menu: Yes
Cuisine: Seafood
Liquor: Full bar
Serving: L, D
Closed: Winter
Credit Cards: D, MC, V
Handicapped Access: Yes
Special Features: Senior's menu; retail fish market; overnight moorage available at the dock

A landmark on the Morehead City waterfront since 1938, when the first 12-seat counter opened in the fish market here, Sanitary now seats 600, and waits can be long when the tour buses roll in. Lunch features fish sandwiches, shrimp and oyster burgers, plus salads made of shrimp and fresh tuna. A long list of seafood, prepared fried, broiled, or steamed, is available all day in numerous combinations. This is a good place to sample some of the more unfamiliar fish favored by locals, such as bluefish, jumping mullet, spots, wahoo, king mackerel, or mahi mahi, all available in season. The hush puppies here are famous: you can buy a bag of mix to take home. Popular entrées include the seafood stuffed potato and the Mixed Grill with rib-eye steak, shrimp, and scallops.

SHEPARD'S POINT

252-727-0815
www.beaufortgrocery.com/spmain.html
925 Arendell St., Morehead City 28557
Price: Expensive
Children's Menu: Yes
Cuisine: American
Liquor: Full bar
Serving: D, SB (summer)
Closed: Tuesday
Credit Cards: AE, D, MC, V
Handicapped Access: Yes
Special Features: Daily specials; lounge; martini menu; Friday happy hour; wine cellar

The sister restaurant of **Beaufort Grocery** provides a sophisticated dining option in downtown Morehead City. A favorite with locals who come for the weekday specials and Friday Happy Hours, the restaurant serves steaks, chops, and seafood in well thought out preparations. Á la carte sides, appetizers, and salads provide delicious options for the lighter appetite. Cigars are available in the lounge where smoking is permitted. On Sundays, a buffet loaded with breakfast specialties, shrimp and grits, carved prime rib, cold salads, and a variety of breads and pastries begins at 11 AM.

SALTER PATH/INDIAN BEACH

★ CARLTON'S FINE DINING AT THE BEACH

252-808-3404
www.carltonsathome.com
1401 Salter Path Rd., NC 58, Salter Path 28575
Price: Expensive
Children's Menu: Yes
Cuisine: American
Liquor: Wine, beer, brown bagging
Serving: L (summer), D, SB
Credit Cards: MC, V
Handicapped Access: Yes
Special Features: Blackboard specials; frequent diners club; bar; clambakes to go; reservations recommended

Patrick Hogan, owner and chef of this fine dining establishment located in the middle of Bogue Banks at MM 11, offers a menu of popular dishes, including appetizer-sized portions of Beef Wellington and Shrimp Scampi, and entrées ranging from Beef Bourguignon to Vietnamese Duck Noodle

Soup. The lump crab cake is Carlton's most famous dish, and is available in a variety of preparations, including atop a filet mignon or under a poached egg. For Sunday Brunch, try the Surf and Turf Benedict, with both crab and steak. The dining room, decorated in simple, bright colors, is the perfect foil for an assortment of local artwork.

SWANSBORO

RIVERSIDE STEAK & SEAFOOD

910-326-8847
506 W. Corbett Ave., NC 24, Swansboro 28584
Price: Expensive
Children's Menu: Yes
Cuisine: Steaks and seafood
Liquor: Full bar
Serving: D
Credit Cards: AE, MC, V
Handicapped Access: Yes
Special Features: Daily specials; reservations recommended

A lengthy list of daily specials supplements a menu of fresh local seafood and hand cut aged beef at this long-time favorite. Try the Carpetbagger, a rib-eye stuffed with jumbo shrimp or, for something light, a salad topped with grilled fish or shrimp and crabmeat, a spinach salad with hot bacon dressing, or Oysters Rockefeller. All meals come with famous homemade sweet potato muffins. Mississippi Mud Pie serves two for dessert.

Food Purveyors

Bakeries and Coffee Shops

Beans-N-Screens Internet Café 252-354-4336; www.beansandscreens.com; 8700 Emerald Dr., Emerald Plantation Shopping Center, Emerald Isle 28594. Cool spot with free WiFi access serves coffees and teas hot and iced, frappes, and lattes, plus homemade muffins.

Church Street Coffee, Deli & Irish Pub 910-326-7572; 105 Church St., Swansboro 28584. In addition to coffee, tea, and pastries, this local favorite with a nice patio is also a deli serving Boar's Head meats and cheeses, and an Irish pub where you can lift a pint of Guinness.

Coffee Affair 252-247-6020; www.coffeeaffair.com; 2302 Arendell St., Morehead City 28557. Internet hotspot has a full menu of coffee and tea drinks, baked goods, box lunches, and terrific chicken salad croissants.

Spouter Inn Bakery 252-728-5190; www.thespouterinn.com; 218 Front St., Beaufort 28516. Freshly baked breads and luscious desserts, including éclairs and napoleons, fill the display case at the in-house bakery.

★ **Taylor's Big Mug** 252-728-0707; 437 Front St., Beaufort 28516. Located across from the town marina, this spacious coffee shop offers a full selection of coffees, juices, bagels, and other fare, as well as free Internet access and occasional live music.

★ **The Tea Clipper** 252-240-2800; www.theteaclipper.com; 1008 Arendell St., Morehead City 28557. Elegant tea room next door to the **History Place** stocks more than 120 whole leaf and herbal teas, and serves light lunches, desserts, and afternoon tea with scones and savories, Tuesday–Saturday.

Breakfast and More

★ **4 Corners Diner** 252240-8855; 100 E. Fort Macon Rd., Atlantic Beach 28512. Breakfast at the most reasonable price is served all day at this classic diner located at the Circle.

Boardwalk Café 252-728-0933, 510 Front St., Beaufort 28516. Popular spot has tables on the dockside boardwalk, or you can eat inside in the comfortable dining room.

Clam Digger Inn Restaurant 252-247-4155, 800-338-1533; www.clamdiggerramadainn.com; 511 Salter Path Rd., Atlantic Beach 28512. Popular with locals for its daily specials, the restaurant serves all the breakfast favorites from 6:30 AM.

Mike's Place 252-354-5277; 8302 Emerald Dr., Emerald Isle 28594. Popular spot in Emerald Isle serves a full breakfast menu, plus a buffet on summer weekends.

Morris Marina Grill 252-225-4261, 877-956-6568; www.capelookoutconcessions.com; 1000 Morris Marina Rd., Atlantic 28511. A favorite stop for breakfast before catching the ferry to North Core Banks for a day of surf fishing. Great burgers, too.

Yanamama's Restaurant & 50's Memorabilia Shoppe 866-766-6845; www.yanamamas.com; 117 Front St., Swansboro 28584. Locals rave about the fruit fritters at this cool restaurant complete with a jukebox loaded with rock-and-roll hits.

Candy and Ice Cream

The Fudge Factory 252-728-6202, 800-551-8066; www.thefudgefactory.com; 400 Front St., Somerset Square, Beaufort 28516. Old-fashioned handmade fudge, ice cream, and frozen yogurt available overlooking the docks.

The General Store 728-7707; 515 Front St., Beaufort 28516. Carries 32 flavors of ice cream, plus souvenirs and gifts, while out back you'll find a coin laundry.

Sweet Spot Ice Cream Parlor and Candy Shoppe 252-354-6201, 8201 Emerald Dr., Emerald Isle 28594; 252-247-6201, Atlantic Station, Atlantic Beach 28512. Two locations feature 42 flavors of Hershey's Premium ice creams, frozen yogurt, Italian ice, saltwater taffy, plus specialty coffees and teas.

Delis and Specialty Foods

Beaufort Grocery Co. 252-728-3899; www.beaufortgrocery.com; 117 Queen St., Beaufort 28516. This popular restaurant has a display case full of goodies, including fresh baked breads, cheesecakes, and homemade salads. Picnic baskets available.

Garden Gate Cafe & Deli 252-247-4061; 278-L NC 24, Morehead City 28557. Sandwich shop next to the Wal-Mart serves great pimento cheese and cookies.

Martha's Spices and Gifts 877-464-7487; www.satansbreath.com; 305 Turner St., Beaufort 28516. Chef Elmo's award-winning hot sauces, spice blends, and handmade sausages.

The Village Market 252-354-6592; www.eideli.com; 7802 Emerald Dr., Emerald Isle 28594. Sandwiches for breakfast or lunch prepared to go, plus salads, cheeses, wine and beer, key lime, pecan, and peanut butter pies, whole or by the piece.

Farms, Farmers Markets, and Vegetable Stands

The farms of Carteret and Onslow counties are mostly small family businesses, producing a variety of crops, depending on the season. A special product of the area to watch for is the Bogue Sound watermelon, noted for its extra sweet taste and ruby red color. For more information on local farm produce, visit www.ncfarmfresh.com.

The Beirut Memorial at Camp Lejeune in Jacksonville

Carteret County Curb Market 252-222-6359; carteret.ces.ncsu.edu; 1213 Evans St., Morehead City 28557. Shop for local produce, fresh seafood, flowers, and baked goods at the oldest continuously operating curb market in North Carolina, 7:30–11:30 AM Saturdays from May to Labor Day. A demonstration garden is located next door.

Guthrie Farm 252-393-2254, 252-241-4918; 195 Guthrie Farm Rd., Bogue 28570. Farmer Guthrie is the founder of the Bogue Sound Watermelon Growers Association.

Winberry Farm 252-393-2281; 1006 Cedar Point Blvd., Cedar Point 28584. An old tobacco barn holds one of the area's best farm stands, a great place to find local tomatoes and Bogue Sound watermelons.

Natural and Vegetarian Foods

CC Ralwiggies 252-240-8646; 3710 Arendell St., Morehead City 28557. All you can eat buffet with more than 50 items at this bright and clean café is 95 percent vegetarian and vegan. Open for weekday lunch only.

Coastal Community Market 252-728-2844; www.coastalcommunitymarket.com; 606 Broad St., Beaufort 28516. Earth-friendly store carries locally grown and organic produce, dried fruits, wines, and soy products; locally baked bread; and free range eggs.

Lebanon Valley Cuisine 252-726-6668; 4219 Arendell St., Morehead City 28557. Mediterranean and Mexican dishes, including many vegetarian selections.

Pizza

Mario's Pizzeria 252-728-6602; 1718 Live Oak St., US 70E, Beaufort Square Shopping Center, Beaufort 28516.

Michaelangelo's Pizza four locations: 252-240-3333, 1010 W. Fort Macon Rd., Atlantic

Beach 28512; 252-393-3333, 315 W. B. McLean Blvd., Cape Carteret 28584; 252-354-7424, 8700 Emerald Dr., Emerald Plantation Shopping Center, Emerald Isle 28594; 910-326-1946, 660 W. Corbett Ave., Swansboro 28584. Local favorite serves pizza whole or by the slice, pasta dishes, salads, gyros, and subs, every day until late at night—a real lifesaver when you arrive in town hungry after all the other family restaurants are closed.

Roma Pizza & Subs 252-247-2040; 100 Charlotte Ave., Atlantic Beach 28512. Delivery available.

Takeout and Fast Food

★ **Big Oak Drive In & Bar-B-Q** 252-247-2588; www.bigoakdrivein.com; 1167 Salter Path Rd., Salter Path 28575. The specialty at this old-time takeout stand is the shrimp burger, reputed to be the best on the coast.

El's Drive-In 252-726-3002; www.elsdrivein.com; 3706 Arendell St., Morehead City 28557. Family-owned fast food joint has been serving burgers since 1959. Waitresses deliver burgers and more, right to your car. Open late.

Mrs. Culpepper's Crab Café & Thai Cuisine 252-240-1960; 5370 US 70 W., Morehead City 28557. Select from the buffet of seafood, spicy curries, pad thai, and other Asian specialties, or order to go at this casual spot with great crab cakes.

No Name Pizza & Subs 252-728-4978; 408 Live Oak St., Beaufort 28516. The No Name serves much more than pizza and subs, including pasta and Greek dishes, in its dining room and at the drive-through window. Beer and wine available.

Roland's Barbecue 252-728-1953; 815 Cedar St., Beaufort 28516. Stop by the takeout window at this top caterer for some eastern North Carolina pulled pork and ribs accompanied by Roland's vinegar-based sauce.

The Shark Shack 252-726-3313; 100 S. Durham Ave., Atlantic Beach 28512. Serving breakfast, burgers, and baskets, this is a drive-in with a difference: live music plus beer and wine.

White Swan Bar-B-Q & Fried Chicken 252-726-9607; www.whiteswanatlanticbeach.com; 2500-A W. Fort Macon Rd., Atlantic Beach 28512. Slow cooked pork ribs and barbecue chicken are the specialties.

Seafood Markets

To combat the rising tide of imported seafood, both in restaurants and markets, the **Carteret Catch** brand has been developed both to insure that consumers receive wild-caught local seafood and to support local fishing families. The Carteret Catch Web site (www.carteretcatch.org) lists restaurants and retail seafood markets where the catch is certified local. You can also find seafood fresh off the boat at roadside stands operated by fishing families.

Atlantic Beach Seafood Market & Tackle Outlet 252-247-2430; 211 Atlantic Beach Causeway, Atlantic Beach 28512. Come by car or boat to pick out some fresh local seafood, or some of the Willis family's famous crab cakes.

Cap'n Willis Seafood Market 252-354-2500; 7803 Emerald Dr., Emerald Isle 28594. A new market opened by the Willis family, providing seafood to the Bogue Banks for four generations.

Captain Jim's Seafood 252-726-3454; 4665 Arendell St., Morehead City 28557. The motto here is, "If it swims, we've got it." A certified Carteret Catch retailer.

Fishtowne Seafood Center 252-728-6644; 100 Wellons Dr., Beaufort 28516. A certified Carteret Catch retailer.

Wines and Beer

★ **The Cru Wine Bar and Store** 252-728-3066; www.thecruwinebar.com; 120 Turner St., Beaufort 28516. Comfortable, sophisticated shop sells bottles and glasses of wine, along with cheese or smoked salmon plates. A coffee shop with handcrafted chocolates is just through the archway.

Emerald Isle Wine Market 252-354-2250; www.htpresort.com; 9102 Coast Guard Rd., Emerald Isle 28594. Located inside the **Holiday Trav-L-Park** RV resort, this wine store stocks microbrews and wines from around the world.

Flip Flops Wine & Gift Shop 252-354-3446; 3305 Emerald Dr., Emerald Isle 28594. This much expanded convenience store stocks a large selection of wines and beers, as well as deli items.

Priscilla's Crystal Coast Wines 252-240-3234, 877-242-7158; www.crystalcoastwines.com; 5370 US 70W, Morehead City 28557. Stocks more than 1,400 wines, plus microbrews, chocolates, cheeses, and gourmet food items. Wine tasting the first Friday of every month.

Somerset Cellars Winery 252-725-0029, 252-727-4800; www.somersetcellars.com; 3906 Arendell St., Morehead City 28557. The Crystal Coast's first federally bonded winery.

TOURING

The **Visitor's Center for Carteret County and the Crystal Coast** (252-726-8148, 877-206-0929; www.crystalcoastnc.org; 3409 Arendell St., Morehead City 28557) has helpful counselors and lots of local information, as well as restrooms, boat ramp, and a pleasant picnic area overlooking Bogue Sound.

A second visitor's center is located in Cedar Point (252-393-3100; 262 NC 58), just before the bridge to Emerald Isle.

For additional information on Swansboro, contact the **Swansboro Area Chamber of Commerce** (910-326-1174; www.swansboroncchamber.com; 502 Church St.), or **Onslow County Tourism** (800-932-2144; www.onslowcountytourism.com; 1099 Gum Branch Rd., Jacksonville 28540).

To become acquainted with the history and lore of the fascinating small fishing villages north of Beaufort, take the virtual **Down East Tour** (www.downeasttour.com) developed by members of the Core Sound Waterfowl and Heritage Museum. Another online tour of the Core Sound region is maintained by the **North Carolina Folklife Institute** at www.ncfolk.org.

By Air

Seagrave Aviation 252-728-2323; www.beaufortairport.com; 150 Airport Rd., Beaufort 28516. For a unique perspective, see Cape Lookout, the wild ponies, and Fort Macon from the air.

The Beaufort waterfront is the center of maritime activities on the Crystal Coast.

By Bicycle or On Foot

★ **Beaufort Ghost Walk** 252-342-0715; www.tourbeaufort.com. A pirate guide leads you to the Hammock House, once the residence of Blackbeard, then on to a 300-year-old cemetery for more tales of horror. Also available: **The Legend of Blackbeard Tour**.

Beaufort Historic Site Tours 252-728-5225; 800-575-7483; www.beauforthistoricsite.org; 130 Turner St., Beaufort 28516. Guides dressed in period costume conduct tours of the site's exquisitely restored homes Monday through Saturday, year round.

Bikes-R-In 252-393-7161, 888-393-7161; www.bikes-r-in.com; 1020 Cedar Point Blvd., Cedar Point 28584. Self-guided tours lead through historic Swansboro, Beaufort, and over the ferry to Ocracoke.

Blackbeard's Amazing Beaufort Adventure 252-342-0715; www.blackbeards adventure.com. Hunt for treasure through the streets of Beaufort as your team seeks to reach the booty first.

North Carolina State Port Tour 252-728-7317; www.ncports.com. Tours offered through the **North Carolina Maritime Museum**. Call for a current schedule. Free tours are also offered during the annual North Carolina Seafood Festival.

Old Burying Ground Tours 252-728-5225; 800-575-7483; www.beauforthistoricsite.org; 130 Turner St., Beaufort 28516. Guided tours of the 300-year-old cemetery are offered June through September, Tuesday through Thursday. You can also take a self-guided tour. Maps are available at the **Beaufort Historic Site** for $1.

★ **Shackleford Wild Horse and Shelling Safari** 252-342-0715; www.tourbeaufort.com. Join a naturalist guide to look for the herds of wild ponies that inhabit the island, then search for shells along the oceanfront.

By Boat

Barrier Island Adventures 252-728-4129; www.outerbanksferry.com; 326 Front St., Beaufort 28516. This company will take you to Carrot Island, Shackleford, or Cape Lookout for island exploration.

Good Fortune Coastal Ecology Tours 252-247-3860, 252-241-6866; www.goodfortune sails.com; 500 Front St., Beaufort 28516. During the summer season, this 41-foot yacht sails on daily coastal ecology cruises conducted by biologist Ron White. Cruises may include snorkeling, shelling, bird and dolphin watching, and kayaking.

Island Ferry Adventure 252-728-7555; www.islandferryadventures.com; 610 Front St., Beaufort 28516. Award-winning boat tours include a dolphin and nature cruise, and a horse and waterfront cruise that circles the islands in front of Beaufort.

Lookout Cruises 252-504-SAIL; www.lookoutcruises.com; 600 Front St., Beaufort 28516. A 45-foot catamaran offers dolphin watching, snorkeling, sunset, and full moon cruises.

Mystery Boat Tours 252-728-7827, 866-230-BOAT; www.mysteryboattours.com; 410 Front St., Beaufort 28516. Two boats, the *Mystery* and the *Diamond City*, cruise daily on narrated harbor tours, dinner cruises, late-night party cruises, dolphin watches, and a special pirate treasure hunt for kids.

Overtime Tours 252-726-6627, 252-259-5283; www.overtimetours.com; Evans St., Morehead City 28557. Depart from the Morehead City waterfront.

Shackleford Charters 252-725-5941; www.shacklefordcharters.com; 2300 E. Fort Macon Rd., Atlantic Beach 28512. Fishing and beachcomber outings, ecology and history tours.

Water Bug Harbor Tours 252-728-4129; www.waterbugtours.com; 324 Front St., Beaufort 28516. Cruise the historic Beaufort waterfront on a one-hour tour.

Waterdog Guide Service 252-728-7907, 919-423-6310; www.waterdogguideservice.com; P.O. Box 2211, Beaufort 28516. Tours offered include historical or sunset cruises; dolphin/pony watches; clamming/crabbing; and a tour of Cape Lookout.

By Bus

★ **Beaufort Historic District Bus Tour** 252-728-5225; 800-575-7483; www.beaufort historicsite.org; 130 Turner St., Beaufort 28516. Tours in a vintage English double-decker bus depart from the Beaufort Historic Site on Monday, Wednesday, and Friday, April through October.

By Kayak

Barrier Island Kayaks 252.393.6457; www.barrierislandkayaks.com; 160 Cedar Point Blvd., Swansboro 28584. Regularly scheduled tours include a marsh eco-tour and a paddle to Bear Island. Trips around the tip of Cape Lookout are also available.

Core Sound Kayaks & Touring Company 252-728-2330; www.capelookoutadventures.com; 1584 Harkers Island Rd., Beaufort 28516. Explore Core Sound, Back Sound, and the Straits with Down East natives, either by kayak or aboard a motorized 22-foot Harkers Island skiff.

Pirate Queen Paddling www.piratequeenpaddling.com; Atlantic Beach location: 252-726-1434, 1010 W. Fort Macon Rd., Atlantic Station; Morehead City location: 252-726-1452, 707 Arendell St. Experienced sea kayakers offer a variety of tours in local waters, including paddles around Sugarloaf Island off the Morehead City waterfront, and up Hoop Pole Creek in Atlantic Beach. The **Wee Pirate Treasure Hunt** takes pirates ages 2–10 and their accompanying adults on a paddle to a secret island.

CULTURE

Drawing on a heritage of hundreds of years, the Crystal Coast has a well-established cultural scene with many arts organizations and annual events.

Architecture

Several recognized historic districts are located in this region, including Cape Lookout Village and Portsmouth Village, both on Core Banks and today deserted. Other historic districts still occupied are the Beaufort, Morehead City, and Swansboro downtowns, all on the National Register of Historic Places.

The Beaufort Historic District contains over 100 buildings bearing plaques with the original owner and date of construction listed. Victorian and Queen Anne influences are reflected in the elaborate millwork found on many of the houses. Beaufort also has a distinctive style of picket fence, characterized by an undulating, up and down top-line and square pickets. **The Beaufort Historical Association** (252-728-5225, 800-575-7483; www.beauforthistoricsite.org) sponsors an Old Homes and Gardens Tour every June.

The Morehead City Historic District running along Fisher Street and Bridges Street, is a mix of Victorian mansions and Craftsman bungalows. Between 10th and 12th Streets, the area known as the Promise Land has cottages in the Banker style, some of them ferried across Bogue Sound after hurricanes in the 1890s. The **Downtown Morehead City Revitalization Association** (252-808-0440; www.downtownmoreheadcity.com; 1001 Arendell St.), housed in a historic 1904 train depot, sponsors an annual Homes and Heritage Tour every May.

Swansboro also has a historic district along its waterfront. The **William Edward Mattocks House**, at 109 Front Street, is listed on the National Register.

Art Museums and Galleries

The Crystal Coast is awash with art, if you know where to look. A good place to start is the Morehead City waterfront district where you'll find the **Fish Walk**, a series of open-air bas-relief sculptures that celebrate the region's maritime heritage. Internationally known local artists Keith Lambert and Willie Baucom created the sculptures. You can find out more about their **Shipyard Earthworks Studio** and the Fish Walk at www.shipyardearthworks.com.

Public art from a different era can be admired at the **Beaufort Post Office** on Front Street. Four large murals painted in 1940, recently restored, depict scenes from local history.

The Arts Council of Carteret County (252-726-9156; www.artscouncilcarteret.org; 812 Evans St., Morehead City 28557) sponsors the Adopt an Artist program which places changing exhibits of artwork in local business. Consult the Web site for current shows.

More local art can be found at the **Morehead City Markets** (252-240-1979; www.mhcmarkets.info) held on Saturdays in Katherine Davis Park on Arendell Street in Morehead City's Waterfront District from spring to fall.

Arts & Things Gallery 252-240-1979, 877-640-ARTS; www.arts-things.com; 704 Evans St., Morehead City 28557. Gallery carries the area's largest selection of art supplies and sponsors a calendar of classes in many media.

Carolina Artists Studio Gallery 252-726-7550; www.carolinaartiststudio.com; 800 Evans St., Morehead City 28557. The area's largest gallery displaying original local art also offers classes and workshops.

Carteret Contemporary Art 252-726-4071; www.twogalleries.net; 1106 Arendell St., Morehead City 28557. Changing exhibits of original, cutting edge artwork.

Down East Gallery 252-728-4410, 800-868-2766; www.alancheek.com; 519 Front St., Beaufort 28516. Displays the works of Alan Cheek, one of North Carolina's premiere coastal artists.

★ **Handscapes Gallery** 252-728-6805, 888-346-8334; www.handscapesgallery.com; 410 Front St., Beaufort 28516. Exquisite selection of pottery, jewelry, art glass, and works in other media created by more than 200 artists across the nation. Special section of Banker pony-themed art.

★ **Mattie King Davis Art Gallery** 252-728-5225; 800-575-7483; www.beauforthistoric site.org; 130 Turner St., Beaufort 28516. Occupying the 1732 Rustell House on the grounds of the Beaufort Historic Site, this gallery displays juried works by over 100 local and regional artists.

Miss Marie's Gallery of Fine Art and Gifts 252-728-0908; www.missmariesgallery.com; 114 Queen St., Beaufort 28516. Jewelry artist Trish Shepherd employs traditional cloisonné techniques.

Vision Gallery 252-247-5550; www.twogalleries.net; 407 Atlantic Beach Causeway, Ste. 6-A, Atlantic Beach 28512. Changing exhibits of original paintings and sculpture by state and regional artists.

Cooking Classes

Coastal Community Market 252-728-2844; www.coastalcommunitymarket.com; 606 Broad St., Beaufort 28516. Classes utilize natural foods and local products.

Elmo's Kitchen 877-464-7487; www.satansbreath.com; 305 Turner St., Beaufort 28516. Enjoy a lesson with Chef Elmo Barnes, author of three cookbooks and the creator of Cajun Blend, a winner in *Chile Pepper* magazine's Fiery Food Challenge.

Succulent Seafood 252-247-4003, 866-294-3477; www.ncaquariums.com; 1 Roosevelt Blvd., Pine Knoll Shores 28512. Local chefs come to the aquarium to demonstrate their favorite seafood dishes.

Historic Homes, Sites, and Gardens

★ BEAUFORT HISTORIC SITE

252-728-5225; 800-575-7483
www.beauforthistoricsite.org
100 Block Turner St., Beaufort 28516
Open: June–Aug. 7 days a week; Sept.–May Mon.–Sat.

The Beaufort Historic Site includes restored buildings from many eras, including a jail and a pharmacy.

Hours: March–Nov. 9:30 AM–5 PM; Dec.–Feb. 10 AM–4 PM
Admission: Grounds and art gallery are free; tours of the historic buildings, Old Burying Ground, and bus tours, $8 for adults, $4 for children.

The Beaufort Historical Association, a private, membership-based organization formed in 1960, has gathered, restored, and furnished six historic buildings—including the 1732 Rustell House, now an art gallery, and Federal and Victorian residences—in the 100 block of Turner Street. They are open to the public year round. Other buildings around the wide green lawn include the 1786 Carteret County Courthouse; the Old Jail, reputed to be haunted; and the 1859 Apothecary Shop and Doctors Office, filled with fascinating medical artifacts. The **Safrit Historical Center** houses exhibits, the museum gift shop, and restrooms, in addition to serving as an information center.

★ CAPE LOOKOUT LIGHTHOUSE & KEEPERS' QUARTERS MUSEUM
252-728-2250
www.nps.gov/calo
South Core Banks
Open: Museum is open Apr.–Nov., 9 AM–5 PM; Lighthouse is under renovation. Call 252-728-5766 to see if it will be open for climbing.
Admission: Free to visit the museum. A $10 ferry ride is required to reach South Core Banks from Harkers Island.

The 169-foot tall Cape Lookout Lighthouse was first lit in 1859, but didn't receive its distinctive black and white diamond paint job until after the Civil War. It was transferred from the U.S. Coast Guard to the National Park Service in 2003, becoming the centerpiece of the Cape Lookout National Seashore. The park service plans to restore the lighthouse so visitors can climb it. The adjacent **Keepers' Quarters** holds a museum that is open daily except during the winter. Private ferries make the run from Harkers Island, the nearest land access, docking near the **Light Station Pavilion**, which houses a ranger station, book store, and restrooms. During the summer months, park rangers conduct free programs on the history of the lighthouse and the surrounding area.

CORE SOUND DECOY CARVERS GUILD HALL
252-838-8818
www.decoyguild.com
P.O. Box 89, Harkers Island Rd., Harkers Island 28531
Hours vary
Admission: Free

Local carvers and waterfowling enthusiasts gather at the historic H. Curt Salter Building, located at the foot of the Harkers Island bridge. Classes for adults and children are available, as well as decoy merchandise.

FORT MACON STATE PARK
252-726-3775, 252-726-2295
www.ncparks.gov
2300 E. Fort Macon Rd., Atlantic Beach 28512
Open: The fort is open all year, 9 AM–5:30 PM; Closed Christmas Day. Hours for the sur-

The Old Burying Ground in Beaufort is a favorite for ghost tours.

rounding grounds, bathhouse, and swimming area vary by season. Check the Web site for current schedule.

Admission: Free to tour fort. Bathhouse fees are $4 a day for ages 13 and older, $3 a day for ages 3–12, free for children under 3.

The eastern tip of Bogue Banks was fortified as early as 1715. The present pentagon-shaped fort was begun in 1826, fell to Union forces in the Civil War, and was garrisoned for the final time during World War II. Today it is the second oldest state park in the North Carolina system, and is the most visited. The 27 vaulted casements in the restored fort house a comprehensive museum detailing the history of the facility and the men who saw service here. Guided tours are offered, and Civil War reenactments take place in April, July, and September.

THE OLD BURYING GROUND
252-728-5225; 800-575-7483
www.beauforthistoricsite.org
Bounded by Ann, Craven, and Broad Streets, Beaufort
Open: Dawn to Dusk
Admission: Free

A leisurely walk beneath the 100-year-old live oaks that shade the Old Burying Ground is a fascinating trip through local history. The nearly 300-year-old cemetery contains some 400 graves dating back to 1731. Two notable occupants are Otway Burns, the famous privateer whose grave is marked with a cannon from his ship, and a young girl buried in a barrel

Tryon Palace in New Bern is an accurate re-creation of the royal governor's residence in colonial times.

of rum, whose grave is decorated with toys and gifts left by visitors over the years. A self-guided tour booklet of the cemetery is available at the **Beaufort Historic Site**, and costumed interpreters offer guided tours with many additional stories several times a week.

SWANSBORO HISTORIC DISTRICT & BICENTENNIAL PARK

910-326-1174
www.onslowcountytourism.com
Bounded by NC 24 and the White Oak River, downtown Swansboro

Listed on the National Register of Historic Places, Swansboro's waterfront is home to an eclectic selection of architectural styles. Highlight of the **Bicentennial Park**, located on the waterfront at the base of the NC 24 bridge, is a statue of native son Otway Burns, captain of the *Snap Dragon* privateer during the War of 1812, and the first person to build a steamboat in North Carolina.

★ TRYON PALACE STATE HISTORIC SITE & GARDENS

252-514-4900, 800-767-1560
www.tryonpalace.org
610 Pollock St., New Bern 28562
Open: 360 days a year, closed Thanksgiving Day, Dec. 24–26, and Jan. 1.
Hours: Mon.–Sat. 9 AM–5 PM; Sunday 1–5 PM; The last tour of the Palace begins at 4 PM;
Academy Museum open Mon.–Sat. 1–4:30 PM
Admission: Governor's Pass giving admission to all buildings and gardens, $15 adults, $6 students grades 1–12; Gardens and Kitchen Pass, $8 adults, $3 student. Tickets are valid for two days.

About 40 miles north of Beaufort is one of North Carolina's historical gems, the colonial capital of New Bern. Tryon Palace, a magnificent Georgian structure designed by architect

John Hawks, has been reconstructed based on the original 1767 plans and archeological evidence, and its 14 acres of gardens replanted in the Colonial-Revival style. The Governor's Pass includes admission to three nearby historic houses, and the New Bern Academy, now a museum detailing the city history through the Civil War. The objects on display in the Palace and other buildings are considered one of the top 10 collections of American and European decorative arts in the United States.

Museums

★ CORE SOUND WATERFOWL MUSEUM AND HERITAGE CENTER

252-728-1500
www.coresound.com
1785 Island Rd., Harkers Island 28531
Open: All year, except Easter Sunday, Thanksgiving Day, Christmas Day, and New Year's Day
Hours: Mon.–Sat. 10 AM–5 PM, Sunday 2–5 PM
Admission: Free

Near the end of the road on Harkers Island, this important new museum is filled with handcarved decoys, boat models, quilts, and other artifacts donated by local families. Each of the Down East communities has its own exhibit, and traditional decoy carvers demonstrate their craft on-site. Outside a nature trail leads to a pond frequented by migrating waterfowl. The center sponsors a full schedule of activities featuring Down East cooking, music, and crafts, including the Waterfowl Weekend every December.

THE HISTORY PLACE

252-247-7533
www.thehistoryplace.org
1008 Arendell St., Morehead City 28557
Open: Tue.–Sat. 10 AM–4 PM
Admission: Free

Operated by the Carteret County Historical Society, this is a museum of both history and art. Exhibits explore the history and traditions of the region including menhaden fishing, the first yacht club, the railroad, the porcelain dolls of Sally Beatty, and artifacts relating to local Confederate spy, Miss Emeline Pigott. The Historical Society sponsors many special events, including the popular "Lunch with a Dash of History" series, featuring storyteller Rodney Kemp.

THE NORTH CAROLINA AQUARIUM AT PINE KNOLL SHORES

252-247-4003, 866-294-3477
www.ncaquariums.com
1 Roosevelt Blvd., Pine Knoll Shores 28512
Open: All year, except Thanksgiving Day, Christmas Day, and New Year's Day
Hours: 9 AM–5 PM daily; until 9 PM Thursdays in July
Admission: $8 adults; $7 seniors 62 and over; $6 children 6–17; children under 6 free. Free admission on Martin Luther King Jr. Day and Veteran's Day

This branch of the state aquariums takes visitors on a journey from a waterfall in the North Carolina mountains, down through many streams and bays, to the deep offshore realm of the big saltwater game fish. Along the way, visitors meet native brown trout, giant catfish, playful river otters, sea turtles, sharks, and red drum. The Living Shipwreck tank holds a replica of a German U-boat inhabited by sharks and other creatures. Outdoors, a boardwalk leads over the marsh to a snake exhibit and Bogue Sound overlook. Free programs are offered daily; kayak trips, marsh explorations, and fishing lessons require a small additional fee.

★ NORTH CAROLINA MARITIME MUSEUM IN BEAUFORT

252-728-7317
www.ncmaritime.org; www.ncmm-friends.org
15 Front St., Beaufort 28516
Open: 360 days a year; closed Thanksgiving, Christmas holidays, and New Year's Day
Hours: Mon.–Fri. 9 AM–5 PM; Sat. 10 AM–5 PM; Sun. 1–5 PM
Admission: Free. Guided tours of "Our Sunken History" exhibit, $5 adults, $2 children.
Reservations required.

The state's Maritime Museum in Beaufort includes three separate facilities: the main galleries on Front Street, the **Watercraft Center** across the street on the waterfront, and the **Gallant's Channel annex**, about 1 mile west of downtown. The main galleries contain an extensive shell collection, examples of traditional boats, and an excellent collection of handcarved decoys. The Watercraft Center specializes in the building and restoration of wooden boats, and houses a ship model-making shop. The annex on Gallant's Channel is open for guided tours of "Our Sunken History," an exhibit featuring artifacts recovered from 15 different shipwrecks, including Blackbeard's *Queen Anne's Revenge*. The Maritime Museum sponsors a wide variety of boatbuilding and environmental education programs throughout the year.

Music, Theater, and Dance

American Music Festival 252-728-4488; www.americanmusicfestival.org; P.O. Box 1099, Beaufort 28516. Chamber music series sponsors performances by top regional and national artists from September to May.

Carteret Arts Forum 252-646-3716, 252-247-1133; www.carteretartforum.com; P.O. Box 462, Morehead City 28557. Annual subscription series brings professional music and theatrical performances to the Crystal Coast.

Carteret Community Theatre 252-726-6340; www.carteretcommunitytheatre.org; P.O. Box 283, Morehead City 28557. Amateur theatrical group with an impressive 50-year history mounts an average of three productions each year, including musicals and children's plays.

Community Contra Dances 252-504-2787; www.downeastfolkarts.org; P.O. Box 328, Beaufort 28516. Dances with live music and callers are held one Saturday evening a month from September to June at the **Duke Marine Lab** in Beaufort.

Crystal Coast Choral Society 910-324-6864, 252-247-5929. This chorus of 70 voices, recently guest artists at New York's Carnegie Hall, performs at least three concerts annually.

Crystal Coast Civic Center 252-247-3883, 888-899-6088; www.crystalcoastcivicctr.com; 3505 Arendell St., Morehead City 28557. Hosts concerts by regional and national touring groups.

The Crystal Coast Jamboree 252-726-1501, 866-580-7469; www.crystalcoastjamboree
.com; 1311 Arendell St., Morehead City 28557. Professional show combines country,
oldies, lots of laughs, and plenty of patriotism. Special Holiday show in December.

★ **Down East FolkArts Society Concert Series** 252-504-2787; www.downeastfolkarts.org;
P.O. Box 328, Beaufort 28516. Held September to June at local venues.

Emerald Isle Beach Jive After Five 252-354-6350; www.emeraldisle-nc.org; Western
Ocean Regional Beach Access. Free live music concerts sponsored by Emerald Isle Parks
and Recreation the third Thursdays of summer months beginning at 5:30 PM.

Fort Macon Summer Concert Series 252-726-8598; www.clis.com/friends. Free concerts
sponsored by the Friends of Fort Macon are held inside the fort Friday evenings, June to
August, 7–8 PM.

Saturday in the Park Concert Series 252-726-5083; www.townofmorehead.com; Jaycee
Park, 9th and Shepard Sts., Morehead City. Free concerts every Saturday evening from
Memorial Day to Labor Day at 7 PM.

Nightlife

★ **Backstreet Pub** 252-728-7108; 124 Middle Ln., Beaufort 28516. Cool little spot behind
Clawson's features a big wine list, cold beer, live music in the courtyard every weekend,
and "Hoot Nite" on Wednesdays.

Ballyhoo's Island Sport Grill 252-354-9397; www.ballyhoos.net; 140 Fairview Dr., Emerald Isle 28594. Upscale bar with TVs tuned to sports, plus late night live music several
times a week.

Bushwackers Restaurant & Lounge 252-354-6300; 100 Bogue Inlet Dr., Emerald Isle
28594. Located on the Bogue Inlet Pier, this smoky bar is noted for its fun jungle decor.

Channel Marker Restaurant & Lounge 252-247-2344; 718 Atlantic Beach Causeway,
Atlantic Beach 28512. Waterfront bar is a favorite summer gathering spot for locals.

Clarita's Tiki Bar at the Sand Bar 252-504-7263; www.clairitastikibar.com; 232 W. Beaufort Rd., Beaufort 28516. Outdoor deck at the Town Creek Marina is a favorite stop for
the sunset crowd, with frequent live bands during the summer.

The Cru Wine Bar 252-728-3066; www.thecruwinebar.com; 120 Turner St., Beaufort
28516. Live music on weekends and Tuesday night jam sessions.

Diamond City Dinner and Party Cruises 252-728-7827, 866-230-BOAT; www.mystery
boattours.com; 410 Front St., Beaufort 28516. Dinner cruises precede the late night
party cruise.

D J Shooters Restaurant & Lounge 252-240-3393; 2604 W. Fort Macon Rd., Atlantic
Beach 28512. A local favorite on Atlantic Beach, both for steaks and nightlife.

The Dock House Restaurant & Bar 252-728-4506; www.beaufortdockhouse.com; 500 Front
St., Beaufort 28516. Dockside pub serves up live sunset music during the summer and fall.

Emerald Club 252-354-2929; www.emeraldclub2001.com; 8102 Emerald Dr., Emerald
Isle 28594. Live beach and classic rock music in a smoke-free atmosphere.

Frank and Clara's Restaurant & Lounge 252-247-2788; NC 58, Indian Beach 28575.
Upstairs lounge offers cocktails and occasional live music.

Memories Beach & Shag Club 252-240-SHAG; www.atlanticbeachshagclub.com; 128 E.
Fort Macon Blvd., Atlantic Beach 28512. DJs spin Beach Rhythm and Blues.

Midnight Rodeo 252-222-0111; www.midnightrodeonc.com; 5386 US 70 W., Morehead
City 28557. Western nightclub hosting live bands every weekend, has a mechanical bull,
pool tables, line dance lessons, and an outdoor Tiki bar where Jimmy Buffett rules.

Raps Grill and Bar 252-240-1213; www.rapsgrillandbar.com; 715 Arendell St., Morehead
City 28557. Historic building makes a stunning sports bar with nightly appetizer and
drink specials, and plenty of TVs.

RECREATION

In a land surrounded by ocean, sound, rivers, and marsh, recreation on the Southern Outer
Banks centers on water sports and fishing. The area has some of the most pristine, undeveloped beaches found on the entire East Coast, protected by their isolation. Fishing, once
the major occupation of the local populace, today provides superior recreational opportunities, including world-class saltwater fly-fishing.

Beaches

Cape Lookout National Seashore (www.nps.gov/calo) has more than 55 miles of pristine,
undeveloped beaches stretching from Portsmouth Island in the north to Cape Point, south
of the lighthouse. Accessible only by boat, the seashore's beaches have few amenities and
can be hard to travel by foot. A boardwalk stretches from the Light Station Pavilion near the
ferry dock, over to the ocean beach and to the Keepers Quarters museum. Drinkable water
and restroom facilities are located at several locations on the various islands. Check the
park service Web site for current amenities and recommended supplies.

The uninhabited islands that make up the **Rachel Carson Reserve,** especially Carrot
Island, are popular beaches, and uncrowded since they are accessible only by boat.

Bogue Banks has about 28 miles of oceanfront beach stretching from Fort Macon in the
east to Emerald Isle in the west. Numerous public access points line NC 58 along the length
of the island. A few of these are detailed below.

The beach at Bear Island, part of **Hammocks Beach State Park** south of Swansboro, is
one of the wildest and least touched of any barrier island. It too can only be reached by boat.

Beach Access

On the causeway between Beaufort and Morehead City, **Newport River Park** is handicapped
accessible with bathhouse, pier, sandy beach, and shallow-water boat ramp. Across US 70
is the entrance to **Radio Island,** where a popular regional beach access has a picnic area
with grills, sandy beach, bathhouse, and a great view of downtown Beaufort and Carrot
Island across the channel.

On Bogue Banks, most Public Beach Access areas are marked by signs with a seagull flying in an orange circle. A complete listing of Bogue Banks beach access points can be found
on the Crystal Coast Tourism Web site: www.crystalcoastnc.org.

In Atlantic Beach, bathhouses are located at **Fort Macon State Park** (fee to use bathhouse); the Les and Sally Moore Public Beach Access (177 New Bern St.), and the West
Atlantic Boulevard Regional Access at the Circle (201 West Atlantic Blvd). Pine Knoll Shores
has a bathhouse at **Iron Steamer Regional Beach Access** (MM 7.5, 345 Salter Path Rd.).

In Indian Beach/Salter Path, public facilities are located at **Salter Path Regional Public
Beach Access** (1050 Salter Path Rd.).

In Emerald Isle, bathhouses are located at the Eastern Regional Access (2700 Emerald
Dr.), and Western Regional Access (299 Islander Dr.). Beaches here don't have lifeguards,
but the Beach Patrol roams the tide line on ATVs from Memorial Day to Labor Day. You can

Quiet times on the beach

find detailed maps of Emerald Isle's numerous public beach accesses at the town's Web site, www.emeraldisle-nc.org.

Down East, public beaches are located at the southeast end of the Harkers Island drawbridge and next to the ferry docks on Cedar Island, but neither offers any facilities besides parking.

Beach Ferries and Water Taxis

During the summer months, many passenger ferries ply the shallow waters of Core Sound and Beaufort Inlet, taking visitors to the offshore, uninhabited islands of the region. Harkers Island is the closest point to the Cape Lookout Lighthouse, and the National Park Service licenses a number of concessionaires to make the 3-mile run. Prices are standardized, so expect to pay about $10 per adult (ages 13 and up), $6 per child (12 and under) for the round-trip to the lighthouse. Fares to other islands vary. Ferries usually operate from mid-March to November, but a few may operate during the winter, weather permitting. Leashed pets are accepted on most ferries, but you may be charged a child's fare for them.

Calico Jack's Ferry 252-728-3575; www.capelookoutferry.com; 1698 Island Rd., Harkers Island 28531. Ferries to Shackleford Banks and Cape Lookout. Food and supplies are available at the marina.

Cape Lookout Concessions 252-225-4261, 877-956-6568; www.capelookoutconcessions.com; 1000 Morris Marina Rd., Atlantic 28511. Ferries carrying pedestrians, vehicles, trailers, and ATVs depart for Long Point on the North Core Banks from Morris Marina in Atlantic, daily from March to mid-December. A beach shuttle is available on Core Banks, with rates calculated by the mile. Another passenger and vehicle ferry departs from Davis to Great Island on South Core.

Core Sound Kayaks 252-728-2330; www.capelookoutadventures.com; 1584 Harkers Island
Rd., Beaufort 28516. Ferry service for campers and kayakers to remote locations around
the region.

Harkers Island Fishing Center 252-728-3907; www.harkersmarina.com; 1002 Island Rd.,
Harkers Island 28531. Passenger shuttles to Cape Lookout and Shackleford. Food and
supplies available at the marina.

Island Ferry Adventures 252-728-7555; www.islandferryadventures.com; 610 Front St.,
Beaufort 28516. Daily passenger service in season from the Beaufort waterfront to Sand
Dollar Island, Carrot Island, Bird Shoals, and the west end of Shackleford Banks. Service from **Barbour's Marina** (252-728-6181; www.barboursmarina.com; 980 Island Dr.)
on Harkers Island to Cape Lookout and the east end of Shackleford.

Local Yokel Ferry and Tours 252-728-2759; 516 Island Rd., Harkers Island 28531. Shuttle
service from Harkers Island to Cape Lookout. Free parking. May operate in winter
months.

Outer Banks Ferry Service 252-728-4129; www.outerbanksferry.com; 326 Front St., Beaufort 28516. Passenger ferry to Carrot Island, Shackleford, or Cape Lookout from Beaufort. May operate in winter.

Waterfront Ferry Service 252-726-7678; 209 Arendell St., Morehead City 28557. Ferries
from Portside Marina on the Morehead City waterfront to Sugarloaf Island just offshore
and to Shackleford Banks.

Bicycling

Best Bike Routes

Local tourist information centers can provide maps of several area bike trails. The **Beaufort
Bicycle Route** makes a 6-mile loop around the historic village. The 25-mile **Swansboro
Bicentennial Bicycle Trail** makes a loop from the fishing village into the Croatan National
Forest. A 19-mile signed route runs from Hammocks Beach State Park to Jacksonville.
Maps of these trails can also be ordered from the North Carolina Department of Trans-
portation Web site, www.ncdot.org.

The town of Emerald Isle is installing wide, multi-use paths along Emerald Drive and
down Coast Guard Road. Ocean Drive, one block back from the beach, is another good biking option in Emerald Isle, with paths connecting the occasional dead ends.

Bike Rental Shops

Beach Butler Rentals 252-354-4272, 252-354-5555; www.beachbutlerrentals.com. Free
delivery within Emerald Isle.

Beach Wheels Bike Rentals 252-240-2453; www.deannahullrealty.com; 607 Atlantic
Beach Causeway, Ste. 103, Atlantic Beach 28512.

Bikes-R-In 252-393-7161, 888-393-7161; www.bikes-r-in.com; 1020 Cedar Point Blvd.,
Cedar Point 28584.

Bogue Banks Beach Gear & Linens www.boguebanksbeachgear.com; Atlantic Beach location: 252-247-4404, 866-933-4404, 407 Atlantic Beach Causeway; Emerald Isle location: 252-354-9449, 866-593-4327, 9106-C Coast Guard Road, Bell Cove Village.

Hwy 58 Bicycles @ E.I. 252-354-9006, 252-393-7762; www.hwy58bicycles.com; 8802-2
Reed Dr., Emerald Isle 28594.

Boats and Boating

The Friends of the Maritime Museum (252-728-1638; www.ncmm-friends.org) sponsor many different boating programs, including the Beaufort Oars Rowing Club, the Beaufort Oars Sliding Seat Program, and family sailing on traditional skiffs or a 30-foot keelboat available by reservation.

Kayaking and Canoeing

The Crystal Coast is richly endowed with established paddle trails. The shallow waters, many rivers, and numerous islands make for some of the best kayaking opportunities on the Eastern seaboard. The Crystal Coast Canoe and Kayak Club (www.ccckc.org) developed four comprehensive maps covering the region. Maps are available free at local outfitters or at regional visitor centers. Additional maps can be downloaded from the club's Web site. Favorite paddles include the route out to Bear Island from the Hammocks Beach State Park dock; to Carrot Island from the Beaufort waterfront; and to Sugarloaf Island from the Morehead City waterfront.

Ambitious paddlers will enjoy the **Croatan Saltwater Adventure Trail**, a 100-mile route that can take up to seven days.

Kayak Rentals

Barrier Island Kayaks 252.393.6457; www.barrierislandkayaks.com; 160 Cedar Point Blvd., Swansboro 28584.

Core Sound Kayaks 252-728-2330; www.capelookoutadventures.com; 1584 Harkers Island Rd., Beaufort 28516.

Morris Marina 252-225-4261; www.portsmouthislandfishing.com; 1000 Morris Marina Rd., Atlantic 28511. Kayak and canoe rentals.

Pirate Queen Paddling www.piratequeenpaddling.com; two locations: 252-726-1434, 1010 W. Fort Macon Rd., Atlantic Station, Atlantic Beach 28512; 252-726-1452, 707 Arendell St., Morehead City 28557.

Water Sports Outfitters 252-247-4386; www.nccoast.com/watersports; 130 Headen Rd., Salter Path 28575.

Marinas

Anchorage Marina 252-726-4423; www.anchoragemarina.net; 517 East Fort Macon Rd., Atlantic Beach 28512. Boat ramp, transient slips, ship's store.

Beaufort Docks 252-728-2503; 500 Front St., Beaufort 28516. Transient slips in the heart of historic Beaufort.

Beaufort Inn & Marina 252-728-2600, 800-726-0321; www.beaufort-inn.com; 101 Ann St., Beaufort 28516. Transient slips adjacent to a 44-room inn with exercise room and large outdoor hot tub.

Barbour's Marina 252-728-6181; www.barboursmarina.com; 1390 Harkers Island Rd., Harkers Island 28531. Boat slip rentals, boat ramp, ship's store, RV-site rentals; the **Fish Hook Grill** and **Noah's Ark** light tackle fishing charters on-site.

Calico Jack's Marina 252-728-3575; www.capelookoutferry.com/marina; 1698 Island Rd., Harkers Island 28531. Boat ramp, overnight mooring, transient slips, ship's store, tackle shop, dry stack storage.

Dudley's Marina 252-393-2204; www.dudleysmarina.com; 106 Cedar Point Blvd., Cedar

Point 28584. Family-owned marina offers dockage for transients, courtesy car, charter fishing fleet, and ship's store.

Harkers Island Fishing Center 252-728-3907; www.harkersmarina.com; 1002 Harkers Island Rd., Harkers Island 28531. Budget hotel rooms and efficiencies, transient slips, boat ramp, fly and light tackle fishing charters (252-504-3823).

Morehead City Yacht Basin 252-726-6862, 888-726-6292; www.moreheadcityyachtbasin .com; 208 Arendell St., Morehead City 28557. Transient slips in the center of downtown Morehead City.

Portside Marina & Miramar Boats 252-726-7678; www.portsidemarina.com; 209 Arendell St., Morehead City 28557. Harbor tours, **Endless Pursuit Sport Fishing** charters, boat rentals, transient slips, and ship's store.

Town Creek Marina 252-728-6111; www.towncreekmarina.com; 232 West Beaufort Rd., Beaufort 28516. Transient slips, restaurant, Tiki bar with live entertainment, and terrific sunset views.

Personal Watercraft

Personal watercraft (PWC) can currently land on the islands of Cape Lookout National Seashore at 10 designated locations. However, these regulations change frequently so check with the Park Service before launching your watercraft. Except when landing at one of these zones, PWCs must stay more than 150 feet off the shore of the National Seashore.

Powerboat and Personal Watercraft Rentals

Ahoy Boat Rentals 252-726-1900; www.ahoyboatrentals.com; 212 Atlantic Beach Causeway, Atlantic Beach 28512. Flat-bottom Carolina skiffs, pontoon boats, and kayaks for rent. Instruction available.

Causeway Marina Motorboat Rentals 252-726-6977; 300 Atlantic Beach Causeway, Atlantic Beach 28512.

Portside Marina & Miramar Boats 252-726-7678; www.portsidemarina.com; 209 Arendell St., Morehead City 28557. Powerboat and pontoon rentals.

Water Sports Outfitters 252-247-4386; www.nccoast.com/watersports; 130 Headen Rd., Salter Path 28575. Banana boat rides, kayak eco-tours, plus kayak, surfboard, and sailboat rentals.

Water Sports Rentals 252-247-7303; www.nccoast.com/watersports; 1960 Salter Path Rd., Indian Beach 28512. Personal watercraft rentals and the Dolphin Deck Tiki Bar, a cool spot to watch the sunset.

Public Boat Ramps

The area has a host of boat ramps, including many free facilities. The North Carolina Wildlife Resources Commission (www.ncwildlife.org) maintains boat ramps at several locations, including two handicapped-accessible facilities, at the Crystal Coast Visitor's Center in Morehead City and at the western end of the bridge to Harkers Island.

In Beaufort, **Curtis A. Perry Park** at the east end of Front Street has four boat ramps, plus a dock, picnic area with grills, and tennis courts. The Town Creek access (Turner St. and W. Beaufort Rd.) has two ramps, plus a boardwalk, fishing pier, and restrooms.

Free boat ramps are located throughout the Croatan National Forest. Those at Catfish Lake, Great Lake, and Oyster Point are best suited to shallow bottom boats.

Sailboat Classes

The Junior Sailing Program offered by the **North Carolina Maritime Museum** (252-728-1638; www.ncmm-friends.org), open to youth ages 8–15, hosts one- and two-week courses, mid-June through mid-August. In addition, the museum's watercraft center offers classes and adventures aboard traditional wooden craft, including spritsails and sharpies. Private lessons for adults are available by appointment.

Family Fun

Emerald Isle Parks and Recreation (252-354-6350; www.emeraldisle-nc.org; 7500 Emerald Dr.) sponsors a year-round program of family-oriented Friday Free Flicks, on the second Friday of the month at 7 PM. Admission is free; popcorn and a drink are just $1.

The Morehead City Parks and Recreation Department (252-726-5083) sponsors an eight-week Summer Camp program for children ages 3–15.

The North Carolina Aquarium at Pine Knoll Shores (252-247-4003) sponsors annual Holiday Adventure Camps at Thanksgiving and Christmas.

The North Carolina Maritime Museum (252-728-1638; www.ncmm-friends.org), offers a week-long Summer Science School for students entering grades 1–10, introducing the natural environments and maritime history of coastal North Carolina.

The Sea Of Dreams public playground, designed by kids for kids, is located at **Shevans Park** (252-726-5083; www.townofmorehead.com) at 16th and Evans Streets in Morehead City.

The Trinity Center (252-247-5600; www.trinityctr.com), located in Pine Knoll Shores, offers a Sound to Sea Summer Day Camp focused on environmental education.

Family Attractions

Carteret County Speedway & Entertainment Complex 910-326-4006; www.carteret countyspeedway.com; 1411 Corbett Ave., Swansboro 28584. NASCAR Racing Series events plus concerts.

Emerald Isle Speedway 252-354-2313; www.emeraldislespeedway.com; 9102 Coast Guard Rd., Holiday Trav-L-Park Resort, Emerald Isle 28594. Naskart racing, 28-foot climbing wall, waterslides, arcade, beach cruiser and three-wheeler rentals.

Golfin' Dolphin Family Recreation Center and Mac Daddy's Bowling Center 252-393-8131; www.thegolfindolphin.com; NC 58 & NC 24, Cape Carteret 28584. Mini-golf, driving range, go-karts, bumper boats, batting cages, bowling center with a huge video game arcade, sports bar and lounge.

Kites Unlimited & Bird Stuff 252-247-7011; www.kitesunlimitednc.com; 1010 W. Fort Macon Rd., Atlantic Station, Atlantic Beach 28512. Full-service kite store sponsors kite-flying events every Sunday morning at Fort Macon State Park.

Mystery Boat Tours 252-728-7827, 866-230-BOAT; www.mysteryboattours.com; 410 Front St., Beaufort 28516. "Pirate Treasure Hunt" cruises for kids include free photos and a visit to a deserted island.

Playland and Lighthouse Golf 252-354-6616; 204 Islander Dr., Emerald Isle 28594. Go-karts, bumper cars and boats, located next to 18 holes of mini-golf and a snack bar.

Professor Hacker's Lost Treasure Golf & Raceway 252-247-3024; 976 Salter Path Rd., Salter Path 28575. 18 holes of mini-golf, a mining train ride, go-karts, bumper boats, arcade games, ice cream parlor, and picnic area.

Water Boggan of Emerald Isle 252-354-2609; 8915 Reed Dr., Emerald Isle 28594. Cool fun for all ages with waterslides, wading pools, and tubing.

Fishing

The Crystal Coast enjoys a great location for all kinds of fishing. The Gulf Stream is just 40 miles away with its big sailfish and bluefin tuna. The inshore waters near Harkers Island are considered some of the finest on the East Coast for light tackle and fly-fishing, especially in the late fall when the giant false albacore (little tunny or "Fat Alberts") run, and in the late summer when tarpon enter the sounds.

Fishing Charters and Outfitters

See our Marinas listing for more charter fishing options.

Captain Sam Sellers 252-728-3907; Atlantic Beach 28512. President Bush's fishing guide will take you out fly-fishing for Fat Alberts and more.

Captain Stacy Fishing Center 252-247-7501, 800-533-9417; www.captstacy.com; Atlantic Beach Causeway, Atlantic Beach 28512. Captain Sonny Davis oversees a fleet of 13 charter fishing boats.

Fish Finder Light Tackle and Fly Fishing Charters 252-240-2744, 800-868-0941; www.capelookoutflyfishing.com; 601-H Atlantic Beach Causeway, Atlantic Beach 28512. Fishing writer Captain Joe Shute specializes in saltwater fly tackle.

Fisherman's Inn Charters 252-726-2273, 800-347-4571; www.fishermansinn.net; Atlantic Beach Causeway, Atlantic Beach 28512. Fishing charters, inexpensive motel rooms, and a bunkhouse are available.

Reel Screamin' Charters 910-389-0064, 910-376-0970; www.reelscreamin.com; 168 Cedar Point Blvd., Swansboro 28584. Inshore and offshore trips include free fish cleaning and pictures. Lodging available at waterfront lodge.

Fishing in Bogue Sound

Fishing Lessons

Captain Bill's Rigging School 252-230-5315. Learn to rig ballyhoo for offshore fishing.

Fishing with a Ranger 252-728-2250; www.nps.gov/calo. Free lessons at the National Seashore during the summer months. Poles and equipment provided.

The North Carolina Aquarium at Pine Knoll Shores 252-247-4003, 866-294-3477; www.ncaquariums.com. Annual Get Hooked Fishing School every March and Surf Fishing Workshop in October, plus regular classes for children and adults in nighttime pier fishing and surf fishing.

The Saltwater Fly-fishing Academy 252-745-3373; www.flyfishcarolina.com; 1313 Old Bay River Rd., Alliance 28509. Novice and intermediate lessons in basic fly-casting, as well as advanced cast and catch classes.

Fishing Piers

Oceanfront fishing piers are endangered along the Crystal Coast. Only three ocean piers still stand, and of these, one is reserved for guests of the Sheraton and the other two face constant siege from developers.

However, there is a movement afoot to save the family tradition of pier fishing, and the state recently announced plans to build a new concrete fishing pier at the former site of the Emerald Isle Pier, currently a public beach access.

In addition, there is a growing number of piers on the sounds and inlets where the public can enjoy crabbing and fishing for the many species found in these waters. Some to check out include the **Newport River Pier** on Radio Island and the **Straits Fishing Pier** on the east side of the Harkers Island bridge, both handicapped accessible; **Brices Creek** and **Haywood Landing** fishing piers, also fully accessible, in the National Croatan Forest; **Town Creek access** in Beaufort; and the **10th St. Pier** in Morehead City. Emerald Isle has a number of piers where you can cast a line, including those at **Cedar Street Soundside Park**, **Bluewater Drive**, and **Cape Emerald**.

Bogue Inlet Fishing Pier 252-354-2919; www.bogueinletpier.com; 100 Bogue Inlet Dr., Emerald Isle 28594. Emerald Isle's last pier, at 932 feet is the state's longest.

Oceanana Fishing Pier 252-726-0863; www.oceanana-resort.com; 700 E. Fort Macon Rd., Atlantic Beach 28512. The centerpiece of the family-friendly **Oceana Resort** is open to the public. A pier grill serves breakfast.

Sheraton Atlantic Beach Pier 800-624-8875; www.sheratonatlanticbeach.com; 2717 W. Fort Macon Rd., Atlantic Beach 28512. Guests at the 200-room, nine-story Sheraton enjoy fishing privileges on the property's 600-foot pier.

Headboats

Captain Stacy IV 252-247-7501, 800-533-9417; www.captstacy.com; Atlantic Beach Causeway, Atlantic Beach 28512. Full day and 24-hour bottom fishing excursions and special night voyages during the summer for sharks.

Carolina Princess 252-726-5479, 800-682-3456; www.carolinaprincess.com; 6th St. Waterfront, Morehead City 28557. Full- and half-day trips to the edge of the Gulf Stream. For hard-core fishers, the *Princess* also offers an 18-hour bottom fishing marathon, and stand-up big game sport fishing.

Continental Shelf 252-726-7454, 800-775-7450; www.continentalshelf.com; 8th St.

Waterfront, Morehead City 28557. Day-long and 24-hour trips, grill on board, fully heated and air-conditioned indoor lounge.

Mystery Boat Tours 252-728-7827, 866-230-BOAT; www.mysteryboattours.com; 410 Front St., Beaufort 28516. Reasonably priced half-day bay fishing trips, with lower rates for children and spectators. Night fishing also available.

Nancy Lee Fishing Center 252-354-3474, 910-326-4304; 128 Corbett Ave., Swansboro 28584. Two headboats, both named *Nancy Lee*, offer 5-hour fishing trips from a dock between the bridges in Swansboro.

Golf

Brandywine Bay Golf Club 252-247-2541; www.brandywinegolf.com; 224 Brandywine Blvd., Morehead City 28557. Award-winning semi-private course.

The Country Club of the Crystal Coast 252-726-1034; www.cccrystalcoast.com; 152 Oakleaf Dr., Pine Knoll Shores 28512. Semi-private course, set amid maritime forest with views of Bogue Sound. Rental clubs available.

The Golf Farm 252-223-3276; www.thegolffarminc.com; 612 Tom Mann Rd., Newport 28570. Driving range set amid old-growth pines offers lessons and clinics with LPGA pro Nina Foust. Special days for ladies, seniors, and military.

North River Club 252-728-5525; www.northrivergolfclub.com; 300 Links Dr., Beaufort 28516.Semi-private course designed by award-winning architect Bob Moore.

Paradise Point Golf Course 910-451-5445; www.mccslejeune.com; Brewster Blvd., Camp Lejeune 28547. The general public is invited to play the two 18-hole courses on the Marine Corps base just west of Swansboro, including the Gold Course designed by George Cobb, renowned architect of Augusta National and a former Marine.

Star Hill Golf Club 252-393-8111; www.starhillgolf.com; 202 Clubhouse Dr., Cape Carteret 28584. Semi-private club offers 27 holes of golf with bent grass greens.

Hiking

For more information about hiking in the area contact **Carteret County Parks and Recreation** (252-808-3301; www.ccparksrec.com). **The Croatan National Forest** (252-638-5628; www.cs.unca.edu/nfsnc; 141 E. Fisher Ave., New Bern 28560) has numerous hiking trails suitable for all abilities.

Alice Hoffman Nature Trail 252-247-4003; www.ncaquariums.com; 1 Roosevelt Boulevard, Pine Knoll Shores 28512. Half-mile trail leads along marsh to a brackish pond frequented by white ibis and other wading birds. Access is through the North Carolina Aquarium with an entrance fee.

Calico Creek Boardwalk 252-726-5083; 1700 Fisher Rd. at N. 20th St., Morehead City 28557. Easy mile-long walk with good bird-watching opportunities.

Emerald Isle Woods Park 252-354-6350; Coast Guard Rd., Emerald Isle. Nature trail leads from Coast Guard Road to Bogue Sound.

Hoop Pole Creek Clean Water Preserve Nature Trail 252-393-8185, 800-232-6210; www.nccoast.org; NC 58, Atlantic Beach. Easy half-mile walk to the shore of Bogue Sound begins in the parking lot of Atlantic Station Shopping Center.

Neusiok Trail 252-638-5628; www.cs.unca.edu/nfsnc; Croatan National Forest. The 21-mile Neusiok Trail features carnivorous plants and cypress wetlands. Camping shelters are located along the trail.

OWLS Nature Trail 252-240-1200; www.owlsonline.org; 100 Wildlife Way, Newport 28570. Half-mile loop passes 40 labeled plant species, duck pond, raptor enclosures, and interactive exhibits. Small fee.

Patsy Pond Nature Trail 252-393-8185, 800-232-6210; www.nccoast.org; 3609 NC 24, Newport 28570. The trailhead for this easy hike through longleaf pines is on NC 24 between Morehead City and Cape Carteret, across from the North Carolina Coastal Federation.

Promise Land Waterfront Walk 252-808-0440; www.downtownmoreheadcity.com. Easy 2.3-mile fitness heritage trail leads from Morehead City Park along Bogue Sound. Maps and restrooms are available at the office of the Morehead City Downtown Revitalization Association at 811 Arendell Street.

Rachel Carson National Estuarine Research Reserve Nature Trail 252-728-2170; www.ncnerr.org; Carrot Island, across from the Beaufort waterfront. Half-mile loop trail introduces this unique island habitat. Access is by boat only. Low tide is the best time to hike.

Sugarloaf Island Nature Trail 252-726-5083; www.townofmorehead.com. Located across from the Morehead City waterfront and accessible only by boat.

★ **Theodore Roosevelt Nature Trail** 252-726-3775; Theodore Roosevelt State Recreation Area, Pine Knoll Shores. The 1.5-mile trail leads through maritime forest and marsh frequented by painted buntings and songbirds. Trailhead is located in the North Carolina Aquarium's parking lot and access is free.

Tideland Trail 252-638-5628; www.cs.unca.edu/nfsnc; Cedar Point, Croatan National Forest. This designated National Recreation Trail winds through the marsh on boardwalks.

Willow Pond Trail 252-728-1500; www.coresound.com; Harkers Island. Easy trail with interpretive signs leads from the Core Sound Waterfowl Museum to the Cape Lookout National Seashore Visitor Center.

Horseback Riding

Equine Country USA 910-347-4511; www.equinecountryusa.com; 1259 McAllister Rd., Jacksonville 28540. Horse resort offers trail and carriage rides, plus lessons with English or Western tack.

Outer Banks Riding Stables 252-225-1185; 120 Driftwood Dr., Cedar Island 28520. Beach rides are offered next to the Cedar Island ferry docks.

Hunting

Regulated hunts are permitted within the Cape Lookout National Seashore (252-728-2250), the Croatan National Forest, and the Rachael Carson Reserve at designated times of the year. Contact the **North Carolina Wildlife Resources Commission** (919-733-7191; www.ncwildlife.org; 512 N. Salisbury St., Raleigh 27604) for current information.

Waterdog Guide Service 252-728-7907, 919-423-6310; www.waterdogguideservice.com; P.O. Box 2211, Beaufort 28516. Join Captains Tom Roller and Scott Crocker on a hunt for sea ducks. Your guides remain with you in the blind and cook up a filet mignon and oyster brunch.

Nature Preserves and Eco-attractions

Cape Lookout National Seashore 252-728-2250; www.nps.gov/calo; 131 Charles St., Harkers Island 28531. Established as a national seashore in 1966, Cape Lookout is a string of ever changing, uninhabited barrier islands stretching for over 50 miles from Ocracoke Inlet to Beaufort Inlet. The extensive dune system along the ocean is backed by areas of maritime forest and scrub, hosting colonies of threatened sea beach amaranth, as well as endangered sea turtle and shorebird-nesting sites. Shackleford Banks is home to a herd of wild horses, proved through DNA studies to be descended from colonial-era Spanish stock. Access to the various islands is by boat only. Exhibits at the visitor's center on Harkers Island explain the ecology and history of area. An award-winning documentary, "Ribbon of Sand," is shown daily. The **Harkers Island Visitor Center** is open daily from 9 AM to 5 PM, except Christmas and New Year's days. The **Cape Lookout Light Station Visitor Center,** accessible only by boat, is open 9 AM–5 PM, April to November. During the summer, rangers and volunteers from the North Carolina Coastal Federation (252-808-3301) lead free programs exploring barrier island ecology.

Cape Lookout Studies Program 252-504-2452; www.capelookoutstudies.org. Overnight field trips covering topics of environmental education and maritime natural history are held at the former Coast Guard Station on South Core Banks, accessible only by boat.

Cedar Island National Wildlife Refuge 252-225-2511, 252-926-4021; www.fws.gov/cedar island; 829 Lola Rd., Cedar Island 28520. This refuge, about 40 miles north of Beaufort, contains nearly 15,000 acres, about 10,000 of it brackish marsh, the rest pocosin and woodland. Kayaks or canoes are the best way to explore the black needlerush marshes, and the best time to visit is in winter when huge numbers of redhead ducks are in residence and the local mosquitoes are least fierce. A number of gated, unimproved roads can be used for hiking, biking, or horseback riding. The refuge is open during daylight hours. No camping or motorized vehicles are allowed.

Croatan National Forest 252-638-5628; www.cs.unca.edu/nfsnc; 141 E. Fisher Ave., New Bern 28560. The 160,000-acre forest is the natural habitat of carnivorous plants such as the Venus fly-trap and pitcher plant. Numerous recreational opportunities include camping, hiking, mountain biking, fishing, paddling, and swimming. The ranger station is about 10 miles south of New Bern on US 70.

★ **Hammocks Beach State Park** 910-326-4881; www.ncparks.gov; 1572 Hammocks Beach Rd., Swansboro 28584. Located just outside Swansboro, this state park includes several uninhabited islands. Bear Island, the most popular, is a barrier island about 3 miles long and less than a mile wide, with a pristine beach, extensive dune system, and pockets of maritime forest. On the beach a boardwalk connects shaded picnic pavilions and a bathhouse with restrooms, drinking water, and cold water showers. A concession stand is open Memorial Day to Labor Day, when lifeguards are also on duty. Primitive camping sites are available for a small fee year round. Kayakers can follow an established paddle trail through the marsh to the islands. The park visitor's center, with ecological exhibits, is free and open daily all year, except for Christmas Day; however, the ferry to Bear Island runs only April to October on a variable schedule. Fares are $5 roundtrip for adults, $3 for seniors ages 62 and up, and for children ages 6–12.

Outer Banks Wildlife Shelter (OWLS) 252-240-1200; www.owlsonline.org; 100 Wildlife Way, Newport 28570. Tours of this hospital that cares for injured, sick, and orphaned wild animals are offered for a small fee.

Rachel Carson National Estuarine Research Reserve 252-728-2170; www.ncnerr.org; 135 Duke Marine Lab Rd., Beaufort 28516. The complex of islands, accessible by boat located directly across Taylor's Creek from the Beaufort waterfront, includes Carrot Island, Town Marsh, Bird Shoal, and Horse Island, all less than a mile wide. Feral horses, not related to the Spanish descendants on Shackleford Banks, roam the islands. A local farmer released them here in the 1940s.

Sea Gate Woods Preserve 252-634-1927; www.coastallandtrust.org. Located about 8 miles west of Beaufort off NC 101, this unique habitat preserves one of the rarest community types, a non-riverine wet hardwood forest, and provides a critical feeding and nesting area for more than 25 species of migrant songbirds. Contact the Coastal Land Trust to join one of their guided walks.

Theodore Roosevelt State Recreation Area 252-726-3775; P.O. Box 127, Atlantic Beach 28512. Located off Roosevelt Drive in Pine Knoll Shores, this 265-acre preserve showcases dense maritime forest and marsh habitats.

University of North Carolina Institute of Marine Sciences 252-726-6841; www.marine.unc.edu; 3431 Arendell St., Morehead City 28557. Seminars on marine topics offered weekly.

Off-Road-Vehicles (ORV) and Trail Bikes

Much of the ocean beach and the unpaved sand roads on North and South Core Banks within the Cape Lookout National Seashore are open to ORV use. Vehicles can reach the seashore aboard ferries located at Davis (for North Core) and Atlantic (for South Core).

In the Croatan National Forest (252-638-5628; www.cs.unca.edu/nfsnc; 141 E. Fisher Ave., New Bern 28560), the 8-mile **Black Swamp Trail** is designed for off-road vehicles. A $5 permit, available at the district office in New Bern, is required.

Dirt trail bikes and mud racing are popular in the Camp Lejeune area west of Swansboro. Two facilities in the area are **Half Moon MX Park** (910-938-1346; www.halfmoonmxpark.com; 1037 Ramsey Rd., Jacksonville 28546) and **Jumping Run Creek Mudbog** (910-326-1511, 910-326-6999; www.promud.com; Riggs Rd., Hubert 28539).

Shelling

The Core and Shackleford Banks of Cape Lookout National Seashore are great places to find shells, including Scotch bonnets, olives, petrified clams, whelks, conchs, and Queen's helmets. Sand dollars are also abundant, especially on the small sand bar called **Sand Dollar Island** that lies between Carrot Island and Shackleford Banks. A limit of two gallons of shells a day may be taken from the national seashore. Shelling is best in the early spring.

Another popular spot for shelling is on Bear Island in Hammock Beach State Park and other islands nearby. One small island here is known for its abundance of shark's teeth.

Spas and Fitness

Cape Carteret Aquatic and Wellness 252-393-1000; www.ccaw.net; 300 Taylor Notion Rd., Cape Carteret 28584. Temporary memberships and day passes are offered at this full-service fitness facility with an indoor pool, hot tub, steam room, and fitness equipment.

Emerald Isle Parks & Recreation Community Center 252-354-6350; www.emeraldisle-nc.org; 7506 Emerald Dr., Emerald Isle 28594. Town-operated recreation center with a fully equipped exercise room and indoor gym. Nonresident passes available.

Morehead City Community Center 252-726-5083; www.townofmorehead.com; 1600
  Fisher St., Morehead City 28557. Nonresident passes available.

★ **The OC Spa** 252-247-2035, 888-237-2035; www.ocspanc.com; 1701 Salter Path Rd.,
  Indian Beach 28575. This world-class spa facility at the Ocean Club offers a wide variety
  of health and beauty treatments in an elegant and tranquil setting.

Tennis

Lighted tennis courts are found at a number of public parks on the Crystal Coast, including
Swinson and **Shevans** parks in Morehead City (252-726-5083); county parks in Smyrna
and Cedar Point (252-808-3301); and at **Blue Heron Park**, behind the Emerald Isle Town
Hall (252-354-6350).

The **Country Club of the Crystal Coast** (252-726-1034, 252-736-1134; www.boguebankscc
  .com; 152 Oakleaf Dr., Pine Knoll Shores 28512), a semi-private club, offers court time
  and lessons to nonmembers on a fee basis.

Water Sports

Parasailing

Beaufort Inlet Watersports & Parasail 252-728-7607; Beaufort waterfront.
Dragonfly Parasail 252-422-5500; 604-A Atlantic Beach Causeway, Atlantic Beach 28512.
  Located at the Anchorage Marina.

Snorkeling and Scuba

The hundreds of ships in the Graveyard of the Atlantic just offshore make this spot the
world's top destination for wreck diving. BFDC, a
club that organizes dive trips, lists over 50 frequently visited wrecks off the North Carolina coast
on its Web site, www.nc-wreckdiving.com. Water
temperatures in the area reach the low 80s, with
visibility to 100 feet during the prime season, May
to October.

Parasailing over Bogue Sound

Dive Shops and Charters

Atlantic Beach Diving Services 252-726-7258;
  www.atlanticbeachdiving.com; 713 Shepard St.,
  Morehead City 28557. Docks at the Olympus Dive
  Center.
Atlantis Charters 252-728-6244; www.atlantis
  charters.net; 145 Intracoastal Dr., Beaufort
  28516. The spacious *Atlantic IV* dive boat carries
  up to six divers in style.
Discovery Diving Company 252-728-2265;
  www.discoverydiving.com; 414 Orange St.,
  Beaufort 28516. Full-service dive shop offers
  charters on three dive boats, as well as classes
  and equipment sales and rentals. A diver's lodge
  is available for groups.

Diver Down Diving Services 252-240-2043; www.diverdownscubadiving.com; 110 Atlantic Beach Causeway, Atlantic Beach 28512. Boat docks at the Fisherman's Inn on the Causeway.

Olympus Dive Center 252-726-9432; www.olympusdiving.com; 713 Shepard St., Morehead City 28557. Two dive boats dock at the Morehead City waterfront, next to a full service dive shop. A divers' lodge nearby provides inexpensive bunkrooms.

Shore Snorkeling and Diving

A few area dive sites can be reached from shore. A Civil War–era wreck lies several yards offshore at the Iron Steamer Beach Access in Emerald Isle in about 15 feet of water. Tropical fish can be seen during the late summer months into October around the Radio Island Jetty. Dive at high-slack tide. The Railroad Bridge along US 70 on Radio Island is another spot to try a shore dive. Depths reach up to 14 feet. Diving is best at low tide.

Surfing

The Buddy Pelletier Foundation (www.buddy.pelletier.com), honoring the memory of a famous local surfer, sponsors a series of competitions and clinics every year, including "The Buddy" Longboard Classic in July.

AB Surf Shop 252-726-9382; www.absurfshop.com; 515 W. Fort Macon Rd., Atlantic Beach 28512. The Crystal Coast's oldest surf shop stocks over 300 boards, including the house brand Outer Banks Custom Shapes.

Action Surf Shop 252-240-1818; www.actionsurf.com; 5116 Hwy 70 W, Morehead City 28557. A big selection of surfboards, skateboards, and accessories.

Bert's Surf Shop www.bertsurfshop.com; 3 locations on Bogue Banks: 252-726-1730, 304 West Fort Macon Rd., Atlantic Beach 28512; 252-354-2441, 252-354-6282; 8202 Emerald Dr., Emerald Isle 28594; 300 Islander Dr., Emerald Isle 28594. The places to find Bert's logo wear.

Hot Wax Surf Shop and Surf Camp 252-354-6466; www.hotwaxsurf.com; 200 Mallard Dr., Emerald Isle 28594. Surfboard and kayak rentals, and surfing instruction, including day- and week-long camps.

Tony's Ice Cream & Surf Shop 252-240-1008; 2518 W. Fort Macon Rd., Atlantic Beach 28512. Covers the classics.

Windsurfing

Windsurfing is growing in popularity in the area. Good spots to sail include Shell Point on Harkers Island near the Cape Lookout National Seashore Visitor Center; next to the ferry docks on Cedar Island; off Radio Island near Beaufort. In Emerald Isle, try the 15th Street sound access, and 3rd Street Park for ocean launches.

Wilderness Camping

You can camp on the beach at **Cape Lookout National Seashore**. There is no trash pickup, so you must carry all your trash out. Fires are permitted below the high tide line. Camping is limited to 14 consecutive days.

Primitive camping is allowed within the **Croatan National Forest** along the Neusiok Trail, and at several primitive campgrounds.

Fourteen primitive campsites, each suitable for up to two tents and six people, are located on **Bear Island in Hammock Beach State Park**. Water and restroom facilities are available on the island except mid-November to mid-March. Fires are not permitted.

Wildlife Spotting

Bird-Watching

Birding is good year round in Carteret County, and especially fine during the winter season. The local birding group meets for monthly field trips and welcomes visitors. Contact Dennis or Robin Chadwick at 252-728-2330 or www.capelookoutadventures.com. You can download birding maps and guides for the area from the Web site of the North Carolina Birding Trail (www.ncbirdingtrail.org).

Wild ponies roam both the Shackleford Banks and Carrot Island.

Wildlife Tours and Charters

Numerous Crystal Coast companies offer dolphin watches and wild pony tours. See our Touring section for a complete listing.

The Foundation for Shackleford Horses 252-728-6308; www.shacklefordhorses.org; 306 Golden Farm Rd., Beaufort 28516. Preserves and protects the herd of wild horses found on the Banks.

SHOPPING

On Evans Street in Morehead City, and the Front Streets in both Beaufort and Swansboro, a stroll takes you past a variety of fascinating shops located in historic surroundings.

In Morehead City, you'll find seafood restaurants and galleries along the docks. On Beaufort's historic Front Street, a multitude of nautically-themed shops carry everything you might need for a life at sea, from books and charts, to Bloody Mary mix and shipboard cat and dog accessories. The equally historic Front Street in Swansboro is home to an eclectic group of gift shops specializing in one-of-a-kind items.

Shopping Centers and Malls

Morehead City in recent years has seen many "big box" stores, such as Wal-Mart and Lowe's, move in, making it the shopping destination for the region. These are concentrated in **Cypress Bay Shopping Center** at the junction of US 70 and NC 24, with Sears, Belk, and a number of specialty stores. Another center, **Pelletier Harbor Shops** at 4426 Arendell Street/US 70, has a concentration of upscale shops.

In Atlantic Beach, shopping options abound in **Atlantic Station Shopping Center** on NC 58 at MM 3, where you'll find a movie theater and several restaurants. Both sides of the causeway to Morehead City are lined with docks, water sports, and fishing tackle stores.

The **Emerald Plantation Shopping Center,** a huge collection of shops and services at 8700 Emerald Drive, MM 20 on NC 58, is an inevitable stop in Emerald Isle. There you'll find a movie theater, as well as a Food Lion supermarket, restaurants, and numerous gift, book, toy, and clothing stores that make for great browsing.

Antiques

Beaufort Antiques 252-504-3838; 126 Turner St., Beaufort 28516. Estate pieces from local and New Orleans' families, plus a selection of folk art.

Olde Towne Theatre Antiques 252-247-7478; 1308 Arendell St., Morehead City 28557. Old coins and silver are specialties.

Swansboro Antique Centre 252-393-6003; 448 Cedar Point Blvd., NC 24, Cedar Point 28584. More than two-dozen dealers.

Taylor's Creek Antiques & Collectibles 728-2275; 513 Front St., Beaufort 28516. Get a peak inside an old Beaufort mansion while shopping for vintage furniture, china, and bottles.

Books and Music

The Book Shelf 910-325-1200; www.thebookshelf.lbu.com; 208 W. Main St., Swansboro 28584. Thousands of books, new and used, in stock for adults and children.

The Book Shop 252-240-1163; Parkway Shopping Center, 4915 Arendell St., Morehead City 28557. New and used books, as well as special orders; trade-ins accepted.

City News Cards & Book Store 252-726-3314; 514 Arendell Street, Morehead City 28557. Convenient stop for regional and national newspapers, magazines, best sellers, maps, and books on local topics.

★ **Dee Gee's Gifts and Books** 252-726-3314, 800-DEE-GEES; www.deegees.com; 508 Evans St., Morehead City 28557. Established in 1934, this is one of the oldest continuously operated bookstores in the state. Selections and events showcase the many writers living in the region.

Emerald Isle Books & Toys 252-354-5323; www.emeraldislebooks.com; 8700 Emerald Dr., Emerald Plantation Shopping Center, Emerald Isle 28594. Family-run independent bookshop sponsors book clubs for children and adults, besides stocking a wide variety of toys, pirate loot, and bath items.

★ **Rocking Chair Bookstore** 252-728-2671; www.rockingchairbookstore.com; 400 Front St., Somerset Square, Beaufort 28516. Independent bookstore on the Beaufort waterfront is owned by writers and specializes in books by North Carolina authors, collectible books, and local interest titles for children and adults.

Clothing

★ **The Bag Lady** 252-728-4200; www.bagladyofbeaufort.com; 413 Front St., Beaufort 28516. Browse Suzie the Bag Lady's huge collection of collectible handbags, ranging from clever to outrageous, or pick up one of Suzie's handmade Sun Totes.

Golden Gull 252-726-2333; 4426 Arendell St., US 70, Morehead City 28557. A favorite for stylish women's apparel since 1976.

Crafts

★ **Harvey & Sons Net & Twine** 252-729-1731; www.harveyandsons.com; 804 US 70, Davis 28524. Visit the shop where Nicky Harvey makes his ingenious crab pot Christmas trees—the must-have souvenir of a trip to the Crystal Coast.

Russell's Olde Tyme Shoppe 910-326-3790; 116 Front St., Swansboro 28584. Marvelous hand-painted objects for every room in the house.

Waterfront Junction 252-726-6283; www.waterfrontjunction.com; 412 Evans St., Morehead City 28557. Supplies for all kinds of needlework and other crafts, plus nautically themed gifts.

Gifts

Captain Henry's Gift Store 252-728-7316; www.capthenrysgiftshop.com; 1341 Island Rd., Harkers Island 28531. A wide variety of gifts and collectibles, including locally carved decoys.

The Old Beaufort Shop 252-728-5225; www.beauforthistoricsite.org; 130 Turner St., Beaufort 28516. Historically related gifts and toys as well as books on local and regional history.

Silver Thimble Gifts & Music 910-326-8558; www.silverthimblegifts.com; 137 Front St., Swansboro 28584. Silver, pewter, and china thimbles and other sewing accessories and gifts, Celtic music, and original folk art.

★ **Yanamama's Memorabilia Shoppe** 910-326-9052, 866-766-6845; www.yanamamas .com; 119 Front St., Swansboro 28584. Fifties memorabilia for fans of Elvis, Marilyn, Betty Boop, and more.

Shops and restaurants along Beaufort's Front Street face directly on the harbor.

Jewelry

Concepts Jewelry Factory Outlet Store 252-247-5244, 800-926-3277; www.concepts jewelry.com; 1000 Arendell St., Morehead City 28557. Earrings guaranteed not to irritate sensitive ears at discount prices.

Stampers Jewelers 252-728-4967; 435 Front St., Beaufort 28516. Full-service jeweler, serving Beaufort since 1955, but still trendy.

Kitchenware and Home Décor

The Quilt Cottage 910-325-1125; 147 Front St., Swansboro 28584. Handmade quilts for bed and baby, plus rugs, linens, and antiques.

Tierra Fina 252-504-2789; 877-504-2789; www.tierrafinanc.com; 119 Turner St., Beaufort 28516. Bright and bold designs, including popular ceramic house number tiles.

Sporting Goods and Clothing

Boater's World/ Outer Banks Outfitters Marine Center 252-240-0055, 877-690-0004; www.outerbanksoutfitters.com; NC 58, Atlantic Station, Atlantic Beach 28512. Every sort of gear for water activities from GPS units to rubber boots.

Captain Joe Shute's Bait & Tackle 252-240-2744, 800-868-0941; www.captjoes.com; 601-H Atlantic Beach Causeway, Atlantic Beach 28512. Full line of equipment, including Captain Joe's Custom Rods. Charters available.

EJW Outdoors 252-247-4725; www.ejwoutdoors.com; 4667 Arendell St., Morehead City 28557. Third generation, family operated hunting, fishing, and biking store also rents bikes. Charters available.

Tea with the Queen, an annual summer event at the Waterside Theatre Photo by Caitlin Snead

9

INFORMATION

Practical Matters

EMERGENCY SERVICES

As in most of the United States, you should dial 911 in an emergency situation for fire, police, or ambulance assistance.

Crisis Assistance

Poison Control 800-222-1222
Carteret County Crisis Hotline 252-725-4040
Dare County Crisis Hotline 252-473-3366
North Carolina State Police 800-441-6127
U.S. Coast Guard 24-Hour Search and Rescue . . 252-247-4570

Disaster/Hurricane Preparedness

Carteret County Emergency Management 252-728-8470
Currituck County Emergency Management 252-232-2115
Dare County Emergency Management 252-475-5655
Hyde County Emergency Management 252-926-4372

AREA INFORMATION

Area Codes

Area code 252 is used from the Virginia border south to Onslow County. In Swansboro, the gateway to Onslow, the area code changes to 910.

County Governments

Carteret County 252-728-8450; www.carteretcountygov.org; Courthouse Square, Beaufort 28516.

Currituck County 252-232-2075; www.currituckgovernment.com; 153 Courthouse Rd., Currituck 28584.

Dare County 252-475-5000; Hatteras Island Complex, 252-475-5878; www.co.dare.nc.us; 962 Marshall C. Collins Dr., Manteo 27954.

Hyde County (Ocracoke) 252-926-9171; 888-493-3826; www.hydecounty.org; 30 Oyster Creek Rd., Swan Quarter 27885.

Onslow County 910-347-4717; www.onslowcountync.gov; 118 Old Bridge St., Jacksonville 28540.

Town Governments

Contact town offices for invaluable information on recycling, beach access, fireworks and fire regulations, and current rules for driving, liquor, and pets on the beach, as well as up-to-the-minute event calendars and recreational opportunities. Several of the town office buildings also house impressive collections by local artists.

Atlantic Beach 252-726-2121; www.atlanticbeach-nc.com; 125 W. Ft. Macon Rd., Atlantic Beach 28512.

Beaufort 252-728-2141; www.beaufortnc.org; 215 Pollock St., Beaufort 28516.

Cape Carteret 252-393-8483; 102 Dolphin St., Cape Carteret 28584.

Cedar Point 252-393-7898; www.cedarpointnc.org; 427 Sherwood Ave., Cedar Point 28584.

Duck 252-255-1234; www.townofduck.com; 1240 Duck Rd., Duck 27949.

Emerald Isle 252-354-3424; www.emeraldisle-nc.org; 7500 Emerald Dr., Emerald Isle 28594.

Indian Beach 252-247-3344; www.indianbeach.org; P.O. Box 306, Indian Beach 28575.

Kill Devil Hills 252-480-4000; www.kdhnc.com; 102 Town Hall Dr., Kill Devil Hills 27948.

Kitty Hawk 252-261-3552; www.townofkittyhawk.org; 101 Veterans Memorial Dr., Kitty Hawk 27949.

Manteo 252-473-2133; www.townofmanteo.com; 407 Budleigh St., Manteo 27954.

Morehead City 252-726-6848; www.townofmorehead.com; 706 Arendell St., Morehead City 28557.

Nags Head 252-441-5508; www.townofnagshead.net; 5401 S. Croatan Highway, Nags Head 27959.

Newport 252-223-4749; www.townofnewport.com; P.O. Box 1869, 200 Howard Blvd., Newport 28570.

Pine Knoll Shores 252-247-4353; www.townofpks.com; 100 Municipal Circle, Pine Knoll Shores 28512.

Southern Shores 252-261-2394; www.southernshores.org; 5375 N. Virginia Dare Trail, Southern Shores 27949.

Swansboro 910-326-4428; www.swansboro-nc.org; 502 Church St., Swansboro 28584.

Chambers of Commerce and Tourism Bureaus

Carteret County Chamber of Commerce 252-726-6350, 800-622-6278; www.nccoastchamber.com; 801 Arendell St., Morehead City 28557.

Carteret County Tourism Development Authority 252-726-8148, 877-206-0929; www.crystalcoastnc.org; 3409 Arendell St., Morehead City 28557.

Currituck Chamber of Commerce 252-453-9497; www.currituckchamber.org; P.O. Box 1160, Grandy 27939.

Currituck Outer Banks Visitor Center 252-453-9612; www.visitcurrituck.com; 500 Hunt Club Dr., Corolla 27927.

Hyde County Chamber of Commerce 252-926-9171, 888-493-3826; www.hydecounty .org; P.O. Box 178, Swan Quarter 27885.

Ocracoke Civic and Business Association 252-928-6711; www.ocracokevillage.com.

Onslow County Tourism 800-932-2144; www.onslowcountytourism.com.

Outer Banks Chamber of Commerce 252-441-8144; www.outerbankschamber.com; 101 Town Hall Dr., Kill Devil Hills 27948.

Outer Banks Tourist Bureau (Dare County) 252-473-2138, 877-629-4386; www.outerbanks.org; 1 Visitors Center Circle, Manteo 27954.

Swansboro Area Chamber of Commerce 910-326-1174; www.swansboronncchamber.com; 774C W. Corbett Ave., Swansboro, NC 28584.

Visit NC 919-733-8372, 800-VISIT NC; www.visitnc.com; in the British isles: www.north carolinatravel.co.uk; in Germany: www.northcarolinatravel.de.

CLIMATE, SEASONS, WHAT TO WEAR

High season on the Outer Banks has traditionally been Memorial Day to Labor Day. However, shoulder seasons are sometimes carved out of this period, and realtors each seem to have their own formula to determine the price of rental properties. While the Banks continue to host the most family groups during the summer, other seasons are becoming more popular and businesses are increasingly open all year.

The coast of North Carolina generally enjoys a temperate climate with very few days on which the temperature goes below freezing. In the Nags Head area, January is the coldest month, with average temperatures ranging from 36 degrees to 51 degrees. July is the hottest month, with lows averaging 72 degrees and highs, 86 degrees. The water is warmest in August, when it reaches 80 degrees. However, a steady wind averaging over 10 mph blows all year, cooling even the warmest days and making cold weather very raw. August is generally the wettest month, when thunderstorms frequently develop in the afternoons.

The Crystal Coast faces south and is generally a little warmer in the summer, when average July temperatures reach 89 degrees.

Some of the best—and worst—weather is experienced in the spring and fall. Hurricane season begins before summer, on June 1. Late summer and fall are prime hurricane season, and storms can approach very quickly. Even outside of the official hurricane season, north-easters and other big storms can have devastating effects on the coast. The Ash Wednesday Storm and the Thanksgiving Storm live on in local lore. You'll find televisions tuned to the Weather Channel everywhere; it's the most watched station on the Outer Banks.

Whatever the season, dress is relentlessly casual on the coast, and the need for a suit jacket is very rare. Most people get comfortable in shorts and sandals in summer, and bundle up when winter comes. A windbreaker is a must all year, and rain gear can come in handy. Closed toed, rubber soled shoes are safest on boats. Hats, sunglasses, and plenty of sunscreen and bug repellent make vacations trouble free, but can be bought at numerous spots if you forget them.

HOSPITALS AND CLINICS

Carteret General Hospital 252-808-6000; www.ccgh.org; 3500 Arendell St., Morehead City 28557. A full-service hospital offering in-patient, out-patient, and emergency services 24-hours a day all year.

Eastern Carteret Medical Center 252-225-1134; US 70, Sealevel 28577. Down East clinic associated with Carteret General.

HealthEast Family Care Avon 252-986-2756; 40894 NC 12, Avon 27915. Center associated with the Outer Banks Hospital offers family medicine by appointment, with a doctor on call 24-hours.

HealthEast Family Care Hatteras 252-986-2756; 57635 NC 12, Hatteras 27943. Associated with the Outer Banks Hospital, this center offers comprehensive care for children and adults, with 24-hour on-call emergency services.

HealthEast Family Care Nags Head 252-441-3177; 4810 S. Croatan Hwy., Nags Head 27959. Located behind the Outer Banks Hospital, this clinic offers primary care for adults and children.

Island Medical Center 252-473-2500; www.albemarlehealth.org; 715 N. US 64-264 Business, Manteo 27954. A family practice associated with Albemarle Hospital in Elizabeth City.

Ocracoke Health Center 252-928-1511, after hours: 252-928-7425(SICK); 305 Back Rd., Ocracoke 27960.

Outer Banks Center for Women 252-449-2100; 4917 S. Croatan Hwy., US 158, MP 14, Nags Head 27959.

The Outer Banks Hospital 252-449-4500, 877-359-9179; www.theouterbankshospital.com; 4800 S. Croatan Hwy., US 158, MP 14, Nags Head 27959. A full-service hospital offering in-patient, out-patient, and emergency services 24-hours a day all year.

Outer Banks Urgent Care Center 252-449-4700; 4923 S. Croatan Hwy, Nags Head 27959. Extended hours are available for walk-ins.

Regional Medical Center 252-255-6000; www.albemarlehealth.org; 5200 N. Croatan Hwy., US 158, MP 1.5, Kitty Hawk 27949. Associated with Albemarle Hospital in Elizabeth City, this center offers out-patient surgery, diagnostic imaging and testing, and the services of doctors representing some 20 specialties.

Tarheel Internal Medicine Associates 252-453-8616; 1123 Ocean Trail, Corolla 27927. Family medicine year round. Walk-ins welcome.

Virginia Dare Women's Center 252-441-2144; 2518 S. Croatan Hwy., US 158, MP 10.5, Nags Head 27959.

BEACH REGULATIONS

North Carolina law says that all the sand below the high-tide line is public property. However you must enter the beach from a public access, not across private property.

Beach Driving

Driving on the beach is a treasured local tradition, and one that has come under increasing pressure due to concern for beach nesting birds and sea turtles. When driving on beaches, especially in the National Seashores, it is vital to observe closings established to protect certain areas.

Driving on the beaches of the National Seashores is especially changeable, with many environmental groups seeking to ban driving completely and locals fighting to maintain their traditional rights. Check with the local park visitor centers to find out areas that are currently available for vehicle and pedestrian access.

Many, although not all, of the communities along the North Carolina coast allow driving on the beach within their townships at certain times of the year. Usually this is October to

March, but there are many variations. Some towns are now asking drivers to buy a permit to drive on the beach. Check the town Web sites listed above to find out the local laws.

When driving on the beach, proceed with extreme caution and follow regular road rules, passing on the right, keeping to the left, wearing seat belts, et cetera. Speed limits are usually 15 miles per hour.

To avoid getting stuck in the sand, lower the air pressure in your tires to about 20 pounds and stick to the hard packed sand below the high-tide line. Enter only at beach access ramps and stay off the dunes if you want to stay out of trouble.

Beach Fires

While the idea of a campfire on the beach during the evening is an appealing idea, many communities along the coast do not permit them, or require that you apply in advance for a permit, usually at the local fire station. Check individual town Web sites for current information and requirements.

Bonfires are permitted in the National Seashores if built below the high-tide line.

Take special precautions when driving in sand.

You should plan to bring your own wood for your fire, as it is illegal to cut any dead trees or use ship timbers that may have washed up on the shore. A fire should be extinguished with water, not sand, so it will not continue to smolder.

FIREWORKS

After a series of near catastrophic brush fires, all fireworks, including firecrackers, torpedoes, sky rockets, and sparklers, have been banned in Dare County, which includes the area from Duck to Hatteras. Ocracoke and Corolla also ban the private use of fireworks. Fines can range as high as $1,000 and are strictly enforced.

Regulations for fireworks on the Crystal Coast vary. Check with each township to discover current laws. In general, the State of North Carolina prohibits the possession of any pyrotechnics that launch or propel into the air, or that explode, making a sound, or "report." Fireworks are also prohibited in all national parks and seashores.

LIQUOR

Bottles of liquor are only available in North Carolina at State ABC Stores. The Web site www .ncabc.com has a complete listing of stores and their hours of operation. Generally, the ABC stores are open Monday to Saturday, 10 AM to 9 PM, and closed on Sunday. While some towns along the coast still don't allow liquor by the drink, beer and wine are universally available at restaurants, groceries, and convenience stores until 2 AM and after 12 noon on Sundays.

PETS

Rules governing pets on the beach vary widely and by season. In general, pets must be leashed. Several communities don't allow pets on the beach at all during the summer season. Again, check each town's Web site for its current rules. Pets on 6-foot leashes or caged are permitted within the national seashores, except at designated swimming beaches. Guide dogs may remain with their owners at all times.

RECOMMENDED READING

The Eastern North Carolina Digital Library contains hundreds of works of fiction and non-fiction, much of it from the 1800s and early 1900s, as well as museum artifacts, maps, and other educational material available free online. You can browse the collection at digital .lib.ecu.edu.

Biographies, Diaries, Oral History and Folklore

Barefoot, Daniel W. *Seaside Spectres: North Carolina's Haunted Hundred, #1*. Winston-Salem, NC: John F. Blair, 2002.

Brown, William K. *Mullet Roar and Other Stories by an Outerbanker*. Manteo: Maritime Kids' Quest Press, 2007. Written by the founder of the Oregon Inlet Fishing Center and the son of Aycock Brown, these fascinating stories of fishing and hunting in the "old days" are illustrated by the author's original artwork.

Carroll, Rick, and Marcie Carroll. *Beaufort-by-the-Sea: Journey Back in Time, The Illustrated Guide to Beaufort, N.C.* Beaufort, NC: Fish Towne Press, 2006.

Mallison, Fred M. *To Ocracoke! Boyhood Summers on the Outer Banks*. Columbia, NC: Sweet Bay Tree Books, 2000.

Mercier, Judith D. *Duck: An Outer Banks Village*. Winston-Salem, NC: John F. Blair, 2001.

Morris, Travis. *Duck Hunting on Currituck Sound: Tales from a Native Gunner*. Charleston, SC: History Press, 2006.

———. *Currituck Memories and Adventures: More Tales from a Native Gunner*. Charleston, SC: History Press, 2007.

Roundtree, Susan Byrum. *Nags Headers*. Winston-Salem, NC: John F. Blair, 2001. Oral histories from Nags Head's oldest families.

Tate, Suzanne. *Bring Me Duck: Folktales and Anecdotes from Duck, N.C. (as told by Ruth Tate)*. Nags Head, NC: Nags Head Art, 1986. Includes many photos and a glossary of local terms.

———. *Memories of Manteo and Roanoke Island, N.C. (as told by the late Cora Mae Basnight)*. Nags Head, NC: Nags Head Art, 1988. Oral history recalls details of Basnight's 25 years performing in *The Lost Colony*.

———. *Whalehead; Tales of Corolla, N.C. (as told by Norris Austin)*. Nags Head, NC: Nags Head Art, 1987. Stories from Corolla's oldest living resident and postmaster for 28 years.

Whedbee, Charles Harry. *Pirates, Ghosts, and Coastal Lore: The Best of Judge Whedbee*. Winston-Salem, NC: John F. Blair, 2004.

Children's Books

Bliven, Jeremy. *Captain Stumpy the Pirate Cat*. Kitty Hawk, NC: Outer Banks Press, 2004.

Garber, Pat. *Little Sea Horse and the Story of the Ocracoke Ponies*. Ocracoke, NC: Ocracoke Preservation Society, 2007.

Harrington, C. S. *The Marsh Runners*. Victoria, BC: Trafford, 2004. Two pre-teens face a stormy summer on the Outer Banks in the 1920s. Based on historical fact and legends.

Lewis, J. Patrick. *Blackbeard the Pirate King*. Washington, DC: National Geographic Society, 2006. Pirate poems and illustrations for grades 4–7.

Runyon, Anne Marshall. *The Sheltering Cedar*. Washington, DC: Portal Press, 2007. A Christmas Eve storm threatens the wildlife on Ocracoke. For ages 4–8.

Taylor, Theodore. *Teetoncey: Cape Hatteras Trilogy, #1*. 1st Odyssey Classics edition. Orlando: Harcourt, 2004. Series aimed at ages 9–12 follows the adventures of an English girl shipwrecked in 1898.

Weatherford, Carole B. *Sink or Swim: African-American Lifesavers of the Outer Banks*. Wilmington, NC: Coastal Carolina Press, 1999. The story of the heroes of the Pea Island Life Saving Station told for young readers.

Cookbooks

Carteret County Home Extension. *Seafood Cookery from Carteret County Kitchens*. New Bern, NC: Owen G. Dunn, 1975.

Davis, Nancy, and Kathy Heart. *Coastal Carolina Cooking*. Chapel Hill, NC: University of North Carolina Press, 1986. Recipes collected by North Carolina's Sea Grant program.

Franklin Memorial Methodist Church. *The Promise Land Cookbook*. Morehead City, NC: Carteret County Historical Association. Old-time Down East recipes.

Harkers Island United Methodist Women. *Island Born and Bred: A Collection of Harkers Island Food, Fun, Fact and Fiction*. New Bern, NC: O. G. Dunn, 1987.

Morehead City Sesquicentennial. *A Little Taste of Heaven Since 1857: Morehead City Heritage Cookbook*. Morehead City, NC: Coastlore, 2007. Traditional recipes are interspersed with bits of Morehead City history.

St. Paul's Episcopal Church Women. *Let Us Keep the Feast in Historic Beaufort*. Beaufort, NC: Wimmer Cookbooks, 2002.

Toth, Ruth Goins. *Café Atlantic Cook Book*. Ocracoke, NC: R.G. Toth, 2006.

Weigand, Elizabeth. *The Outer Banks Cookbook: Recipes and Traditions from North Carolina's Barrier Islands*. Guilford, CT: Globe Pequot Press 2007.

Cultural Studies

Beal, Candy, and Carmine Prioli, eds. *Life at the Edge of the Sea; Essays on North Carolina's Coast and Coastal Culture*. Wilmington, NC: Coastal Carolina Press, 2002.

Bishir, Catherine. *Unpainted Aristocracy: The Beach Cottages of Old Nags Head*. Raleigh, NC: Division of Archives and History, North Carolina Department of Cultural Resources, 1978. .

Carlson, Tom. *Hatteras Blues: A Story from the Edge of America*. Chapel Hill, NC: University of North Carolina Press, 2005. Memoirs of deepwater fishing and the families of Hatteras.

Conoley, Neal. *Waterfowl Heritage: North Carolina Decoys and Gunning Lore*. Wendell, NC: Webfoot, 1982.

Garrity-Blake, Barbara. *The Fish Factory: Work and Meaning for the Black and White Fisherman of the Menhaden Industry*. Knoxville, TN: University of Tennessee Press, 2005.

Maiolo, John. *Hard Times and a Nickel Bucket: Struggle and Survival in North Carolina's Shrimp Industry*. Chapel Hill, NC: Chapel Hill Press, 2004.

McNaughton, Marimar. *Outer Banks Architecture: An Anthology of Outposts, Lodges & Cottages*. Winston-Salem, NC: John F. Blair, 2000.

Wolfram, Walt, and Natalie Schilling-Estes. *Hoi Toide on the Outer Banks: The Story of the Ocracoke Brogue*. Chapel Hill, NC: The University of North Carolina Press, 1997.

Fiction

Duncan, Pamela. *The Big Beautiful*. New York: Dial Press, 2007. Romantic comedy set in Salter Path.

Egghart, Chris. *The Tannhauser Contingency*. Riverdale, GA: Riverdale Electronic Books, 2006. Suspense thriller centers on the discovery of a sunken German U-boat.

Fletcher, Inglis. *Men of Albemarle*. New York: Bantam Books, 1970. Prolific author Inglis Fletcher wrote a dozen meticulously researched historical novels covering 200 years of North Carolina history (1585–1789).

Mills, Wendy Howell. *Death of a Mermaid: A Callie McKinley Outer Banks Mystery*. Wilmington, NC: Coastal Carolina Press, 2002.

Morris, Bill. *Saltwater Cowboys*. Wilmington, NC: Coastal Carolina Press, 2004. A fun fish tale set on the Crystal Coast.

Siddons, Anne Rivers. *Outer Banks*. New York: HarperCollins Publishers, 1992. This best-seller introduced the Unpainted Aristocracy to the world.

Sparks, Nicolas. *Nights in Rodanthe*. New York: Grand Central Publishing, 2003. Also a 2008 film from Warner Bros. starring Richard Gere and Diane Lane.

Birds have the right of way along most beaches.

History

Balance, Alton. *Ocracokers*. Chapel Hill, NC: The University of North Carolina Press, 1989. Written by an island native.

Butler, Lindley S. *Pirates, Privateers, and Rebel Raiders of the Carolina Coast*. Chapel Hill, NC: University of North Carolina Press, 2000.

Carr, Dawson. *Cape Hatteras Lighthouse: Sentinel of the Shoals*. Chapel Hill, NC: University of North Carolina Press, 2000. New edition details the effort to move the lighthouse inland.

Cheney, Richard L., III, *Old Coast Guard Stations, North Carolina: Currituck Beach to Cape Fear*. Richmond, VA: Dietz Press, 2004.

Click, Patricia. *Time Full of Trial: The Roanoke Island Freedmen's Colony 1862–1867*. Chapel Hill, NC: University of North Carolina Press, 2001.

Crouch, Tom. *The Bishop's Boys: A Life of Wilbur and Orville Wright*. New York: W.W. Norton, 1989.

Davis, Susan Joy. *The Whalehead Club: Reflections Of Currituck Heritage*. Virginia Beach: Donning Company Publishers, 2004.

Duffus, Kevin. *The Last Days of Black Beard the Pirate: Within Every Legend Lies a Grain of Truth*. Raleigh, NC: Looking Glass Productions, 2008. New revelations about Blackbeard, researched by a leading history detective.

———. *The Lost Light: The Mystery of the Missing Cape Hatteras Fresnel Lens*. Raleigh, NC: Looking Glass Productions, 2003. A factual account of how the author found the lens lost in the Civil War, now in the Graveyard of the Atlantic Museum.

Hickam, Homer. *Torpedo Junction: U-Boat War Off America's East Coast, 1942*. Annapolis, MD: US Naval Institute Press, April 1996.

houston, lebame, and Barbara Hird, eds. *Roanoke Revisited: The Story of the First English Settlements in the New World and the Fabled Lost Colony of Roanoke Island*. Manteo, NC: Penny Books, 1997. houston and Hird, the team behind the successful Elizabeth R theatrical troupe, translate the documents relating to the Lost Colony into modern English.

Hudson, Marjorie. *A Journey Into History, Memory, and the Fate of America's First English Child*. Winston-Salem, NC: Press 53, www.searchingforvirginiadare.com, 2007

Mallison, Fred M. *The Civil War on the Outer Banks: A History of the Late Rebellion Along the Coast of North Carolina from Carteret to Currituck*. Jefferson, NC: McFarland & Company, 2005.

Mobley, Joe A. *Ship Ashore! The U.S. Lifesavers of Coastal North Carolina*. Raleigh, NC: Division of Archives and History, North Carolina Department of Cultural Resources, 1994.

Noble, Dennis L. *That Others Might Live: The U.S. Life-Saving Service, 1878–1915*. Annapolis, MD: Naval Institute Press, 1994.

Pullen, Drew. *The Civil War in New Bern & Fort Macon, North Carolina*. Mt. Holly, NJ: Aerial Perspective, 2008.

———. *Portrait of the Past: The Civil War on Hatteras Island, North Carolina*. Mt. Holly, NJ: Aerial Perspective, 2001.

———. *Portrait of the Past: The Civil War on Roanoke Island North Carolina*. Mt. Holly, NJ: Aerial Perspective, 2002.

Quinn, David Beers. *Set Fair for Roanoke: Voyages and Colonies, 1584–1606*. Chapel Hill, NC: University of North Carolina Press, 1985. Sir Walter Raleigh's other expeditions and attempts colonize the New World.

Simpson, Bland. *Ghost Ship of Diamond Shoals: The Mystery of the Carroll A. Deering*. Chapel Hill, NC: University of North Carolina Press, 2005.

Stick, David, ed. *An Outer Banks Reader*. Chapel Hill, NC: University of North Carolina Press, 1998. Excerpts from nearly five centuries of writings about the region, selected by the Banks' top scholar.

———. *Dare County: A History*. Raleigh, NC: Division of Archives and History, North Carolina Dept. of Cultural Resources, 1970.

———. *Graveyard of the Atlantic: Shipwrecks of the North Carolina Coast*. Chapel Hill, NC: University of North Carolina Press, 1952.

———. *The Outer Banks of North Carolina, 1584–1958*. Chapel Hill, NC: University of North Carolina Press, 1990. Originally published in the 1950s, this landmark work remains a best seller and the definitive work on the region's history.

———. *Roanoke Island: The Beginnings of English America*. Chapel Hill, NC: University of North Carolina Press, 1983.

Wright, David, and David Zoby. *Fire on the Beach: Recovering the Lost Story of Richard Etheridge and the Pea Island Lifesavers*. New York: Oxford University Press, USA, 2002. The bravery and exploits of the first all-black unit of the Life Saving Service.

Music CDs

Darden, Mark Fielding. *Will This Town Survive? Songs and Stories from Salter Path*. Salter Path Records, www.salterpathnc.com, 2004. CD of songs comes with a 60-page book recounting the fast disappearing life of one of the Banks' original fishing villages.

Golden, John. *Hatteras Memories*, Soundside Records, 2005.

Molasses Creek, *Ocracoke Island*, Soundside Records, 2008 (remastered). New version of the original 1993 recording by the group that is the guiding force behind the folk music revival on Ocracoke, with seven other CDs to date.

Parsons, Roy, *Songs and Tales from Ocracoke Island*, Soundside Records, 1999. An Ocracoke original.

Temple, Rob, *The Rumgagger*, 2006. Sea stories, pirate poetry, and nautical tunes from the captain of the schooner *Windfall*.

Various artists, *CoastalFolk*, Soundside Records, 2002.

———. *Ocrafolk 3*, Soundside Records, 2006.

Natural History

Alexander, John, and James Lazell. *Ribbon of Sand: The Amazing Convergence of the Ocean & the Outer Banks*. Chapel Hill, NC: University of North Carolina Press, 2000.

Barnes, Jay. *North Carolina's Hurricane History*. Chapel Hill, NC: University of North Carolina Press, 2001.

Cleary, William J., and Tara P. Marden. *Shifting Shorelines: A Pictorial Atlas of North Carolina Inlets*. Raleigh, NC: NC Sea Grant, 1999.

Daniels, Jaret C. *Butterflies of the Carolinas Field Guide*. Cambridge, MN: Adventure Publications, 2003.

DeBlieu, Jan. *Hatteras Journal*. Winston-Salem, NC: John F. Blair, 1998. A naturalist writes evocatively about the barrier island ecology.

Frankenberg, Dirk. *The Nature of the Outer Banks: Environmental Processes, Field Sites, and Development Issues, Corolla to Ocracoke*. Chapel Hill, NC: University of North Carolina Press, 1995.

Fussell, John O. *A Birder's Guide to Coastal North Carolina*. Chapel Hill, NC: University of North Carolina Press, 1994.

Gerber, Pat. *Ocracoke Odyssey: A Naturalist's Reflections on her Home by the Sea*. Winston-Salem, NC: John F. Blair, 1999.

Houser, Lynn. Edited by Jeannie Norris. *Seashells of North Carolina*. Raleigh, NC: NC Sea Grant, 2000.

Kaufman, Wallace. *The Beaches Are Moving: The Drowning of America's Shoreline*. Durham, NC: Duke University Press, 1983.

Kraus, E. Jean Wilson, and Sarah Friday, eds. *Guide to Ocean Dune Plants Common to North Carolina*. Chapel Hill, NC: University of North Carolina Press, 1988.

Meyer, Peter K. *Nature Guide to the Carolina Coast: Common Birds, Crabs, Shells, Fish, and Other Entities of the Coastal Environment*. Wilmington, NC: Avian-Cetacean Press, 1991.

Pilkey, Orrin H. *How to Read a North Carolina Beach: Bubble Holes, Barking Sands, and Rippled Runnels*. Chapel Hill, NC: University of North Carolina Press, 2004

Prioli, Carmine. *The Wild Horses of Shackleford Banks*. Winston-Salem, NC: John F. Blair, 2007.

Waugaman, Sandra. *Mustangs on the Beach: The Wild Horses of Currituck*. Corolla, NC: Carova Beach Volunteer Fire Dept. Auxiliary, 2005.

Numerous festivals attract kites both big and small.

Photographic Studies and Art Books

Alterman, Steve, and Tricia Ibelli. *Outer Banks Wild: A Winged Horse Extravaganza Pictorial. Volumes I & II.* Kitty Hawk, NC: Outer Banks Press, 2003, 2004. Color photographs of the winged horses on display during the Centennial of Flight.

Shelton-Roberts, Cheryl, and Bruce Roberts. *North Carolina Lighthouses: A Tribute of History and Hope.* Greensboro, NC: Our State Books, 2004.

Stick, David. Photos by Aycock Brown & Walter V. Gresham III. *Ash Wednesday Storm, March 7, 1962.* Kill Devil Hills, NC: Gresham Publications, 1987.

Recreation and Travel

Goldstein, Robert J. *Coastal Fishing in the Carolinas: From Surf, Pier, & Jetty.* Winston-Salem: John F. Blair, 2000.

Harrison, Molly, and Meredith Vaccaro. *Corolla: Then and Now.* Manteo, NC, One Boat Guides, 2006. Walking tour and old photos of Corolla Village, plus Norris Austin's Corolla memories.

———. *Roanoke Island: Then and Now.* Manteo, NC, One Boat Guides, 2004. Walking tour with map and many old photos of Manteo.

Malat, Joe. *Let's Go Crabbing!* York, PA: Wellspring, 2004.

———. *Pier Fishing: How to Catch More Fish from Atlantic and Gulf Coast Piers.* York, PA: Wellspring, 1999.

———. *Surf Fishing.* York, PA: Wellspring, 1993.

Malec, Pam. *Guide to Sea Kayaking in North Carolina: The Best Trips from Currituck to Cape Fear.* Guilford, CT: Globe Pequot, 2001.

Marsh, Mike. *Inshore Angler: Coastal Carolina's Small Boat Fishing Guide.* Wilmington, NC: Coastal Carolina Press, 2000.

———. *Offshore Angler: Carolina's Mackerel Boat Fishing Guide.* Wilmington, NC: Coastal Carolina Press, 2004.

Roundtree, Susan Byrum, and Meredith Vaccaro. *Nags Head: Then and Now*. Manteo, NC, One Boat Guides, 2004. Walking tour of the Unpainted Aristocracy district.

Scarborough, Jenny. *Ocracoke Walking Tour & Guide Book*. Manteo, NC, One Boat Guides, 2005. Tour of Ocracoke Village with many old photos.

Simpson, Bland. *The Inner Islands: A Carolinian's Sound Country Chronicle*. Chapel Hill, NC: University of North Carolina Press, 2006. A guide to the often forgotten islands of the North Carolina sounds.

Young, Claiborne S. *Cruising Guide to Coastal North Carolina*. Winston-Salem, NC: John F. Blair, 2005. An invaluable guide for boaters.

Media

Newspapers and Magazines

Carolina Currents: The North and South Carolina Sailor's Magazine 252-745-6507; www.carolinacurrents.com; P.O. Box 1090, Oriental 28571. Free bimonthly covering the boating scene in the Carolinas.

Carteret County News-Times 252-726-7081, 800-849-6397; www.carteretnewstimes.com; P.O. Box 1679, Morehead City 28557. Published Sunday, Wednesday, and Friday covering the entire county.

Coaster Magazine 252-247-7442; www.nccoast.com; 201 N. 17th St., Morehead City 28557. Free publication published seven times a year with information on the Crystal Coast.

Coastland Times 252-473-2105; www.thecoastlandtimes.net; 503 Budleigh St., Manteo 27954. Published continuously since 1935, three times a week, Tuesday, Thursday, and Sunday.

The Gam 252-728-2435; www.thegam.com; P.O. Box 300, Beaufort 28516. Weekly publication distributed on Thursdays in Carteret County and Swansboro.

Island Breeze 252-986-2421; www.islandbreezepublishing.com; P.O. Box 598, Hatteras 27943. Free monthly newspaper covers the islands of Hatteras and Ocracoke. Summer "Just for Kids" special section.

Island Free Press www.islandfreepress.org; P.O. Box 414, Buxton 27920. Extensive online coverage of Hatteras and Ocracoke islands.

North Beach Sun 252-449-2222; www.northbeachsun.com; 4425 N. Croatan Hwy., Kitty Hawk 27949. Quarterly tabloid with a large real estate section covers Southern Shores to Carova.

Ocracoke Observer 252-928-2565; www.ocracokeisland.com; P.O. Box 427, Ocracoke 27960. Monthly free publication.

Outer Banks Free Press www.outerbanksfreepress.com. Online publication with an interesting history section.

Outer Banks Press 252-261-0612; www.outerbankspress.com; P.O. Box 2829, Kitty Hawk 27949. Publishes *The Edge Outer Banks*, a slick annual magazine available by mail or in bookstores, as well as other annuals and books.

Outer Banks Sentinel 252-480-2234; www.obsentinel.com; P.O. Box 546, Nags Head 27959. Local newspaper publishes on Sundays and Wednesdays. Online and mail subscriptions available. A blog, Outer Banks Onstage (www.obxonstage.com), covers local entertainment events.

ReelFisher News 252-261-8210; www.reelfisher.com; P.O. Box 1146, Kitty Hawk 27949.

Online and quarterly print guides to saltwater fishing options and conditions.

Sunny Day Guides 800-786-6932; www.sunnydayguide.com; 800 Seahawk Circle, Suite 106, Virginia Beach, VA 23452. Free annual guides contain maps, coupons, and informative articles. Outer Banks and Hatteras–Ocracoke editions can be downloaded or ordered online.

This Week Magazine 252-726-6016; www.thisweekmag.com; P.O. Box 1679, Morehead City 28557. Free weekly covers entertainment and dining on the South Banks.

Tideland News 910-326-5066; www.nccoastonline.com/TidelandNews.html; P.O. Box 1000, Swansboro 28584. News and fishing reports from the Swansboro area.

The Virginian-Pilot 252-441-1620; www.pilotonline.com; 2224 S. Croatan Hwy, Nags Head 27949. Daily paper from Hampton Roads, Virginia, has a section of news from the North Carolina coast. A free section called *The Coast* with Outer Banks entertainment listings and news is published weekly March to December, monthly January–February.

Visitors Guide Network 800-422-0742; www.vgnet.com; 1264 Perimeter Pkwy., Virginia Beach, VA 23452. Free magazines contain coupons and articles on attractions and dining. Crystal Coast and the Outer Banks editions available by mail or download.

LOCAL RADIO STATIONS

The National Weather Service broadcasts on frequency 162.425.

WBJD 91.5 FM 252-672-7522, 800-222-9832; www.publicradioeast.org; Atlantic Beach. Programming from Public Radio East, a National Public Radio (NPR) affiliate.

WBUX 90.5 800-556-5178; www.theclassicalstation.org; Buxton. North Carolina Public Radio affiliate broadcasts classical music.

WCMS Water Country 94.5 FM 252-449-2837; www.wcms.com; P.O. Box 1897, Kill Devil Hills 27948. Country hits and Oregon Inlet First Light fishing reports.

WCXL Beach 104.1 FM 252-449-4104; www.beach104.com; 103D W. Woodhill Dr., Nags Head 27959.

Each beach has its own set of dog regulations.

WERX The Shark 102.5 FM 252-441-1025, 888-75-SHARK; www.1025theshark.com; 2422 S. Wrightsville Ave., Nags Head 27959.

WFMZ Classic Hits 104.9 FM 252-473-4588; www.classichits1049.com; 637 Harbor Rd., Wanchese 27981.

WGAI 560 AM 252-480-4655; 102 W. Woodhill Dr., Nags Head 27959. News radio.

WJCD Smooth Jazz 107.7 FM 757-466-0009; www.wjcd.com; 1003 Norfolk Square, Norfolk, VA 23502.

WOBR Christian Radio 1530 AM 252-473-5402; 129 Old Schoolhouse Rd., Wanchese 27981.

WOBR 95.3 FM 252-480-9530; www.wobr.com; 2422 S. Wrightsville Ave., Nags Head 27959. Classic rock.

WOBX 98X 98.1 FM 252-441-9810; www.wobx.net; 2422 S. Wrightsville Ave., Nags Head 27959. Today's rock.

WRSF Dixie 105.7 FM 252 441-4566, 800-422-DIXI; www.dixie1057.com; 2422 S. Wrightsville Ave., Nags Head 27959. Country hits.

WRVS 89.9 FM 252-335-3517; www.wrvsfm.org; 1704 Weeksville Rd., Elizabeth City 27909. NPR affiliate operated by Elizabeth City State University carries local cultural programs, jazz, gospel, and R&B.

WTFK 107.1 FM & WJNC 1240 AM Talk Radio 252-247-6343; www.wtkf107.com; P.O. Box 70, Newport 28570.

WUND 88.9 FM 252-475-9862, 800-962-9862; www.wunc.org; Manteo. North Carolina Public Radio affiliate broadcasts NPR shows.

WURI 90.9 FM 800-556-5178; www.theclassicalstation.org; Manteo. Classical music.

WVOD 99.1 FM The Sound 252-473-9863; www.991thesound.com; 637 Harbor Rd., Wanchese 27981. Alternative music: acoustic, world music, fusion, blues, punk.

WYND Your Country 97.1 FM 252-475-1888; www.yourcountry971.com; 637 Harbor Rd., Wanchese 27981. Country hits.

WZPR ESPN 92.3 FM 252-475-1888; www.capsanmedia.com; 637 Harbor Rd., Wanchese 27981. Sports radio broadcasts 24/7.

Local Television Stations

Local station **WSKY-TV 4** (252-491-4242; www.wsky4.com) broadcasts on channel 4.

Charter Communications (877-728-3121; www.charter.com; 2400 S. Virginia Dare Trail, Nags Head 27959) provides cable service to the northern and central sections of the Outer Banks. Several channels feature local programming, including 12, 19, and 20.

On Ocracoke Island, cable service is provided by Belhaven Cable TV (252-928-1551, 252-943-3736; www.belhavencabletv.com).

In Carteret and Onslow counties, Time Warner (252-223-6400; www.timewarnercable.com; 500 Vision Cable Dr., Newport 28570) is the cable provider. Local programming can be found on Channel 10.

Calendar of Annual Events

January

Central Banks and Roanoke Island

Frank Stick Memorial Art Show 252-473-5558; www.darearts.org; Glenn Eure's Ghost Fleet Gallery, Nags Head. Displays local works through mid-February.

Outer Banks Wedding Weekend and Expo 252-305-0978; outerbanksweddingassoc.org.

Hatteras Island

Old Chrismas 252-987-1303; www.rwscivic.org; Rodanthe Waves Salvo Community Building. Celebrated on the Saturday closest to January 6, this 100-year-old custom includes an appearance by "Old Buck" plus oyster roasts, music, and bonfires.

South Banks

Bridal Fair 252-247-3883; www.crystalcoastcivicctr.com; Crystal Coast Civic Center, Morehead City.

February

Central Banks and Roanoke Island

The Elizabethan Rendezvous 252-473-1061; www.elizabethr.org; Penguin Isle Restaurant, Nags Head. Fun-filled gala produced by Elizabeth R and Company includes an Elizabethan seven-course feast and cabaret entertainment. Reservations required.

Freedman's Colony Celebration 252-475-1500; www.roanokeisland.com; Roanoke Island Festival Park, Manteo.

Stumpy Point Oyster Feast 252-473-5869; Stumpy Point Civic Center. All-you-can-eat down-home feast on the Dare County mainland.

South Banks

Art From The Heart 252-726-9156; www.accc.wordpress.com; Morehead City.

★ **Carolina Chocolate Festival** 877-848-4976; www.carolinachocolatefestival.com; Crystal Coast Civic Center and other venues, Morehead City. Chocolate dinners, cooking demonstrations, and other events surround the main tasting festival at the Civic Center.

Empty Bowls Fundraiser 252-354-5278; www.bridgesstreetpottery.com; Crystal Coast Civic Center, Morehead City.

Taste of Core Sound–Winter Edition 252-728-1500; www.coresound.com; Core Sound Waterfowl Museum and Heritage Center, Harkers Island. Enjoy a dinner of Down East specialties.

March

Regional

★ **Taste of the Beach** www.obxtasteofthebeach.com; Duck, Kill Devil Hills, Kitty Hawk, Manteo, Nags Head. Four-day festival for foodies with dozens of events including wine-pairing dinners, pig and oyster roasts, chowder cook-off, cooking classes, tapas crawl, brewing lessons, a tasting expo, and more.

Central Banks and Roanoke Island

Kelly's Restaurant and Tavern's St. Patrick's Day Parade 252-441-4116; www.kellys restaurant.com; MP 12-10.5, Beach Road, Nags Head.

Outer Banks Family YMCA Polar Plunge 252-449-8897; www.obxpolarplunge.com; Ramada Inn, Kill Devil Hills.

Priceless Pieces Past & Present Quilt Extravaganza 252-475-1500; www.roanokeisland .com; Roanoke Island Festival Park Gallery, Manteo. Annual quilt show includes a vendor day.

Roanoke Island 1862—A Civil War Living History Weekend 252-475-1500; www.roanoke island.com; Roanoke Island Festival Park Gallery, Manteo.

South Banks

Coastal Home and Garden Show 252-247-3883; www.crystalcoastcivicctr.com; Crystal Coast Civic Center, Morehead City.

Crystal Coast Culinary Challenge 252-222-6034; Coral Bay Club, Atlantic Beach.

Crystal Coast Half Marathon and 5K Race 252-247-3883; www.ncraces.com; www.crystal coastcivicctr.com; Crystal Coast Civic Center, Morehead City.

Oyster Roast and Pig Out 910-326-6175; www.swansbororotary.com; Swansboro Rotary Civic Center, NC 24, Swansboro.

St. Patrick's Day Celebration 252-354-6350; www.emeraldisle-nc.org; Emerald Plantation Shopping Center, Emerald Isle.

April

Regional

THE Studio Tour 252-473-5558; www.darearts.org; Corolla to Hatteras. Over 40 local artists open their studios during this two-day event.

North Banks

Easter Egg-Stravaganza 252-453-9040; www.whaleheadclub.org; Currituck Heritage Park, Corolla.

Central Banks and Roanoke Island

First Friday on Roanoke Island 252-473-2133; www.firstfriday-roanokeisland.com; Downtown Manteo Waterfront. Live music, family activities, and more, 6–8 PM.

Green Party for the Planet—Earth Day 252-473-3494; www.ncaquariums.com; North Carolina Aquarium on Roanoke Island, Manteo.

Kitty Hawk Kites Easter Eggstravaganza 252-441-4124, 877-FLY-THIS; www.kittyhawk.com; Kitty Hawk Kites, MP 12.5, Nags Head. The largest egg hunt on the Outer Banks.

Kitty Hawk Kites Fly Into Spring Kite Festival 252-441-4124, 877-FLY-THIS; www.kittyhawk.com; Jockey's Ridge State Park, Nags Head. Kite flyers from around the country demo stunt kites and teach lessons.

Kitty Hawk Woods Earth Day 8K Race 252-261-8891; www.cerf.us; Kitty Hawk Woods. Benefits the Carolina Estuarine Reserve Foundation.

Land of Beginnings Festival 252-473-2127; www.thelostcolony.org; various venues. Week-long festival includes a fun run, Children's Faire, story-telling, lectures, Living Legend Luncheon, and final gala.

Outer Banks Bike Week 757-397-5550; www.outerbanksbikeweek.com; various venues. Bike show, treasure hunt, stunt show, live bands, bikini contests, tattoo art show, and more.

Outer Banks Triathlon & Kids Triathlon 252-599-0911; www.obxtri.com; Manteo waterfront. Running, biking, and swimming events.

Oyster Fool Eating Contest 252-473-3222; www.stripersbarandgrille.com; Stripers Bar & Grille, Manteo. Locals compete on April Fool's Day.

Tour de Cure 757-455-6335, 888-DIABETES; tour.diabetes.org; Roanoke Island Festival Park, Manteo. Bike 100 miles from Chesapeake, VA, to Manteo to benefit the American Diabetes Association.

Wilbur Wright's Birthday 252-441-7430; www.nps.gov/wrbr; Wright Brothers National Memorial, Kill Devil Hills.

HATTERAS ISLAND

Frisco Woods WindFest 252-995-5208; www.outer-banks.com/friscowoods; Frisco Woods Campground, Frisco. Weekend of windsurfing and kiteboarding.

★ **Inter-Tribal Powwow: Journey Home** 252-995-4440; www.nativeamericanmuseum.org; Frisco Native American Museum. Sharing of cultures includes dancing, drumming, crafts, and foods from many tribal traditions.

OCRACOKE ISLAND

★ **Portsmouth Village Homecoming** 252-728-2250, 252-728-3242; www.nps.gov/calo; Portsmouth Village, Cape Lookout National Seashore. Held in even-numbered years, this old-fashioned homecoming brings together descendants of residents and visitors for music, fellowship, and a picnic-style dinner. Open to all.

SOUTH BANKS

★ **Beaufort Wine and Food Weekend** 252-728-5225; www.beaufortwineandfood.com; various venues. Five-day event includes wine and food tastings, seminars, dinners, art shows, and more.

Easter Egg Hunt 252-728-5225, 800-575-7483; www.beauforthistoricsite.org; Beaufort Historic Site. Free event for children seven and under.

Newport Pig Cookin' 252-223-3112; www.newportpigcooking.com; Newport Community Park. Newport goes whole hog with more than 80 pigs on the grill.

Publick Day 252-728-5225, 800-575-7483; www.beauforthistoricsite.org; Beaufort Historic Site. Colonial-style flea market and period children's games. Free.

Spring Home Tour and Art Show 252-354-2916, 252-393-6500; Lands End Clubhouse, Coast Guard Rd., Emerald Isle.

Women's Fair 252-247-3883; www.crystalcoastcivicctr.com; Crystal Coast Civic Center, Morehead City.

May

North Banks

Picnic in the Park 252-255-1234; www.townofduck.com; Town of Duck Municipal Park.

Central Banks and Roanoke Island

Carolina Outdoors OBX Surf Kayak Competition 252-441-4124, 877-FLY-THIS; www .kittyhawk.com; 1st Street Beach Access, Kill Devil Hills.

Coastal Gardening Festival 252-473-4290; Outer Banks Arboretum and Teaching Garden, Kill Devil Hills. Educational lectures plus plant sale and vendors.

First Friday on Roanoke Island (See April listing.)

International Miniature Art Show 252-441-5418, 800-828-2444; www.seasideart.com; Seaside Art Gallery, MP 11, Beach Rd., Nags Head.

Kitty Hawk Kites Hang Gliding Spectacular 252-441-4124, 877-FLY-THIS; www.kitty hawk.com; Jockey's Ridge State Park, Nags Head.

The Lost Colony **Preview Night** 252-473-3414; www.thelostcolony.org; Waterside Theatre, Manteo. Attending the final dress rehearsal before opening night is a local tradition.

Mollie Fearing Memorial Art Show 252-473-5558; www.darearts.org; Roanoke Island Festival Park Gallery, Manteo. Juried show honors the founder of the Dare County Arts Council.

Outer Banks Beach Music Festival 252-384-3494; www.outerbanksbeachmusicfestival.com; Roanoke Island Festival Park, Manteo. Memorial Day weekend event brings out shaggers and lovers of old time R & B.

Roanoke Island House and Garden Tour 252-473-3234; www.elizabethangardens.org; Elizabethan Gardens, Manteo.

Tux and Topsiders Ball 252-475-1750; www.obxmaritime.org; North Carolina Maritime Museum, Manteo. Benefit for the local branch of the Maritime Museum.

Hatteras Island

Hatteras Village Offshore Open 252-986-2579; www.hatterasoffshoreopen.com; Hatteras Village Civic Association. Cash and trophies for largest billfish and blue marlin, followed by evening events, including a "Taste of the Village."

Ocracoke Island

British Cemetery Military Honors Ceremony 888-493-3826; www.hydecounty.org; British Cemetery. Graveside ceremony followed by a reception and pig pickin' at the Ocracoke Community Center.

Ocracoke Invitational Surf Fishing Tournament 252-928-5491; www.hydecounty.org; Ocracoke Community Center.

South Banks

Beaufort Music Festival www.beaufortmusicfestival.com; Downtown Beaufort. A weekend of free music and family fun featuring national and local performers.

Coastal Stars Quilt Show 252-247-2316; www.crystalcoastcivicctr.com; Crystal Coast Civic Center, Morehead City.

King Mackerel Blue Water Fishing Tournament 910-326-3474; www.kingbluewater.com; Hammocks Beach State Park, Swansboro. Memorial Day weekend competition is one of the country's largest.

Loon Day 252-838-8818; www.decoyguild.com; Core Sound Decoy Carvers Guild, Harkers Island. Decoy competition and auction.

★ **Wooden Boat Show** 252-728-7317; www.ncmaritimemuseum.org; N.C. Maritime Museum, Beaufort.

JUNE

NORTH BANKS

"Under the Oaks" Arts Festival 252-453-9040; www.whaleheadclub.org; Currituck Heritage Park, Corolla.

Whalehead Club Wine Festivals 252-453-9040; www.whaleheadclub.org; Currituck Heritage Park, Corolla. Wednesday afternoon events include live music, a souvenir glass, and tour of the Whalehead Club.

CENTRAL BANKS AND ROANOKE ISLAND

★ *Bloody Mary and the Virgin Queen, Elizabeth R, Shepherd of the Ocean* 252-475-1500; www.roanokeisland.com; Film Theatre, Roanoke Island Festival Park, Manteo. Theatrical productions are free with admission to the Festival Park.

Dare Day 252-475-5629; www.townofmanteo.com; Downtown Manteo. Annual free festival takes place on the waterfront.

Evening Under the Stars with the North Carolina Symphony 252-475-1500, 877-629-4386; www.roanokeisland.com; Roanoke Island Festival Park, Manteo. Free event.

First Friday on Roanoke Island (See April listing.)

Kitty Hawk Kites Kiteboarding Competition 252-441-4124, 877-FLY-THIS; www.kittyhawk.com; Kitty Hawk Kites Kiteboarding Center, MP 15.5, Nags Head.

Kitty Hawk Kites Wil-Bear Wright's Festival of Fun 252-441-4124, 877-FLY-THIS; www.kittyhawk.com; Kitty Hawk Kites, MP 12.5, Nags Head. Kick-off event for Kitty Hawk Kites' summer Kids Day series, held every Wednesday.

★ *The Lost Colony* 252-473-3414; www.thelostcolony.org, Waterside Theatre, Manteo. Performed nightly except Sundays and July 4th.

North Carolina School of the Arts Summer Performance Festival 252-475-1500; www.ncsasummerfest.org; Roanoke Island Festival Park, Manteo. Free performances.

Rogallo Kite Festival 252-441-4124, 877-FLY-THIS; www.kittyhawk.com; Jockey's Ridge State Park, MP 12.5, Nags Head. Honors the inventor of the flexible wing.

★ **Tea with the Queen** 252-473-3414; www.thelostcolony.org, Backstage Courtyard, Waterside Theatre, Manteo.

HATTERAS ISLAND

Hatteras Marlin Club Invitational Tournament 252-986-2454; www.hatterasmarlinclub.com; Hatteras Marlin Club, P.O. Box 218, Hatteras 27943. The state's oldest billfish tournament.

Pea Island Crabbing and Fishing Rodeo 252-987-2394; www.fws.gov/peaisland; Pea Island National Wildlife Refuge.

OCRACOKE ISLAND

★ **OcraFolk Music and Storytelling Festival** 252-928-4280 www.ocrafolkfestival.org; Deepwater Theater and other venues. A free weekend of acoustic music, storytelling, art exhibits, live auction, potluck dinner, and community square dance.

SOUTH BANKS

Art by the Sea and Storytelling Festival 910-326-7370, 910-326-1174; www.swansboro festival.zoomshare.com; Downtown Swansboro.

Beaufort Old Homes & Gardens Tour 252-728-5225, 800-575-7483; www.beaufort historicsite.org; Beaufort Historic Site.

Big Rock Blue Marlin Fishing Tournament 252-247-3575; www.thebigrock.com; Crystal Coast Civic Center and other venues. Week-long event includes men's and ladies' divisions, social mixers and a fireworks display.

Kids' Day 252-838-8818; www.decoyguild.com; Core Sound Decoy Carvers Guild, Harkers Island. Hunting and fishing safety, wildlife preservation, decoy painting, and other fun activities.

★ **MCAS Cherry Point Air Show** 866-WINGS-NC; www.cherrypointairshow.com; Marine Air Corps Station Cherry Point, Havelock. The state's largest air show features two days of military and civilian aerobatic demonstrations, aircraft on display, live music, and the famous "Night Show" featuring skydivers and aerial pyrotechnics topped off by the region's largest fireworks display.

JULY

Fourth of July fireworks from ocean piers are a treasured and spectacular Banks tradition. Look for fireworks displays off Nags Head Fishing Pier, Avalon Pier in Kill Devil Hills, Avon Pier, and on the South Banks, off Oceana and Bogue Inlet piers.

NORTH BANKS

Fourth of July Parade and Afterparty 252-255-1234; www.townofduck.com; Town of Duck Municipal Park Green.

Independence Day Festival of Fireworks 252-453-9612; www.visitcurrituck.com; Currituck Heritage Park, Corolla.

Summer Concert Series on the Lawn 252-453-9040; www.whaleheadclub.org; Currituck Heritage Park, Corolla. Free concerts are held every Thursday evening in July and August.

Whalehead Club Wine Festivals (See June listings.)

Wild Horse Days 252-453-8002; www.corollawildhorses.com; Wild Horse Museum, Old Corolla Village.

CENTRAL BANKS AND ROANOKE ISLAND

Dare County Boat Builders Challenge 252-473-1015, 800-367-4728; www.fishpiratescove .com; Pirates Cove Marina, Manteo. Fishing tournament open only to those with boats hand-crafted in Dare County.

First Friday on Roanoke Island (See April listing.)

Fourth of July Celebration and Fireworks 252-475-5629; www.townofmanteo.com; Downtown Manteo.

The Lost Colony (See June listing.)

North Carolina School of the Arts Summer Performance Festival (See June listing.)

One Design Regatta 252-475-1750; www.obxmaritime.org; N.C. Maritime Museum,

Tea with the Queen (See June listing.)

Wright Kite Festival 252-441-4124, 877-FLY-THIS; www.kittyhawk.com; Wright Brothers National Memorial, MP 8, Kill Devil Hills.

HATTERAS ISLAND

Kitty Hawk Kites Hatteras Kite Festival 252-441-4124, 877-FLY-THIS; www.kittyhawk.com; Hatteras Landing.

OCRACOKE ISLAND

Ocracoke Island Independence Day Celebration 252-928-6711; www.ocracoke village.com; various venues. A sand sculpture contest, patriotic parade, and fireworks.

SOUTH BANKS

Fourth of July Fireworks 910-326-7370, 910-326-4428; www.swansborofestival. zoomshare.com; Downtown Swansboro.

Barta Boys & Girls Club Billfish Tournament and Art Show 252-808-2286; www.barta billfish.com; Beaufort Docks.

N.C. Ducks Unlimited Band The Billfish Tournament 252-237-3717; www.bandthe billfish.com; Crystal Coast Civic Center, Morehead City.

AUGUST

NORTH BANKS

Corolla Surf Shop Longboard Invitational 252-453-9283; www.corollasurfshop.com; Corolla.

Summer Concert Series on the Lawn (See July listing.)

Whalehead Club Wine Festivals (See June listing.)

CENTRAL BANKS AND ROANOKE ISLAND

Alice Kelly—Ladies Only—Tournament, 252-473-1015, 800-367-4728; www.fishpirates cove.com; Pirates Cove Marina, Manteo. Billfish tournament benefits the Outer Banks Cancer Support Group.

Bloody Mary and the Virgin Queen, Elizabeth R, Shepherd of the Ocean (See June listing.)

First Friday on Roanoke Island (See April listing.)

Herbert Hoover's Birthday Celebration 252-473-1221; www.manteobooksellers.com; Manteo Booksellers, 101 Sir Walter Raleigh St., Manteo.

Kitty Hawk Kites Ocean Games 252-441-4124, 877-FLY-THIS; www.kittyhawk.com; Ramada Plaza, Kill Devil Hills. Family beach day includes a kayak race, sand castle contest, and kite boarding demos.

Life Is Good Watermelon Festival 252-441-4124, 877-FLY-THIS; www.kittyhawk.com; Kitty Hawk Kites, MP 12.5, Nags Head.

The Lost Colony (See June listing.)

National Aviation Day 252-441-7430; www.nps.gov/wrbr; Wright Brothers National Memorial, Kill Devil Hills. Orville Wright's birthday.

New World Festival of The Arts 252-473-2838; www.townofmanteo.com, Manteo waterfront.

North Carolina School of the Arts Summer Performance Festival (See June listing.)

OBX Sandbar 5K 252-441-7752; www.outerbanksrelieffoundation.com; Beach Access at MP 4.5, Kitty Hawk. Run/walk takes place on the sand.

Roanoke Island American Indian Cultural Festival & Powwow 757-477-3589; www.nc algonquians.com; Airport Pavilion Lawn, Airport Rd., Manteo.

Tea with the Queen (See June listing.)

★ **Virginia Dare Faire** 252-473-3414; www.thelostcolony.org; Fort Raleigh National Historic Site, Manteo. Free family festival celebrates the birthday of the first English child born in America.

HATTERAS ISLAND

★ **American Heroes Day** 252-987-1552; www.chicamacomico.net; Chicamacomico Life-Saving Station Historic Site, Rodanthe. Flyovers and demonstrations of lifesaving techniques, both historic and modern, by military organizations.

SOUTH BANKS

★ **Beaufort Pyrate Invasion** 252-728-3917; www.beaufortpyrateinvasion.com; Beaufort. Captain Sinbad fires on the town docks then invades with his buccaneer crew for a weekend of feasting, dancing, and other pirate merriment.

SEPTEMBER

NORTH BANKS

Whalehead Club Wine Festivals (See June listing.)

CENTRAL BANKS AND ROANOKE ISLAND

Blackbeard's Pirate Festival 252-441-4124, 877-FLY-THIS; www.kittyhawk.com; Kitty Hawk Kites, MP 12.5, Nags Head. Week-long festival at various venues.

Currituck Wine & Jazz Festival 252-491-2387; www.sanctuaryvineyards.com; The Cotton Gin, Jarvisburg.

First Friday on Roanoke Island (See April listing.)

Kitty Hawk Kites Kayak Jamboree 252-441-4124, 877-FLY-THIS; www.kittyhawk.com; Kitty Hawk Kites, Manteo Waterfront.

★ **Outer Banks Coastal Land Trust Festival** 252-449-8289; www.coastallandtrust.org; various venues. Weekend of eco-activities, including hikes, kayak eco-tours, and social mixers, benefiting the Land Trust.

Weeping Radish Oktoberfest 252-491-5205; www.weepingradish.com; Weeping Radish Farm Brewery, N. Caratoke Hwy., Jarvisburg.

HATTERAS ISLAND

★ **Day at The Docks—A Celebration of Hatteras Island Watermen** 252-986-2515; www.dayatthedocks.org; Hatteras Village. Chowder cook-off, kids' fishing contest, crab races, traditional wooden boat exhibits, and a working boat parade followed by the Blessing of the Fleet.

ESA Eastern Surfing Championships 757-233-1790, 800-937-4733; www.surfesa.org; Cape Hatteras National Seashore, Buxton.

Hatteras Village Invitational Surf Fishing Tournament 252-986-2579; www.hatterason mymind.com; Hatteras Village Civic Association.

OCRACOKE ISLAND

★ **Ocracoke Art Walk** 252-928-2598; www.art-on-ocracoke.com; Ocracoke Village. Held on the last Saturday of September, over 40 artists' studios are open to the public. Free shuttle and a Meet the Artists reception.

SOUTH BANKS

Beaufort Offshore Celebrity Classic 252-504-2640, 800-760-7278; www.fishbocc.com; Beaufort. Held annually on Labor Day weekend.

Davis Island Fishing Foundation Surf Fishing Tournament www.diffclub.com; Great Island Camp and Core Banks South, Cape Lookout National Seashore.

OCTOBER

REGIONAL

Outer Banks Home Builders Parade of Homes 252-449-8232; www.obhomebuilders.org. Tour dozens of new homes situated from Corolla to Hatteras.

NORTH BANKS

★ **Duck Jazz Festival** 252-255-1286, 252-255-1286; www.townofduck.com; Town of Duck Municipal Park Green. Free admission.

Haunted Corolla Village 252-453-9040; www.whaleheadclub.org; Currituck Heritage Park and Old Corolla Village. Evening hayrides and treasure hunts.

CENTRAL BANKS AND ROANOKE ISLAND

Artrageous Art Extravaganza 252-473-5558; www.darearts.org; various venues.

Beach Book Cover Art Competition 252-473-5558; www.darearts.org; Sea & Sounds Gallery, Manteo.

Coastival Harvest Fest 252-491-8166, 252-491-5205; www.coastival.org; Weeping Radish Farm Brewery, N. Caratoke Hwy., Jarvisburg. Celebrates local food and music.

Elizabethan Tymes: A Country Faire 252-475-1500; www.roanokeisland.com; Roanoke Island Festival Park, Manteo. Living history event; admission included with entrance to the Festival Park.

First Friday on Roanoke Island (See April listing.)

Kayak Fishing Tournament 252-449-2210, 877-FLY-THIS; www.kittyhawk.com.

Outer Banks International Wine Festival 252-491-5311; www.nativevine.com; Big City Wine/Native Vine, 9132 Caratoke Hwy., Point Harbor 27964.

Outer Banks Pig Stein 252-449-8229; www.pigstein.com; MP 2, Beach Rd., Kitty Hawk. BBQ cook-off and international beer festival.

Outer Banks Stunt Kite Competition 252-441-4124, 877-FLY-THIS; www.kittyhawk.com; Wright Brothers National Memorial, MP 7.5, Kill Devil Hills.

Trick or Treat Under the Sea 252-473-3494, 866-332-3475; www.ncaquariums.com; N.C. Aquarium at Roanoke Island, Manteo.

WildFest 252-987-1118; www.wingsoverwater.org; College of the Albemarle Roanoke Island Campus, Manteo. Exhibits on red wolves and black bears, critter calls, and many fun activities.

Hatteras Island

Frank and Fran's Red Drum Tournament 252-995-4171; www.hatteras-island.com; Avon.

Teach's Lair Shootout King Mackerel Tournament 252-986-2460, 888-868-2460; www.teachslair.com; Teach's Lair Marina, Hatteras Village.

Ocracoke Island

★ **OcraFolk School** 252-928-1541; www.ocrafolkschool.org; Deepwater Theater. Week-long school offers classes in traditional music, arts, crafts, cooking, and history, plus an immersion in local culture.

South Banks

Atlantic Beach King Mackerel Tournament 252-247-2334; www.abkmt.com; Atlantic Station Shopping Center, Atlantic Beach. Largest all-cash tournament in the United States.

Beaufort Historical Association Fall Gala and Art Show 252-728-5225, 800-575-7483; www.beauforthistoricsite.org; Beaufort.

Carolina Kite Fest 252-247-7011; www.kitesunlimitednc.com; Sheraton Oceanfront Hotel, Atlantic Beach. Includes a Night Fly with illuminated kites, and a Candy Drop.

Emerald Isle Triathlon 252-354-6350; www.emeraldisle-nc.org; Emerald Isle.

★ **North Carolina Seafood Festival** 252-726-6273; www.ncseafoodfestival.org; Morehead City waterfront. Weekend celebrating the commercial fishing industry includes seafood tastings, live music, fishing and sailing competitions, a free boat show, and Blessing of the Fleet.

Swansboro Mullet Festival 910-326-7370; Downtown Swansboro.

Trick Or Treat Under the Sea 252-247-4003; www.ncaquariums.com; N.C. Aquarium at Pine Knoll Shores.

November

Regional

★ **Wings Over Water** 252-441-8144; www.wingsoverwater.org; various venues. Week-long birding festival includes over 100 birding tours, plus special photography workshops, an art show, and social events.

North Banks

Advice 5K Turkey Trot 252-255-1050; www.outerbanksrunningclub.org; Scarborough Lane, Duck. Thanksgiving Day fun run.

Black Friday Porch Sale 252-453-9040; www.whaleheadclub.org; Whalehead Club, Corolla. Holiday open house features special sales.

CENTRAL BANKS AND ROANOKE ISLAND

First Friday on Roanoke Island (See April listing.)

Holiday Small Works Show 252-473-5558; www.darearts.org; Sea & Sounds Gallery, Manteo.

Kites with Lights 252-441-4124, 877-FLY-THIS; www.kittyhawk.com; Jockey's Ridge State Park, MP 12.5, Nags Head. Illuminated kites fly over Jockey's Ridge at sunset.

Kitty Hawk Kites Hanging with Santa 252-441-4124, 877-FLY-THIS; www.kittyhawk.com; Kitty Hawk Kites, MP 12.5, Nags Head. Free pictures with Santa in a demonstration hang glider.

OBX Marathon, Half Marathon & Fun Run 252-261-6296; www.obxmarathon.org; Kitty Hawk to Manteo. An expo, art show, and social events are included in this Veteran's Day weekend of races.

HATTERAS ISLAND

End of Season Festivities 252-987-1552; www.chicamacomico.net; Chicamacomico Life-Saving Station Historic Site, Rodanthe.

Hatteras Island Arts and Craft Guild Holiday Show 252-441-1850; Cape Hatteras Secondary School, Buxton. Free admission, local food and artworks.

United Methodist Women's Holiday Craft Bazaar 252-986-2149; Hatteras Civic Center, Hatteras Village. Community lunch.

OCRACOKE ISLAND

OcraFolk Festival Fall Fundraiser 252-928-7375;www.ocrafolkfestival.org; Ocracoke Community Center. Thanksgiving weekend tradition.

SOUTH BANKS

Antique-A-Thon 252-247-7533; www.thehistoryplace.org; The History Place, Morehead City. Experts evaluate treasures for the public.

Emerald Isle Holiday Parade 252-354-2916; www.emeraldisle-nc.org; Merchant's Park, Emerald Isle. Caroling, visits with Santa, the Lighting of the Town Tree, and merchant open houses.

Holiday Flotilla 910-326-7370; Downtown Swansboro. Decorated boats parade along the Swansboro waterfront on Thanksgiving weekend.

DECEMBER

NORTH BANKS

Currituck Heritage Park Tree Lighting Celebration 252-453-9040; www.whaleheadclub .org; Currituck Heritage Park, Corolla. Free tours of the Whalehead Club, caroling, and carriage rides.

CENTRAL BANKS AND ROANOKE ISLAND

★ **Christmas by the Sea** 252-473-2133; www.townofmanteo.com; Downtown Manteo. Friday night Lighting of the Town Tree; Saturday Christmas Parade featuring Queen Elizabeth I and Santa.

Christmas in the Park: A Holiday Open House 252-473-3234; 252-473-5772; www

.elizabethangardens.org; Fort Raleigh National Historic Site, Elizabethan Gardens and The Lost Colony.

Elizabethan Christmas 252-475-1500; www.roanokeisland.com; Roanoke Island Festival Park, Manteo. Post-Christmas celebration.

Festival of Trees 252-473-5121; www.obhotline.org; various venues.

★ **First Flight Anniversary** 252-473-2111; www.nps.gov/wrbr; Wright Brothers National Memorial, MP 8, Kill Devil Hills. Free December 17th celebration includes fly-bys and guest speakers.

First Friday on Roanoke Island (See April listing.)

Holiday Tour of Homes 252-473-5548; www.manteopt.com; 108 Budleigh St., Manteo.

Manteo Rotary Rockfish Rodeo 252-473-6644; www.rockfishrodeo.com; Outdoor Pavilion, Roanoke Island Festival Park.

Man Will Never Fly Memorial Society Annual Banquet www.manwillneverfly.com. Spoofs the "legend" of flight. Open to the public.

New Year's Eve 3-Miler 252-441-7299; www.tortugaslie.com; Tortuga's Lie Restaurant, MP 11.5, Beach Rd., Nags Head.

HATTERAS ISLAND

Christmas Parade 252-986-2579; www.hatterasonmymind.com; Hatteras Village. Parade is followed by open houses at area businesses.

OCRACOKE ISLAND

Island Caroling 252-928-5541; villagecraftsmen.blogspot.com; Meet at the United Methodist Church.

Ocracoke Seafood Company Fish Fry and Oyster Roast 252-928-5601; www.ocracoke watermen.org, www.ocracokeseafood.com; Fish House, Ocracoke Village.

Wassail and Tree Lighting 252-928-7375; www.ocracokepreservation.org; Ocracoke Preservation Museum.

SOUTH BANKS

Core Sound Decoy Festival 252-838-8818; www.decoyguild.com; H. Curt Salter Building, Harkers Island Rd., Harkers Island. Weekend of decoy competition includes an auction, retriever demonstrations, loon calling, and children's decoy painting.

★ **Core Sound Waterfowl Weekend** 252-728-1500; www.coresound.com; Core Sound Waterfowl Museum and Heritage Center, Harkers Island. Held the same weekend as the Decoy Festival. Celebrates island traditions of boatbuilding, fishing, music, arts and crafts, cooking, and fellowship.

Festival of Trees 252-247-3883; www.crystalcoastcivicctr.com; Crystal Coast Civic Center, Morehead City.

WRIGHT CHOICES
(Best Bets)

If time is short on your trip to the Banks (and when is any vacation too long?), we offer these suggested itineraries tuned to different interests. They include many of our Wright Choices, marked with stars throughout the text.

Wright Choices Road Trip Sampler

This trip goes down the Outer Banks, over the ferries to the South Banks, then loops back north on US 17. You can, of course, reverse the order, or just go one way. The trip can be comfortably done in a week.

Start with a trip to **Corolla** on the northern end of the Outer Banks, where you can visit the elegant **Whalehead Club**, climb the **Currituck Beach Lighthouse**, and take an off-road adventure to see the wild horses of **Carova**. Traveling south on US 158, visit the **Wright Memorial** in **Kill Devil Hills**, and climb the dunes at **Jockey's Ridge State Park** in **Nags Head** to see the sunset.

Cross the causeway to **Manteo**, where the **Roanoke Island Festival Park** brings you up to speed on the region's early history. On the way back across the causeway, stop for some fresh local seafood at the **Lone Cedar Restaurant**, owned by Marc Basnight, long time President Pro Tem of the North Carolina Senate.

Crossing to Hatteras Island, seek out the **Chicamacomico Life-Saving Station** in **Rodanthe**, and climb the famous **Cape Hatteras Light** for a bird's eye view of Diamond Shoals. After a stop in **Hatteras Village** to tour the **Graveyard of the Atlantic Museum**, take the free ferry to **Ocracoke Island**. While there, visit the country's number one beach, stop for a meal or beverage at famous **Howard's Pub**, and watch the sun set over **Silver Lake**.

Take the ferry to Cedar Island, and visit the historic town of Beaufort, where you'll find the main campus of the **N.C. Maritime Museum**. Take in a meal at the famous **Sanitary Seafood** in Morehead City, before heading back north. You can take US 70 out to US 17 in New Bern, North Carolina's colonial capital, or turn off in Havelock to take the Cherry Branch–Minnesott Beach ferry and the Aurora–Bayview ferry to Bath, another colonial town, with a stop in Aurora to see some excellent fossils.

History Lover's Tour

Visit the **Whalehead Club** in **Corolla**; have lunch at the **Life-Saving Station Restaurant** at the **Sanderling Resort**; drive down the Beach Road in **Nags Head** to see the famous "Unpainted Aristocracy" of **Cottage Row**. **Manteo** has many historic highlights including **Fort Raleigh National Historic Site**; the summer drama *The Lost Colony*; and **Roanoke**

Island Festival Park, home of the *Elizabeth II* replica ship. On **Hatteras Island**, visit the **Chicamacomico Life-Saving Station** in **Rodanthe**, and the **U.S. Weather Station** and **Graveyard of the Atlantic Museum**, both in **Hatteras Village**. For an insider's take on local lore, consider a tour with historian David Couch. The **Ocracoke Preservation Association Museum** and the **Beaufort Historic Site** are must-sees further south. About an hour from Manteo on US 64, **Plymouth** has a working replica of the Confederate ironclad, *CSS Albemarle*.

Nature Lover's Tour

Visit the **Outer Banks Center for Wildlife Education** and the nearby boardwalk at the **Currituck Banks National Estuarine Preserve** in **Corolla**; paddle the salt marshes of **Currituck Sound** and the maritime forest in **Kitty Hawk Woods**; walk the nature trails in **Nags Head Woods** and **Buxton Woods**. Look for bears or go on a Red Wolf Howling tour at the **Alligator River National Wildlife Refuge**. On the **South Banks**, the **Croatan National Forest** offers exceptional outdoor options, including the chance to explore the unique pocosin ecosystem with its carnivorous plants, while the islands of **Core and Shackleford Banks**, and the **Rachel Carson Preserve**, form the largest uninhabited island chain on the East Coast, with wild horses and birds their only year-round residents.

Food Connoisseur's Tour

On the Currituck mainland, visit the **Weeping Radish** to sample "farmer to fork" local foods. Other dining experiences not to miss: the elegant **Left Bank** at the **Sanderling Resort**, the acclaimed **Blue Point** in **Duck**, the seafood at **Owen's Restaurant** in **Nags Head**, the she-crab soup at **Marc Basnight's Lone Cedar Café Restaurant** on the causeway to **Manteo**, and, on the Manteo waterfront, **1587**, another stronghold for local foods.

On the South Banks, you can't go wrong in historic **Beaufort**, known for its many fine restaurants, including the **Blue Moon Bistro, Beaufort Grocery, Sharpies, the Front Street Grill at Stillwater**, and **Aqua**. On **Bogue Banks**, try **Clawson's** for Sunday brunch or **Kathryn's** for appetizers and cocktails.

Wine Lover's Tour

Schedule a visit to the two vineyards on **Knott's Island**. Taste unique vintages at the **Native Vine** or the **Outer Banks Wine University**. Make reservations for a wine-pairing dinner with expert Leonard Logan at **Elizabeth's Café and Winery** in **Duck**. Stop by the copper-topped bar in Manteo's **1587 Restaurant** to sample its extensive selection of wines by the glass. In **Beaufort**, the **Cru Wine Bar and Store** provides a wine lover's retreat where you can enjoy a glass or half-bottle complemented by a light meal of cheese or smoked salmon and some relaxing jazz music.

Surfing Enthusiast's Tour

Corolla on the North Banks is a surfing hotspot. Stop by one of the locations of the **Corolla Surf Shop** to find out where the waves are breaking. **Zero's** sandwich shop nearby is a favorite surfer hangout. On the **Central Beaches**, you'll find surfers gathering at **The Pit**. **Hatteras Island** has attracted many board shapers. Visit one of the many surf shops to find the best boards and breaks. On **Ocracoke**, surfers meet up at **Howard's**, where they can watch the waves from the rooftop deck.

Art Lover's Tour

You'll see painted horses decorated by local artists all over the Outer Banks, part of the Winged Horses project held in conjunction with the Centennial of Flight celebration. The **Sanderling** displays an outstanding collection of bird art by all the modern masters. Other places to enjoy local artwork include the **KDH Cooperative Gallery** in **Kill Devil Hills**; **Gallery Row**, near MP 10 in **Nags Head**; and the **Pea Island Gallery** in **Salvo** on Hatteras Island. The historic villages of **Manteo, Ocracoke**, and **Beaufort** all have numerous galleries and sponsor art walks and open studio tours on a regular basis.

Decoy Collector's Tour

The region has several museums exhibiting antique decoys, as well as waterfowl created by contemporary carvers. **The Outer Banks Center for Wildlife Education** in **Corolla** contains the important Neil Conoley collection, with examples from all the most famed Currituck Sound school of carvers, and offers classes in carving. You can browse antique and modern decoys, as well as much other wildlife art, for sale at the **Bird Store** in **Kill Devil Hills**. Look especially for hollow canvas-covered decoys, a local style carried on today by **Wanchese** carver Nick Sapone. Farther south on **Harkers Island**, the **Core Sound Waterfowl Museum and Heritage Center** contains numerous examples of decoys donated by local families who have carved waterfowl for generations. Many of today's carvers gather at the **H. Curt Salter Building**, headquarters of the **Core Sound Decoy Carvers Guild**, just down the road from the museum. You'll often find carvers at work at these two locations and auctions are held several times a year. Other decoy collections are housed at the **N.C. Maritime Center** in **Beaufort** and the **History Place** in **Morehead City**.

OBX for Kids Tour

Thanks to their summer beach patrols, the best beaches for families with young children are the Central Beaches of **Kitty Hawk, Kill Devil Hills**, and **Nags Head,** and on the South Banks, **Emerald Isle**. Both areas also have many other kid-friendly activities, such as minigolf, bumper boats, and go-karts. Skate parks can be found at **Corolla, Kill Devil Hills,** and **Manteo**. The Beach Road running along the **Central Beaches** still has several old-fashioned ice cream and burger hangouts, such as the **Snowbird** and **Dune Burger.** The state aquariums in **Manteo** and **Pine Knoll Shores** offer great rainy day options, and the **Roanoke Island Festival Park** is fun rain or shine. The region's many headboats provide an easy and inexpensive introduction to fishing for all ages, as well as an exciting day on the water. Lessons for kids in sailing, snorkeling, kayaking, crabbing, and ecology are available free or for nominal fees at **Corolla's Wildlife Education Center, Jockey's Ridge State Park** in **Nags Head**, the **N.C. Aquariums, Cape Hatteras** and **Cape Lookout National Seashores**, and the **N.C. Maritime Museums** in **Manteo** and **Beaufort**. Check their online schedules in advance as pre-registration is often required.

Playing Pirate Tour

Ocracoke, Beaufort, and the Inner Banks village of **Bath** are the towns most associated with Blackbeard and his fellow pirates. On **Ocracoke**, visit the **Teach's Hole Blackbeard Exhibit**, then take a sail on the **schooner** *Windfall*, where Captain Temple will entertain you with tales of pirate lore, and point out the spot where Blackbeard met his end. In **Beaufort**, you can see artifacts recovered from the presumed wreck of Blackbeard's ship, *Queen*

Anne's Revenge, in the **Maritime Museum**, and take a ghost tour to the pirate's former home, said to be haunted by the one of his unfortunate "wives." Three Web sites where you can find out more about Blackbeard's activities in North Carolina are www.blackbeardthepirate .com, www.blackbeardlives.com, and www.qaronline.org.

Bird Lover's Tour

Among the many exceptional birding locations on the Banks are **Pea Island National Wildlife Refuge**, which offers free birding walks all year, and the **Pine Island Audubon Sanctuary**, just north of **Duck**. Stop by the nearby **Sanderling Resort** to see its outstanding collection of bird art. If you are visiting in summer, be sure to see the huge flock of purple marlins returning to roost at the **Umstead Memorial Bridge** in **Manteo** at sunset. In the winter, plan a visit to **Lake Mattamuskeet** to be amazed at the flocks of swans and other waterfowl that visit there. One of the largest colonies of the endangered red-cockaded woodpeckers can be seen at **Palmetto-Peartree Preserve** on the mainland. The **Wings Over Water Festival** held every November offers many escorted birding tours. At any time of year, a kayak trip through **Kitty Hawk Woods** rewards paddlers with serene views of wading and other birds. You can download detailed maps of birding sites in the area from www.ncbirdingtrail.org.

General Index

Lodging by Price

Inexpensive: Up to $80
Moderate: $80 to $150
Expensive: $150 to $200
Very Expensive: $200 and up

North Beaches

Inexpensive to Very Expensive
The Inn at Corolla Light, 55

Moderate to Expensive
Hampton Inn and Suites Outer Banks Corolla, 55

Moderate to Very Expensive
The Duck Inn, A Bed and Breakfast, 55–56
Sanderling Resort & Spa, 56

Central Beaches

Inexpensive to Moderate
Atlantic Street Inn, 94
Colonial Inn Motel, 97
Fin 'n Feather Waterside Inn, 98
Sea Foam Motel, 98

Inexpensive to Expensive
Days Inn Oceanfront-Wilbur and Orville Wright, 95
Nags Head Beach Inn Bed and Breakfast, 97

Inexpensive to Very Expensive
Best Western Ocean Reef Suites, 94
Colony IV by the Sea, 94–95
First Colony Inn, 97

Moderate to Expensive
Cypress House Inn, 95
Cypress Moon Bed and Breakfast, 96

Moderate to Very Expensive
Colington Creek Inn, 93–94
Hilton Garden Inn, 96
Ramada Plaza Resort and Conference Center, 95–96

Expensive to Very Expensive
Oasis Suites, 98

Roanoke Island

Inexpensive
Duke of Dare Motor Lodge, 151

Inexpensive to Moderate
The Scarborough House, 152–53
Scarborough Inn, 153
Wanchese Inn Bed and Breakfast, 154–55

Inexpensive to Expensive
Elizabethan Inn, 151
The Inn at Marshes Light, 151

Inexpensive to Very Expensive
Island Guesthouse and Cottages, 152

Moderate to Expensive
Cameron House Inn, 150–51
Island House of Wanchese Bed & Breakfast, 154
Roanoke Island Inn, 152

Moderate to Very Expensive
Tranquil House Inn, 153

Expensive to Very Expensive
The White Doe Inn, 153–54

Very Expensive
Burrus House Inn Waterfront Suites, 150

Hatteras Island

Inexpensive to Moderate
Breakwater Inn, 196
Cape Pines Motel, 195
Sea Side Inn, 196–97
Sea Sound Motel, 197

Inexpensive to Expensive
Lighthouse View Motel, 195–96

Moderate
Cape Hatteras Bed and Breakfast, 194–95
Sea Gull Motel, 196

Moderate to Expensive
The Villas at Hatteras Landing, 197

Moderate to Very Expensive
The Inn on Pamlico Sound, 195

Expensive to Very Expensive
Hatteras Landing Rooftop Residences, 196

Ocracoke Island

Inexpensive
Crews Inn Bed & Breakfast, 241
Oscar's House, 242

Inexpensive to Moderate
Beach House Bed and Breakfast, 239
Pelican Lodge, 242

Inexpensive to Expensive
Blackbeard's Lodge, 239–40

Inexpensive to Very Expensive
The Island Inn and Villas, 241

Moderate
Harborside Motel, 241

Moderate to Expensive
The Castle on Silver Lake Bed and Breakfast and Castle Villas, 240

Moderate to Very Expensive
The Anchorage Inn & Marina, 238–39

Expensive to Very Expensive
Captain's Landing, 240
The Cove Bed & Breakfast, 240–41

South Banks

Inexpensive
Calico Jack's Inn and Marina, 278–79
Caribbe Inn, 276
William and Garland Motel, 279

Moderate
Best Western Silver Creek Inn, 278
County Home Bed & Breakfast, 276–77
Inlet Inn, 277
Otway House Bed & Breakfast, 279
Pecan Tree Inn, 277–78

Moderate to Expensive
Anchorage House, 276
Cedars by the Sea, 276

Expensive to Very Expensive
Harborlight Guest House, 278
The Ocean Club, 279

Dining by Price

Inexpensive:	under $10
Moderate:	$10 to $20
Expensive:	$20 to $25
Very Expensive:	$25 and up

Dining by Cuisine